READINGS

Professional Essays

Student Essays

Student Sketches

A TEXT & TECHNOLOGY SYSTEM FOR WRITING & RESEARCH SUCCESS

***The Curious Writer* offers a unique, integrated text and technology learning system that combines the power of the textbook's instruction with the interactive tools of MyCompLab, Longman's market-leading online composition resource.**

A book-specific version of MyCompLab includes an **E-book of *The Curious Writer,* Second Edition by Bruce Ballenger** that links you to relevant **MyCompLab activities, quizzes, tutorials and instruction.** The MyCompLab multimedia tutorials enable you to learn about grammar, writing and research topics in a new way, while the self-grading quizzes and in-depth exercises allow you to practice and improve skills. All scores and work are captured in MyCompLab's **Grade Tracker** so you can assess your progress and track your success.

Set yourself on the path to writing and research success today. Register for the *The Curious Writer* version of MyCompLab!

www.mycomplab.com

PLEASE NOTE:
Access to MyCompLab comes packaged with your text at no additional cost only if your instructor has ordered it that way. If your text did not come with an access card, you can ask your bookstore to order one for you, or you can purchase access at www.mycomplab.com using a credit card.

RESOURCES TO HELP YOU SUCCEED!

Not all resources are listed here. For the full list of resources, go to www.mycomplab.com

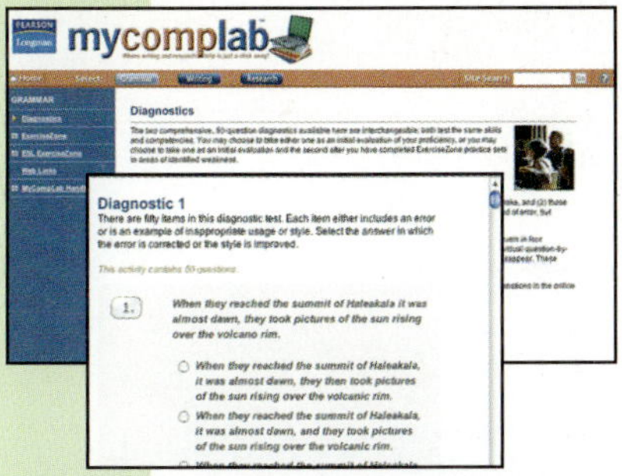

- **My Book Resources.** Additional activities and materials (downloadable worksheets, additional readings) that supplement Ballenger's *The Curious Writer.*

GRAMMAR

- **Diagnostics.** Two Comprehensive and four Targeted Diagnostics test student skills in basic grammar, sentence grammar, style/usage and punctuation/mechanics. For both types of Diagnostics, results pages provide a study plan for the student with overall proficiency scores, question-by-question feedback, and links to appropriate areas in ExerciseZone to improve skills.

- **ExerciseZone.** Over 4,600 self-grading questions allow students to improve skills in basic grammar, sentence grammar, punctuation and mechanics, and usage and style.

- **Grammar Video Tutorials.** For each of the 20 most common grammar errors, an animated clip with voiceover shows students on-screen editing, including tips for identifying and correcting errors.

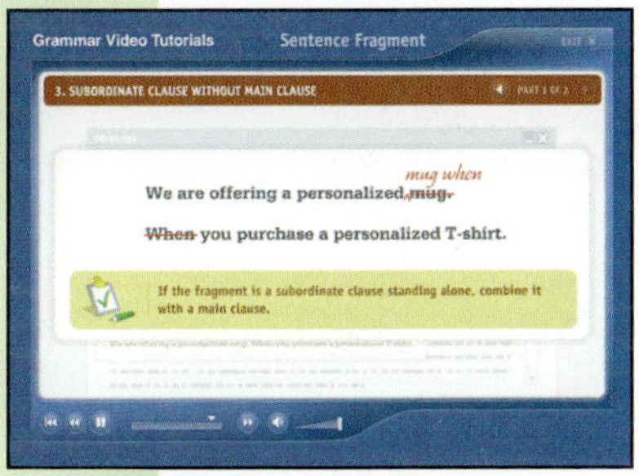

WRITING

- **"Office Hours" Writing Video Tutorials.** This unique and engaging video series shows real students tackling the stages of the writing process (prewriting, drafting, editing, revising, peer review) and learning useful strategies from their instructor.

- **Writing Process Exercises.** Offering in-depth instruction and practice opportunities for each stage of the writing process, this section also provides a series of "guided" exercises that walk students from one step to the next, allowing them to bring a writing project to completion.

RESEARCH

- **Citation Diagnostics and Exercises.** Offering 2 MLA diagnostic tests and 2 APA diagnostic tests, this new section features follow-up, self-grading exercises in both styles.

- **Evaluating Sources Tutorial.** This section features instruction, exercises and an interactive tutorial that helps students master the challenging skills of using and evaluating sources.

- **Avoiding Plagiarism.** These self-guided tutorials—in both MLA and APA formats—offer strategies, self-tests and quizzes to help students recognize plagiarism and avoid it.

- **"Office Hours" Research Video Tutorials.** These videos show real students tackling stages of the research process (Avoiding Plagiarism, Evaluating Sources, Citing Sources, Finding and Narrowing a Topic) and learning useful strategies from their instructor.

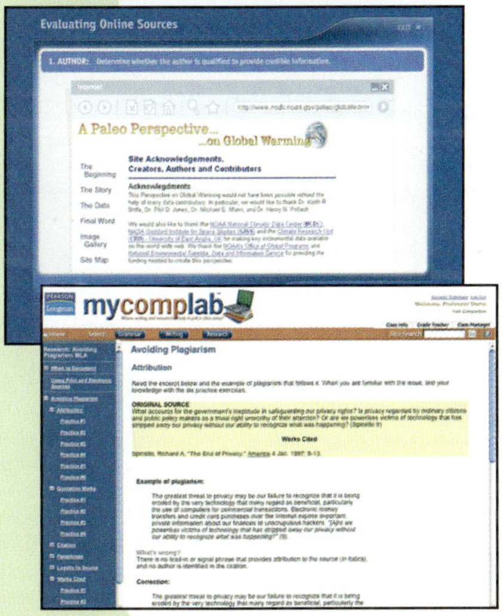

The Curious Writer

Now Includes Essays from Students at the University of Montana

Bruce Ballenger

Second Custom Edition for the University of Montana

Taken from:
The Curious Writer, Second Edition
by Bruce Ballenger

Custom Publishing

New York Boston San Francisco
London Toronto Sydney Tokyo Singapore Madrid
Mexico City Munich Paris Cape Town Hong Kong Montreal

Cover Art: Courtesy of Photodisc/Getty Images

Taken from:

The Curious Writer, Second Edition
by Bruce Ballenger

A Pearson Education Company
Boston, Massachusetts 02116

Printed in the United States of America

10 9 8 7 6 5 4 3 2 1

2008240324

AM

Pearson Custom Publishing is a division of

PEARSON

www.pearsonhighered.com

ISBN 10: 0-555-00945-9
ISBN 13: 978-0-555-00945-1

Brief Contents

Part Two
INQUIRY PROJECTS 89

Part Three

INQUIRING DEEPER 427

Detailed Contents

Chapter 5
Writing a Profile 133

Chapter 12
Research Techniques 491

Preface

A few years ago, the Carnegie Foundation asked a group of leading scholars, teachers, and intellectuals to investigate the current state of undergraduate education at America's research universities. The Boyer Commission report was unequivocal about the problems: "The experience of most undergraduates at most research universities is that of receiving what is served out to them. In one course after another they listen, transcribe, absorb, and repeat, essentially as undergraduates have done for centuries." The investigators called for a "new model" of undergraduate education that would "turn the prevailing undergraduate culture of receivers into a culture of inquirers, a culture in which faculty, graduate students, and undergraduates share an adventure of discovery. . . ." In particular, they added, "The first year of university experience needs to provide new stimulation for intellectual growth and a firm grounding in inquiry-based learning."

The "adventure of discovery" is what many of us love about writing. Our students often enter our composition classrooms with little experience using language as a tool of learning. Then we help them understand that writing can be a means for finding out what they didn't know they knew, and that the process of revision can lead to a fresh way of seeing things; pretty soon even some resistant writers welcome the invitation to sit down and write. They've discovered that they can write to learn.

Most of us *already* teach inquiry, although not all may realize it. For instance, our writing classes invite students to be active participants in making knowledge in the classroom through peer review workshops. When we ask students to fastwrite or brainstorm we encourage them to suspend judgment and openly explore their feelings or ideas. And when we ask students to see a draft as a first look at a topic, and revision as a means of discovering what they may not have noticed, we teach a process that makes discovery its purpose. Indeed, most composition classrooms create a "culture of inquirers" rather than passive recipients of what their teachers know.

That's why the Boyer Commission's call for an inquiry-based freshman year resonated with me and so many others. Initially, I saw its relevance to one of the most common writing assignments in the composition course—the research paper—and this led me to write my book *The Curious Researcher*. But an inquiry-based approach can and should permeate every assignment in the entire sequence of freshman writing courses. I also thought that although much of what we already do involves inquiry-based learning, we should explicitly make the spirit of inquiry—its practices, methods, and purposes—the focus of the writing course, generating ideas that students can apply not only in our classrooms but in their work in other disciplines.

INQUIRY IN THE WRITING CLASSROOM

Historically, composition teachers have struggled to decide what besides reading and writing skills students could export to their other classes and, later, into their lives. Often we vaguely refer to "critical-thinking" skills. *The Curious Writer* offers a comprehensive approach for teaching *inquiry*. This idea also may seem vague until you consider the following.

First, think about what is required to create a culture of inquirers in the composition course. How do we create the learning environment that will foster such a culture? I believe there are at least five key features of an inquiry-based classroom on nearly any subject.

1. *Create an atmosphere of mutual inquiry.* Students are used to seeing their teachers as experts who know everything that students need to learn. But in an inquiry-based classroom instructors are learners, too. They ask questions not because they already know the answers but because there might be answers they haven't considered.
2. *Emphasize questions before answers.* The idea that student writers begin with an inflexible thesis or a firm position on a topic *before* they engage in the process of writing and thinking is anathema to inquiry-based learning. Questions, not preconceived answers, lead to new discoveries.
3. *Encourage a willingness to suspend judgment.* Student culture at most schools works against this. Papers get written at the last minute, multiple deadlines in multiple classes compete for students' time, and multiple-choice tests or lecture courses imply that there is one true answer and the teacher knows it. To suspend judgment demands that we trust the process that will lead us to new insights. This requires both faith in the process and the time to engage in it. The composition course, with its emphasis on process, is uniquely suited to nurture such faith.
4. *Introduce a strategy of inquiry.* It's not enough to simply announce that we're teaching an inquiry-based class. We have to introduce students to the *strategy of inquiry* we'll be using. In the sciences, the experimental method provides a foundation for investigations. What guidance will we give our students in the composition course? *The Curious Writer* features a strategy that is genuinely multidisciplinary, borrowing from science, social science, and the humanities.
5. *Present inquiry in a rhetorical context.* An essay, a research project, an experiment, any kind of investigation is always pursued with particular purposes and audiences in mind. In an inquiry-based class, the *situation* in which the inquiry project is taking place is always considered.

You'll find all of these elements of inquiry-based learning integrated in *The Curious Writer*. For example, each assignment in Part Two, "Inquiry Projects," leads students toward writing subjects that offer the most potential for learning. Rather than write about what they already know, students are always encouraged to choose a topic because they want to find out more about it. In addition, the discussion questions that follow the student and professional essays are crafted to do more than simply test their comprehension of the piece or reduce it to a single theme. In many cases, questions are open ended and can lead students in many directions as they analyze a reading. *The Curious Writer* maintains a voice and persona throughout the book that suggests that I am working along with the students as a writer and a thinker, which is exactly the experience of mutual inquiry I try to create in my classes. Finally, *The Curious Writer* is organized around a strategy of inquiry that is present in every assignment and nearly every exercise. Introduced in Part One, "The Spirit of Inquiry," I call on the model often in every subsequent chapter. The inquiry strategy is the thematic core of the book.

THE INQUIRY STRATEGY OF *THE CURIOUS WRITER*

A strategy of inquiry is simply a process of discovery. In the sciences, this process is systematic and often quite formal. The model I use in this book borrows from science in some ways through its insistence on continually looking closely at the "data" (sensory details, facts, evidence, textual passages, and so on) and using it to shape or test the writer's ideas about a subject. But the heart of the model is the alternating movement between two modes of thinking—creative and critical—in a dialectical process. One way of describing this is shifting back and forth between suspending judgment and making judgments (see Figure A).

To help students see how questions can help them see their writing subjects in new ways, I offer four categories of questions—those that explore, explain, evaluate, and reflect—and return to these frequently, particularly in the early stages of the inquiry process. These will be most evident in the follow-up questions to the many readings throughout *The Curious Writer.* A strategy of inquiry is useful only if it makes sense to students; I've tried very hard, particularly in the first section of the book, to make the model comprehensible.

OTHER FEATURES

Because the inquiry-based approach is central to *The Curious Writer*, it's crucial for students to work through the first three chapters in Part One, "The Spirit of Inquiry." Part Two—the largest—focuses on "inquiry projects." The range of assignments in this part should satisfy the needs of most composition instructors. If your university is lucky enough to have a two-semester sequence, *The Curious Writer* includes assignments suitable for both courses, including personal, argument, and research essays. Also included is the ethnographic essay, a form that engages students in field research; *The Curious Writer* is the first major text to include ethnography.

The book's focus on genres of writing also makes it appealing for advanced composition courses. For example, assignments such as the profile, review, and

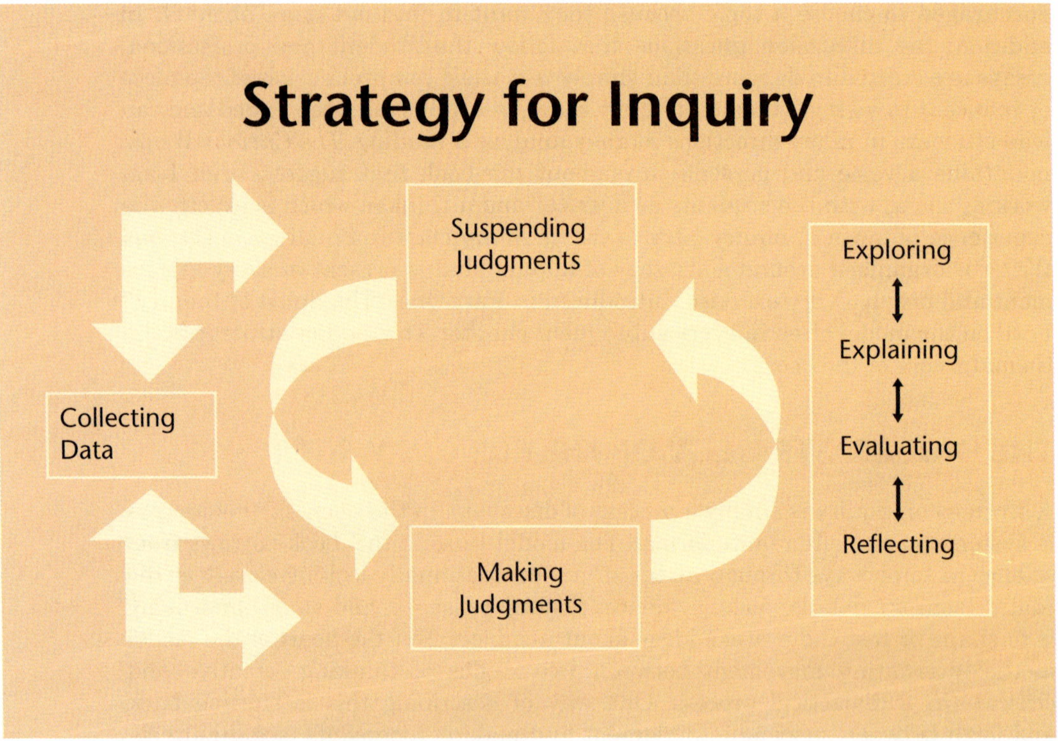

FIGURE A In nearly every assignment in *The Curious Writer*, students will use this strategy of inquiry.

proposal help students see how to apply what they've learned to distinct rhetorical situations and help them to understand how those situations shape the genres.

In recent years, I've become interested in reading strategies, a topic that I never mentioned as a novice teacher. There was simply so much to say about the writing process that I didn't think reading was a topic that should get much airtime. Yet as in writing, students bring many prior beliefs and assumptions about reading into our classrooms, and because reading is always an important part of teaching writing, I've come around to talking more about it. *The Curious Writer* reflects this. Chapter 2, "Reading as Inquiry," is devoted to the topic. The best thing about this is that the inquiry model I promote for writing applies just as easily to reading. I've also expanded the discussion to reading images. This emphasis on visual rhetoric echoes the latest developments in composition in response to the growth of the Web and the growing visual literacy of our students.

Finally, the approach of *The Curious Writer* grows in part from my own scholarship on research writing, particularly the criticism that research is too often isolated in the writing course. Students understandably get the idea that research is reserved only for the research paper if they're asked to do it only when they're assigned a research project. This book makes research a part of every assignment, from the personal essay to the proposal, emphasizing that it is a useful source of information, not a separate genre.

This is the third textbook I've written with the "curious" moniker. Because all are inquiry-based, the word is a natural choice. And although I'm very interested in encouraging my students to be curious researchers, readers, and writers, I also hope to remind my colleagues who use the books that we should be curious, too. We should model for our students our own passion for inquiring into the world. We should also celebrate what we can learn from our students, and not just about writing, or the many topics they might choose to write about. I'm curious every time I walk into the writing classroom what my students will teach me about myself. That's a lifetime inquiry project for all of us, as teachers and as people.

NEW TO THE SECOND EDITION

I have made a number of changes to the second edition in an effort to refine the book further. These changes, many made at the request of the book's users and reviewers, include the addition of twenty-seven new readings (twenty-two professional and five student); new material on visual analysis in Chapter 2; a clarified and streamlined discussion of the four ways of inquiring in Chapter 3; expanded treatment of revision in each of the inquiry project chapters in Part Two; new material on the literacy narrative in Chapter 4; expanded treatment of formal argument techniques in Chapter 8; upgraded research models in Chapter 11; and new and improved versions of the *Seeing the Form, Writing with Computers,* and *Inquiring into the Details* features throughout the book.

APPROACHES TO TEACHING WITH THE BOOK

The Instructor's Manual, written by my colleague Michelle Payne, will give you detailed suggestions about ways to teach *The Curious Writer*. Here are a few additional suggestions drawn with a much broader stroke.

I organized the book to span, if necessary, a two-semester composition course, though it can easily be adapted to one semester. Typically, in a two-semester sequence the first course focuses on writing process, exposition, critical analysis, writing to learn, and so on. The second semester often focuses on argument and research. A single-semester composition course tries to combine them all. Fortunately, *The Curious Writer* is extremely flexible, with ample material to keep students busy for one or two semesters.

Sequence

Whether you use this book for one course or two, it's wise to introduce *The Curious Writer* to students by first working through Part One, "The Spirit of Inquiry," because this section lays the foundation for all that follows. The many exercises in these chapters will help students experience firsthand what we mean by inquiry. Part Two, "Inquiry Projects," is the heart of the book. I've organized chapters in an order that roughly follows typical composition courses, beginning with genres that draw heavily on students' personal experiences and observations and then moving them outward toward other sources of information and encounters with other people's experiences and ideas. In a one-semester course, for example, you might begin with the personal essay, and then move to the profile, followed by the review, and then the argument or research essay. This builds nicely by challenging students to work with more sources of information and leads to a more sophisticated understanding of persuasion and rhetoric. A two-semester course has the luxury of more assignments, of course, allowing you to potentially use most of the Inquiry Projects in Part Two.

Certain assignments clump together. For example, while arguably all writing is persuasive, the following genres are most explicitly so: proposal, review, argument, critical essay, and often the research essay. A course that focuses on argument might emphasize these assignments. A research-oriented course might exploit the wealth of material with a strong emphasis on outside sources, including the proposal, review, argument, research essay, and ethnography. A single-semester composition course that attempts coverage of critical thinking and writing as well as research and argument might move from personal essay to profile, and then cover persuasion through the review or critical essay, move on to the argument, and finish with the ethnographic and research essays.

Integrating the Research and Revision Sections

An unusual feature of the book is its treatment of research skills and revision. Research is an element of every assignment but it receives special attention in Part Three, "Inquiring Deeper," in which students are introduced not only to the research essay but to research strategies and skills. Hopefully, you will find that this section, particularly Chapter 12, "Research Techniques," is immediately relevant because students will be encouraged to consider research angles in every assignment they tackle. Consider assigning this chapter early in your course, particularly the sections on developing a working and focused knowledge of a subject.

Similarly, revision is an element of every assignment. That's hardly a novel idea, but what is unusual is that *The Curious Writer* devotes an entire section of the book—Part Four, "Re-inquiring"—to revision. Like the section on research, the chapters on revision are relevant to students from their very first assignment. The first half of Chapter 14, "Revision Strategies," is a useful introduction to what it means to revise, and you might assign this material early on in your course. The chapter also features specific revision strategies that your students will use in every assignment.

Chapter 15, "The Writer's Workshop," can also be assigned at any time and in sections. Consider having your students read the first half of that chapter—an introduction to peer review—before the first class workshops. The second half of the chapter focuses on "Methods of Responding," specific workshop formats that are most helpful for drafts at different stages in the writing process. Ask students who are responsible for presenting their work to read about the method of response they'll use in their workshop as preparation for it.

Using the Exercises

Learning follows experience, and the exercises in *The Curious Writer* are intended to help students make sense of the ideas in the text. I often plan the exercises as an in-class activity, and then assign the relevant reading to follow up that experience. Sometimes the discussion following these in-class exercises is so rich that some of the assigned reading becomes unnecessary. The students get it without having to hear it again from the author. More often, though, the reading helps students deepen their understanding of what they've done and how they can apply it to their own work.

However, assigning all of the exercises isn't necessary. Don't mistake their abundance in the book as an indication that you must march your students in lockstep through every activity or they won't learn what they need to. *The Curious Writer* is more flexible than that. Use the exercises and activities that seem to emphasize key points that *you* think are important. Skip those you don't have time for or that don't seem necessary. If you're like me, you also have a few rabbits of your own in your hat, exercises and activities that may work better with the text than the ones I suggest.

FOR INSTRUCTORS

The following resources are free to qualified adopters of Longman English textbooks.

The Instructor's Resource Manual

ISBN 0-205-52077-4

This manual includes several sample syllabi, as well as a helpful introduction that will offer general teaching strategies and ideas for teaching writing as a form of inquiry. It also gives a detailed overview of each chapter and its goals, ideas for discussion starters, handouts and overheads, and a large number of additional writing activities that teachers can use in their classrooms to supplement the textbook.

E-book of *The Curious Writer,* Second Edition

An E-book of *The Curious Writer*, Second Edition is now available within MyCompLab, Longman's premier online composition resource. In MyCompLab, students and teachers will find the best multimedia resources for writing, research, and grammar in one easy-to-use site. Added to this, the E-book of *The Curious Writer* includes hyperlinks to relevant MyCompLab tutorials, quizzes, and instruction, providing an engaging multimedia learning experience for students. Also in the E-book, students will find unique, book-specific materials that supplement the text, including downloadable worksheets, writing activities, additional visual analysis exercises, and more. Tour the site at www.mycomplab.com.

ACKNOWLEDGMENTS

I owe the success of the first edition of *The Curious Writer* to many people, particularly my Development Editor, Adam Beroud, whose savvy judgment, sharp eye, and imaginative thinking influenced me every step of the way. He's been similarly helpful with this second edition. None of the *Curious* books would be possible if the Senior Vice President and Publisher of Longman, Joe Opiela, weren't a force behind them.

I've also been fortunate to have the help of other bright and generous people, particularly my colleague and friend Michelle Payne, with whom I coauthored an inquiry book. Michelle developed the Instructor's Manual for this book and wrote the appendixes. I'm a lucky author to have a partner in these projects with such a rich understanding of what I'm trying to do, and what I might do better.

In addition to Michelle, I've benefited from the insights of other colleagues as well, including Devan Cook, Brock Dethier, Bonnie Sunstein, Elizabeth Chiseri-Strater, Mike Mattison, Karen Uehling, Gail Shuck, Lad Tobin, and many others in the field whose work informed my understanding of how writers get better.

My students always contribute to my work. Several whose own exemplary writing is featured here include Julia Arrendondo, Jon Butterfield, Gordon Seirup, Kersti Harter, Margaret Parker, Lana Kuchta, Amy Garrett-Brown, Julie Bird, Kelly Sundberg, Gina Sinisi, and Christy Claymore.

Reviewers of books like these can be crucial to their development. I was lucky enough to have some excellent reviewers for the second edition, including the following: Melissa Batai, Triton College; Jennifer Black, McLennan Community College; Mark Browning, Johnson County Community College; Jo Ann Buck, Guilford Technical Community College; Jason DePolo, North Carolina A&T State University; John Christopher Ervin, University of South Dakota; Greg Giberson, Salisbury University; Nels P. Highberg, University of Hartford; William Klein, University of Missouri–St. Louis; Mary C. Leahy, College of DuPage; Lynn Lewis, University of Oklahoma; Steve Luebke, University of Wisconsin–River Falls; Michael Lueker, Our Lady of the Lake University; Jacqueline L. McGrath, College of DuPage; Betty Porter, Indiana Wesleyan University; Kristie Rowe, Wright State University; Kathleen J. Ryan, University of Montana; and Heath Scott, Thomas Nelson Community College.

Finally, I want to thank my daughters, Rebecca and Julia, who allow themselves to be characters in all of my books. They are both actors, and like good theater people, they are more than willing to play their parts in these texts, no matter what role I assign. I'm especially grateful to Karen, my wife, who has endured multiple editions of these books and their hold on my attention, which has often come at her expense. She's the beacon I follow through this blizzard of words, always guiding me home.

BRUCE BALLENGER

The Curious Writer

Second Edition

Brief Edition

Part One
THE SPIRIT OF INQUIRY

Chapter 1
Writing as Inquiry

Chapter 2
Reading as Inquiry

Chapter 3
Ways of Inquiring

Writing as inquiry is an invitation to wonder again.

Writing as Inquiry

1

Just the other night I was writing a card to my old friend Linda, someone I went to college with and haven't seen in twenty-five years. As I wrote, my words scribbled in a heavy black pen, she began to appear before me again. I saw her in geology class, a few rows up, wearing a black raincoat and rubber boots, carefully putting her straight black hair behind an ear so she could see her notes. I hadn't seen her so clearly in years, and the writing brought her back. Most of us have had this experience—the power of words to summon images, memories, and feelings—which is why we sometimes indulge, often with pleasure, in writing letters, cards, and e-mails to friends and family.

Yet many of us admit that we really don't like to write, particularly when forced to do it, or we clearly prefer certain kinds of writing and dislike others: "I just like to write funny stories" or "I like writing for myself, and not for other people" or "I hate writing research papers." I can understand this, because for years I felt much the same way. I saw virtually no similarities between my note to Linda and the paper I wrote for my philosophy class in college. Words that had power in one context seemed flimsy and vacant in another. One kind of writing was fairly easy; the other was sweating blood. How could my experience as a writer be so fundamentally different? In other words, what's the secret of writing well in a range of contexts *and* enjoying it more? Here's what I had to learn:

1. All writing can offer the joy of discovery, the opportunity to speak and be heard, and the satisfaction of earned insight.
2. A key to writing well is understanding the *process* of doing it.

I'm not really sure they are particularly novel, but both ideas were a revelation to me when I finally figured them out late in my academic career, and they changed the way I wrote for good. These two

What You'll Learn in This Chapter

- Why it pays to spend time thinking about your writing process.
- Why learning to write well often involves *unlearning* things you already believe.
- How understanding rhetoric will help you analyze writing situations.
- What it means to be a writer who is motivated by a spirit of inquiry.
- How to harness both creative and critical ways of thinking to come up with new ideas.

insights—that the pleasures of writing can span genres and situations, and that thinking about *how* we write matters—are guiding principles of this book. After they read *The Curious Writer,* I won't guarantee that haters of writing will come to love it, or that lovers of writing won't find writing to be hard work. But I hope that by the end of the book you'll experience some of the same pleasures I found writing to my friend Linda in most writing situations, and that you'll be able to adapt your own writing process to meet the demands of whatever situation you encounter.

The process of becoming a more flexible and insightful writer must begin by exploring what you already believe it means to write well and learning a bit about how we can talk about writing as a process. In this chapter, I'll also introduce you to an idea that will be at the heart of every activity and assignment in *The Curious Writer:* the habits of mind and practices that will encourage you to adopt the "spirit of inquiry" as a motive for writing. This may sound a bit lofty and abstract. But by chapter's end I hope you'll recognize some practical implications of this approach that will help you with any writing assignment.

MOTIVES FOR WRITING

Why write? You could probably build a long list of reasons in a minute or two, perhaps beginning facetiously: "Because I *have* to!" But as you consider the many situations that call for writing and the purposes for doing it, I suspect that most will fall under a broad and obvious category: to say something to someone else. I'm less confident that you will see another broad motive for writing, partly because it gets less attention: we write to *discover* what we want to say.

These two motives for writing—to *share* ideas with others and to *discover* what the writer thinks and feels—are equally important.

But both these motives may arise from a still deeper spring: a sense of wonder and curiosity or even confusion and doubt, a desire to touch other people, or an urge to solve a problem. These feelings can inspire what I call the *spirit of inquiry,* a kind of perspective toward the world that invites questions, accepts uncertainty, and makes each of us feel some responsibility for what we say. This inquiring spirit should be familiar to you. It's the feeling you had when you discovered that the sun and a simple magnifying glass could be used to burn a hole in an oak leaf. It's wondering what a teacher meant when he said that World War II was a "good" war and Vietnam was a "bad" war. It's the questions that haunted you yesterday as you listened to a good friend describe her struggles with anorexia. The inquiring spirit even drives your quest to find the best DVD player, an effort that inspires you to read about the technology and visit *Consumer Reports Online.*

BELIEFS ABOUT WRITING

Most of us have been taught about writing since the first grade. We usually enter college with beliefs about how best to write a paper, which rules govern school writing, and even how to improve at composing. As I mentioned earlier,

I've learned a lot about writing since my first years in college, and a big part of that learning involved unraveling some of my prior beliefs about writing. In fact, initially, I'd say that my development as a writer had more to do with *unlearning* some of what I already knew than it did with discovering new ways to write. Actually, that's one of the central findings of learning theorists: When learners have considerable prior knowledge of a subject, they often need to reexamine their beliefs to determine whether those beliefs are accurate or helpful. Until they do this, any new learning in the subject can be limited. In keeping with this philosophy, we need to evaluate what you already believe about writing. Only after you articulate your beliefs can you begin to examine whether those beliefs are obstacles or aids to new learning about writing.

EXERCISE 1.1

What Do You Believe?

STEP ONE: From the following list, identify *the one belief* about writing that you agree with most strongly, and *one* that you're convinced isn't true.

1. Writing proficiency begins with learning the basics and then building on them, working from words to sentences to paragraphs to compositions.
2. The best way to develop as a writer is to imitate the writing of the people you want to write like.
3. People are born writers. Either you can do it or you can't.
4. The best way to develop as a writer is to develop good reading skills.
5. Practice is the key to a writer's development. The more a writer writes, the more he or she will improve.
6. Developing writers need to learn the modes of writing (argument, exposition, description, narration) and the genres (essays, research papers, position papers, and so on).
7. Developing writers should start with simple writing tasks, such as telling stories, and move to harder writing tasks, such as writing a research paper.
8. The most important thing that influences a writer's growth is believing that he or she can learn to write well.
9. The key to becoming a better writer is finding your voice.

STEP TWO: Spend five minutes writing in your notebook or journal about *why* you agree with the one belief and disagree with the other. This is an open-ended "fastwrite." You should write fast and without stopping, letting your thoughts flow in whatever direction they go. Try not to think about what you want to say before you write it, and don't worry about whether you're writing well or making sense (see the following "One Student's Response" for an example).

Journal Prompts

- *When* did you first start agreeing or disagreeing with the belief? Can you remember a particular moment or experience as a student learning to write that drove this home?
- *What* do you mean, exactly, when you say you agree or disagree with the belief? Can you explain more fully why you think the belief is true or false?
- *Who* was most influential in convincing you of the truth or falsity of the belief?

Rules for Fastwriting

1. There are no rules.
2. Don't try to write badly, but give yourself permission to do so.
3. To the extent you can, think through writing rather than before it.
4. Keep your pen moving.
5. If you run out of things to say, write about how weird it is to run out of things to say until new thoughts arrive.
6. Silence your internal critic to suspend judgment.
7. Don't censor yourself.

ONE STUDENT'S RESPONSE

JON'S JOURNAL

EXERCISE 1.1

STEP TWO

I agree that writing is a natural human activity that we are all capable of. Anyone capable of thinking understands language. That's truly all that one needs to begin. The only problem that arises is that writing for one's self contains limitations. He is the rare person that can be satisfied with his own praise. There is something within the human spirit that understands that other people may know more than we do. This drives us on for a response from others. This requires a set standard for communication. This, in turn, requires rules. These are things that a successful writer must learn.

I don't agree with the next statement about imitation. Mr. Studabacher is a good man and a good writer and he pushes this theory a little bit. He says that we should learn to borrow without plagiarism. Imitation can only be a beginning—a starting block for the creation of our own voice and ideas . . .

Inquiring into the Details

JOURNALS

Throughout *The Curious Writer,* I invite you to write in a journal. Some people hate journals. These are usually students who were forced to keep a journal in some class and found it a chore, or who tried to keep a journal at home and had little to show from the experience but blank pages. If you suffer from this condition, use a notebook instead of a journal. The two terms are synonymous. It's not what you call it that counts—it's what you do inside it!

Why do I want you to use a journal? One reason is that it is easier to write freely in this medium than it is when confronting the first page of a rough draft. Also, it's okay to write badly in journals and, as you will see later in this chapter, that's a good thing.

What kind of journal should you use? That's up to you. The writer Natalie Goldberg advises that a journal with a cartoon character on the cover will help you take yourself and your writing less seriously, which will help loosen up your writing. Some students just use the ubiquitous spiral notebook, which works just fine. For a variety of reasons, others find the digital journal best. They may be able to write faster and with more ease using a keyboard instead of pen; keeping a journal on the computer might even be required if you're taking your class in a computer lab.

Unlearning Unhelpful Beliefs

You shouldn't be surprised when I say that I have a lot of theories about writing development; after all, I'm supposedly the expert. But we are *all* writing theorists, with beliefs that grow out of our successes and failures as students who write. Because you don't think much about them, these beliefs often shape your response to writing instruction without your even knowing it. For example, I've had a number of students who believe that people are born writers. As far as I can tell, they mean that there is some kind of writing gene that some folks have and some don't. This belief, of course, would make any kind of writing course a waste of time because writing ability would be a genetic problem.

A much more common belief is that learning to write is a process of building on basics, beginning with words, and then working up to sentences, paragraphs, and perhaps whole compositions. This belief was very common when I was taught writing. I remember slogging my way through Warriner's *English Grammar and Composition* in the seventh and eighth grade, dutifully working through chapter after chapter, beginning with parts of speech, parts of sentences, sentences, and then paragraphs. It wasn't until page 377 that I was urged to write a whole composition, a topic whose section was the smallest in the book.

Along with a lot of experts on writing instruction, I don't think that this foundational approach to writing development is very effective. I know it didn't help me become a better writer, and while I can still diagram a sentence, that's never a skill I call on when I'm composing. As a matter of fact, fifty years of research confirms that teaching formal grammar separately from writing essays is largely a waste of time. Despite this, formal grammar instruction persists, testimony to the subversive power of common sense. (Isn't it common sense that we should always learn the basics first?)

Unlearning involves rejecting common sense if it conflicts with what actually works.

Unlearning involves rejecting common sense *if* it conflicts with what actually works. Throughout this book, I hope you'll constantly test your beliefs about writing against the experiences you're having with it. Pay attention to what seems to work for you and what doesn't; mostly, I'd like you at least initially to play what one writing instructor calls the believing game. Ask yourself, *What do I have to gain as a writer if I try believing this is true?*

The Beliefs of This Book

One of the metaphors I very much like about writing development is offered by writing theorist Ann E. Berthoff. She said learning to write is like learning to ride a bike. You don't start by practicing handlebar skills, move on to pedaling practice, and then finally learn balancing techniques. You get on the bike and fall off, get up and try again, doing all of those separate things all at once. At some point, you don't fall and you pedal off down the street. Berthoff said writing is a process that involves *allatonceness* (all-at-once-ness), and it's simply not helpful to try to practice the subskills separately. This is one belief about writing development shared by this book. Obviously, then, *The Curious Writer* is nothing like Warriner's *English Grammar and Composition,* but what other beliefs *does* it embrace?

Any number of beliefs—the importance of critical thinking, the connection between reading and writing, the power of voice and fluency, and the need to listen to voices other than your own—all guide the structure of this book. One belief, though, undergirds them all: *the most important thing that influences a writer's growth is believing that he or she can learn to write well.* Faith in your ability to become a better writer is key. From it grows the motivation to learn how to write well.

Faith isn't easy to come by. I didn't have it as a writer through most of my school career because I assumed that being placed in the English class for underachievers meant that writing was simply another thing, like track, that I was mediocre at. For a long time, I was a captive to this attitude. But then, as a college freshman, I wrote a paper I cared about and the writing started to matter, not because I wanted to impress my instructor but because I discovered something I really wanted to say, and say well. I didn't settle for mediocrity after that.

As someone who wasn't too keen on writing for a very long time, I know how difficult it is to develop compelling reasons to write, particularly when the writing is required. I had to learn, among other things, that my teacher wasn't responsible for supplying the motivation (though I acknowledge that deadlines can help). I had to find a way to approach a writing assignment that made it seem like an opportunity to learn something.

It turns out that the way you *initially* see a writing assignment—any assignment, really—influences your attitude toward it. To illustrate this point, consider the following questions. Which one of the two responses *best* describes your own feelings when confronted with a writing assignment?

Which opening question are you most likely to ask yourself?

- ❑ How can I be successful at this?
- ❑ What can I learn?

How do you feel when problems arise as you're writing?

- ❑ I don't have the necessary skills.
- ❑ I expect challenges.

How do you view your instructor?

- ❑ Someone who should tell me exactly what he or she wants.
- ❑ Someone who can help solve my writing problems.

What do you consider your main goal?

- ❑ I want to show I'm a decent writer.
- ❑ I want to develop my writing skills.

It may have been hard to limit yourself to just these responses because our attitudes are much more complex than this. You may also have found yourself checking the responses in both columns. But if your choices tended toward the left column, it's likely that your attitude toward writing is driven by *performance* goals. In other words, you want to perform well on a writing assignment for your instructor, for your peers, for your friends, for yourself. If you found yourself agreeing with the items in the right column, *learning goals* seem to dominate how you feel about writing assignments; that is, you are less interested in how well you perform than you are in developing your writing abilities. You see the challenge of a writing assignment as a learning opportunity.

There is nothing wrong with your attitude if it leans more toward performance than learning. Each type of goal has its place. Just remember this about performance-oriented writing: along with the desire for success inevitably comes anxiety about failure. Fearfulness is not a very comfortable place from which to write or to learn. If you're willing to consider making learning rather than performance goals a priority as you work through *The Curious Writer,* you're much more likely to develop your writing abilities. And you might even find that you can use writing in ways you never thought possible. Consider, then, beginning your study of college writing with the opening question, *What can I learn?*

Inquiring into the Details

PORTFOLIOS

One method for evaluating your development as a writer is to use a *portfolio,* which is a collection of work you assemble throughout a semester and submit to your instructor at the end of the course. If your instructor uses portfolios, he or she may grade some of your work as you go along, but will mainly assess your writing abilities by reviewing the total body of work in your portfolio. This means that until you hand in your final drafts, everything is pretty much a work in progress, and for much of the course you can focus on learning goals—say, finding new methods to begin and end your essays, or improving your editing skills. Performance goals, such as getting a decent grade, become a priority only at the end of the course. I'll have much more to say about portfolios later (see Appendix A).

WRITING SITUATIONS AND RHETORICAL CHOICES

Good writing is good writing, right? Well, it depends on the situation. For instance, here's what a friend of my daughter wrote as a comment on her blog the other day:

> im happy to be back w/ u guys it was a too long of a weekend- dancing friday then? u hailey and i runnin tomorrow- sounds fun 2 me

This isn't necessarily bad writing for MySpace.com and sites like it. The message uses online conventions that most of us are familiar with—text messaging abbreviations like "u" for *you* and "2" for *two*—and it possesses a level of informality and intimacy that seems appropriate for its context. Would it be good writing for a college essay? Obviously not.

Part of learning to write well, then, isn't simply learning how to craft transitions, organize information, and follow grammatical rules; it's learning to recognize that each writing situation asks you for something different. Actually, you know this already. You know, for example, that composing a letter to a landlord who refuses to return your security deposit will be fundamentally different from a letter to your sister describing your problem with the landlord. What you may not know is what to call this kind of knowledge: rhetoric.

One way of analyzing any writing situation is by using *the rhetorical triangle,* which reveals the dynamic relationships among the writer, the subject, and the reader (see Figure 1.1).

What the triangle implies is pretty straightforward—to write effectively, you must simultaneously address three main factors: your own perspective as the writer, the topic you are writing about, and the people you are writing for. The word *rhetorical,* of course, comes from *rhetoric,* the classical term for the study and practice of written and verbal communication. In fact, the rhetorical triangle

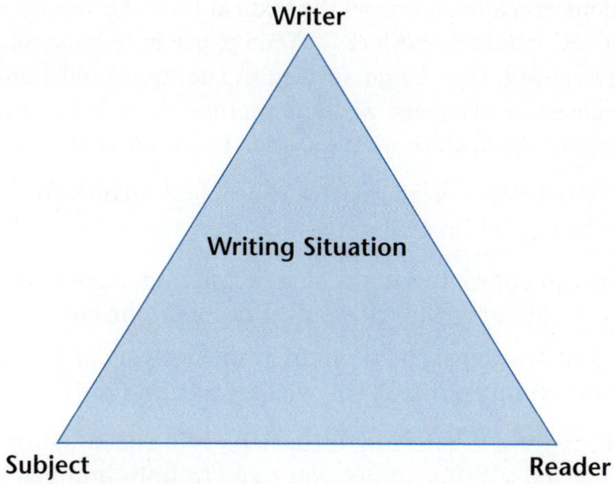

FIGURE 1.1 The rhetorical triangle.

has its origins in ancient Greece and the thinking of Aristotle, who first set down the principles of effective communication more than 2,000 years ago.

The three legs of the rhetorical triangle come together to shape the writing situation. The particularities of each leg—the writer, the subject, and the reader—determine the context of the writing situation. Consider again the security deposit problem. In that scenario, one thing is clear: both of the proposed letters has a distinct—and different—*audience*. While the writer and the subject would seem to be the same for both letters, given the different audiences, the approach will be fundamentally different. In the letter to the landlord, the writer might adopt a formal, even legalistic tone. The letter would be specific about what the writer is asking and when. The letter to the writer's sister would likely be informal, possibly more emotional. Its purpose would be to enlist a sibling's emotional support, not to persuade a landlord to return $500.

I'm pretty sure this is intuitively obvious to you. What may not be apparent is that you can use the same rhetorical knowledge to understand all kinds of writing situations, including academic ones. For example, consider next the opening two paragraphs from a writing assignment in Political Science 141: Contemporary Political Ideologies.

> This assignment aims to encourage students to connect the arguments being made by the thinkers in class to the issues and themes of our politics today. It aims to help students understand the relevance of political thinking for our political practice. Students are encouraged to share their judgments about the authors, only after they have shown that they understand the authors as the authors would understand themselves.
>
> Use one of the following questions as the basis for a short essay. Your essay should be lucid and concise, and your argument should be thoroughly supported by

> relevant citations and allusions from the texts at hand. Grammar, spelling, punctuation, and syntax should be perfect . . . Your paper is to be three to five pages in length, double-spaced, typed, and stapled in the upper left-hand corner. Please number your pages. A title page with an appropriate title must also be included, and all title pages should show what question the student is answering.

Using your own instincts about the rhetorical situation in this example, answer the following questions:

1. How would you characterize the instructor, and, based on that characterization, what kind of reader do you think he might be?
2. If you were in this class, how might your analysis of the rhetorical situation influence your approach the writing assignment?

Writing well involves evaluating situations like these using your rhetorical knowledge. *The Curious Writer* offers you tools to help analyze various writing and reading situations and explores a range of choices that might be appropriate in each, choices that will make you a more persuasive writer and a more sophisticated reader.

HABITS OF MIND

When I first started teaching writing, I noticed a strange thing in my classes. What students learned about writing through the early assignments in the class didn't seem to transfer to later assignments, particularly research papers. What was I doing wrong, I wondered? Among other things, what I failed to make clear to my students was how certain "essential acts of mind" were present in every assignment, from the very first to the very last. What bound the writing course together was the idea of academic inquiry and the habits of mind—or *dispositions*, as one writer describes them—that lead students to see how writing can be a process of discovery.

Start with Questions, Not Answers

A lot of people think that writing is about recording what you already know, which accounts for those who choose familiar topics to write on when given the choice. "I think I'll write about ____________," the thinking goes, "because I know that topic really well and already have an idea what I can say." Unfortunately, the result of writing about what you already know is too often an uninspired draft full of generalizations and clichés.

What do you do about this problem? *Make the familiar strange.* This means finding new ways to see what you've seen before. For years, I've asked some of my writing students to take photographs of any subject they want. Predictably, most students choose to take pictures of familiar things—their rooms or apartments, the trees outside the window, campus buildings, local landscapes—and they almost always take one picture of each subject. The result is that these photographs are rarely surprising. They see these familiar subjects in very familiar ways. But when I ask them to return to a single subject and take multiple pictures of it there are almost always surprises, and fresh ways of seeing the subject.

It's apparent that there are multiple ways of seeing the same thing, and of course this is one thing that we often admire about good writing—it offers a perspective on something familiar that we hadn't considered before. One of the ways writers accomplish this is by using questions. Questions shift a writer's perspective on a subject much as distance, angle, and light alter a photographer's ways of seeing a tree or a building.

Therefore, in an inquiry-based approach to writing, you'll choose a writing topic that raises questions about how you think or feel over one that you have all figured out. Almost any topic can raise interesting questions. *There are no boring topics, only boring questions.* The key is to approach any topic with a sense of wonder and curiosity: *Why are houseflies so hard to kill? What distinguishes the cultures of skaters and snowboarders? When do most marriages fail and what can be done about it? Why do young people join gangs?*

Suspend Judgment

What's one of the most common problems I see in student writers? Poor grammar? Lack of organization? A missing thesis? Nope. *It's the tendency to judge too soon and too harshly.* A great majority of my students, including really smart, capable writers, have powerful internal critics, or as the novelist Gail Godwin once called them, "Watchers at the Gates." This is the voice you may hear when you're starting to write a paper, the one that has you crossing out that first sentence or that first paragraph over and over until you "get it perfect." As you'll see later, this voice isn't demonic; you need it. "Watchers at the Gates" are, as Godwin said, "excellent critics after inspiration has been captured" and "dependable, sharp-eyed readers of things already set down." The problem, of course, is that many of us allow our Watchers to keep us from setting down much of anything. The blank page or screen offers nothing for our internal critics to scrutinize except the glaring failure to get words on the page or screen in the first place.

I've seen bad writing transform students who once hated writing into people who see writing as a useful tool for thinking, and even a source of pleasure.

The only way to overcome this problem is to suspend judgment. In doing so, you essentially tell your Watchers this: *It's okay to write badly.*

I never try to write badly, of course, but whenever I'm stuck in the middle of something, or can't figure out what to say or where to begin, or even when I don't have a clue about my subject, I simply start writing. Sometimes it's absolutely horrible. But just as often, there's a glint of an idea, or direction, or topic, and away I go, trying to keep up with the vein of thought branching in all directions. The British novelist E. M. Forster once said, "How do I know what I think until I see what I say?" I've come to have a lot of faith in this idea. Rather than trying to use my journal the way I used to—to try to write beautiful, eloquent prose—I use the journal simply to think things through; that the prose sometimes stinks doesn't bother me anymore.

We know how powerful our internal critics can be, insisting that every word be spelled right, and every thought sharp. Our Watchers can't abide bad writing. One of the conditions that makes bad writing possible for me is that my Watchers are not voices I honor in my journal, at least not when I want to use my journal to think something through.

Now I know it must seem odd that a book on writing would talk about the virtues of writing badly, but it can be a useful tool for solving all kinds of writing problems. I encourage you to use this approach throughout *The Curious Writer.* I've seen bad writing turn slow writers into faster ones, procrastinators into initiators. I've seen bad writing help students who always wrote short papers begin to generate longer, more thoughtful essays. Best of all, I've seen bad writing transform students who once hated writing into people who see writing as a useful tool for thinking, and even a source of pleasure.

Conditions That Make "Bad" Writing Possible

1. Willingness to suspend judgment.
2. Ability to write fast enough to outrun your internal critic.
3. Belief that confusion, uncertainty, and ambiguity help thought rather than hinder it.
4. Interest in writing about "risky" subjects, or those that you don't know what you want to say about until you say it.

Search for Surprise

One of the key benefits of writing badly is *surprise.* This was a revelation for me when I first discovered the virtues of bad writing in graduate school. I was convinced that you never pick up the pen unless you know what you want to say, which may account for my struggles with journal writing. Suddenly I stumbled on a new way to use writing—not to *record* what I already knew about a subject, but to *discover* what I actually thought. This way of writing promised a feast of surprises that made me hunger to put words on the page.

EXERCISE 1.2

A Roomful of Details

STEP ONE: Spend ten minutes brainstorming a list of details based on the following prompt. Write down whatever comes into your mind, no matter how silly. Be specific and don't censor yourself.

> Try to remember a room you spent a lot of time in as a child. It may be your bedroom in the back of the house at the edge of the field, or the kitchen where

your grandmother kneaded bread or made thick red pasta sauce. Put yourself back in that room. Now look around you. What do you see? What do you hear? What do you smell?

STEP TWO: Examine your list. If things went well, you will have a fairly long list of details. As you review the list, identify one detail that surprises you the most, a detail that seems somehow to carry an unexpected charge. This might be a detail that seems connected to a feeling or story. You might be drawn to a detail that confuses you a little. Whatever its particular appeal, circle the detail.

Brainstorming

- Anything goes.
- Don't censor yourself.
- Write everything down.
- Be playful but stay focused.

STEP THREE: Use the circled detail as a prompt for a seven-minute fast-write. Begin by focusing on the detail: What does it make you think of? And then what? And then? Alternatively, begin by simply describing the detail more fully: What does it look like? Where did it come from? What stories are attached to it? How does it make you feel? Avoid writing in generalities. Write about specifics—that is, particular times, places, moments, and people. Write fast, and chase after the words to see where they want to go. Give yourself permission to write badly.

One Student's Response

MARGARET'S JOURNAL

EXERCISE 1.2

STEP THREE

Detail: Pillows that spelled our names

The pillows that spelled our names sat on our beds against the wall. I slept on the top bunk, I think. Mostly I think I wanted the bunk that she got—if she was on the bottom then I wanted it. If she wanted the top then that was inevitably the coolest bunk. My pillows spelled out "Margy" in red, green fabric, with white lace tracing the edges. They were ugly, Christmassy shades, antiquish. Freckly. Our mom made them just for us girls, not the three boys. I didn't get my whole name spelled out because it is eight letters long, but Chelsea got all seven of hers. Her colors were blue-yellow, a color scheme that to this day I find elegant and beautiful. Her colors were fresh and alive and mine seemed dusty, old, plain, like my old-lady name . . . But they were fun, they made bed-making an exercise in identity, these are my colors—red, green, brown like my hair and eyes and freckles and hers were gold like her almost white blond hair and bright blue eyes. This is us . . .

"Did anything surprise you?" That's one of the first questions I ask my students after an open-ended fastwriting exercise. With any exercise, some students answer, "No, nothing surprised me." But almost always an equal number of students nod, or simply ignore the question because they haven't stopped writing even after the time is up. This is the experience I most want my students to have, particularly early in a writing course, because they discover, often for the first time, that they can write to learn more about something.

You may experience at least three kinds of surprise after completing a fastwriting exercise like the preceding one:

1. Surprise about *how much* writing you did: "I never thought I had that much to say about that." Even if the writing doesn't lead to an essay or provide material for an assignment, this discovery is crucial. Remember, the fastwriting was prompted by just one detail. "Who would have guessed that I could write three pages about a broken old chair!"

2. Surprise about discovering an *unexpected topic:* The poet Richard Hugo wrote that there were two kinds of these—triggering topics and generated topics. Writers often begin with one idea about their subject, but the writing leads them to another, better idea, one they wouldn't have discovered without following the trail of words.

3. Surprise about discovering a *new way of understanding a topic:* Consider Margaret's response to Exercise 1.2 in the preceding "One Student's Response." Margaret writes about embroidered pillows she and her sister received from their mother, a seemingly innocuous detail until her writing suddenly takes a reflective turn: *they made bed-making an exercise in identity* . . . Quite unexpectedly, Margaret has discovered a new way of understanding her childhood bed pillows.

The kind of surprises you encounter doing this sort of writing may not always be profound. They may not even provide you with obvious essay topics. With any luck, though, by hunting for surprises in your own work you will begin to experience the pleasure of writing *to learn.* That's no small thing, particularly if you've always believed that writers should have it all figured out before they pick up the pen.

Finally, remember that *the more you look, the more you see.* Memories, texts, objects, data, experiences, art, whatever, are all much more likely to yield surprise if we prolong our gaze, resisting the temptation to rush to easy conclusions.

Inquiring into the Details

INVENTION STRATEGIES

Perhaps without knowing it, you have already practiced some writing techniques designed to help you generate material. These *invention strategies* include fastwriting, listing, brainstorming, questioning, and even conversation. You can use these techniques in any writing situation when you need to gather more information, find a topic, or explore what you think. We call on these strategies often in the exercises and assignments that follow.

At first, spending time doing all this writing and thinking before you actually begin a draft may seem like waste of time. After all, your goal is to finish the assignment. But if you want to find a focused topic that means something to you and write it with enough information, then invention strategies such as fastwriting will prove invaluable. They produce the raw material that can be shaped, like clay on a potter's wheel, into something with form and meaning. But really the best thing about invention strategies is that they often generate material that is ripe with surprise.

Invention Strategies

- ***Fastwriting:*** The emphasis is on speed, not correctness. Don't compose, don't think about what you want to say before you say it. Instead, let the writing lead, helping you discover what you think.
- ***Listing:*** Fast lists can help you generate lots of information quickly. They are often in code, with words and phrases that have meaning only for you. Let your lists grow in waves—think of two or three items and then pause until the next few items rush in.
- ***Clustering:*** This nonlinear method of generating information, also called *mapping,* relies on *webs* and often free association of ideas or information. Begin with a core word, phrase, or concept at the center of a page, and build branches off it. Follow each branch until it dies out, return to the core, and build another. (See page 113.)
- ***Questioning:*** Questions are to ideas what knives are to onions. They help you cut through to the less obvious insights and perspectives, revealing layers of possible meanings, interpretations, and ways of understanding. Asking questions complicates things but rewards you with new discoveries.

- ***Conversing:*** Conversing is fastwriting with the mouth. When we talk, especially to someone we trust, we work out what we think and feel about things. We listen to what we say, but we also invite a response, which leads us to new insights.
- ***Researching:*** This is a kind of conversation, too. We listen and respond to other voices that have said something or will say something if asked about topics that interest us. Reading and interviewing are not simply things you do when you write a research paper but activities to use whenever you have questions you can't answer on your own.
- ***Observing:*** When we look closely at anything, we see what we didn't notice at first. Careful observation of people, objects, experiments, images, and so on generates specific information that leads to informed judgment.

WRITING AS A PROCESS

Hunting is not those heads on the wall. This is the title of an essay by Amiri Baraka, a writer and intellectual, who argues that the *process* of bringing art into being is the essential element of a creative act, not the end product. In other words, the *act* of painting, not the painting itself, matters most. I wouldn't go quite that far when describing writing—the process and the final product are inseparable—but generally students pay far too little attention to the writing process in their rush to get the writing done. The result is that rich possibilities, including new ideas and perspectives, are short-circuited before they have a chance to be explored. The key to writing well is to understand the writing process. That way we get more control over it.

Recognizing the Challenges

All writers, including those who publish, face challenges in their writing. The difference between an experienced writer and a less experienced one is that the experienced writer recognizes the challenges and has figured out ways to solve them.

Consider, for example, the process of John McPhee, a writer of creative nonfiction articles and books on topics ranging from birch bark canoes to oranges. Pulitzer Prize winner McPhee is of the "stone-kicking school" of journalism; its philosophy is that if you want to discover the story you want to tell, you must spend a lot of time just hanging around with the people who know something about your subject. McPhee does this, spending as much as a year interviewing and observing people and things, as well as reading up on his subject. The result of this kind of investigation is pages and pages of notes, a mother lode of information, and this is McPhee's writing challenge: how to organize all that information and find the story he wants to tell. Over the years, McPhee has worked this out. When his notes get lengthy, he organizes them by topic in three-ring binders, and then he transfers the topics to index cards, which he

The writer John McPhee, winner of the Pulitzer Prize.

posts on a bulletin board above his desk. McPhee constantly plays with the order of the cards, experimenting with different beginnings, middles, and ends, constantly on the hunt for a structure that will bring all the information to life. When he finds it, he begins writing the piece, following the trail he worked out on the bulletin board in front of him.

John McPhee established this process through trial and error. He stuck with the strategies that seemed to improve the results and abandoned the strategies that didn't. I offer you this story not because McPhee's process is one I recommend. It's an approach that's peculiar to this one writer in a particular situation, a writer who must figure out how to organize a tremendous amount of information in a meaningful way. I want to suggest that if you recognize your writing challenges as solvable issues that are often related to *how* you approach a particular writing task, then you will become a more versatile and more skilled writer. Seeing the link between writing challenges and the writing process means that most writers can improve if they become more aware of *how* they approach a particular writing situation that creates the challenges for them.

EXERCISE 1.3

What Is Your Process?

Take a moment and analyze your own writing challenges. The following questions might help you develop a profile of your writing process in certain situations, and help you identify problems you might want to address by altering your process.

STEP ONE: Complete the Self-Evaluation Survey.

Self-Evaluation Survey

1. When you're given a school writing assignment, do you wait until the last minute to get it done?

   Always——Often——Sometimes——Rarely——Never

2. How often have you had the experience of learning something you didn't expect through writing about it?

   Very often——Fairly often——Sometimes——Rarely——Never

3. Do you generally plan out what you're going to write before you write it?

   Always——Often——Sometimes——Rarely——Never

4. *Prewriting* describes activities that some writers engage in before they begin a first draft. Prewriting might include freewriting or fastwriting, making lists, brainstorming or mapping, collecting information, talking to someone about the essay topic, reading up on it, or jotting down ideas in a notebook or journal. How much prewriting do you tend to do for the following types of assignments? Circle the appropriate answer.

   - A personal essay:

     A great deal——Some——Very little——None——Haven't written one
   - A critical essay about a short story, novel, or poem:

     A great deal——Some——Very little——None——Haven't written one
   - A research paper:

     A great deal——Some——Very little——None——Haven't written one
   - An essay exam:

     A great deal——Some——Very little——None——Haven't written one

5. At what point in writing an academic paper do you usually get stuck? Check all that apply.

   - ❑ Getting started
   - ☑ In the middle
   - ❑ Finishing
   - ❑ I never get stuck (go on to Question 9)
   - ❑ Other ______________________

6. If you usually have problems getting started on an academic paper or essay, which of the following do you often find hardest to do? Check all that apply. (If you don't have trouble getting started, go on to Question 7.)

   - ❑ Deciding on a topic
   - ❑ Writing an introduction

- ❑ Finding a good place to write
- ❑ Figuring out exactly what you're supposed to do for the assignment
- ❑ Finding a purpose or focus for the paper
- ❑ Finding the right tone
- ❑ Other ______________________________

7. If you usually get stuck in the middle of a paper, which of the following causes the most problems? (If writing in the middle of a paper isn't a problem for you, go on to Question 8.)

- ❑ Keeping focused on the topic
- ☑ Finding enough information to meet page length requirements
- ❑ Following my plan for how I wanted to write the paper
- ☑ Bringing in other research or points of view
- ❑ Organizing all my information
- ❑ Trying to avoid plagiarism
- ❑ Worrying about whether the paper meets the requirements of the assignment
- ❑ Worrying that the paper just isn't any good
- ❑ Messing with citations
- ❑ Other ______________________________

8. If you have difficulty finishing an essay or paper, which of the following difficulties are typical for you? Check all that apply.

- ❑ Composing a last paragraph or conclusion
- ❑ Worrying that the paper doesn't meet the requirements of the assignment
- ❑ Worrying that the paper just isn't any good
- ❑ Trying to keep focused on the main idea or thesis
- ❑ Trying to avoid repeating yourself
- ❑ Realizing you don't have enough information
- ❑ Dealing with the bibliography or citations
- ❑ Other ______________________________

9. Rank the following list of approaches to revision so that it reflects the strategies you use *most often to least often* when rewriting academic papers. Rank the items 1–6, with the strategy you use most often as a 1 and least often as a 6.

__1__ I usually just tidy things up—editing sentences, checking spelling, looking for grammatical errors, and other proofreading activities.

3 I mostly look for ways to reorganize existing information in the draft to make it more effective.

2 I generally try to fill holes by adding more information.

4 I do more research.

6 I often completely change the focus or even the main idea in the revision, rewriting sections, adding or removing information, and rearranging the order of things.

5 I rarely do any rewriting at all.

10. Finally, do you tend to impose a lot of conditions on when, where, or how you think you write most effectively? For example, do you need a certain pen, do you always have to write on a computer, must it be quiet or noisy, or do you often write best under pressure? Do you need to be in certain kinds of places to write effectively? Or can you write under a range of circumstances, with few or no conditions? Circle one.

    Lots of conditions——Some——A few——No conditions

    If you do impose conditions on when, where, or how you write, list some of those conditions here:

    1.
    2.
    3.
    4.

STEP TWO: In small groups, discuss the results of the survey. Begin by picking someone to tally the answers to each question. Post these on the board or a sheet of newsprint so they can be added to the class totals. Analyze the results for your group. In particular, discuss the following questions:

- Are there patterns in the responses? Do most group members seem to answer certain questions in similar or different ways? Are there interesting contradictions?
- Based on these results, what "typical" habits or challenges do writers in your class seem to share?
- What struck you most?

Thinking About Your Process

We are creatures of habit. This applies to writing, too. Even experienced writers have deeply ingrained habits, some of them quite sensible, some quirky. Donald Murray always works in the morning and always in his basement office with a view of the river. Novelist Mitch Wieland always writes with a No. 2 pencil and a yellow legal pad; only later does he compose on the computer. Some writers must smoke, chew gum, or drink. Some must write in bed. Rachel, a former student, always came to class on the day a draft was due with dark circles under her eyes; she insisted that the only way she could write good papers was to pull an all-nighter before the assignment was due.

When we do something more than a few times we often develop habits like these. Sometimes we don't even think about them. But we develop other habits with some awareness—waiting until the last minute to write a draft seemed to work for Rachel the first time she tried it, an accidental strategy she first used when she forgot a paper was due and was forced to crank it out at the last minute. Likewise, Mitch Wieland developed his fondness for pencils and legal pads to draft a short story or novel early on without much deliberation. He likes the way he thinks with a pencil in his hand, and perhaps the feel and sound of the lead scratching on paper.

The habits we consciously develop become less conscious as time goes on, and pretty soon it isn't even a question whether television and schoolwork mix well together, or if last-minute drafts are the only way to compose. When we *do* scrutinize these habits, we often immediately assume that they are part of the best—if not the *only*—way to proceed with a task. "It's always worked for me," Rachel said every time.

However, reflecting on *how* we do something is as central to intellectual activities as it is to athletic ones. Coaches often help a tennis player deconstruct and then revise a backhand, or a swimmer refine a flip turn, but consider how infrequently we do this kind of reflection when it comes to our academic writing. *Metacognitive thinking,* or thinking about thinking, is a fairly sophisticated intellectual activity but it's an essential one for this simple reason: *the more we think about a process, the more control we get over it.*

Reading and writing are two processes that are central to life—including academic life—and the time you spend reflecting on how you engage in both activities is time well spent. That's why the composition course emphasizes discussion and analysis of the writing process, and will include many moments like the one I had with Rachel after she told me that she wrote her best stuff at the last minute.

"Are you sure?" I asked.

"I think so," she said. "But I never really thought about it much."

The survey you completed is the beginning of reflection on your own writing process. You will do this kind of reflection again and again throughout this book so that by the end you will have written a narrative of thought that tells the story of your reading and writing processes, and how you change those processes to produce better writing more efficiently. The reflective letter in your portfolio (see Appendix A) might be where you finally tell that story in full, perhaps beginning with what the survey revealed about your own habits, rituals, and challenges as you began this book.

Linear Versus Recursive Models

No single writing process—a kind of recipe every writer can follow—will reliably produce "good" writing. But certain elements of the writing process are fairly common to all writers. What distinguishes one writer's process from another's is *when* they invoke an element and in what situations. Timing is crucial in the writing process, as in any process from making fudge to building space shuttles. But what are these elements of the writing process? Many experts have proposed models to describe it. You may be familiar with some of them. For example, one of the simplest models for the writing process is depicted in Figure 1.2, which shows a linear process that moves, step by step, from prewriting to writing to rewriting. Typically, prewriting represents things a writer does to generate information and clarify intention. The term from classical rhetoric that roughly equates with prewriting is *invention*. As we discussed earlier, prewriting can include a range of activities from brainstorming and fastwriting to note taking, conversation, and formal research. Writing is the process of producing the draft. Rewriting, of course, is revision and all that it entails, from tidying up sentences to entirely changing a paper's focus or even its topic.

FIGURE 1.2 A linear model of the writing process.

The only problem with the linear model is that it moves in one direction, and most writing theorists agree that the writing process just doesn't work that way. Instead, movement within the process proceeds in a *recursive* fashion—that is, it moves back and forth from one stage to the next. Writers do not simply march forward, step by step, completing one stage of the writing process and then moving on to a subsequent stage. Writing, like life, is more complicated than that. For example, I initially drafted this chapter fairly quickly, relying on what I already knew about writing process models. Only later did I consult the books on my shelf and collect more information about the writing process—double-checking what I had said and adding information I may not have thought of at the time of my initial draft. When I have some background knowledge about my subject my approach often is to draft *and then* prewrite *and then* rewrite.

In other words, writers don't always begin at the "beginning" of the writing process, and they may return to a step they've already attempted. Sometimes they leap over a step or return to it later. A better description of the writing process, then, looks like Figure 1.3.

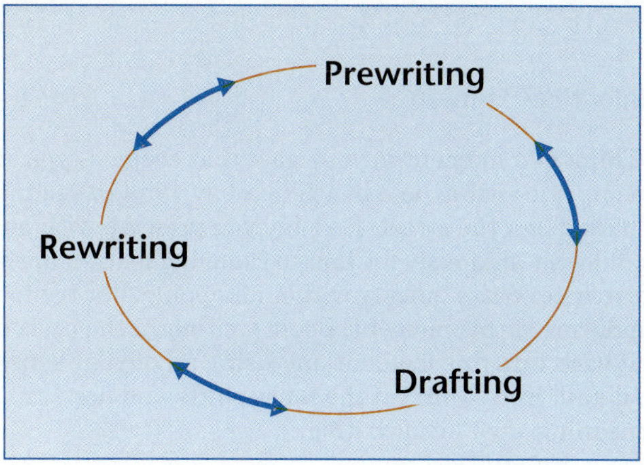

FIGURE 1.3 A recursive model of the writing process.

Dialectical Thinking

The recursive model of the writing process focuses on the back-and-forth movement between the different stages of process. The sort of thinking writers do as they move through the process also is done in a back-and-forth manner, but instead of moving between the different stages of the process, *dialectical thinking* shifts between two contrasting modes of thought, one creative and the other critical.

The word *dialectical* has several meanings, many of which focus on the relationship between opposing ideas or forces. In dialectical thinking, the relationship between creative and critical modes of thought is important. Why? Because the interplay between the creative and the critical can foster new and deeper ways of understanding.

Dialectical thinking does not come naturally to most people and, while you might think otherwise, the critical mode of thought isn't the problem. I mentioned earlier that most writers have strong internal critics—the "Watchers at the Gates" who are quick to criticize and judge. "That's a stupid sentence," they hiss. "You really don't know what you're trying to say, do you?" The critical self is all too present for most of us. What we tend to be less aware of is our creative self. This side may surface in a fastwrite that uncovers an unexpected subject, or in the pleasure of making lists of places you remember from childhood. Much like children, our creative selves are playful, open to surprise and discovery.

One of the key benefits of writing badly is surprise.

Unfortunately, for many writing students these two selves are often at war with each other. This is a pity. Imagine the results if you could get the creative and the critical to collaborate. As a writer, you could be both playful *and* judgmental, open things up *and* narrow them down. That's the key to dialectical thinking when it's applied to the writing process.

EXERCISE 1.4

Practicing Dialectical Thinking

STEP ONE: Think of a moment in your past that seemed typical for you. Perhaps you spent time sitting on a bench in a bay window reading or playing football at the park down the street. Possibly you grew up with an alcoholic parent, and would wait anxiously for him to come home. Use this moment as the topic of a fastwrite. Write quickly without stopping, but try to remain within the boundaries of this moment. Begin writing in the present tense, putting yourself back into this moment and using all of your senses. Describe the moment in detail. Don't worry if the tense shifts and don't try to explain the moment's meaning. Just keep writing.

STEP TWO: Reread your initial fastwrite, underlining words, lines, or passages that seem significant in some way. Now compose a short paragraph that begins with the following words:

As I look back on this moment now, I realize that . . .

STEP THREE: After completing your short paragraph, skip a few lines in your journal and compose a response to one or more of the following questions about your writing experience.

- How differently, if at all, would you have approached the fastwrite if you knew that you would read the results aloud to others?
- Did you imagine an audience other than yourself?
- What, if anything, surprised you?
- What problems arose during the fastwrite, if any, and how did you resolve them?
- Was there anything different about the ways you approached the writing from the ways you usually do?

ONE STUDENT'S RESPONSE

JON'S JOURNAL

EXERCISE 1.4

STEP ONE

Birds chirp overhead as the squirrels quickly dash through the branches like school-children would burst through the door at recess. Directly behind me, Aunty Val is hanging her laundry out to dry. Directly in front of me lies the sort of structure that all children would dream of having. It's as tall as my house! A rope dangles from the top down to the ground. I have never climbed this to the top and I don't think that I ever will. If I ever got to the top of this structure, I would climb the wooden ladder built on the side. Or maybe take the few steps up to the monkey bars, swing to the end, and try to climb up from there. But I rarely paid any attention to this structure at all. Today is no exception. I am sitting in the sandbox with my springer spaniel and the dismembered corpses of hundreds of GI Joes that felt the heat of battle and now lay in shallow, unmarked sand graves . . . I can hear my brothers and the neighbor kid fight over who shot first, why he didn't die, and whether or not he was wearing Kevlar. That was the beauty of the GI Joes, they didn't whine, or cheat. When it was their time they simply snapped and died. Then, they were satisfied with mass burials . . .

STEP TWO

As I look back on this moment now, I realize that as a child, I was extremely self-contained. I could keep myself entertained as easily, if not better than I could be entertained by others. I wonder what changed between now and then? Now, I hate being alone . . .

Writing with Computers

KNOWING WHEN TO STEP AWAY FROM THE COMPUTER

Computers make many time-consuming tasks more efficient, but there are times when it's important to step away from the computer.

- Some writers prefer the experience of writing with paper and pen. If a computer makes you feel disconnected from your writing or makes you feel anxious, then by all means step away from it.
- Some invention strategies are best done with paper and pen. For instance, one of your invention strategies might be carrying a small notepad and pen with you and jotting notes about your ideas and observations as you go about your day. Doing this with a computer, even a very small one, would be unnatural.
- Computers are tools of both productivity and recreation. Many writers sit down with great intentions of working diligently and find themselves checking their e-mail, visiting social networking sites, shopping, or playing games. Thus, the computer can become a source of procrastination or a scapegoat for avoiding the apprehension of starting a new project. Either way, if you are distracted when sitting down at a computer, it may be best to step away.
- Sitting down at a computer without initial thinking, note taking, and invention causes writers to bypass one of the most critical stages of writing. While it is perfectly fine to use the computer to invent, we must distinguish invention and drafting. Skipping the invention stage and jumping into drafting may seem productive at first, but it usually results in a shallow draft that will require substantial revision. When you start a new writing project, choose an invention strategy that works for you before sitting down at the computer to write a first draft.

Calling the two opposed modes of thought creative and critical is a helpful shorthand for the different *types* of thought. But let's look at this idea more closely. When students reflect on their experience with Exercise 1.4, they often say that Step One and Step Two were quite different. In Step One, when they plunged into a fastwrite remembering a moment from their past, the writing often led them to unexpected places. They remembered surprising details, or discovered a new subject, or found a new way of seeing something they'd seen before. This is a kind of *creative thinking;* it is open ended, digressive, and often surprising. It might even engage feelings as well as thoughts. Step Two of Exercise 1.4 begins with the phrase, *As I look back on this moment now . . .*, and this frame often thrusts writers into a much more reflective, thoughtful, and detached stance. When writers are instructed to *compose* rather than fastwrite—that is, think about what they're going to say before they say it—their writing process frequently slows down, their language becomes more precise, and the writing becomes more focused. This is *critical thinking.*

Combining these two modes of thinking gives both thinking and writing more range and depth. Creative thinking creates the conditions for discovery—new insights or ways of seeing—while critical thinking helps writers refine their discoveries and focus on the most significant of them.

Figure 1.4 lists other ways you can visualize creative and critical thinking. In narrative writing, for instance (the kind of writing you likely did in the previous exercise), creative thinking helps you generate information about *what*

Creative Thinking	⟷	**Critical Thinking**
Fastwriting	⟷	Composing
Showing	⟷	Telling
Specifics	⟷	Generalities
Collecting	⟷	Focusing
Observations of	⟷	Ideas about
What happened	⟷	What happens
Then	⟷	Now
Generating	⟷	Criticizing
Exploring	⟷	Reflecting
Seeing	⟷	Interpreting
Playing	⟷	Judging

FIGURE 1.4 When writers use dialectical thinking, they move back and forth between two opposing modes of thought—the creative and the critical. One seems playful and the other judgmental; one feels open ended and the other more closed. Certain activities such as fastwriting or brainstorming promote one mode of thought, and careful composing or reflection promotes another.

happened, while critical thinking may lead you to insights about *what happens.* Note in the excerpt from Jon's journal how a seemingly meaningless scene describing play with toy soldiers acquires substance when Jon is forced to place the experience in perspective. Jon finds a larger significance in his simple recollection by shifting to critical thinking. Likewise, in research writing, investigators often move back and forth between their *observations of* things and their *ideas about* them. More broadly speaking, when we think creatively we collect, and when we think critically we evaluate what we have collected.

Note that in Figure 1.4 double-ended arrows link each of the two pairs. The process is *dialectical*; it consists of a back-and-forth movement between the two opposing modes of thought. Many writers do this instinctively. As they compose, they constantly shift between contrasting modes of thought, from collecting to focusing, from generating to criticizing, from showing to telling, from exploring to reflecting, from believing to doubting, from playing to judging.

Certain activities—such as fastwriting and composing—encourage one way of thinking or the other. Learning to balance these opposing forces is what dialectical thinking is all about. In practice, however, many beginning writers give too much emphasis to either one mode of thinking or the other, a tendency that accounts for many of the challenges these writers face within their own writing processes.

Spend too much time locked in the critical mode of thinking and your internal critic takes over. This voice pinches off the flow of material generated by creative thinking. The writing then comes slowly and painfully, and it rarely yields surprise. Topics are abandoned before the writer has fully explored their potential. Working from scarcity, the writer is compelled to use all the material he or she has at hand, often resulting in writing that feels forced, incomplete, or obvious.

On the other hand, give too much free rein to creative thinking and the artist runs wild. The problem here isn't scarcity but rather overabundance. It's a poverty of riches, for without a critical eye to provide shape and direction, the writer cannot present all of his or her material in a coherent and meaningful fashion.

Other challenges result when writers fail to move back and forth between creative and critical modes. One excursion into creative thinking followed by a second into critical thinking is rarely enough to produce good writing. Writers need to move back and forth between the two modes until they come to see their topics in interesting ways that differ from what they might have creatively or critically thought about the topic when they started the writing process.

Put simply, the goal of this dialectical thinking is to address a question that ultimately all writing must answer:

So what?

So what? can be a pretty harsh question, and I find that some students tend to ask it too soon in the writing process, before they've fully explored their topic or collected enough information. That may have been your experience when you suddenly found yourself high and dry, forced to reflect on possible meanings of a moment you've written about for only eight minutes. When you can't come up with an answer to *So what?,* the solution is usually to generate more information.

There's another danger, too. In their enthusiasm to answer *So what?,* some writers seize on the first convenient idea or thesis that comes along. This abruptly ends the process of inquiry before they've had a chance to explore their subjects. These writers squander the opportunity to be surprised by what they discover.

EXERCISE 1.5

Overcome Your Own Challenges

STEP ONE: Consult again the Self-Evaluation Survey you completed in Exercise 1.3. Based on what you've learned so far, answer the following questions:

- What are the biggest challenges to your writing process?
- How can you overcome these challenges?

Using What You Have Learned

When I was in college I used to say this to anyone who asked how I felt about writing: *I don't like writing but I love having written.* What I meant, of course, is that I often felt satisfaction with the product of writing—the paper or essay—but didn't like the work that it took to produce it. This belief didn't help me improve as a writer because it prevented me from finding things about the process that could actually be okay, and even pleasurable, things like discovery. I never imagined surprise was possible. I hope this chapter initiated a reexamination of your own beliefs about writing. I hardly expect a revolution in your thinking, but maybe one or two things you once thought were true of writing may at least be in doubt, particularly if you think those beliefs get in the way of your progress. Carry that openness to revise your thinking into every assignment in this book and you may be surprised at what you can do.

You now know more about your writing process. You've identified what seems to go well and when you get into trouble. The habit of reflecting on your process will be invaluable as you face each new writing situation because each one presents different problems and choices. Understanding the basic rhetorical principles—considering how to present yourself to particular audiences on particular subjects—will help. You already know more than you think about rhetoric.

You'll also have the chance to try out dialectical thinking, a process that may seem a little dizzying. In a way, it should, because both the writing process and dialectical thinking involve a great deal of back-and-forth movement, the sort of mental gymnastics you perform with the pen in your hand or your fingers on the keyboard.

Does it feel natural? Probably not. At least not yet. But I hope you'll find that your understanding of the writing process becomes more intuitive as you read further in the book. You may modify your writing process, add a step here or skip one there, prolong the process or cut it short, depending on the writing situation and your rhetorical concerns. Whatever you do, though, you need to make choices based on an understanding of how they will influence your process. This is the key to making you a productive, confident writer.

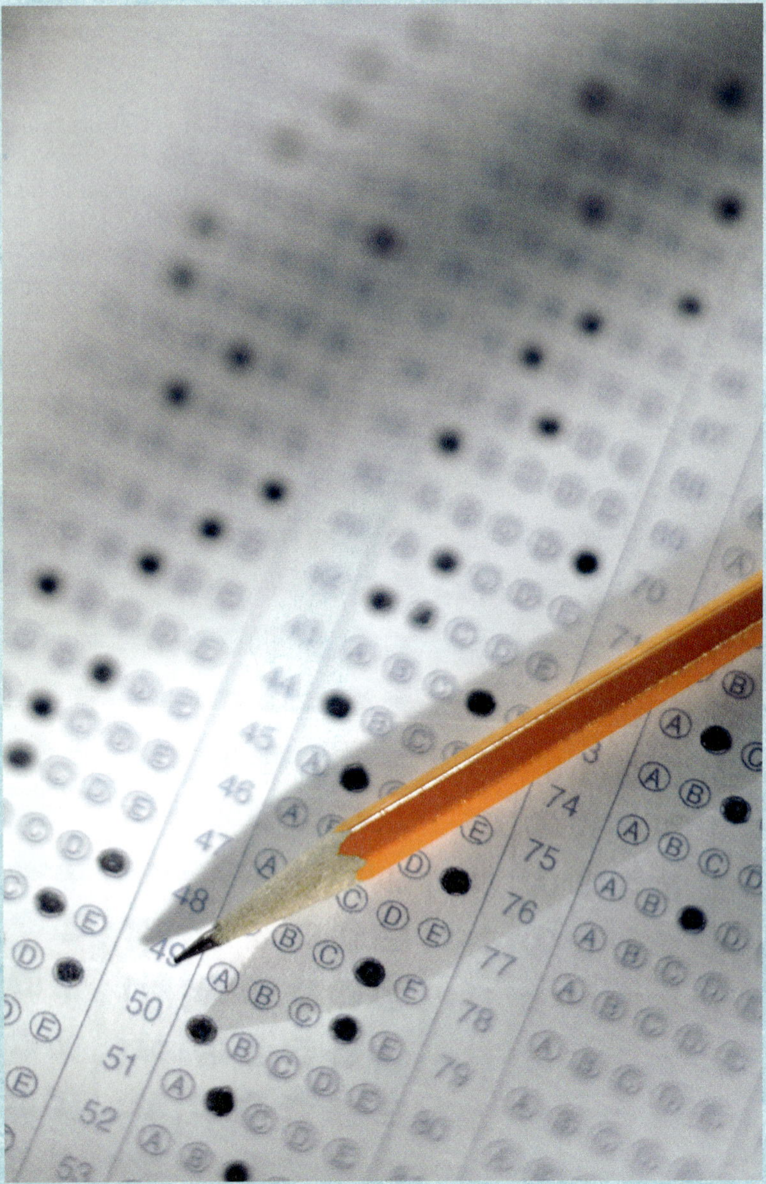

On Saturday mornings across America, students read a passage on an aptitude test and answer a question about it by darkening a circle on a bubble sheet. In contrast, reading to inquire opens a conversation with a text in which the words on the page are only a part of the dialogue between the author and the reader.

Reading as Inquiry

2

Here's what you might be thinking as you read this sentence: *this is a chapter about reading (in a textbook about writing) and I'm really hungry and could eat some potato chips and I already know about reading; I've been reading for years; this guy has a strange way of opening a textbook chapter how does he know what I'm thinking, he probably doesn't want to know* . . . Okay, so I don't know exactly what you're thinking. But I do know that you're not simply sitting there decoding the meaning of each word I've written. For one thing, you're reading faster than that, looking at chunks of language. However, a lot of what is going on in your head isn't directly related to the words here. You are thinking about what kind of book you are reading—the textbook genre—and making mental predictions about what is going to come next. You are thinking about the subject—"reading as inquiry"—and considering what you may already know about it. And you are thinking about your purpose in reading these sentences or this book, trying to use that purpose as a guide to help you navigate my meaning and its relevance to you. However, I'm probably wrong about the potato chips.

I hope the image you get of reading from this account is that what *you* bring to the reading situation is much more powerful than the words on the page. Experienced readers are aware of this, and like experienced writers, they can bring this knowledge to a range of reading situations and make choices about *how* to read. This rhetorical knowledge of reading is especially important in college. First, you'll be reading a lot, and you'll be introduced, in classes across campus, to new genres and specialized writing that are entirely new to you. Sometimes you might feel as if you're in a wrestling match with texts whose moves are so novel that they threaten to pin you every time you confront them. But you can learn the moves, and in many cases you already know them. My students fret about writing. But they don't seem to get very worked up

What You'll Learn in This Chapter

- How your existing beliefs about reading might be obstacles to reading rhetorically.
- What connections exist between the writing and reading process.
- How to use the double-entry journal to encourage dialectical thinking.
- How to apply some of the same strategies to reading pictures that you do to reading texts.
- How to understand the unique grammar of images.
- How to design the "look" of your writing.

about the challenges of reading. As you've seen, however, reading is complex, and in this chapter I'll show you how the writing process involves some of the same mental activities and even similar rhetorical choices used in reading. I'll also show you how writing can help you read better.

When we think of reading we usually associate the act exclusively with written texts, but so many of the images we encounter are, like written texts, crafted to communicate and persuade and so, whether we recognize it or not, we read images, too. In this chapter we'll use images as a metaphor to talk about all kinds of reading strategies, but we'll also focus on the unique grammar of visual literacy and how images work to influence a "reader."

MOTIVES FOR READING

Why read? In the case of best-selling popular fiction such as *The Da Vinci Code* or the Harry Potter books, the answer seems pretty clear: these are entertaining books. But pleasure is not a motive that seems to apply to most academic reading—we usually regard such reading as something we have to do to study for the test or write the paper. However, reading to inquire, while not always a source of pleasure, can offer the satisfaction of surprise and discovery, just as writing to inquire can. This is because what's behind an encounter with a text can be a desire to answer a question that interests you. Reading to inquire is, like writing to inquire, an open-ended process in which you set out to discover what you think, and along the way welcome confusion and ambiguity as a natural condition of the search. In other words, you never read just to collect information; you read to have a conversation with the information. You go back and forth between what an author says and what you think about what he or she says. *Does this help answer a question I've posed? Does it inspire me to see things differently? Does it complicate what I already believe?*

Reading with the spirit of inquiry turns books, essays, and articles into one side of a dialogue that you're having with yourself and an author.

Reading with the spirit of inquiry turns books, essays, and articles into one side of a dialogue that you're having with yourself and an author. The meaning of a text (or an image) isn't fixed forever—engraved in stone tablets like a message from above—but worked out between the two of you, the author and the reader. This turns reading into a much more complicated intellectual activity, but it also makes reading more interesting because you create the conditions for surprise, for learning, and for discovery.

BELIEFS ABOUT READING

Most of us aren't very aware of our reading strategies and habits. Why should we be? After all, isn't reading just reading? How many ways can you do it? The way we go about learning how to read, however, is similar to the way we learn how to write. We start at an early age, perhaps even before we get to school. Along with the learning, we acquire beliefs that inform our response to *how* we read. These beliefs, though, can help or hinder our progress as readers. Once again, then, we need to assess our beliefs. Only by understanding *how* we read in certain situations can we acquire more control over what we get out of the reading experience.

EXERCISE 2.1

What Do You Believe?

STEP ONE: From the following list, choose two qualities that you believe best characterize a "good" reader.

1. Needs to read things only once to understand what an author is saying.
2. Can find the hidden meanings in the text.
3. Takes notes while reading.
4. Reads slowly and carefully, and doesn't proceed unless she understands the meaning of every word.
5. Pays attention to his feelings about what he is reading.
6. Tries to find support for what she already believes.
7. Understands that all sources and all authors are biased.
8. Tries to find the author's theme or thesis.
9. Focuses mostly on the important parts of the text, such as the beginning, ending, and titles.
10. Pays most attention to details, facts, statistics.
11. Avoids reading things that don't interest him.
12. Reads with certain questions or goals in mind.

STEP TWO: Answer the following questions in your journal.

- Do you think you're a good reader? Why or why not?
- How would you describe your own reading habits and methods?

STEP THREE: Share the results of the previous two steps in a class discussion and then consider the following questions:

- Did you find that your beliefs were widely shared by others in the class?
- Did you find that others generally considered themselves competent readers?
- Did all competent readers have similar beliefs and reading habits?
- How important were your early reading experiences in shaping your beliefs about reading?

Most reading instruction seems to focus on comprehension—you know, the SAT- or ACT-inspired kind of situation in which you are asked to read something and then explain what it means. This often becomes an exercise in recall and vocabulary, an analytical challenge in only the most general way. Essentially, you train yourself to distinguish between specifics and generalities and to loosely follow the author's reasoning. In English classes, sometimes we are asked to perform a similar exercise with stories or poems—what is the theme or what does it mean?

Questions such as these send students off on what is essentially an archaeological expedition where they must dig for hidden meaning. The "right" answers to the questions are in the text, like a buried bone; you just have to find them. Sometimes the expedition is successful, sometimes not. The trouble with this type of exercise has less to do with its success rate than with the belief that it tends to foster, which is that *all meaning resides in the text and the reader's job is merely to find it.* This belief limits the reader's interaction with the text. If meaning is fixed within the text, embedded like a bone in antediluvian mud, then all the reader has to do is dig to find that meaning. Digging isn't a bad thing, but reading can be so much more than laboring at the shovel and sifting through dirt.

Only by understanding how we read in certain situations can we acquire more control over what we get out of the reading experience.

Our many experiences with reading in and out of school inevitably lead us to develop assumptions about what reading demands. That's why it's so crucial to draw those beliefs into the open where you can examine them in the light.

READING SITUATIONS AND RHETORICAL CHOICES

It's impossible to decide how you should read without knowing the reading situation. *What are you reading? Why are you reading it?* For example, consider the box score from the 2006 Major League Baseball All-Star Game, pictured here. Those who love baseball are familiar with this particular reading "genre" and how to decipher its meaning quickly and easily. A reader of this sort who is interested in how many runs batted in (RBIs) Alex Rodriguez had during the game knows exactly where to find this information. In the process, that reader might also cull additional relevant information about Rodriguez's performance, like at bats (ABs), statistics that illuminate the significance of his RBIs (or in this case, his lack of RBIs).

However, for a reader who is not a baseball fan and is unfamiliar with the conventions by which the sport communicates its statistics in print, interpreting the information in this box score would be a chore. Obviously then, reading in unfamiliar genres is not easy. Let's consider another, very different genre. For example, those not used to "reading" abstract art are often unmoved by a work like *One (Number 31, 1950).* Not surprisingly, students often have a similar reaction to academic writing, a reaction that can usually be summed up in two words: "It's boring!" But when you read rhetorically you learn not to stay with such initial reactions. You recognize that one reason you can't relate to the text is that you don't know the genre or its conventions. The language may be unfamiliar because you aren't the audience for whom the writing was originally intended.

AL All-Stars	AB	R	H	RBI	BB	SO	LOB	AVG
Suzuki, RF	3	0	0	0	0	1	0	.000
Dye, RF	1	0	0	0	0	0	0	.000
Jeter, SS	3	0	0	0	0	2	0	.000
Tejada, SS	1	0	0	0	0	0	0	.000
Ortiz, 1B	2	0	0	0	0	1	0	.000
Konerko, 1B	2	0	2	0	0	0	0	1.000
1-Lopez, PR-3B	0	1	0	0	0	0	0	.000
Rodriguez, 3B	2	0	0	0	0	0	0	.000
Glaus, 3B-1B	2	1	1	0	0	0	1	.500
Guerrero, LF	2	1	1	1	0	0	0	.500
Young, 2B	2	0	1	2	0	0	0	.500
Rodriguez, C	2	0	0	0	0	0	0	.000
Mauer, C	2	0	0	0	0	1	1	.000
Wells, CF	2	0	1	0	0	0	0	.500
Matthews, LF	1	0	1	0	0	0	0	1.000
Loretta, 2B	2	0	0	0	0	0	1	.000
Zito, P	0	0	0	0	0	0	0	.000
Kazmir, P	0	0	0	0	0	0	0	.000
Santana, P	0	0	0	0	0	0	0	.000
b-Thome, PH	1	0	0	0	0	0	1	.000
Ryan, P	0	0	0	0	0	0	0	.000
Rivera, P	0	0	0	0	0	0	0	.000
Rogers, P	0	0	0	0	0	0	0	.000
a-Ordonez, PH	1	0	0	0	0	1	0	.000
Halladay, P	0	0	0	0	0	0	0	.000
Sizemore, CF	2	0	0	0	0	1	1	.000
Totals	**33**	**3**	**7**	**3**	**0**	**7**	**5**	

a-Struck out for Rogers in the 3rd. b-Grounded out for Santana in the 8th.
1-Ran for Konerko in the 9th.

BATTING
2B: Glaus (1, Hoffman).
3B: Young (1, Hoffman).
HR: Guerrero (1, 2nd inning off Penny, 0 on, 1 out).
TB: Konerko 2; Glaus 2; Guerrero 4; Young 3; Wells; Matthews.
RBI: Guerrero (1), Young 2 (2).
2-out RBI: Young 2.
Runners left in scoring position, 2 out: Sizemore; Mauer.
GIDP: Glaus.
Team LOB: 3.

FIELDING
E: Lopez (1, fielding).
Outfield assists: Wells (Soriano at home).
DP: 3 (Rogers-Jeter-Ortiz, Loretta-Jeter-Ortiz, Young-Tejada-Konerko).

NL All-Stars	AB	R	H	RBI	BB	SO	LOB	AVG
Soriano, LF	2	0	1	0	0	0	0	.500
Webb, P	0	0	0	0	0	0	0	.000
Sanchez, SS-2B	2	0	0	0	0	0	0	.000
Beltran, CF	4	1	2	0	0	0	0	.500
Pujols, 1B	3	0	0	0	0	1	1	.000
Howard, 1B	1	0	0	0	0	0	1	.000
Bay, RF-LF	3	0	1	0	0	2	1	.333
Lee, LF	1	0	0	0	0	0	1	.000
Renteria, SS	2	0	0	0	0	0	1	.000
Arroyo, P	0	0	0	0	0	0	0	.000
Fuentes, P	0	0	0	0	0	0	0	.000
Turnbow, P	0	0	0	0	0	0	0	.000
b-Berkman, PH	0	0	0	0	1	0	0	.000
Cabrera, 3B	0	0	0	0	0	0	0	.000
Wright, 3B	3	1	1	1	0	0	1	.333
Gordon, P	0	0	0	0	0	0	0	.000
Hoffman, P	0	0	0	0	0	0	0	.000
Utley, 2B	2	0	1	0	0	0	0	.500
McCann, C	1	0	0	0	0	0	0	.000
Lo Duca, C	2	0	0	0	0	0	1	.000
Eckstein, SS	1	0	0	0	0	1	0	.000
Penny, P	0	0	0	0	0	0	0	.000
Oswalt, P	0	0	0	0	0	0	0	.000
a-Holliday, PH-RF	3	0	0	0	0	0	0	.000
Totals	**30**	**2**	**6**	**1**	**1**	**4**	**7**	

a-Grounded out for Oswalt in the 3rd. b-Walked for Turnbow in the 7th.

BATTING
2B: Beltran (1, Rogers).
HR: Wright (1, 2nd inning off Rogers, 0 on, 1 out).
TB: Soriano; Beltran 3; Bay; Wright 4; Utley.
RBI: Wright (1).
Runners left in scoring position, 2 out: Bay; Lee.
GIDP: Lo Duca; Renteria; Wright.
Team LOB: 2.

BASERUNNING
SB: Soriano (1, 2nd base off Halladay/Rodriguez), Beltran (1, 3rd base off Halladay/Rodriguez).

FIELDING
DP: (Wright-Sanchez-Howard).

AL All-Stars	IP	H	R	ER	BB	SO	HR	ERA
Rogers	2.0	3	1	1	0	1	1	4.50
Halladay	2.0	3	1	1	0	1	0	4.50
Zito	1.0	0	0	0	0	0	0	0.00
Kazmir	1.0	0	0	0	0	0	0	0.00
Santana	1.0	0	0	0	1	1	0	0.00
Ryan (W, 1-0)	1.0	0	0	0	0	1	0	0.00
Rivera (S, 1)	1.0	0	0	0	0	0	0	0.00

NL All-Stars	IP	H	R	ER	BB	SO	HR	ERA
Penny	2.0	1	1	1	0	3	1	4.50
Oswalt	1.0	0	0	0	0	1	0	0.00
Webb (H, 1)	1.0	0	0	0	0	1	0	0.00
Arroyo (H, 1)	1.0	1	0	0	0	0	0	0.00
Fuentes (H, 1)	1.0	0	0	0	0	1	0	0.00
Turnbow (H, 1)	1.0	1	0	0	0	0	0	0.00
Gordon (H, 1)	1.0	1	0	0	0	1	0	0.00
Hoffman (BS, 1)(L, 0-1)	1.0	3	2	2	0	0	0	18.00

WP: Halladay.
Pitches-strikes: Rogers 30-20, Halladay 22-13, Zito 8-7, Kazmir 9-6, Santana 11-5, Ryan 10-10, Rivera 17-12, Penny 38-24, Oswalt 13-7, Webb 16-10, Arroyo 10-7, Fuentes 9-8, Turnbow 14-8, Gordon 14-8, Hoffman 13-13.
Ground outs-fly outs: Rogers 3-2, Halladay 4-0, Zito 1-2, Kazmir 1-2, Santana 2-0, Ryan 1-1, Rivera 2-1, Penny 1-2, Oswalt 1-1, Webb 1-1, Arroyo 0-3, Fuentes 2-0, Turnbow 2-1, Gordon 2-0, Hoffman 3-0.
Batters faced: Rogers 8, Halladay 7, Zito 3, Kazmir 3, Santana 3, Ryan 3, Rivera 4, Penny 7, Oswalt 3, Webb 3, Arroyo 4, Fuentes 3, Turnbow 3, Gordon 4, Hoffman 8.
Umpires: HP: Jerry Crawford. 1B: Randy Marsh. 2B: Fieldin Culbreth. 3B: Jeff Nelson. LF: Mike Everitt. RF: Alfonso Marquez.
Weather: 79 degrees, cloudy.
Wind: 8 mph, R to L.
T: 2:33.
Att: 38,904.

Box score official statistics approved by Major League Baseball Office of the Commissioner

Box score from 2006 Major League Baseball All-Star Game.

One (Number 31, 1950). 1950. Oil and enamel on unprinted canvas, 8′10″ × 17′5 5/8″. Sidney and Harriet Janis Collection Fund (by exchange). (7.1968) Location: The Museum of Modern Art, New York, NY, U.S.A.

What do you do? Look for clues in the text about how to read it, prepare for the encounter by learning as much as you can about the text's subject, and always keep in mind your purposes for reading the piece in the first place. Only by keeping these things in mind can you make informed choices about *how* you should read. In this sense, reading situations demand the same sort of rhetorical choices that writing situations do. What's surprising, though, is that we rarely talk about choices when we discuss reading.

As a matter of fact, we rarely talk much about reading at all except to practice the reading skills that might help students do well on the reading comprehension section of the SAT or ACT. This is probably a good thing because those are high-stakes tests for college-bound students. But the Saturday morning computerized placement test is only one very specific rhetorical situation. Recall the rhetorical triangle—it also applies to reading situations.

In the reader's rhetorical triangle, the reader moves to the apex of the triangle and the writer (or text's author, in this case) moves down to one of the lower legs (see Figure 2.1). The reader's portion of the triangle includes the reader's purpose for reading the text and the particular habits and strategies he brings to his reading. The subject includes not only the main topic of the reading but the form or genre in which it is presented. The author's purpose shapes the third portion of the triangle. Combined, the three work to determine the context of each reading situation. The verbal SAT exam, for instance, in part involves reading short passages and answering multiple-choice comprehension questions. Speed is important. The significance of the test and the speed required to complete it influence the reader's portion of the triangle. So too does the subject, which is presented in the form of multiple-choice questions. The author's intent in composing the questions—to test comprehension—also shapes the reading situation.

A test situation differs greatly from one in which the same person is asked to read a Ralph Ellison short story and write a critical essay about it for her English

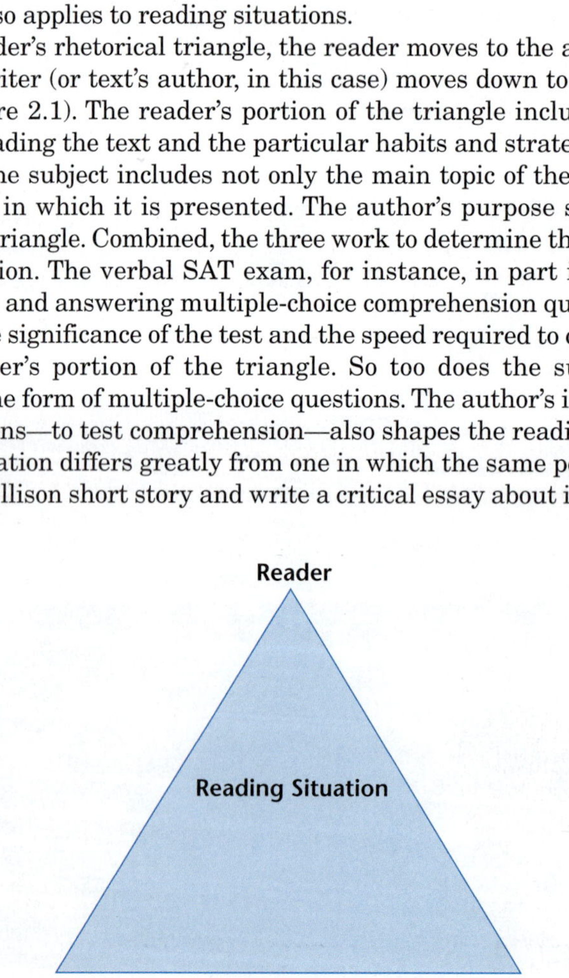

FIGURE 2.1 The reader's rhetorical triangle.

class. Here the author's perspective may be harder to interpret. The subject, presented in short-story form, is also likely to be more ambiguous in its message than multiple-choice questions. The reader also brings different reading habits to the text, reading slowly and perhaps repeatedly, to tease out the meaning.

Each reading situation, then, requires its own rhetorical choices. But how do you know which rhetorical choices to make? A recent study of reading strategies used by college undergraduates found that what distinguished academically successful readers from those who were less successful was agreement with the following statement: *I evaluate whether what I am reading is relevant to my reading goals.*[1] Students with lower GPAs generally didn't consider goals when they were reading and rarely varied their reading strategies. The less successful readers made the same rhetorical choices regardless of the reading situation. The more successful readers, on the other hand, tailored their rhetorical choices to address the needs of the reading situation.

READING AS A PROCESS

Rhetorical reading begins with understanding reading as a process. As with the writing process, the more we know about our own reading process, the more control we have over it and the more we are likely to get out of our reading. There's nothing difficult about understanding reading as a process, but doing so may challenge some of your existing beliefs about how reading works.

Linear Versus Recursive Models

In the last chapter, I discussed two models for understanding the writing process. The first model moved in one direction from prewriting to writing to rewriting. The second model moved back and forth among these three stages. The two models of the reading process that I want you to consider here operate in a similar fashion. The conventional model is linear—information flows in one direction from the text to the readers (see Figure 2.2). Here, while readers

FIGURE 2.2 A linear model of the reading process.

1. Roman, Taraban, Kimberly Rynearson, and Marcel Kerr, "College Students' Academic Performance and Self-Reports of Comprehension Strategy Use," *Reading Psychology* 21, no. 4 (2000): 283–308.

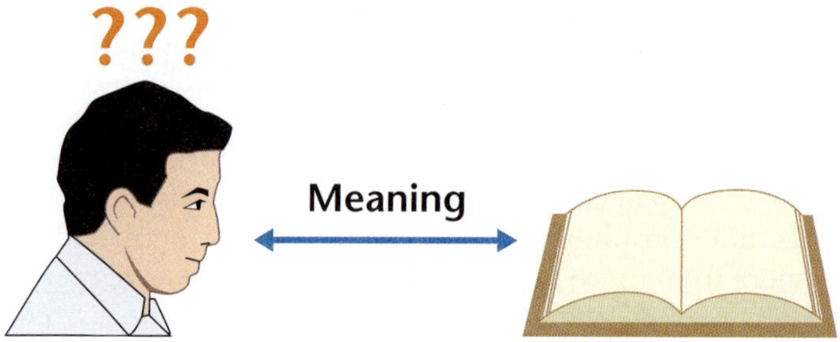

FIGURE 2.3 A recursive model of the reading process.

may have to actively dig within the text for information, the manner in which they receive the information is relatively passive. Meaning resides squarely within the text. Most reading comprehension tests exclusively evaluate this type of reading.

The second model is recursive. It suggests that our understanding of what a text means exists as a two-way *transaction* between the reader and author, the product of a back-and-forth dialogue between what the author is saying and what the reader thinks the author is saying (see Figure 2.3). In this model, the reader interprets, analyzes, reflects on, and thoroughly questions the information in the text; the meaning that emerges doesn't reside on the pages, but somewhere between the reader and the text. As you will see, the recursive model of the reading process often involves writing *while* you read. You will also learn that the back-and-forth movement represented by this model is guided by the reading situation and the rhetorical choices that the reader makes in response to the situation.

EXERCISE 2.2

Reading Strategies

Henry David Thoreau's *Walden*, a classic of American literature, is an account of his relatively brief time living in a one-room cabin on the shore of Walden Pond, just outside Concord, Massachusetts. The book continues to influence new generations of Americans, sometimes with tragic consequences. Writer Jon Krakauer's best seller *Into the Wild* is an account of a young man, Chris McCandless, who used *Walden* as his inspiration to live alone in Alaska, where he starved to death. The excerpt that follows is a famous passage from Thoreau's book in which he establishes his purposes for living alone. You can find a copy of this passage on the companion Web site (http://ablongman.com/ballenger) if you don't want to mark up your book.

STEP ONE: Read the excerpt as you normally would if your purpose was to understand what the author is saying.

WALDEN

"Where I Lived and What I Live For"

Henry David Thoreau

I went to the woods because I wished to live deliberately, to front only the essential facts of life, and see if I could not learn what it had to teach, and not, when I came to die, discover I had not lived. I do not wish to live what was not life, living is so dear; nor did I wish to practice resignation, unless it was quite necessary. I wanted to live deep and suck out all the marrow of life, to live so sturdily and Spartan-like as to put to rout all that was not life, to cut a broad swath and shave close, to drive life into a corner, and reduce it to its lowest terms, and, if it proved to be mean, why then to get the whole and genuine meanness of it, and publish its meanness to the world; or if it were sublime, to know it by experience, and be able to give a true account of it in my next excursion. For most men, it appears to me, are in a strange uncertainty about it, whether it is of the devil or of God, and have *somewhat hastily* concluded that it is the chief end of man here to "glorify God and enjoy him forever." 1

Still we live meanly, like ants; though the fable tells us that we were long ago changed into men; like pygmies we fight with cranes; it is error upon error, and clout upon clout, and our best virtue has for its occasion a superfluous and evitable wretchedness. Our life is frittered away by detail. An honest man has hardly need to count more than his ten fingers, or in extreme cases he may add his ten toes, and lump the rest. Simplicity, simplicity, simplicity! I say, let your affairs be as two or three, and not a hundred or a thousand; instead of a million count half a dozen, and keep your accounts on your thumb nail. 2

STEP TWO: It might seem criminal to distill such a rich passage into two or three sentences, but compose a summary in your journal. *In your own words,* explain what you understand Thoreau to be saying here. Identify, if you can, the main ideas you cull from the passage.

STEP THREE: Review the list of reading perspectives in the "Inquiring into the Details" box on page 43. Which perspectives did you use to complete the exercise? Also, list the reading behaviors you used, if any, to complete the previous two steps. Reading behaviors include underlining, highlighting, note taking, writing in the margin, listing, rereading, skimming, exploratory writing, conversing with others about the text, taking a break, or copying passages (see the accompanying list). When you are done, answer the following questions:

- Did you note any pattern to the way you used the behaviors (when, how much, which ones)? Were the perspectives you adopted pretty typical for you?
- Would you have used different behaviors or perspectives if your purpose had not been to summarize the passage but instead had been to write a one-page argument against the author's claims in the passage?

Types of Reading Behaviors

What do you actually *do*, if anything, when you read for school?

- Underline
- Highlight
- Make marginal notes
- Write in your journal
- Converse with someone about the text
- Reread
- Skim
- Take lots of breaks
- Copy down important passages or facts

A good first step to using the recursive model of the reading process is to find ways to *actively* interact with the text so that you're having a conversation with the material. Simple strategies such as underlining, highlighting, note taking, writing in the margins, listing, and rereading help begin this conversation. Doing nothing—the default mode for many readers—is the intellectual equivalent of being a couch potato. Conversations also work best when *both* participants listen and respond to each other—and as in any conversation, how you listen and respond depends on the stance or perspective you take toward what you're hearing.

The behaviors and perspectives that you use when reading depend on the rhetorical situation. For example, you'll likely mark up a poem in *The Longman Anthology of World Literature* differently from an article in *Sociology Quarterly.* If your motive is simply to summarize an article on Canada's drug laws, you'll ask yourself different questions than if you're analyzing the claims of an editorial on the ethics of downloading free music. But certain "essential acts of mind" occur in almost all reading situations, and you'll find them mighty familiar.

INQUIRING INTO THE DETAILS

READING PERSPECTIVES

When we read, we always adopt certain perspectives toward a text, usually unconsciously. But one of the best ways to read strategically is to consciously *shift* our perspective while we read. Like changing lenses on a camera or changing the angle, distance, or time of day to photograph something, this shift in reading perspective illuminates different aspects of a text. Here are some of the perspectives you might take:

- ***Believing:*** What the author says is probably true. Which ideas can I relate to? What information should I use? What seems especially sound about the argument?
- ***Doubting:*** What are the text's weaknesses? What ideas don't jibe with my own experience? What are the gaps in the information or the argument? What isn't believable about this?
- ***Updating:*** What does this add to what I already know about the subject?
- ***Hunting and gathering:*** What can I collect from the text that I might be able to use?
- ***Interpreting:*** What might be the meaning of this?
- ***Pleasure seeking:*** I just want to enjoy the text and be entertained by it.
- ***Connecting:*** How does this information relate to my own experiences? What is its relationship to other things I've read? Does it verify, extend, or contradict what other authors have said?
- ***Reflecting:*** How was this written? What makes it particularly effective or ineffective?
- ***Resisting:*** This doesn't interest me. Why do I have to read it? Isn't *Survivor* on television right now?

Dialectical Thinking

The sort of thinking we do while engaged in the reading process is comparable to the thinking we do when involved in the writing process. We move back and forth between creative and critical modes of thought, shifting between specifics and generalities, collecting and focusing, narrating and criticizing, generating and reflecting. Many of the questions we asked for writing are the same for reading: *What does this mean? Why might this fact or detail be significant? How does this connect with what I already know? What do I understand from reading this that I didn't understand when I began? Is this believable and convincing?*

Like writers, readers often consider their motives before they plunge into the text. For example, one reader might begin with a particular purpose: He just bought a handheld computer and must read the instructions to find out how it works. In this particular reading situation, it wouldn't make much sense to use creative thinking to interpret the instructions. Instead, the reader, with clear purpose in mind, uses critical thinking to decipher the instructions and apply them to the task at hand. But many texts we read in college are either much less explicit or much more challenging to understand than the instructions to a handheld computer. Nor is the sense of purpose so obviously clear. How do we make sense of texts like these? Move back and forth between the two contrary modes of thought, trying to answer the same essential question that nags us as writers: *So what*? There are some very practical ways to encourage this kind of thinking when you read, including the *double-entry* or *dialogue journal*, which is introduced later in the chapter.

Writing with Computers

REFLECTION AND DIALECTICAL THINKING ON A COMPUTER

The comments function of your word processor is a great tool for practicing reflection and dialectical thinking in electronic documents. If you're reading a Web site or other electronic source, you can copy the text into your word processor and use the comments function to make notes as you critically analyze the text while you are reading it. As a writer you can use the feature to reflect on your own writing without altering your draft. Some writers use the comments feature as they write their initial draft to make notes that they want to have available later. For instance, instead of spending ten minutes trying to revise a passage that seems a bit unclear, make a note to yourself saying you think it is unclear and then get back to writing your draft. This will prevent getting caught up with surface-level revision when your objective is to generate new ideas and text.

When you use the comments feature, you don't need to create a second file of your draft for making comments. Comments can be hidden by changing your display settings. In addition, the print menu has options to show or hide comments in printouts. These options allow you to have a presentable copy for your peer-editing groups and keep all of your comments in a single file with your draft.

Believing and Doubting

Another way to engage dialectical thinking is to move back and forth between believing and doubting the author's claims as we read. Writing teacher Peter Elbow introduced the terms *believing game* and *doubting game* to describe how we might look at texts or experiences.[2] Elbow argues that our tendency to doubt or be critical of what we hear or read is only half of what we need to be able to reason and inquire well. He suggests we also need to play the believing game, to "try on" accepting the truth of another's arguments, claims, or experiences, and to search for "virtues or strengths we otherwise might miss," even if we disagree.

2. Peter Elbow, "Methodological Believing and Doubting: Contraries in Inquiry," in *Embracing Contraries: Explorations in Learning and Teaching* (New York: Oxford University Press, 1986).

Believing and doubting are opposed stances, obviously, and adopting both of them when reading a book or an article isn't always easy, particularly when you have strong feelings about a topic or an author. But I think you'll be amazed at how the shift between the two sparks new ways of thinking.

Other stances were described in the "Inquiring into the Details: Reading Perspectives" box. These may come into play depending on what you're reading and why. But believing and doubting can be particularly useful, especially in academic situations.

EXERCISE 2.3

Practicing Dialectical Thinking

STEP ONE: Read the essay that follows.

THE IMPORTANCE OF WRITING BADLY

Bruce Ballenger

I was grading papers in the waiting room of my doctor's office the other day, and he said, "It must be pretty eye-opening reading that stuff. Can you believe those students had four years of high school and still can't write?" 1

I've heard that before. I hear it almost every time I tell a stranger that I teach writing at a university. 2

I also hear it from colleagues brandishing red pens who hover over their students' papers like Huey helicopters waiting to flush the enemy from the tall grass, waiting for a comma splice or a vague pronoun reference or a misspelled word to break cover. 3

And I heard it this morning from the commentator on my public radio station who publishes snickering books about how students abuse the sacred language. 4

I have another problem: getting my students to write badly. 5

Most of us have lurking in our past some high priest of good grammar whose angry scribbling occupied the margins of our papers. Mine was Mrs. O'Neill, an eighth-grade teacher with a good heart but no patience for the bad sentence. Her favorite comment on my writing was "awk," which now sounds to me like the grunt of a large bird, but back then meant "awkward." She didn't think much of my sentences. 6

I find some people who reminisce fondly about their own Mrs. O'Neill, usually an English teacher who terrorized them into worshipping the error-free sentence. In some cases that terror paid off when it was finally transformed into an appreciation for the music a well-made sentence can make. 7

8 But it didn't work that way with me. I was driven into silence, losing faith that I could ever pick up the pen without breaking the rules or drawing another "awk" from a doubting reader. For years I wrote only when forced to, and when I did it was never good enough.

9 Many of my students come to me similarly voiceless, dreading the first writing assignment because they mistakenly believe that how they say it matters more than discovering what they have to say.

10 The night before the essay is due they pace their rooms like expectant fathers, waiting to deliver the perfect beginning. They wait and they wait and they wait. It's no wonder the waiting often turns to hating what they have written when they finally get it down. Many pledge to steer clear of English classes, or any class that demands much writing.

11 My doctor would say my students' failure to make words march down the page with military precision is another example of a failed education system. The criticism sometimes takes on political overtones. On my campus, for example, the right-wing student newspaper demanded that an entire semester of Freshman English be devoted to teaching students the rules of punctuation.

12 There is, I think, a hint of elitism among those who are so quick to decry the sorry state of the sentence in the hands of student writers. A colleague of mine, an Ivy League graduate, is among the self-appointed grammar police, complaining often about the dumb mistakes his students make in their papers. I don't remember him ever talking about what his students are trying to say in those papers. I have a feeling he's really not that interested.

13 Concise, clear writing matters, of course, and I have a responsibility to demand it from students. But first I am far more interested in encouraging thinking than error-free sentences. That's where bad writing comes in.

14 When I give my students permission to write badly, to suspend their compulsive need to find the "perfect way of saying it," often something miraculous happens: Words that used to trickle forth come gushing to the page. The students quickly find their voices again, and even more important, they are surprised by what they have to say. They can worry later about fixing awkward sentences. First, they need to make a mess.

15 It's harder to write badly than you might think. Haunted by their Mrs. O'Neill, some students can't overlook the sloppiness of their sentences or their lack of eloquence, and quickly stall out and stop writing. When the writing stops, so does the thinking.

16 The greatest reward in allowing students to write badly is that they learn that language can lead them to meaning, that words can be a means for finding out what they didn't know they knew. It usually happens when the words rush to the page, however awkwardly.

I don't mean to excuse bad grammar. But I cringe at conservative educational reformers who believe writing instruction should return to primarily teaching how to punctuate a sentence and use *Roget's Thesaurus*. If policing student papers for mistakes means alienating young writers from the language we expect them to master, then the exercise is self-defeating. 17

It is more important to allow students to first experience how language can be a vehicle for discovering how they see the world. And what matters in this journey—at least initially—is not what kind of car you're driving, but where you end up. 18

STEP TWO: Carefully copy lines or passages from the essay that you found interesting, puzzling, provocative, or central to its argument, as you understand it. Copy these passages onto a blank page on the left side of your notebook or journal.

STEP THREE: PLAY THE BELIEVING GAME. To start with, assume the truth of the author's claims. *What evidence from your own experience or knowledge, or from the text itself, might lead you to believe some of the things said in the essay?* Explore this in a fastwrite on the right page of your journal, opposite the page on which you copied the passage. If the writing stalls, look left and find something to respond to in one of the quoted passages you collected.

STEP FOUR: PLAY THE DOUBTING GAME. Skip a few lines, and shift your stance to one that is critical of the essay's claims. What do you suspect might be the weakness of the argument? What do you know from your own experience and knowledge that contradicts the claims? What does the essay fail to consider? Do this in a fastwrite just below the one you completed from Step One. Again, if your pen slows, look on the left for quotations from the excerpt that will get you going again.

STEP FIVE: MAKE A CLAIM OF YOUR OWN. Based on what you've learned from these two contrary perspectives—believing and doubting—compose a paragraph that states what you believe about the idea that "bad" writing is important.

STEP SIX: REFLECT ON THE PROCESS. Reflect on your experience with this exercise. Make an entry in your journal that explores some of the following questions:

- What, if anything, do you understand about your reading habits or perspectives now that you didn't fully understand before this exercise?
- Which came more easily—doubting or believing? What perspectives on the topic might not have emerged if you hadn't been forced to shift stances?
- Can you see any similarities between your writing and reading processes? Differences?

One Student's Response

TODD'S JOURNAL

EXERCISE 2.3

COLLECTING	FOCUSING
STEP TWO: Writing Down Quotations "I find some people who reminisce fondly about their own Mrs. O'Neill, usually an English teacher who terrorized them into worshipping the error-free sentence. In some cases that error paid off when it was finally transformed into an appreciation for the music a well-made sentence can make." "There is, I think, a hint of elitism among those who are so quick to decry the sorry state of the sentence in the hands of student writers." "If policing student papers for mistakes means alienating young writers from the language we expect them to master, then the exercise is self-defeating." "It is more important to allow students to first experience how language can be a vehicle for discovering how they see the world. And what matters in this journey—at least initially—is not what kind of car you're driving, but where you end up."	**STEP THREE: The Doubting Game** I know enough people who have had a strong grammar background to believe that this happens more often than the author implies. Some people really like to study grammar and mechanics, and isn't it common sense that you should learn the basics before you learn how to put them all together? I also wonder what the writer means about "elitism." What is elitist about helping students to write correctly, something that will help a lot of students get better jobs. After all, even if teaching grammar doesn't help some people write better, the world expects correctness. And writers quickly get into trouble if they can't punctuate, spell, or dangle their modifiers . . . **STEP FOUR: The Believing Game** On the other hand, making people afraid to write doesn't seem like a good idea either. In a way it can be elitist if grammar is taught as rules, handed down by the grammar god (someone invented by these "defenders" of the language). You get the impression that if you dangle a modifier you're a bad person. There's something moral about the whole thing that bothers me. I really like the idea that "policing" essays can be "alienating for your writers" because I've felt that way at times. I hand in a paper to a professor and I don't feel he or she has paid any attention to my ideas . . .

COLLECTING	FOCUSING
	STEP FIVE: Making a Claim So-called "bad" writing can be useful for some writers who struggle with perfection. But students who lack basic grammar skills will be punished for it in school and in the workplace. Therefore, teachers have an obligation to teach it. **STEP SIX: Reflecting on the Exercise** It was weird to shift stances. I really wanted to spend more time playing the "believing game" because I basically agreed with the article. This suggests that when I read something I agree with, I automatically read it looking for confirmation of what I already believe. The "doubting game" shook me out of that, and . . .

INQUIRING INTO THE DETAILS

THE DOUBLE-ENTRY JOURNAL

A double-entry journal is essentially a written dialogue between a reader and a text. As a reader you ask questions, make connections, and note memories and associations.

Here's how it works: You can either draw a line down the middle of a page to make two columns, or you can use the spine of your notebook for the line and use two opposing pages.

What the Text Says	What I Think
In the left column, write out the passages from the reading that confuse you, surprise you, make you think of other ideas, seem key to your understanding of what it says, and so on.	Then in the right column, write out your response to those passages. Sometimes you'll do a fastwrite, other times you may simply jot down quick thoughts.

(continued)

THE DOUBLE-ENTRY JOURNAL ***(Continued)***

What the Text Says	What I Think
■ Jot down direct quotes, paraphrases, summaries, facts, claims. ■ Note page numbers next to each passage or summary/paraphrase. Put them in the far right margin next to the borrowed material or ideas.	Play the doubting game, questioning the source; play the believing game, trying to find its virtues, even if you disagree. ■ Shift to other reading perspectives. ■ Tell the story of your thinking about what you're reading: *My initial reaction to this is . . . but now I think . . . and now I think . . .* ■ List questions you have about the source's ideas; your emotional responses; other ideas or readings it connects to.

Continue this process for the entire reading, moving back and forth across the columns. Remember that you want to explore your response to a text, make connections to other works and your own writing, and analyze the writer's choices in terms of language, style, detail, and so forth. *Be sure to note all the bibliographic information from the source at the top of the page.*

Adapting to Unfamiliar Reading Situations

Studies on reading are unambiguous about one thing: What most affects readers' comprehension of a text is their prior knowledge of its topic. Texts on familiar subjects are clearly easier to read and respond to, but generally the reading you're required to do in college demands that you confront books and articles about things you may know little about. Frequently, these texts adopt the *discourse,* or language and conventions, of the field for which they were written, a field with which you may have little experience. Other times you'll be asked to read primary sources—the original writings of important thinkers—which may be written in the style and structure of another time or place. Reading situations such as these require us to modify our reading process.

Of course, it's quite common when reading in such situations to feel little connection to the author or her ideas, at least initially. *What is this person talking about? What does this mean to me? How boring!* In adapting our reading process to these rhetorical situations, then, the challenge is to use dialectical thinking to actively seek out the connections between your own experiences and knowledge and the author's text. The key is to use *writing* to help you to work out what you think about what you've read, focusing especially on what you find confusing, puzzling, or significant.

I realize that getting you to write as you read can be a tough sell. You're pressed for time, and you just want to get the reading done. But I'm confident that if you take a little time to use writing to hold up your end of the conversation with a text, you'll discover the pleasures of seeing the story of your own thinking unfold before you, and if you have to write about what you read, you're essentially beginning a draft. In other words, not only will you come up with better ideas, you may also work more efficiently.

EXERCISE 2.4

Further Practice: Untangling Academic Prose

Frequently you'll be asked to read some pretty difficult texts in your college classes, books or articles that are a thicket of ideas that may be hard to see through. Try using the dialectical thinking method to analyze the following passage, one that is typical of the kind of texts you'll encounter.

STEP ONE: COLLECT. As you read the following excerpt from David F. Noble's book, use the double-entry journal technique to collect lines or passages that you find significant, interesting, or puzzling. Carefully copy these on the left page of your journal. Consider reading the excerpt through at least once *without* taking notes and then begin collecting in your journal during the second or third reading.

THE FORCES OF PRODUCTION

A Social History of Industrial Automation

David F. Noble

It is a staple of current thinking about technological change that such a "successful" technology, having become dominant, must have evolved in some "necessary" way. Implicit in the modern ideology of technological progress is the belief that the process of technological development is analogous to that of natural selection. It is thus assumed that all technological alternatives are always considered, that they are disinterestedly evaluated on their technical merits, and that they are then judged according to the cold calculus of accumulation. Any successful technology, therefore—one which becomes the dominant and ultimately the only solutions to a given problem—must, by definition, be the best, for it alone has survived the rigors of engineering experimentation and the trials of the competitive marketplace. And, as the best, it has become the latest, and necessary, step along the unilinear path of progress. 1

2 This dominant "Darwinian" view of technological development rests upon a simple faith in objective science, economic rationality, and the market. It assumes that the flow of creative inventions passes progressively through three successive filters, each of which further guarantees that only the "best" alternatives survive. The first, the objective technical filter, selects the most scientifically sound solutions to a given problem. The second, the pecuniary rationality of the hard-nosed businessman, screens out more fanciful technical solutions and accepts only those which are practical and economically viable. The third, the self-correcting mechanism of the market, dooms the less savvy businessman and thus insures that only the best innovations survive.

3 But this facile faith assumes too much, and explains too little. It portrays technological development as an autonomous and neutral technical process, on the one hand, and a coldly rational and self-regulating economic process, on the other, neither of which accounts for people, power, institutions, competing values, or different dreams. Thus it begs and explains away all important historical questions: The best technology? Best for whom? Best for what? Best according to what criteria, what visions, according to whose criteria, whose visions?

STEP TWO: EXPLORE. When you feel satisfied that you've collected enough, use the lines or passages you've gathered on the left page as prompts for fastwriting on the right. When the writing stalls, skip a line, look to the left, and find something else to jump-start your writing. *When you can, write about your own observations and experiences with technology that might help you think about what Noble is trying to say. Tell stories.* Remember, questions, not answers, should direct your fastwriting. Keep writing until you feel you have a grip on some of what Noble seems to be saying about technology and your own response to his ideas.

STEP THREE: FOCUS. Adopt a critical mode of thinking for a moment. Use the writing and information you've collected so far to compose a paragraph response that summarizes, in your own words, Noble's argument and offers your own response to it. This response should complete the following sentence: *Based on my understanding, the most significant thing Noble has to say is . . .*

STEP FOUR: REFLECT. Finally, make an entry in your journal that reflects your experience with this exercise. The following questions may prompt your thinking:

- Did your reading process in this exercise differ significantly from the process you used when you read "The Importance of Writing Badly" in Exercise 2.3?
- What did you find most helpful about the double-entry journal method? What was least helpful?

- Can you connect any moments of insight or discovery in your journal with particular moves you made, perhaps asking a certain question or shifting the focus of your writing?
- How did you struggle with this reading? How did it come easily? What might you do differently when you encounter texts like these?

Inquiring into the Details

ENCOUNTERING UNFAMILIAR GENRES

An ad for the film *Memento*.

The only time most of us ever really pay attention to genre is when we encounter one that defies our expectations. When the low-budget film *Memento* was released several years ago, its puzzling narrative structure (beginning at the end of the story and proceeding to the beginning), its use of an unreliable narrator, and its alternation between black-and-white and color took audiences by surprise and generated lots of print by movie critics. Ultimately, the film became a phenomenal success, partly because its approach was so unexpected. *Memento* got people talking about a completely different way to think about filmmaking.

The response to the movie was so significant because we are a nation of moviegoers who are quite familiar with the genre, and *Memento* made us wonder how much we really know about film. These kinds of *Memento* moments happen to readers all the time, especially when we're in an academic setting and aren't familiar with the genres we're asked to read—a poem, a lab report, an academic argument, a minimalist painting. Our first response might be to question how well we can read, even though we've all been reading for a very long time.

One way of dealing with this is to simply apply reading strategies that we've used successfully in other genres. For example, because your verbal score on the reading comprehension portion of the SAT was so high, then why not approach reading the essay on the need for a new immigration policy the same way, and try to decode exactly what the writer must have meant and leave it at that? Well, your instructor will likely say, "Fine, but I want to know what you think about his argument."

A better approach when you encounter kinds of readings that are new to you is to let the reading situation be your guide.

- Ask yourself, *Why am I reading this? How is it relevant to my inquiry question?* or *What exactly is my instructor asking me to do with this text?*
- Are there clues in the text about how it might be efficiently read? For instance, do subheadings provide guidance? Is there a preface that reviews the argument? Does the concluding section have the most weight?
- Who is the intended audience for this text and what clues does that provide about the writer's purpose? Might that explain not only how she composed the text—its language, organization, and so on—and what she hoped to accomplish with it?
- Whenever possible, "frontload" before you read something challenging; that is, learn as much as you can about the subject and even the writer's relation to the subject. This knowledge will make a big difference in how much you understand.

"READING" THE VISUAL

That famous cliché—"a picture is worth a thousand words"—has apparently evolved slightly from the original Chinese proverb, "one picture is worth ten thousand words," but the theme is the same: images are more powerful than words. However, our experience tells us that this dichotomy is often false—verbal text *and* images, when used together, can be most powerful of all. Advertisers, perhaps the most skilled practitioners of modern rhetoric, know this well as they work to associate certain values or desires with a product by combining words and pictures. In the iPod advertisement on page 55, Apple has successfully married its famous silhouette images of young men and women to the pure white pleasure of the iPod. There is little text. But in this case it isn't needed because the association, by now, is firmly cemented in the public imagination. The success of our reading of this ad—and of any ad—has to do not only with its repetition but how it appeals to certain of our cultural

Chinese proverb.

Apple iPod advertisement.

values and beliefs. In this case, what are they? Answering that question must begin, as always, with another question: *Who is the intended audience here?*

Of course, you asked these same questions when analyzing verbal texts. These questions guide our reading of the visual, too, because reading images is also a rhetorical act. Why should we pay attention to this? For much the same reason we apply rhetorical knowledge to reading an article or essay: we can approach the reading with more understanding and on a more equal footing. Visual rhetoric gives us a language to talk about what we see, not simply to guard us from manipulation but to help us expose the assumptions we bring to our consumption of images. There's another reason, too. While you probably won't be designing advertisements this semester or next, you may have opportunities to craft how your writing looks, not just how it reads. We'll briefly explore both aspects of reading the visual—how images work and the "look" of writing—in the following section.

Learning the Grammar of Images

It's pretty obvious that images and texts have a lot in common. For example, a good picture is *composed*—the visual elements are arranged a certain way with a certain idea in mind. Images also have their own *grammar,* but rather than using words and syntax, images use color, lines, shape, and texture, all of which combine for a certain effect. The rhetorical reading triangle (Figure 2.1) applies to images as it applies to any other text because these elements—composition and grammar—are combined for a certain purpose and for a certain audience. And, just like writing, visual images take a range of forms, from advertisements to oil paintings, and each of these genres asks to be "read" differently (see Exercise 2.5).

Visual rhetoric gives us a language to talk about what we see, not simply to guard us from manipulation but to help us expose the assumptions we bring to our consumption of images.

Finally, the meaning of an image isn't fixed. Earlier in the chapter, I mentioned that we work out the meaning of what we read by having a conversation with it, one that is always conducted in a particular context. Each reader brings certain experiences and knowledge to a reading that influence what that reader thinks the text means. The same is true of reading images. For example, your reading of the 1950s advertisement for Wildroot Cream-Oil that follows will be quite different from the reading its designers intended.

For all of these reasons, the recursive process and dialectical thinking both apply to analyzing pictures just as they do to reading and writing texts.

Some Strategies for Reading Images

You can analyze images and written texts in many of the same ways, but because each has a different "language"—one works with words and the other with visual elements—the actual practices of analysis differ a bit. Here are some things to keep in mind:

- *Look closely.* Pictures, naturally, appeal to sight. Your skills of close observation, consequently, are probably as important when reading images as rereading is when analyzing a written text.
- *Find the subject.* Like a piece of writing, an image usually focuses on a particular visual subject that can be seen in the context of other elements of the picture. We intuitively look first at the very center of an image for the

An ad for Wildroot Cream-Oil Hair Tonic from the 1950s.

main subject, but some images may be designed to draw our eyes in other directions. Why would they do this? What might be the motive?

- *Understand the context.* It helps to know when and where an image was created. This knowledge helps shape our response and helps us understand the designer's motives. For example, knowing which magazine a particular advertisement appeared in also can provide valuable clues about purpose and audience. But the context of an image also includes the experiences and knowledge *the viewer* brings to the image, too. How might your interpretation of an image be influenced by your own history and historical vantage point and your own cultural beliefs and assumptions?
- *Understand the genre.* You are already an expert on the many forms that images take. You intuitively know that you should "read" an advertisement differently from an oil painting, a movie differently from a documentary photograph. Like written forms, visual genres give readers clues about how they should be read, and we typically know the purposes behind different forms. It's not hard, for example, to recognize the persuasive purpose of a car ad, but the purposes of other genres may be more ambiguous. For instance, what is the purpose of a painting by Van Gogh?
- *What's the story?* Images can tell stories, too. For example, the 1950s ad for Wildroot Cream-Oil on page 57 has a strong narrative element that isn't too hard to figure out: If you've got a really swell gal, she'll send you Wildroot instead of a letter because it's your hair she really cares about. Happy users of the product will also enjoy that "successful look," which has everything to do with sex appeal. Sometimes discovering the story in an image is a good starting point for analyzing its message: is this story designed to appeal to a certain audience? Does it reflect certain cultural values? Is the story current?
- *Analyze the interaction of words and pictures.* Web pages typically combine words and pictures. Some pictures have captions or are positioned carefully near certain text. Words and images are intended to work together—to *reinforce* each other. Notice how text and image elaborate on and extend a particular message. Also notice which element exploits emotions and which emphasizes reason.

EXERCISE 2.5

Reading Images

If an image is a kind of text that can be read like writing can, then the recursive reading model and dialectical thinking should help you analyze pictures, paintings, and ads, too. Try to apply those methods to the images that follow.

STEP ONE: Closely examine each of the five images that follow. Choose one you want to work with.

STEP TWO: Begin "reading" the image as you would a printed text, using the dialectical approach. Open your journal to two blank opposing pages. Begin on the left page and jump into the sea. Fastwrite about the image, letting the writing wander wherever it leads you. But begin with the following prompt: *When I first look at this picture, I think or feel_______. And then I think_______. And then . . . And then. . . .* Whenever the writing stalls, repeat the phrase *and then.* Write for five minutes without stopping.

STEP THREE: Now work on the right page with your more critical mind. Reread your fastwrite, and then try to focus your thinking about the picture by answering the question, *What story or stories does the image seem to be telling*? Remember that what makes a picture powerful is that it tells stories that transcend the moment the image captures, trying to say something larger about its subject, about our lives, or about a product. The most persuasive of these stories probably echo some cultural narrative we want to believe about ourselves, ideas about family, or patriotism, or racial harmony, or health, and so on.

STEP FOUR: Now return to the image, looking at it again closely. On the left page of your journal, collect information—specific details—from the picture or ad that seems to support the story or stories you believe the image inspires. Here's where it helps to know a little about the grammar of images.

- As you look at the pictures, pay attention to color. How does color contribute to feeling?
- What is the main visual subject? Where are your eyes drawn, and how is that accomplished?
- Are there clues about context, things like *when* or *where* the image was created?
- Are there rhetorical clues? What do you see in the image (or text) that suggests it targeted a particular audience? Does it include text or visual details that suggest a certain story, theme, or message?
- How does the image appeal to certain cultural values or beliefs? What are they? To what extent do you share these values and beliefs?

STEP FIVE: On the right page of your notebook, compose a 250-word response that explains, using supporting evidence from the picture you chose, your interpretation of its meaning and your analysis of how the image tries to communicate that meaning. Make sure you talk about rhetorical aspects of your image—what is it trying to do for what audiences?

Edward Hopper, *Nighthawks*, 1942. (Oil on canvas, 84.1 × 152.4 cm. Friends of American Art Collection, 1942.51. Reproduction, The Art Institute of Chicago.)

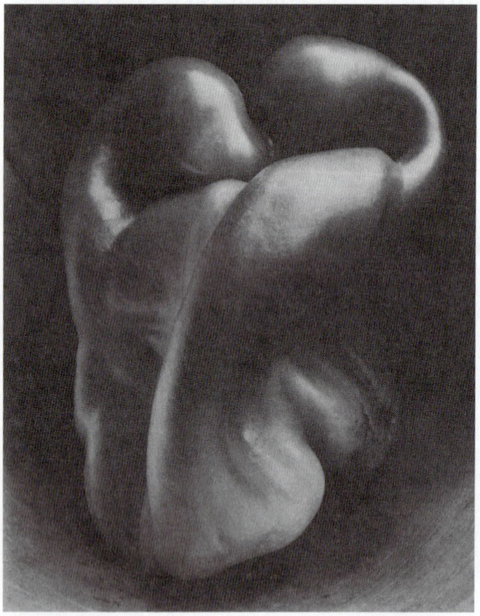

Edward Weston, *Pepper No. 30*.

A movie poster promoting the original 1933 film version of *King Kong*, starring Fay Wray.

Johnnie & Zeek from the Lower West Side series by Milton Rogovin. Photo courtesy of the Rogovin Collection (MiltonRogovin.com). Copyright 1952–2002 Milton Rogovin.

C. R. Miller, *America's Strength, All of Us Pulling Together*, c. 1950.

The "Look" of Writing

Back in my typewriter days, I didn't think about how my writing looked except to worry over whether my whited-out corrections were ugly and my margins were straight. As you know, word-processing software opened a new world of graphic possibilities. It's a world you may not have much opportunity to explore in college because the format of your papers is often limited by the assignment. However, this is changing. Many instructors welcome some use of graphic elements *if they serve a useful purpose.* Does the graphic design of your work clarify your information and ideas, and, especially, does it make your argument more persuasive?

Five graphic elements are under your control:

1. Layout
2. Images
3. Graphic representations (charts, tables, graphics)
4. Color
5. Typefaces and fonts

This is too brief a treatment of visual rhetoric to explore these elements thoroughly, but we'll focus on a few key principles to give you an idea of how the visual and the verbal can work together to make writing persuasive.

Typefaces and Fonts. In the early days of computers, I could immediately tell which of my students owned a Mac. They were the students who handed in their papers with unusual fonts. PC users like me didn't mess with fonts much back then. Of course, all that has changed. The document I'm working on at this very moment includes at least four different fonts and sizes, and I'm constantly trying to manage them all. The reason, of course, is that how writing looks can influence how it is read. Imagine, for instance, I want to incorporate a concern for visual rhetoric in my course syllabus. The course is English 102, English Composition, and I'd like the syllabus to reinforce the idea that the class will be informal, intimate, and friendly. Which of the following fonts would be likely to suggest these?

1. *Dr. Bruce Ballenger*

   English 102: English Composition

   Course Syllabus

2. Dr. Bruce Ballenger

   English 102: English Composition

   Course Syllabus

3. Dr. Bruce Ballenger

English 102: English Composition

Course Syllabus

4. Dr. Bruce Ballenger

English 102: English Composition

Course Syllabus

The two broadest categories of fonts are *serif* and *sans serif.* Serif typefaces include flourishes that sans serif typefaces lack (see Figure 2.4). In general, graphic artists believe that serif fonts are more formal than sans serif. We also respond to certain typefaces because of our previous experience with them. For example, we naturally associate example 4 above, Old English, with old books, while those of us who have had experience working with typewriters usually recognize example 3, Courier. Figure 2.5, which associates various fonts with personality traits, takes this inquiry into the effect of fonts much further. It is based on a recent study of adjectives readers consistently associated with a certain typeface.

Layout. Of course, the typeface is only one aspect of the "look" of writing, and probably not the most important. Layout is perhaps the broadest category of graphic design, and in many cases may be the element least under your control with academic writing. Your papers in English, for example, will often be guided by the design prescriptions of the Modern Language Association (MLA), while in fields like education and psychology you'll toil under the guidelines of the American Psychological Association (APA). But even then, you can enhance the layout of your papers by adding bulleted lists and headings. If you've got more liberty to play with the graphic design of your work then there's a lot to consider. Begin by understanding the following four design principles suggested by Robin Williams[3] in *The Non-Designer's Design Book:*

FIGURE 2.4 Serif versus san serif fonts.

	Top Three		
Stable	Times New Roman	Arial	Palatino
Flexible	Lisa	Giddyup	Palace Script
Conformist	Courier New	Times New Roman	Arial
Polite	Monotype Corsiva	Times New Roman	Palatino
Mature	Times New Roman	Courier New	Palatino
Formal	Times New Roman	Monotype Corsiva	Georgia
Assertive	Impact	Rockwell Xbold	Georgia
Practical	Georgia	Times New Roman	Palatino
Creative	Giddyup	Lisa	Palace Script
Happy	Lisa	Giddyup	Tekton
Exciting	Giddyup	Lisa	Palace Script
Attractive	Monotype Corsiva	Palace Script	Giddyup
Elegant	Monotype Corsiva	Palace Script	Giddyup
Cuddly	Lisa	Giddyup	Tekton
Feminine	Giddyup	Monotype Corsiva	Lisa
Unstable	Giddyup	Lisa	Palace Script
Rigid	Impact	Courier New	Futura Cond
Rebel	Giddyup	Lisa	Palace Script
Rude	Impact	Rockwell Xbold	Futura Cond
Youthful	Lisa	Giddyup	Tekton
Casual	Lisa	Tekton	Giddyup
Passive	Lisa	Giddyup	Tekton
Impractical	Giddyup	Palace Script	Lisa
Unimaginative	Courier New	Arial	Melior
Sad	Impact	Courier New	Futura Cond
Dull	Courier New	Melior	Helvetica
Unattractive	Impact	Courier New	Rockwell Xbold
Plain	Courier New	Impact	Rockwell Xbold
Coarse	Impact	Rockwell Xbold	Courier New
Masculine	Impact	Rockwell Xbold	Courier New

FIGURE 2.5 The results of a study that identified reader perception of the "personality" of various fonts.

Proximity. This principle concerns how much you "chunk" material and how well you use white or "negative" space. The idea here is that when you put similar or related things together they become an understandable "visual unit." For example, in the "Ten Things to Do" fact sheet about global warming below, notice how information about what actions to take is visually discrete from the information about the film, *An Inconvenient Truth.* There are at least two major visual units on the page, each containing related information.

Contrast. A page that lacks contrast is dull. Using different font types and sizes, colors, spaces, lines, and so on, establishes very noticeable (not subtle) contrasts. That isn't hard to see in the "Ten Things to Do" fact sheet. Notice the large, colored font with the black background that proclaims that there are things you can do about the problem. This is a noticeable contrast from the list of activities, which use a smaller font size and lack the shading. At the bottom of the page, a black background and graphic again provides a striking contrast with the list of actions.

Repetition. Repeated design elements makes the page look unified; this is particularly important in multipage documents. Typically, we consistently use the same headings or subheadings, varying the size to signal a hierarchy of importance. But there are plenty of other things you can do, including repetition of colors, lines, boxes, white spaces, margins, bolding, and so on. It's not hard to see where the designers of the "Ten Things to Do" fact sheet use repetition. It's particularly striking, for example, in the repeated color pattern and font of the top head—"Ten Things to Do" and the head at the bottom, "An Inconvenient Truth."

Alignment. The eye loves order. When designing the look of a page, always consider arrangement of visual elements. You do this already when you use margins, or center titles, or align a table to the left or to the right. The key to alignment is the sense that there is a reason for the placement of everything on the page. Even visual elements that represent different material should all feel a sense of belonging to the single page, and alignment is the way we do this. For example, the "Ten Things to Do" fact sheet is aligned by centering most of the text. This is one of the most common methods of aligning material. You can also align edges of text chunks, or pictures and graphics.

3. Robin Williams, *The Non-Designer's Design Book: Design and Typographic Principles for the Visual Novice* (Berkeley, CA: Peachpit Press, 1994).

"Ten Things to Do" fact sheet accompanying Al Gore's global warming film, *An Inconvenient Truth.*

USING WHAT YOU HAVE LEARNED

Inquiry-based writing and reading begins with an open-eyed sense of wonder. Instead of initially asking, *What should I say?* you ask, *What do I think?* You begin by trying to find questions that interest you, knowing that there isn't necessarily a single right answer. At the same time, you know that just as you open up possible meanings, at some point you need to narrow them. You are both creative *and* critical, moving back and forth between collecting and focusing, exploring and evaluating, narrating and reflecting.

As you continue in *The Curious Writer*, I'll encourage you to apply this process to nearly every assignment. Before long, it will become second nature to you; you'll find yourself naturally shifting back and forth between the creative and the critical, whether you're exploring a topic for an assignment, reading an essay that you'll discuss in class, or analyzing an advertisement. Techniques that you've already practiced such as fastwriting and listing, the double-entry journal, and generating questions will help this along.

Dorothea Lange's famous Great Depression–era photograph *Migrant Mother.*

3

Ways of Inquiring

In March 1936, while the Great Depression still gripped the nation, documentary photographer Dorothea Lange was driving along a quiet California road when she passed a sign that said, "Pea Picker's Camp." Lange already had finished a project for the federal Resettlement Administration that focused on migrant families devastated by the depression, but twenty miles after passing the sign she turned her car around to get just a few more photos. At the camp, Lange was "drawn like a magnet" to a mother and her children. Lange later recalled that she did "not remember how I explained my presence or my camera to her,"

> . . . but I do remember she asked me no questions. I made five exposures, working closer and closer from the same direction. I did not ask her name or her history. She told me her age, that she was thirty-two. She said that they had been living on frozen vegetables from the surrounding fields, and birds that the children killed. She had just sold the tires from her car to buy food. There she sat in that lean-to tent with her children huddled around her, and seemed to know that my pictures might help her, and so she helped me. There was a sort of equality about it.

Lange's last-minute decision to return to take a few more pictures proved opportune. Her image *Migrant Mother* is perhaps the most famous twentieth-century American documentary photograph, and it remains among the most requested pictures in the Library of Congress archive.

In the last chapter, we discussed the correlation between textual and visual literacy. A photograph, like an essay, involves composition and visual grammar. In Lange's photograph of the migrant mother, for example, she consciously arranged certain visual elements to create an emotional effect. Like writing, a good photograph is full of information, too. There are

What You'll Learn in This Chapter

- How questions create fresh perspective on any subject.
- How you can use certain categories of questions—those that explore, explain, evaluate, and reflect—to think more deeply about any subject.
- How you can combine question asking with dialectical thinking to discover what you want to say.

exactly three children in this picture surrounding Florence Thompson, and they are wearing similar rough-fabric clothing. None faces the camera. Florence's gaze seems fixed on some distant place, her mouth is set, and her brow seems furrowed. All of these details work together to say more than they say individually, to tell a story not just about the impact of the Great Depression but about motherhood and family.

You can develop your own interpretation of *Migrant Mother* using dialectical thinking, perhaps beginning by openly exploring how the picture connects with your own experiences and observations. This might lead you to focus on a "reading" of the photograph that emphasizes the anxieties of mothering or the shame of poverty in America. But there are ways to make the inquiry process a bit more methodological, ways that you can deliberately shift your perspective to see a subject freshly. How? Ask the right questions.

Years ago, I spent an afternoon taking photographs of an old wagon on a rolling New Hampshire hill. I got up early on a September morning hoping to take advantage of the slanting light and the shreds of mist that hung on the hayfield. I resolved to take an entire roll of the wagon, and I literally circled it, taking shot after shot. By the fourth or fifth shot, I started to see the wagon in ways I'd never seen it. I saw how the beads of dew covered the bleached wood of the wagon's wheel. I saw how the ironwork of the driver's bench created a shadow on the grass that was a tangle of geometric shapes.

What I'm describing is the process of revision. But the anecdote also comes to mind now because it illustrates how different questions shift your gaze on a topic. They help you circle the wagon, changing your angle and revealing certain aspects of the subject and not others. Behind each question is a different perspective.

All inquiry begins with questions. Indeed, the opening questions we ask largely determine our response to a subject.

In this chapter, I'll suggest four ways of seeing, each prompted by a different opening question. Combined with dialectical thinking, these stances—*exploring, explaining, evaluating,* and *reflecting*—are a foundation of inquiry-based learning that will help you with every assignment in this book, and in any situation in which you want to figure out what you think. We'll apply these ways of seeing to a range of texts, both written and visual, and I hope you'll find yourself circling the wagon in much the same way I did years ago.

OPENING QUESTIONS FOR INQUIRY

All inquiry begins with questions. Indeed, the *opening questions* we ask largely determine our response to a subject. These questions shape the stance we take toward both the writing process and the reading process. These opening questions are situational. For example, in writing they depend on our particular subject, on who we're writing for, and our purposes at any given moment in the process. Recall the rhetorical triangle from Chapter 1: the rhetorical choices we make are informed by the questions we ask in response to the writing situation. While opening questions vary from one writing situation to the next, we can group them into categories that conform to four different ways of inquiring into a subject: exploration, explanation, evaluation, and reflection. Each of these four ways of inquiring compels writers to take a different stance toward a subject, be it a text, a memory, an observation, a conversation, a photograph, or another process. Each shapes how writers see a subject (or themselves), much like taking a series of different photographs of the wagon on the hill that was mentioned earlier.

EXPLORATION

To explore is to see a topic with wide-eyed wonder. *What might this mean to me? What do I feel or think about this?* Through these questions, the writer can openly investigate his or her feelings and thoughts and find a personal point of attachment to the subject. This way of inquiring is easiest when you're writing on something about which you're uncertain. After all, it's not hard to suspend judgment when you don't have one. But exploration can also be useful when you want to reexamine what you already believe, when you're open to the possibility of changing your mind. Why would you want to do that? Because you can learn and discover things, even if you end up feeling more strongly about your initial belief.

This way of inquiring isn't just for fastwriting or journal work. Exploration can also inform much more publicly oriented inquiry into a subject. Historically, the personal essay is a genre that relies heavily on exploration (see Chapter 4, "Writing a Personal Essay"). Writers of personal essays constantly take measure of their emotional relationship with their subjects, much the way we do when we're writing for ourselves in our journals. This public performance of the inquiring *I* has an interesting effect on readers—we feel a sense of intimacy with the writer that is often absent in other writing genres. Ironically, questions that would seem to free us from concern for our audience can also wind up making our writing more accessible to that audience.

When should you try exploration as a way of inquiring?

1. When you want to discover what you think.
2. When you have time to take a more circuitous path to these discoveries.
3. When the topic is new to you or when you'd like to look critically at your existing ideas or beliefs about a subject.

Exploring Questions

- What does this mean to me, or how do I think or feel about it?
- What do I notice first? And then what? And then?
- What interests me most about this? What additional questions does it raise?
- How do my own personal knowledge and experiences affect the way I feel and what I see?
- What surprises me about the way I see or think about this?

EXPLANATION

We explain things all the time. This is something parents are acutely aware of, especially if they have a kid like my daughter Julia.

"Who are the Israelis?" she asks as we listen to National Public Radio on the way to school, "and why are they always talking about them?"

"Who is talking about them?"

"The people on the radio," she says. "They are always talking about the Israelis and the Palestinians."

How do I begin to explain a conflict that has its roots in several thousand years of history, one complicated by religious differences and political alliances that seem to defy resolution? What Julia knows seems much simpler: a Palestinian family in Gaza was killed by Israeli soldiers who were retaliating for a suicide attack in Jerusalem that killed thirteen. Do I begin by explaining Moses' exodus from Egypt and the Jews' historic claims to the Holy Land or the Muslims' conquest of the region in the seventh century? Or do I explain the creation of the Israeli state following World War II and the demise of Palestine? What I realize, as Julia impatiently waits for me to say something, is that I know much less than I thought I knew about the history of this conflict.

As this example suggests, we tend to use explanation with an audience in mind. But by explaining things to ourselves we can learn a lot, too, because this way of inquiring exposes gaps in our knowledge. Clearly, in attempting to explain the conflict between the Israelis and the Palestinians to my daughter I was forced to confront the limits of my own knowledge on the subject.

A common technique in psychotherapy is something called "say back." In couples counseling, for example, one partner may be required to listen carefully to his or her spouse talk, and then say back what he or she heard. The method is great for helping couples really listen to and understand each other, something that is ordinarily difficult to do amid life's daily distractions. The explanatory power of say back is much like the power of summarizing or paraphrasing something you've read or experienced. By challenging writers to use their own words, summarizing and paraphrasing allow writers to take possession of the information, to make it their own by articulating their understanding of the information in their own words. Summarizing and paraphrasing can also expose the gaps in our knowledge. You thought you understood a subject, but upon reading over your summary or paraphrase of the subject, you now aren't so sure that's the case. Is there another way to understand the subject so you can explain it better? Have you missed something you need to know in order to understand the subject?

This way of inquiring involves much more than simply reporting information. It's a way of clarifying thought, enhancing understanding, making useful comparisons, and exposing gaps. For me, trying to explain the Middle East conflict to Julia and writing this book were two experiences that involved discoveries that made them much more than mere recitations of fact and detail.

When should you try explaining as a way of inquiring?

1. When you want to understand what you think you know.
2. When you want to clarify that understanding for yourself and others.
3. When you want to define, describe, categorize, or compare things.

Explaining Questions

- What is this?
- What is its purpose?
- How does this work? Why does it work? How does this clarify things?
- What does it look like?
- How does it compare to something else?
- What do I understand this to be saying?

EVALUATION

To evaluate something is to judge it or to form an opinion about it. Evaluating things—restaurants, the quality of play in the NBA, the religious motives of terrorists such as Osama bin Laden—is something we all do naturally. These evaluations tend to lead us to do and say certain things to support our opinions or to make our claims convincing, first to ourselves and then to others. Indeed, evaluation is really the driving force behind argument.

As a way of inquiring, evaluation shares much with exploration. Both hinge on the writer's emotional response to a subject. Exploration, however, is much more open ended in its approach, more receptive to doubt and uncertainty about the subject. Evaluation, on the other hand, is focused exclusively on making and supporting a judgment about the subject. In sum, you use exploration when your purpose is *to discover* and you use evaluation when your purpose is *to prove,* although both ways of inquiring can be used together to great effect.

While we constantly evaluate things for ourselves, we usually reserve written evaluation for an audience. Our concern, then, is to persuade others to feel the same way we do about the subject. To do so, we usually have to clarify and elaborate on our thinking.

Indeed, because all evaluation stems from what are essentially subjective value judgments, a tension always exists between our *desire* to prove our point and our *need or willingness* to learn more about the subject. Most if not all issues worth arguing about are complex. In learning more about them, we can actually make it harder to prove our point. We might even be compelled to change our minds about the subject. This may be a good thing in terms of fostering a deeper understanding of the world, but it's bound to slow down the writing process. You may not have the time required to fully explore the complexities of a subject. Charged with evaluating the impact of the war in Afghanistan on the U.S. relationship with Uzbekistan or the meaning of the water imagery in Kate Chopin's story "The Awakening," you might feel compelled to come up with an assertion you can prove right away. Will you ignore evidence that doesn't support your claim? Will you allow the evidence to shape your understanding? Will you use it only to confirm your claim?

When used as a way of inquiring, evaluation should never be used merely to support a claim. Evaluation involves making judgments *and* testing them against the evidence. The discoveries that result should shape the claims you make. Evaluation, then, is essentially a form of dialectical thinking.

When should you turn to evaluation as a way of inquiring?

1. When you are more interested in proving something than finding more out about it.
2. When you're ready to judge the quality, relevance, or significance of something.
3. When you're looking for the reasons why you believe something is true.

Evaluating Questions

- What's my judgment about the value of this?
- What are my reasons?
- Do I see it the way most other people do?
- What's most convincing here? What's least convincing?
- What do I see that supports what I believe? What do I see that complicates or contradicts what I believe?

REFLECTION

Some of you may remember the television program *The Wonder Years.* Set in the turbulent 1960s, the show offered a glimpse of a boy and his middle-class family navigating the cultural upheavals of the time as well as the ordinary challenges of growing up. What was interesting about the show, though, was its narration. While viewers watched the boy Kevin deal with his family and friends in a changing society, the voice of a much older Kevin reflected on the meaning of those relationships and events, providing perspective that was unavailable to the boy while he was actually experiencing them.

As a way of inquiring, reflection is a lot like playing the part of the adult Kevin. Through reflection it is possible to increase the learning and self-knowledge we get from writing by looking back on the experience of writing and thinking about something. This means finding the right distance from which to see what's not necessarily apparent in the moments of engagement. It also means learning to ask the questions that help us see not just what we've written or what it means, but *how* we've done the writing and how we might be able to do it better. You've already had a fair amount of practice with this in *The Curious Writer* as you've reflected on the processes you used to complete the exercises and assignments. Indeed, one of the book's central claims is that only by reflecting on your process can you control it.

This way of inquiring may not yet come naturally to you. Reflection, in some ways, seems quite different from exploration, explanation, and evaluation. The object of reflection is not *what* you're writing or reading about, but *how* you are writing and reading about the subject. This way of inquiring requires us *to witness and report on ourselves.* Reflection is a form of self-assessment. By employing it, we can learn to identify and overcome our writing challenges. *What problems do you have in this writing situation? What might be some of the ways you could solve them? What's working? What's not? What's typical about your process? What's unique about your process in this situation?*

All of these questions force you backward, away from the immediate demands of the writing task, and encourage you to see *how* you write and think. Remember, writing *is* thinking. The payoff for reflecting is much more than figuring out when to resort to fastwriting or how to revise. It's discovering your patterns of thought and how they can be extended or changed to let you write with more insight.

When should you use reflection as a way of inquiring?

1. When you're interested in *how* you've done something and learning ways you can make the process better.
2. When you consistently have problems with the process.
3. When you're disappointed with the product.

Reflecting Questions

- What do I notice about how I think about or do this?
- How do I compare how I approach this task with how I approach another one?
- When did I have the most—and the fewest—problems?
- If I were going to do this again, what might I do differently?
- What do I understand now about how to do this that I didn't understand when I started?

PRACTICING INQUIRY

In Twin Falls, Idaho, a city of 38,000, people have taken to jumping off a bridge that spans the Snake River canyon. The Perrine Bridge, once the highest in the world, is 486 feet above the Snake, and it's a popular destination for BASE jumpers, thrill seekers who look for very tall stationary objects from which to jump with a parachute strapped to their backs. What fascinates me about this and other extreme sports is how successfully people apparently overcome the normal instincts that suggest, quite simply, that what you are about to do is a really, really bad idea because it could kill you.

Psychologists who study extreme athletes hear some of the same things over and over again. Some thrill seekers pursue extreme sports because life-threatening risk "makes them feel alive." Others talk about getting in a "zone" while climbing mountains or jumping off bridges, a feeling of being completely engaged in the moment. One study pointed to a particularly interesting finding: people with experience taking risks not only keep taking them but ultimately stop seeing what they do as all that risky.

While engaging in academic inquiry is hardly as risky as jumping off the Perrine Bridge, inquiry is also an activity that goes against instinct. It's a kind of thinking that will probably run counter to what you've learned in school so far. Rather than forming conclusions quickly, inquiry urges you to suspend judgment. Rather than avoiding uncertainty, inquiry works best when you accept ambiguity as a natural part of the discovery process. Rather than a quick look at a topic, inquiry involves a more prolonged engagement. What's the risk? That you'll become so wrapped up in your subject that you'll fail to open your parachute before you reach bottom. Fortunately, unlike BASE jumping, your life usually isn't at stake when you practice inquiry but your early drafts could be a real mess. But like an extreme athlete, the more you experience the open-ended approach to inquiry, the less risky it seems.

Rather than avoiding uncertainty, inquiry works best when you accept ambiguity as a natural part of the discovery process.

Before you move on to the writing assignments in Part Two of this book, you need to practice the four ways of inquiring. In preparation for that practice, first consider the following short reading.

HOW MUCH SHOULD WE CARE WHAT HAPPENS TO ANIMALS?

1 Whenever my family packs bags for a trip we're all convinced that Bear, our yellow lab, is depressed. He curls up on his dog bed, tail tucked under his back legs, nose parked on the cushion, and looks up at us through his eyebrows. Only his eyes move, following our every movement. It's pathetic, and we all feel sorry for Bear, and guilty that we're daring to go somewhere without him. We imagine all of this, of course. We can't ask Bear how he's feeling. But like most pet owners and animal lovers across the world we naturally presume to believe that our animals feel some of the things we do—sadness, loneliness, joy, or in the case of cats, contempt. *Anthropomorphism* is the

To what extent do animals feel emotions as we do?

habit of attributing human qualities to non-human animals, and scientists rightly point out that this is often presumptuous and even arrogant. How can we know what an orangutan feels if we can't ask her?

2 But confronted with Bear's long face in the presence of luggage it's enormously hard not to sense feeling. I don't think I've ever met a pet owner who doesn't believe his pet can feel, or even think. The conversations between dog owners in the park down my street run the gamut: This pug is a loner, that collie loves only the owner's wife, this poodle is incredibly intelligent, and that lab is dopey. We often simply assume that the emotional landscapes of our pets are just like ours. Just look at that face!

3 However, this is more complicated than it seems. What do we mean by feeling or emotion? How do we define consciousness? In the absence of a means to communicate with a non-human animal, how can we determine the presence of feeling or thought? If we grant some animals like dolphins, dogs, cats, and the great apes special status because of their intelligence and emotionality, where do we draw the line? What other animals might deserve special consideration? And, of course, there's this question: who cares? If we can't definitively prove that an elephant can cry or a lab can be depressed, why worry about it? Well, think about it for a moment. If some animals can experience human-like emotion and others, including, say, a pig, are self-aware—I am this pig and not that one—then doesn't that raise some interesting ethical and moral questions? If we're able to determine, or even if we simply suspect, that an animal feels and thinks should we treat it differently? On the other hand, where do we draw the line? I suspect rats are plenty intelligent and are probably even good parents, but I much prefer them dead than alive.

The best inquiry projects deal with complicated issues like those that involve our treatment of animals. Such projects raise challenging questions and offer few simple answers. That's exactly what draws an inquiring writer to a subject—he might discover something new about what he thinks and add something to an important conversation. In the next few pages, you'll get a chance to try using the ways of inquiring discussed earlier by examining the controversy over whether non-human animals can feel and think, and in particular, whether their presumed feelings should influence how we treat them. I'm hoping that you'll find the topic interesting. Because many of us have pets, appreciate wildlife, and have definite attitudes about eating meat, this controversy touches us all in some way.

All inquiry projects are fueled by questions. An important part of the process, once you discover your topic, is to craft the questions that will initially power your investigation. In this case, I'll make it easy for you by providing the inquiry question that will get you started.

Those who argue about the "rights" of animals often claim that the issue comes down to this question:

> *Do people possess some inherent qualities that might make their lives have greater moral significance than the lives of other animals?*

In the exercises that follow, you'll pursue your own investigation into this question, exploring your own feelings, experiences, and ideas; explaining the significance of the issue; evaluating the evidence; and finally reflecting on the whole process.

EXERCISE 3.1

Exploring Within and Without

To explore is open things up rather than nail them down. More than any other method of inquiry, exploration asks that you suspend judgment, at least for a while, and ask, *What might this mean to me? What do I feel or think about this?* Changing your mind is fine. Don't hesitate to ask yourself questions you can't readily answer. Expect surprise and discovery.

STEP ONE: EXPLORING WITHIN. Return to the inquiry question. Do people possess some inherent qualities that might make their lives have greater moral significance than the lives of other animals? What are your first thoughts about it? Do you agree that human life has greater moral value than the lives of other animals? What questions does this raise for you personally? Fastwrite about this for five minutes, keeping your pen moving.

STEP TWO: EXPLORING WITHOUT. Explore your response to the following claim: *One of the things that distinguish people from other animals is that we think and they don't.* Fastwrite for three minutes. Begin by playing the "believing game"; that is, think about what makes sense to you about this claim. Then shift to the "doubting game," thinking more critically about this claim and what about it doesn't seem quite right to you.

STEP THREE: EXPLORING WITHIN AND WITHOUT. Consider the following passage from a recent article, which explores the new movement in the United States to extend animal rights to certain food items such as lobster and chickens. After reading the excerpt, fastwrite for five minutes about it. What are your first thoughts? And then what? And then?

IT DIED FOR US

Frank Bruni

Do oysters have little bivalve souls? Do they dream briny dreams, scream briny screams? On a level that I suppose is selfish and somewhat silly, I hope not, because they are alive when they are shucked right in front of us, their deaths more proximal than those of so many creatures we eat. 1

They don't thrash like the lobster in its scalding pot, but should we nonetheless worry about how they meet their end? And whether that end is a sufficiently compassionate one? 2

These questions seem less ridiculous than they once did. This month Whole Foods announced that it would no longer sell live lobsters, saying that keeping them in crammed tanks for long periods doesn't demonstrate a proper concern for animal welfare. The Chicago City Council recently outlawed the sale of foie gras to protest the force-feeding of the ducks and geese that yield it. California passed a similar law, which doesn't take effect until 2012, and other states and cities are considering such measures. 3

All of these developments dovetail with a heightened awareness in these food-obsessed times of what we eat: where it came from, what it was fed, how it was penned, how it perished. If the success of best sellers like *Fast Food Nation* and *The Omnivore's Dilemma* and stores like Whole Foods is any indication, more Americans are spending more time mulling the nutritional, environmental and, yes, ethical implications of their diets. 4

If you eat an animal, should you be morally concerned about the animal's welfare prior to its winding up on your dinner table?

5 They prefer that their beef carry the tag "grass fed," which evokes a verdant pasture rather than a squalid feed lot, and that their poultry knew the glories of a "free range," a less sturdy assurance than many people believe.

6 But these concerns are riddled with intellectual inconsistencies and prompt infinite questions. Are the calls for fundamental changes in the mass production of food simply elitist, the privilege of people wealthy enough to pay more at the checkout counter? Does fretting about ducks give people a pass on chickens? Does considering the lobster allow seafood lovers to disregard the tuna?

One Student's Response

DANIEL'S JOURNAL

EXERCISE 3.1

STEP THREE

The first thing I think about after reading this is that it really does raise "infinite questions" to consider where to draw the line. What animals are worthy of our concern and which aren't? Lobsters? And then I think that the whole movement to be concerned about what we eat is probably good. After all, until recently I never thought at all about eating organic food, and certainly had no idea about how chickens were raised. And then I think that the danger here is that we make everyone feel guilty about what they eat, and I'm not at all convinced that making people guilty makes them ultimately change what they do. And then I think that the agricultural industry does seem to respond to strong consumer movements; after all didn't the whole organic movement, which is now a multibillion dollar industry (I think), arise because more and more people demanded chemical free foods? If we make food ethics a part of our consumer demands, wouldn't the industry respond? And then I wonder again about the elitist thing mentioned in the article. Organic food is more expensive, and wouldn't ethically grown or raised chickens cost more? Doesn't that mean that some people can afford to care more and others simply don't have that choice?

EXERCISE 3.2

Explaining to Yourself, Explaining to Others

To explain is to ask, *What is this? How does it fit into what I know? How do I understand its significance?* Initially, we often ask ourselves these questions when we encounter something new. Later, we may need to explain what we know to others. When we explain things to ourselves, we do it privately, working things out in the absence of an audience. But an audience helps sharpen our thinking because to explain to others we must be clear and sensible.

STEP ONE: EXPLAINING TO YOURSELF. Review the information and ideas that you generated in the previous exploring exercise, particularly your entry from Step One, which asked for your "first thoughts" in response to the inquiry question: *Do people possess some inherent qualities that might make their lives have greater moral significance than the lives of other animals?* In your notebook, spend five minutes explaining to yourself how your thinking has evolved since then. Begin your fastwrite with the following phrase: *What I understand now about this question that I didn't understand then is . . .* See where this line takes you.

STEP TWO: EXPLAINING TO OTHERS. Craft a temporary thesis that reflects what you currently think about the inquiry question, explaining what you currently believe about the moral significance of what happens to people versus what happens to other animals.

ONE STUDENT'S RESPONSE

DANIEL'S JOURNAL

EXERCISE 3.2

STEP TWO

Overall, the lives of human beings have greater moral significance than the lives of other animals except those that show a recognizable human-like consciousness. Whales and other marine mammals and certain other primates should enjoy greater "rights" than other non-human animals.

EXERCISE 3.3

Evaluating the Arguments

Here are a few of the expert voices that are attempting to influence the debate about the inquiry question we're considering. Typically, when you do academic research you stride into an ongoing discussion about your topic, first trying to understand the conversation and then trying to find your own place in it. It's a two-step process: Listen carefully to what knowledgeable people are saying to make sure you understand it, and then make some judgments about what you find valid or questionable about their claims.

STEP ONE: Begin with an empty left page of your notebook. Then read each of the following four passages in turn, and *in your own words*, explain (paraphrase) what you understand the author's argument or point to be. Jot this down on the left page only, moving on to subsequent left pages as necessary.

1 "Although most humans may be superior in reasoning or in other intellectual capacities to nonhuman animals that is not enough to justify the line we draw between humans and animals. Some humans—infants and those with severe intellectual disabilities—have intellectual capacities inferior to some animals, but we would, rightly, be shocked by anyone who proposed that we inflict slow, painful deaths on these intellectually inferior humans in order to test the safety of household products. Nor, of course, would we tolerate confining them in small cages and then slaughtering them in order to eat them. The fact that we are prepared to do these things to nonhuman animals is therefore a sign of 'speciesism'—a prejudice that survives because it is convenient for the dominant group—in this case not whites or males, but all humans."[1]

* * *

1. Peter Singer, "Animal Liberation at 30," *New York Review of Books* (May 15, 2003), http://www.nybooks.com/articles/16276.

"I am a speciesist. Speciesism is not merely plausible; it is essential for right conduct, because those who will not make the morally relevant distinctions among species are almost certain, in consequence, to misapprehend their true obligations. The analogy between speciesism and racism is insidious. Every sensitive moral judgment requires that the differing natures of the beings to whom obligations are owed be considered. If all forms of animate life—or vertebrate animal life?—must be treated equally, and if therefore in evaluating a research program the pains of a rodent count equally with the pains of a human, we are forced to conclude (1) that neither humans nor rodents possess rights, or (2) that rodents possess all the rights that humans possess. Both alternatives are absurd. Yet one or the other must be swallowed if the moral equality of all species is to be defended. Humans owe to other humans a degree of moral regard that cannot be owed to animals. Some humans take on the obligation to support and heal others, both humans and animals, as a principal duty in their lives; the fulfillment of that duty may require the sacrifice of many animals. If biomedical investigators abandon the effective pursuit of their professional objectives because they are convinced that they may not do to animals what the service of humans requires, they will fail, objectively, to do their duty. Refusing to recognize the moral differences among species is a sure path to calamity."[2] 2

* * *

"People have always exalted certain 'higher' feelings that are claimed to single us out among animals. Only humans, it is said, feel noble emotions such as compassion, true love, altruism, pity, mercy, reverence, honor, and modesty. On the other hand, people have often attributed so called 'negative' emotions to animals: cruelty, pride, greed, rage, vanity, and hatred. At play here appears to be a seemingly unbearable injury to our sense of uniqueness, to our entitlement to the special nobility of our emotional life. Thus not only whether animals can feel, but what they feel, is used to strengthen the species barrier. What lies behind this 'us/them' mentality—the urge to define ourselves by proving we are not only different, but utterly different, including emotionally? Why should this distinction between man and beast be so important?"[3] 3

* * *

"The concept of the person belongs to the ongoing dialogue which binds the moral community. Creatures who are by nature incapable of entering into this dialogue have neither rights nor duties nor personality. If animals had rights, then we should require their consent before taking them into captivity, training them, domesticating them or in any way putting them to our uses. But there is no conceivable process whereby this consent could be delivered or withheld. 4

2. Carl Cohen, "The Case for the Use of Animals in Biomedical Research," *New England Journal of Medicine* 315, no. 4 (1986): 865–870.
3. Jeffrey Moussaieff Masson and Susan McCarthy, *When Elephants Weep: The Emotional Lives of Animals* (New York: Dell, 1995), pp. 26–27.

Furthermore, a creature with rights is duty-bound to respect the rights of others. The fox would be duty-bound to respect the life of the chicken and the whole species would be condemned out of hand as criminal by nature. Any law which compelled persons to respect the rights of non-human species would weigh so heavily on the predators as to drive them to extinction in a short while."[4]

STEP TWO: Now that you understand the arguments and ideas advanced by each of these four experts, determine which of them you find most compelling and how that might support or change your tentative thesis from Exercise 3.2. Begin by writing your tentative thesis on the top of the right page that faces your initial entry from Step One. Now fastwrite for seven full minutes on the right facing pages, using the following questions to focus for your thinking:

- Which of these claims or ideas do I find most persuasive? Which seem least persuasive? Why?
- What new questions do these authors raise for me?
- Which arguments seem to support what I initially believed in my thesis, and which challenged me to rethink my position?
- What do I believe now might be the best answer to the inquiry question?

STEP THREE: Finish by composing one or two paragraphs that best articulate your *current* thoughts on the inquiry question. What is your position on the question? What other questions do you have that you might investigate if you had more time? What do you understand now about the issue of speciesism that you didn't understand when you began?

One Student's Response

DANIEL'S JOURNAL

EXERCISE 3.3

STEP ONE

To be a "speciesist" is to insist that there are "essential" distinctions to be made between humans and other animals. The author argues that if we collapse these distinctions and distribute similar rights to all living things then we're stuck with a situation where the basic idea of "rights" is made meaningless, or we have to accept that a lab animal has the same rights as we do. The author believes that humans' "principal duty" is to each other. As a result, if other animals must suffer or even be sacrificed in the service of that duty, then this is the way things should be.

4. Roger Scruton, *Animal Rights and Wrongs* (London: Demos, 1996), p. 80.

EXERCISE 3.4

Reflecting on the Process

When athletes want to improve their performance—perfect their swing, improve their strategy at the track, improve the accuracy of their throw—they reflect on *how* they do something. The same idea applies to writing and thinking. If you want to get better at both, you set aside some time to consider what you did, how it worked, and what you might do differently.

STEP ONE: WHAT'S THE STORY? On a left page of your notebook, fastwrite the story of your experience writing and thinking about the inquiry question: *Do people possess some inherent qualities that might make their lives have greater moral significance than the lives of other animals?* Begin your fastwrite with the phrase, *When I first started investigating this issue, I began by . . .* When the writing stalls, use the phrase, *And then I . . .* Tell yourself the story of your experience until you feel there is nothing more to tell.

STEP TWO: On the right page of your notebook, begin with the following phrase and follow it for three minutes. Try to be specific as possible.

1. *As I reflect on my experience doing this, what I understand now about my methods of writing and thinking that I didn't understand when I began was . . .*

Finish by following this phrase for another three minutes:

2. *If I was going to do this again, I would . . .*

ONE STUDENT'S RESPONSE

DANIEL'S JOURNAL

EXERCISE 3.4

STEP ONE

When I first started investigating this issue I realized that it wasn't something I'd thought about at all, and I was a little surprised by the whole thing. I wasn't aware that there was all this controversy over whether a lobster has feelings or has rights. And then I spent some time working through the exercises, writing about what I thought, and I started to believe that maybe it was possible to think about this whole animal rights thing in a new way. I began to think that certain animals that have a consciousness might deserve some special consideration. And then I began to think about the whole idea of consciousness. What do I mean by that exactly? And how do you measure it? And then I thought this was something that would be interesting to research if I had more time . . .

SYMPHONIC INQUIRY

When we write, we rarely use just one of the four ways of inquiring. Instead, we explore, explain, evaluate, and reflect in concert, unconsciously shifting from one to the other. Even in a fastwrite, the seeming refuge of exploration, writers often use explanation, evaluation, and reflection as they circle a subject and discover their feelings and motives.

When you bring all four ways of inquiring together you achieve symphonic inquiry. But how do you do that? Learning the opening questions to ask yourself helps a lot. Soon, asking these questions becomes second nature. Taking time to reflect on how you're approaching a task also helps, particularly for an apprentice to inquiry-based learning. For instance, perhaps your essays come up a bit short on information and your instructor complains that your ideas are fairly obvious. Reflecting on this, you realize that you tend to short-circuit exploration in a rush to judgment. Next time, you try doing more open-ended writing in your journal before you try to come up with a thesis.

You're both a composer and the conductor of this orchestra, and your task is to create the music of surprise and discovery.

You also can incorporate some practical techniques into your reading and writing processes that promote symphonic inquiry. The double-entry journal, or some variation of it, can really help you shift back and forth between creative and critical thinking. You also might establish the habit of writing summaries or other explanations of the things you're reading in your notebook or in the margins of the article you're reading. Shifting from one way of inquiring to another is like shifting from one instrument to another. You're both a composer and the conductor of this orchestra, and your task is to create the music of surprise and discovery.

INQUIRING INTO THE DETAILS

TIME TO WRITE

A model for the writing process, like most models, tries to simply describe something that is exceedingly complex. That became obvious the more I have learned, over the years, about the lives of my students. They often hold down full-time jobs, live in chaotic dormitories, have children, or juggle heavy credit loads. While many are willing to write, what these students lack most of all is the time to do it.

There is no simple solution to this problem. College students, no matter what their circumstances, must make time to write. But here are some suggestions about how to make the most of the time you have.

1. *Don't waste time staring off into space waiting for the words to come.* What you must do instead is to hold your internal critic at bay, lower your standards, and get something down, no matter how bad it is, so you have

something to work with. Fastwriting and listing are excellent techniques to help with this.

2. *Accept the gift of revision.* Gift, you say? Yes. While the prospect of rewriting might not inspire, it does allow you to embrace a draft that doesn't meet your expectations. Remember, a draft is a thing the wind blows through. Don't waste time trying to make it "perfect" when you first write it. Leave that for revision.

3. *Exploit your notebook.* One of the great advantages of a journal or notebook is that it gives you a way to make good use of five minutes. Short bursts of writing—perhaps making a list of topics for your next essay, rehearsing an introduction to your paper, fastwriting your thoughts about the reading—can be enormously productive.

4. *Find your time to write.* Students rarely have this luxury. But when you can, decide what part of the day, or which days of the week, you can set aside for writing. Announce it to yourself and others. That's when your husband gets the kids to school, or the roommate turns off the boombox, or you retire to that cubicle in the fifth floor of the campus library. That's a sacred time when it's just you and the blizzard of words on the page.

Using What You Have Learned

Part Two, "Inquiry Projects," which follows, introduces a range of genres and writing assignments. Although each has different features and purposes, I believe you'll find that the *process* of composing these essays draws heavily on what you've learned about writing in these first three chapters. Whether you're writing a personal essay or a research paper, some of the same things will guide you:

- The spirit of inquiry will guide your writing.
- You will use the power of questions to help you to see what isn't immediately obvious.
- You will employ constructive habits of mind, such as making the familiar strange, suspending judgment, and searching for surprise.
- You will make rhetorical choices based on the needs of the writing or reading situation.
- You will use dialectical thinking to guide your writing and reading processes, moving back and forth between the creative and the critical.
- You will use exploration, explanation, evaluation, and reflection to get the most out of your inquiry projects.
- You will experience the pleasure of using writing not only to say what you already know but to discover what you didn't know you knew.

Part Two
INQUIRY PROJECTS

Chapter 4
Writing a Personal Essay

Chapter 5
Writing a Profile

Chapter 6
Writing a Review

Chapter 7
Writing a Proposal

Chapter 8
Writing an Argument

Chapter 9
Writing a Critical Essay

Chapter 10
Writing an Ethnographic Essay

Writing a personal essay is often like seeing an old picture of yourself. It thrusts you back into a particular time and place, but at the same time you see yourself from a certain distance, bringing knowledge and understanding to past events that you didn't have when they occurred. This publicity photograph of my mother, brother, and me in the 1950s returns me to that world and at the same time I see what I couldn't have seen then: a time when fathers were often missing from the picture while working mothers, like mine, had to move gracefully from family to job, proving themselves at both.

4

Writing a Personal Essay

WRITING ABOUT EXPERIENCE

Most us were taught and still believe that we need to know what we are going to write before we actually pick up the pen or sit in front of the computer. My student Lynn was typical.

"I think I'll write about my experience organizing the street fair," she told me the other day. "That would be a good topic for a personal essay, right?"

"Do you think so?" I said.

"Well, yes, because I already know a lot about it. I'll have a lot to write about."

"Okay, but is there anything about this experience that you want to understand better?" I said. "Anything about it that makes you curious?"

"Curious? It was just a street fair," she said.

"Sure, but is there something about what happened that makes you want to look at the experience again? Is there a chance that you might learn something about yourself, or about street fairs, or about the community, or about people, or . . ."

Lynn was clearly sorry she asked. What I should have said was much more to the point: the best essay topics are those that are an itch you need to scratch. These tend not to be topics you have already figured out. While the topics can be familiar to you, the results of your inquiry are usually much better if you don't yet know what you think about your topics and you're interested to learn more about them. The best topics ask to be written about because they make you wonder *Why did I do that? What does that mean? Why did that happen? How did I really feel? What do I really think?*

Unlike most other forms of inquiry, the personal essay invites an initial display of confusion or uncertainty from writers regarding their

What You'll Learn in This Chapter

- How personal essays can help you with academic writing.
- What distinguishes a personal essay from other forms.
- How to write a sketch.
- Why a confusing topic may be better than one you have all figured out.
- Questions for revising personal essays.

subjects. In other words, writers do not have to have their subjects figured out when starting a personal essay. This form of inquiry is a vehicle for writers to work through their thinking and feeling on a subject directly in front of their readers.

As a form, the *personal* essay places the writer at center stage. This doesn't mean that once she's there, her responsibility is to pour out her secrets, share her pain, or confess her sins. Some essays do have these confessional qualities, but more often they do not. Yet a personal essayist, no matter the subject of the essay, is still *exposed.* There is no hiding behind the pronoun "one," as in "one might think" or "one often feels," no lurking in the shadows of the passive voice: "This paper will argue. . . ." The personal essay is first-person territory.

The personal essay is a vehicle for writers to work through their thinking and feeling on a subject directly in front of their readers.

In this sense, the personal essay is much like a photographic self-portrait. Like a picture, a good personal essay tells the truth, or it tells *a* truth about the writer/subject, and it often captures the writer at a particular moment of time. Therefore, the experience of taking a self-portrait, or confronting an old picture of oneself taken by someone else, can create the feeling of exposure that writing a personal essay often does.

But it does more. When we gaze at ourselves in a photograph we often see it as yanked from a larger story about ourselves, stories that thread their way through our lives and give us ideas about who we were and who we are. This is what the personal essay demands of us: we must somehow present ourselves truthfully and measure our past against the present. In other words, when we hold a photograph of ourselves we know more than the person we see there knew, and as writers of the personal essay, we must share that knowledge and understanding with readers.

MOTIVES FOR WRITING A PERSONAL ESSAY

Essai was a term first coined by the sixteenth-century French nobleman Michel de Montaigne, a man who had lived through occurrences of the plague, the bloody civil war between French Catholics and Protestants, and his own ill health. These were tumultuous and uncertain times when old social orders and intellectual traditions were under assault, and it proved to be ideal ferment for the essay. The French verb *essaier* means "to attempt" or "to try," and the essay became an opportunity for Montaigne to work out his thoughts about war, the education of children, the evils of doctors, and the importance of pleasure. The personal essay tradition inspired by Montaigne is probably unlike the essays you are familiar with in school. The school essay is often formulaic—a five-paragraph theme, or thesis-example paper—while the personal essay is an open-ended form that allows for uncertainty and inconclusiveness. It is more about the process of coming to know than presenting *what* you know. The personal essay attempts *to find out* rather than *to prove.*

It is an ideal form of inquiry if your purpose is exploratory rather than argumentative, and if you're particularly interested in working out the possible relationships between your subject and yourself. Because the personal essay is openly subjective, the writer can't hide. The intruding *I* confronts the writer with the same questions, over and over again: *Why does this matter to me? What do I make of it? How does this change the way I think of myself and the way I see the world?* Because of this, one of the principal dangers of the personal essay is that it becomes narcissistic; it goes on and on about what the writer thinks and feels, and the reader is left with that nagging question—*So what?* The personal essayist must always find some way to hitch the particulars of his or her experience to something larger—an idea, a theme, or even a feeling that readers might share.

On the other hand, one of the prime rhetorical advantages of the personal essay is its subjectivity. Because it is written with openness and honesty, the essay is often a very intimate form, inviting the reader to share in the writer's often concealed world. In the personal essay, we often get to see the face sweating under the mask. Honesty is one of the essay's primary virtues, and because the form allows for uncertainty and confusion, the writer doesn't need to pretend that he has *the* answer, or that he knows more than he lets on about his subject.

THE PERSONAL ESSAY AND ACADEMIC WRITING

In some ways, the personal essay might seem like a dramatic departure from the kind of academic writing you've done in other classes. Openly subjective and sometimes tentative in its conclusions, the personal essay is a relatively open form that is not predictably structured, like much academic writing. Additionally, the tone of the personal essay is conversational, even intimate, rather than impersonal and removed. If your sociology or economics professor will never ask for a personal essay, why bother to write one in your composition class?

It's a fair question. While the pleasures of personal essay writing can be significant, and reason alone to write essays, there are other important reasons to practice the form. The most obvious is that the essay, more than any other form, gives you an opportunity to use exploration as a method of inquiry, and to practice those habits of mind that are so important to academic inquiry: suspending judgment, tolerating ambiguity, and using questions to challenge easy assumptions.

But the purpose of writing personal essays in your composition class goes beyond this. For one thing, the essay emphasizes the *process* of coming to know about yourself and your subject, exposing your reasoning and the ways you use knowledge to get at the truth of things. Reflecting on these things in a personal essay can tell you a lot about how you think. The *dialectical thinking* required by the personal essay—the movement back and forth between critical and creative thinking—is a useful mental exercise for a range of academic situations. Finally, much of what you are asked to write in college depends on your

> The dialectical thinking *required by the personal essay—the movement back and forth between critical and creative thinking—is a useful mental exercise for a range of academic situations.*

willingness to step forward and express a belief, make an assertion, or pose a relevant question. The personal essay is a form that puts the writer in the spotlight. You can't hide in the wings, concealed in the shadow of other people's opinions or someone else's findings. What *you* think is what the essay is all about.

FEATURES OF THE FORM

There are many different kinds of personal essays, of course, but certain conventions are present in most of them. Keep these in mind as you read the professional essays that follow. Which of the conventions listed here seem to be present? Can you detect any others?

- *Personal essays are usually written in the first person.* There is no pretense of scientific objectivity in personal essays. What makes them work is the tension between the subject and the writer as the writer reaches for new understandings.
- *The subject of the essay is often commonplace.* Although essayists sometimes write about dramatic things, they most often are interested in the drama of everyday life. Fine essays have been published, for example, about hats, houseflies, and summer lakes. The essayist's thoughts about such things may catapult her beyond the ordinary, but the topic is often humble.
- *Narrative is often the primary method of development.* Personal essays often tell two kinds of stories—they relate narratives of the writer's experiences and observations, and they tell the story of the writer's thinking about what those experiences and observations might mean.
- *The thesis can be implicit, and it frequently emerges late, rather than at the beginning, of the essay.* In some ways, the personal essay is the most literary of the academic forms—it tells stories, it relies heavily on details, it shows *and* tells. As a result, the meaning of an essay can be implied rather than stated directly, and because essays are often used to describe *the process* of coming to know something, insight is usually earned later rather than at the beginning of the telling.
- *Of the four sources of information, the personal essay relies on memory and observation most of all.* Because of the subjectivity of the essay, the writer often reports *what has happened* to her as a means to account for *what happens*. However, interview and research can enrich a personal essay by challenging the writer to consider other voices and other information (see Chapter 11, "Writing a Research Essay").
- *The essay often mimics the dialectical process that helped the writer compose it, shifting back and forth from the then and now, what happened to*

what happens, and showing and telling. Because the personal essay, more than any other form of inquiry, often focuses on the process of coming to know, essays themselves often capture this process in action. See if you can see evidence of this movement in the essays that follow.

PERSONAL ESSAY

When I first met Anne-Marie Oomen in the late eighties, she was working on a collection of essays on her rural childhood in Michigan. She was a student in one of my summer graduate classes back then, and in the New Hampshire heat we all toiled on our personal essays, trying to give voice to our longings, joys, and sorrows. Anne-Marie's was the voice I most remember from that summer twenty-five years ago. I was hardly surprised, then, to discover that in 2004 she had published *Pulling Down the Barn: Memories of a Rural Childhood.* "The Barn," the essay that follows, was drawn from that essay collection.

"The Barn" exemplifies the personal essay tradition in a number of ways: it's about a commonplace subject and experience, and it finds in ordinary moments some significant meanings that makes familiar things new. Imagine Anne-Marie writing about the barn of her childhood, trying to figure out why it lurks there so monumentally in memory. The answers she discovers begin with the very first line.

THE BARN

Anne-Marie Oomen

Barns place the farmer squarely in the middle of dirt, animals, and reverence. Barns are where things die openly but not serenely: stillborn calves, drowned swallows, frost-bitten kittens. Our barn is a place of largesse and work, open mows and high arching spaces. They are the cathedrals of farms, where all the great rituals are housed. 1

On days when we can leave the fields and play, Tom and I dare each other to walk the high crossbeams, balancing on the old cross-cut, ax-hewn ten-by-tens. 2

The first time I hesitate, and Tom taunts me. "Hey you, you're gonna get stuck up there, and somebody'll have to come getcha." 3

"Yeah, scaredy-cat, fraidy, can't walk the high beam," Rick joins him. 4

And then I remember what my mother, who is afraid of heights, has said: "Don't look down." I look directly at the beam, at the ladder brace in the middle, and take tentative, wobbly steps all the way across the high beam. 5

When I am good enough to climb like a cat, I curl onto the ladder and laugh down at my little sisters. Though I am too young to know the words to describe the experience, I love sending dust and pigeon droppings down into the shafts of light. 6

I take pleasure in the way my stomach feels if I nearly lose my balance. Walking that ten-inch-wide beam across the open bays has nothing to do with death, only with the thrill of risk. Walking the crossbeam is a chosen dare. Though my brothers and I say to each other, "You could fall and die," what we mean is "You could fall and hurt yourself." We do not believe ourselves immortal, as teenagers do; we haven't thought of death yet at all.

7 One day my foster brother, Bobby Barnes, who lives with us while he finishes high school, holds a heavy work rope in his young hands. The rope is winched to an iron eye at the very peak of the barn. Bobby is tall and lanky, with dark brown hair, and in a way that I don't yet understand I like him. He is from a downstate city, Muskegon. He is much older than the other children who sometimes stay with us, and he works long hours with my father. He often plays with me, and he is willing to teach me things. On this day he is teaching me to swing the bay.

8 The rope hangs and drops loosely down into the center of the bay, that open space where we pull the wagons to unload the hay. Bobby and I take turns hauling the rope up into the north mow. We wrap our legs around it, grab it with our dirty hands, and leap off the high-stacked bales. We swing wildly across the bay to the other side, dropping into the softer, lower mow on the south. The trick is to let go at the right time, before the rope starts its pendulum swing back. And because we are swinging from a high place, the rope, even at the lowest point of its arc, is many feet above the floor of the barn. But we never think of falling, only of the wild swinging and the shrieking as we land in the softer, lower hay on the other side.

9 Even though I am clumsy, the swing through the dusty air is pure addiction. Bobby does it better than I do. Swinging farther and farther out, he whoops and waves. It becomes a dare, him swinging, then me swinging, seeing if I can fly as high, as far as he can before dropping off onto the other side.

10 Though I am tired and sweating, I grab the rope. "I want to go higher. Higher than you." I am full of bravado.

11 "You probably can. You're lighter." He grins. For him the competition is no issue.

12 This time I twist the rope twice around my foot. This time, as I pull the rope up and back tightly onto the mow, he grabs my hips and lifts me higher, so I can leap from a greater distance. Then he lets go, and I lean back and fly. I slip into the air like a fish, swinging fast, the dusty speed cooling my face. But way out, somewhere in the space between one mow and another, leaning too far back into the slim beams of light, my hands come loose, slipping in their own grime and sweat. Because my feet are wrapped in the rope, the trunk of my body falls first, my ankles untangling last. From several feet in the air, I free-fall, landing on the floor of the barn on my back.

13 I feel no impact. I know where I am. Staring up through the dust motes in the sprawl of light, I experience a sense of floating, as though I have gained the weightlessness of being under water. And then, in that dim way awareness returns when one is stunned, I realize that I cannot breathe. I cannot breathe. My body tightens. I feel

pain in my chest so foreign that a streak of panic rushes through me like nothing I have known in my life. *I cannot breathe*.

I know that I have died. 14

This sense of not being able to inhale is fiery and alien. No other awareness enters my small intellect. I thrash and roll on the floor, then somehow I stand. Without knowing how or where, I am running, trying to scream, unable to scream. 15

Somewhere between the barn and the house, I do inhale and scream. The screams bring my mother from the clothesline. Through some wild buzz in my body I see her running too, wiping her hands on the faded apron. In her brown saddle shoes, she clomps down the sunny driveway. She moves closer and closer to me in an odd silence that is also a huge noise in my head, covering the sound of her thudding steps. I do not remember entering her arms. I am simply there, screaming strange, incongruous utterances over and over. 16

As sense pulls me back into the world, I look down at my chest. My hands are spread across it like wings, as though something in it would break open and escape from my body. I hear my breath at last, rasping but real. I say the words again, more softly, winding down: "I died. I died." 17

And for every time I say the words, I hear her soft chant, a methodical response to my claim. She is kneeling in the sand on the edge of the barnyard, rocking me, answering over and over, every time. Each time I say "I died," she responds "You're not dead." 18

I begin to believe her. 19

But if I am not dead, what was that? 20

In half-sobbed nonsense, I try to say how we were swinging, how I have fallen. I mutter. My words wind down like a mechanical toy. How can I tell her? I know enough about death to know that breathing is life. If I couldn't breathe, I must have been dead. 21

"You got the wind knocked out of you." She pulls away and looks into my face. 22

"The wind knocked out of me?" I am trembling. 23

"When you fell and hit the barn floor, it knocked all the air out of your chest. It takes a minute for it to come back." She nods. 24

The wind knocked out of me! Breathing, like wind in a tree, can leave the body and go away and then come back? Is this true? I stare at her for so long that she must look away. 25

Together, we walk back to the barn. It is still calm and huge, but I am changed. I point tenderly to the rope but do not touch it. I show her where I fell. She explains what happened, the rudiments of a person's lungs. Bobby joins us; he is shy and worried until he realizes that she does not blame him. She says she is glad I am not hurt, asks him not to play this game with me anymore. She walks us back to the house, where she pours Kool-Aid and tells us to find something more constructive to do. My chest and my back hurt, but I know my body is not seriously hurt. However, there is this other awareness, and I am just old enough to think about it. 26

The awareness comes to rest in the words, the abrupt phrase, *knocked the wind out of you*. I say the phrase over and over. It comes to represent a moment so formative it 27 is forever associated with the thick part of me where breathing is housed. The words and their meaning are linked now in cellular knowing. On that day my mother named for me something that was so like death it negated coming back to the innocence of mere risk. I never again walked the crossbeams or swung on the rope because, with a child's commitment to knowing, I understood that I could die.

Inquiring into the Essay

Throughout *The Curious Writer,* I'll invite you to respond to readings such as "The Barn" using questions based on the four methods of inquiry discussed in Chapter 3. The following questions, therefore, encourage you to explore, explain, evaluate, and reflect to discover and shape what you think about the reading. If you're using a double-entry journal, use these questions to prompt writing on the right page of your notebook. Use the opposing left page to collect passages, details, and quotations from the reading that you think might be important.

1. We all want some structure in our lives. I mean that literally, of course. Many of us, like Anne-Marie Oomen, are drawn again and again to some building—a house, a cabin, a city apartment, a museum, a school, the firehouse down the street—that lives on in memory. But why? Explore places like that in your past. First brainstorm a list of them. Then choose one to write about in a seven-minute fastwrite. Describe the place with as much detail as you can.
2. Personal essays often tell two stories: the story of what happened, and the story of what the writer came to understand about the meaning of what happened. In your own words, explain your understanding of that second story in "The Barn."
3. Coming up with a good title for an essay is a vexing problem for most of us. Perhaps one reason is that we know how important they are. The title of this essay is quite simple: "The Barn." Based on your understanding of the essay, argue for an alternative title that you think is at least as good.
4. Oomen writes at the end of the essay that after she had the wind knocked out of her, "I understood that I could die." Do you find that assertion convincing and believable? *Why or why not?*
5. While "The Barn" is not a confessional essay, it is quite personal. Reflect on how comfortable are you writing, as Anne-Marie Oomen did, about the details of your life.
6. Create a graph of your interest in this essay, as shown in Figure 4.1. Put the paragraph numbers on the horizontal axis and your level of interest, scored from 1 to 5 (with 5 being highest interest and 1 lowest interest), on the vertical axis. Plot the graph and compare your graph with others in the class. Discuss which paragraphs seemed to generate the highest and lowest levels of reader interest. What are the particular qualities of each? Reflect on what your own graph says about you as a reader.

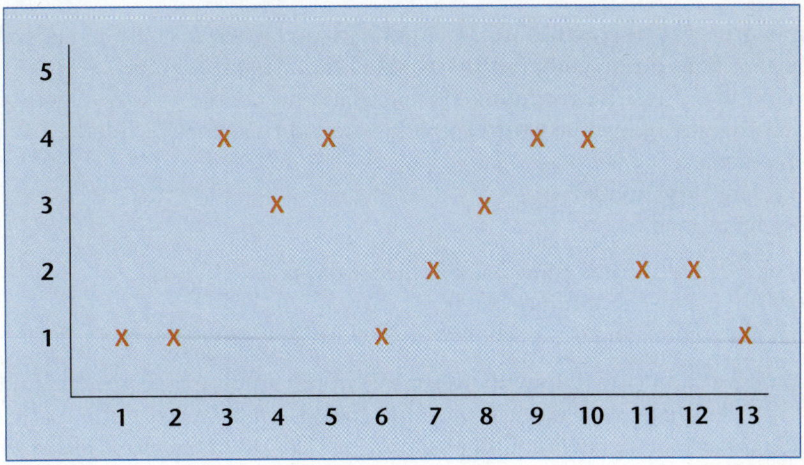

FIGURE 4.1 An example of a graph of reader interest. The horizontal axis lists paragraph numbers and the vertical axis lists the level of interest.

PERSONAL ESSAY

Naomi Shihab Nye is a poet, and the essay that follows, "Long Overdue," has some of the qualities of a poem—spare language, breaks or white spaces between sections of the narrative, and an emphasis on the line. That makes her essay unusual, yet compelling. Nye, the daughter of a Palestinian father and an American mother, writes here about confronting the prejudice of others and being unable to find the words to speak up.

While most of us have probably not been on the receiving end of bigotry, we commonly find ourselves offended by the words of others and unable to find the words to respond. In a larger sense, this essay explores those moments, as Nye attempts to write to the heart of the nagging question, *Why do we say nothing?*

LONG OVERDUE

Naomi Shihab Nye

A gardener stares at our raggedy front yard. More weeds than grass. The star jasmine vine has died in the drought, leaving its bony spine woven through the frets of the wire fence. A young hackberry presses too close to the house. A bedraggled pomegranate tree crowds the banana palms. 1

The gardener shakes his head. Hands on hips. He is large and blond as a Viking. He wears no shirt. When I ask what he thinks about laying flat stones on the beaten 2 path from driveway to porch so we don't track in mud when it rains, he nods silently, then puts his arms out to embrace this troubled yard. "Long overdue."

3 Excuse me? And the trimming? What would he charge to take out that tree? Could he edge this flowerbed with smooth rounded river rocks while he's at it? He stares into my face.

4 *Long, long, long overdue.*

5 I laugh out loud.

6 His few well-chosen words come back to me for days.

7 That's how I feel about lives bereft of poetry.

8 That's how I feel about the whole Middle East.

9 The words we didn't say. How many times? Stones stuck in the throat. Endlessly revised silence. *What was wrong with me? How could I, a person whose entire vocation has been dedicated one way or another to "the use of words," lose words completely when I needed them? Where does vocal paralysis come from? Why does regret have such a long life span?* My favorite poet William Stafford used to say. "Think of something you said. Now write what you *wish you* had said."

10 But I am always thinking of the times I said nothing.

11 In England, attending a play by myself, I was happy when the elderly woman next to me began speaking at intermission. Our arms had been touching lightly on the arm rest between our seats.

12 "Smashingly talented," she said of Ben Kingsley, whose brilliant monologue we'd been watching. "I don't know how he does it—transporting us so effortlessly, he's a genius. Not many in the world like him. " I agreed. But then she sighed and made an odd turn. "You know what's wrong with the world today? It's Arabs. I blame it all on the Arabs. Most world problems can really be traced to them."

13 My blood froze. Why was she saying this? The play wasn't about Arabs. Ben Kingsley was hardly your blue-blooded Englishman, either, so what brought it up? Nothing terrible relating to Arabs had happened lately in the news. I wasn't wearing a kef' fiyeh around my neck.

14 But my mouth would not open.

15 "Why *did so* many of them come to England?" she continued, muttering as if we were sharing a confidence. "A ruination, that's what it is."

16 It struck me then she might be a landlady having trouble with tenants. I tried and tried to part my lips. *Where is the end of the tangled thread? How will we roll it into a ball if we can't find an end?*

17 She chitted on about something less consequential, never seeming to mind our utterly one-sided conversation, till the lights went down. Of course I couldn't concentrate on the rest of the play. My precious ticket felt wasted. I twisted my icy hands together while my cheeks burned.

18 Even worse, she and I rode the same train afterwards. I had plenty of time to respond, to find a vocabulary for prejudice and fear. The dark night buildings flew by.

I could have said, "Madam. I am half Arab. I pray your heart grows larger someday." I could have sent her off, stunned and embrassed, into the dark.

My father would say, *People like that can't be embarrassed.* 19

But what would he say *back to her?* 20

Oh I was ashamed for my silence and I have carried that shame across oceans, through a summer when it never rained, in my secret pocket, till now. I will never feel better about it. Like my reckless angry last words to the one who took his own life. 21

Years later my son and I were sitting on an American island with a dear friend, the only African American living among eighty or so residents. A brilliant artist and poet in his seventies, he has made a beautiful lifetime of painting picture books, celebrating expression, encouraging the human spirit, reciting poems of other African American heroes, delighting children and adults alike. 22

We had spent a peaceful day riding bicycles, visiting the few students at the schoolhouse, picking up rounded stones on the beach, digging peat moss in the woods. We had sung hymns together in the resonant little church. Our friend had purchased a live lobster down at the dock for supper. My son and I became sad when it seemed to be knocking on the lid of the pot of boiling water. "Let me out!" We vowed quietly to one another never to eat a lobster again. 23

After dinner a friend of our friend dropped in, returned to the island from her traveling life as an anthropologist. We asked if she had heard anything about the elections in Israel—that was the day Shimon Peres and Benjamin Netanyahu vied for prime minister and we had been unable to pick up a final tally on the radio. 24

She thought Netanyahu had won. The election was very close. But then she said, "Good thing! He'll put those Arabs in their places. Arabs always want more than they deserve." 25

My face froze. Was it possible I had heard incorrectly? *An anthropologist speaking. Not a teenager, not a blithering idiot.* I didn't speak another word during her visit. I wanted to, I should have, but I couldn't. My plate littered with red shells. 26

After she left, my friend put his gentle hand on my shoulder. He said simply, "Now you know a little more what it feels like to be black." 27

So what happens to my words when the going gets rough? In a world where certain equities for human beings seem long, long, long, overdue, where is the magic sentence to act as a tool? Where is the hoe, the tiller, the rake? 28

Pontificating, proving, proselytizing leave me cold. So do endless political debates over coffee after dinner. I can't listen to talk radio, drowning in jabber. 29

The poetic impulse—to suggest, hint, shape a little picture, to find a story, metaphor, scene—abides as a kind of music inside. Nor can I forget the journalist in Dubai who called me a donkey for talking about vegetables when there was injustice in the world. 30

I can talk about sumac too. When a friend asks what's that purple spice in the little shake-up jar at the Persian restaurant, tears cloud my eyes. 31

32 *Is it good for you?*

33 Are vegetables, in some indelible way, smarter than we are? Are animals?

34 But then the headlines take the power. The fanatical behavior.

35 *Problem is, we can't hear the voices of the moderates*, said the Israeli man, who assured me his home was built on a spot where Arabs had never lived. Where are *they?* Why *don't* they *speak louder?*

36 (They don't like to raise their voices.)

37 (Maybe they can't hear you either.)

38 The men haven't fixed it. Lose their turn. Their turn was long enough. Hanan stepped back. Anyone can understand why. Too many men. Pass the power to the women. And the children. And the eggplants. But it *was women who said stupid things both times to me*. No one exempt from stupidity. Is there a cure?

39 I love when the poet Wislawa said we have to honor anew those humble words *I don't know*.

40 Then we start out fresh. Like the soft dampness of a new morning.

41 I don't know. How. To tell the whole story. No one tells the whole story. No one knows it! *Still, don't those guys seem to talk forever?*

42 EVERY VIOLENT ACT SETS US BACK. SETS US BACK. Say it louder.

43 What to contain. To honor, leave unspoken. People will talk and talk while the almond tree is blooming. But something crucial is always too big, or too obvious, to say. Obviously, it is the thing which could save people, if we could only learn its name.

44 The gardener laid the stones. He cut the trees back. He turned over the soil around the plants so their roots could breathe. He used no language doing it. His skin glistened in the sun.

45 What he has suffered in his life remains a mystery to me. Rumors in the neighborhood say it has been much, and extreme. What did Aldous Huxley say toward the end of his life when someone asked him for advice? *After so much study, after so much research and discussion, it comes to this: be a little kinder to one another.*

46 Before leaving, the gardener mentioned the grass would grow up soon between the stepping stones to help them look much nicer, as if they had been there for years.

Inquiring into the Essay

As with the previous essay, think about "Long Overdue" by shifting your perspective on it using the four methods of inquiry: exploring, explaining, evaluating, and reflecting.

1. After you've read through Nye's essay once, read through it again, but this time stop at every line break, or white space that divides each segment, and fastwrite in your journal for sixty seconds. Each time, begin with this

phrase: *The most important thing I understand from this is . . .*"Usc these multiple responses to compose the story of your understanding of the meaning of Nye's essay from beginning to end.

2. Explain what you take to be the significance of the repeated phrase *Long, long, overdue.*
3. Evaluate the effectiveness of the "line breaks" in this essay. We are used to unbroken narratives—this happened and then this happened and so on. "Long Overdue," like many contemporary personal essays, defies this expectation. What do you think about the effect of this on you as a reader?
4. An important part of academic inquiry—whether it's doing scientific research or writing a critical essay on literature—is trying to identify the prejudices you bring as an investigator to your project. Reflect on what prejudices you brought to your reading of this essay.

PERSONAL ESSAY

America is a nation of immigrants, and their stories often haunt their children. Judith Ortiz Cofer moved from Puerto Rico as a child with her family in the mid-1950s to a barrio in Paterson, New Jersey. There she became both part of and witness to a familiar narrative, that of the outsider who finds herself wedged between two worlds, two cultures, and two longings: the desire to return "home" and the desire to feel at home in the new place. While this is a story most immigrants know well, it is also a deeply personal one, shaded by particular places, prejudices, and patterns.

In "One More Lesson," Cofer describes both the places that competed for her sense of self—the Puerto Rico of her childhood, where she spent time as a child while her Navy father was away at sea, and an apartment in New Jersey where she would go when he returned.

ONE MORE LESSON

Judith Ortiz Cofer

I remember Christmas on the Island by the way it felt on my skin. The temperature dropped into the ideal seventies and even lower after midnight when some of the more devout Catholics—mostly older women—got up to go to church, *misa del gallo* they called it; mass at the hour when the rooster crowed for Christ. They would drape shawls over their heads and shoulders and move slowly toward town. The birth of Our Savior was a serious affair in our *pueblo*. 1

At Mamá's house, food was the focal point of *Navidad*. There were banana leaves brought in bunches by the boys, spread on the table, where the women would pour coconut candy steaming hot, and the leaves would wilt around the sticky lumps, 2 adding an extra tang of flavor to the already irresistible treat. Someone had to watch the candy while it cooled, or it would begin to disappear as the children risked life and limb for a stolen piece of heaven. The banana leaves were also used to wrap the traditional food of holidays in Puerto Rico: *pasteles*, the meat pies made from grated yucca and plantain and stuffed with spiced meats.

3 Every afternoon during the week before Christmas Day, we would come home from school to find the women sitting around in the parlor with bowls on their laps, grating pieces of coconut, yuccas, plantains, cheeses—all the ingredients that would make up our Christmas Eve feast. The smells that filled Mamá's house at that time have come to mean anticipation and a sensual joy during a time in my life, the last days of my early childhood, when I could still absorb joy through my pores—*when I had not yet learned that light is followed by darkness, that all of creation is based on that simple concept, and maturity is a discovery of that natural law.*

4 It was in those days that the Americans sent baskets of fruit to our barrio—apples, oranges, grapes flown in from the States. And at night, if you dared to walk up to the hill where the mango tree stood in the dark, you could see a wonderful sight: a Christmas tree, a real pine, decorated with lights of many colors. It was the blurry outline of this tree you saw, for it was inside a screened-in-porch, but we had heard a thorough description of it from the boy who delivered the fruit, a nephew of Mamá's, as it had turned out. Only, I was not impressed, since just the previous year we had put up a tree ourselves in our apartment in Paterson.

5 Packages arrived for us in the mail from our father. I got dolls dressed in the national costumes of Spain, Italy, and Greece (at first we could not decide which of the Greek dolls was the male, since they both wore skirts); my brother got picture books; and my mother, jewelry that she would not wear, because it was too much like showing off and might attract the Evil Eye.

6 Evil Eye or not, the three of us were the envy of the pueblo. Everything about us set us apart, and I put away my dolls quickly when I discovered that my playmates would not be getting any gifts until *Los Reyes*—the Day of the Three Kings, when Christ received His gifts—and that even then it was more likely that the gifts they found under their beds would be practical things like clothes. Still, it was fun to find fresh grass for the camels the night the Kings were expected, tie it in bundles with string, and put it under our beds along with a bowl of fresh water.

7 The year went by fast after Christmas, and in the spring we received a telegram from Father. His ship had arrived in Brooklyn Yard. He gave us a date for our trip back to the States. I remember Mother's frantic packing, and the trips to Mayagüez for new clothes; the inspections of my brother's and my bodies for cuts, scrapes, mosquito bites, and other "damage" she would have to explain to Father. And I remember begging Mamá to tell me stories in the afternoons, although it was not summer yet and the trips to the mango tree had not begun. In looking back I realize that Mamá's stories were what I packed—my winter store.

8 Father had succeeded in finding an apartment outside Paterson's "vertical barrio," the tenement Puerto Ricans called *El Building*. He had talked a Jewish candy

store owner into renting us the apartment above his establishment, which he and his wife had just vacated after buying a house in West Paterson, an affluent suburb. Mr. Schultz was a nice man whose melancholy face I was familiar with from trips I had made often with my father to his store for cigarettes. Apparently, my father had convinced him and his brother, a look-alike of Mr. Schultz who helped in the store, that we were not the usual Puerto Rican family. My father's fair skin, his ultra-correct English, and his Navy uniform were a good argument. Later it occurred to me that my father had been displaying me as a model child when he took me to that store with him. I was always dressed as if for church and held firmly by the hand. I imagine he did the same with my brother. As for my mother, her Latin beauty, her thick black hair that hung to her waist, her voluptuous body which even the winter clothes could not disguise, would have been nothing but a hindrance to my father's plans. But everyone knew that a Puerto Rican woman is her husband's satellite; she reflects both his light and his dark sides. If my father was respectable, then his family would be respectable. We got the apartment on Park Avenue.

Unlike El Building, where we had lived on our first trip to Paterson, our new home was truly in exile. There were Puerto Ricans by the hundreds only one block away, but we heard no Spanish, no loud music, no mothers yelling at children, nor the familiar *¡Ay Bendito!*, that catch-all phrase of our people. Mother lapsed into silence herself, suffering from *La Tristeza,* the sadness that only place induces and only place cures. But Father relished silence, and we were taught that silence was something to be cultivated and practiced. 9

Since our apartment was situated directly above where the Schultzes worked all day, our father instructed us to remove our shoes at the door and walk in our socks. We were going to prove how respectable we were by being the opposite of what our ethnic group was known to be—we would be quiet and inconspicuous. 10

I was escorted each day to school by my nervous mother. It was a long walk in the cooling air of fall in Paterson and we had to pass by El Building where the children poured out of the front door of the dilapidated tenement still answering their mothers in a mixture of Spanish and English: "Sí, Mami, I'll come straight home from school." At the corner we were halted by the crossing guard, a strict woman who only gestured her instructions, never spoke directly to the children, and only ordered us to "halt" or "cross" while holding her white-gloved hand up at face level or swinging her arm sharply across her chest if the light was green. 11

The school building was not a welcoming sight for someone used to the bright colors and airiness of tropical architecture. The building looked functional. It could have been a prison, an asylum, or just what it was: an urban school for the children of immigrants, built to withstand waves of change, generation by generation. Its red brick sides rose to four solid stories. The black steel fire escapes snaked up its back like an exposed vertebra. A chain-link fence surrounded its concrete playground. Members of the elite safety patrol, older kids, sixth graders mainly, stood at each of its entrances, wearing their fluorescent white belts that criss-crossed 12 their chests and their metal badges. No one was allowed in the building until the bell rang, not even on rainy or bitter-cold days. Only the safety-patrol stayed warm.

13 My mother stood in front of the main entrance with me and a growing crowd of noisy children. She looked like one of us, being no taller than the sixth-grade girls. She held my hand so tightly that my fingers cramped. When the bell rang, she walked me into the building and kissed my cheek. Apparently my father had done all the paperwork for my enrollment, because the next thing I remember was being led to my third-grade classroom by a black girl who had emerged from the principal's office.

14 Though I had learned some English at home during my first years in Paterson, I had let it recede deep into my memory while learning Spanish in Puerto Rico. Once again I was the child in the cloud of silence, the one who had to be spoken to in sign language as if she were a deaf-mute. Some of the children even raised their voices when they spoke to me, as if I had trouble hearing. Since it was a large troublesome class composed mainly of black and Puerto Rican children, with a few working-class Italian children interspersed, the teacher paid little attention to me. I re-learned the language quickly by the immersion method. I remember one day, soon after I joined the rowdy class when our regular teacher was absent and Mrs. D., the sixth-grade teacher from across the hall, attempted to monitor both classes. She scribbled something on the chalkboard and went to her own room. I felt a pressing need to use the bathroom and asked Julio, the Puerto Rican boy who sat behind me, what I had to do to be excused. He said that Mrs. D. had written on the board that we could be excused by simply writing our names under the sign. I got up from my desk and started for the front of the room when I was struck on the head hard with a book. Startled and hurt, I turned around expecting to find one of the bad boys in my class, but it was Mrs. D. I faced. I remember her angry face, her fingers on my arms pulling me back to my desk, and her voice saying incomprehensible things to me in a hissing tone. Someone finally explained to her that I was new, that I did not speak English. I also remember how suddenly her face changed from anger to anxiety. But I did not forgive her for hitting me with that hard-cover spelling book. Yes, I would recognize that book even now. It was not until years later that I stopped hating that teacher for not understanding that I had been betrayed by a classmate, and by my inability to read her warning on the board. I *instinctively understood then that language is the only weapon a child has against the absolute power of adults*.

15 I quickly built up my arsenal of words by becoming an insatiable reader of books.

Inquiring into the Essay

Explore, explain, evaluate, and reflect on Cofer's "One More Lesson."

1. In the 1950s and 1960s, many saw America as a "melting pot." The idea then was that although we may have many different immigrant

backgrounds, we should strive toward some common "Americanism." For some, this is still a powerful idea, but for others the melting pot is a metaphor for cultural hegemony or even racial prejudice, a demand that differences be ignored and erased rather than celebrated. In your journal, write about your own feelings on this controversy. Tell the story of a friend, a relative, a neighbor who was an outsider. Tell about your own experience. What did it mean to assimilate, and at what cost?

2. Personal essays, like short fiction, rely heavily on narrative. But unlike fiction, essays both *show* and *tell;* that is, they use story to reveal meaning (*show*) and they also explain that meaning to the reader (*tell*). Identify several places in the essay where Cofer "tells." What do you notice about the placement of these moments of reflection?
3. Does this essay make an evaluation, and if so, what is it asserting about cultural assimilation in America during the 1950s and 1960s? Is Cofer's evaluation still relevant?
4. One of the most common reasons students cite for liking a story is that "they could relate to it." Does that criterion apply here? Reflect on whether it's a standard you often use as a reader to judge the value of something. What exactly does it mean to "relate to" a text?

SEEING THE FORM

SELF-PORTRAIT BY FRANCES BENJAMIN JOHNSTON

In the striking self-portrait that follows, American photographer Frances Benjamin Johnston represents herself in ways in which most nineteenth-century women wouldn't dare. Her skirts are hiked up to her knees, she holds a burning cigarette between her fingers, and she clutches a beer mug on her lap. Johnston carefully composed the picture to offer a very particular version of herself. Photographic self-portraits like this one are similar to personal essays in a number of respects. They often tell a story, and the photographer, like the essayist, is a subject of the work, sometimes *the* subject. We also consider a photograph to be "authentic." We assume, for instance, that this is the real Frances Benjamin Johnston, not someone else's impression or interpretation of her. When we read a personal essay, a work of nonfiction, we also assume that the *I* of the essay is the author of the piece, not some character or other invention.

As writers of personal essays, don't we attempt to represent ourselves as authentically and honestly as we can? Aren't we basically trying to present verbal pictures of ourselves and our experiences? But how accurate are these self-representations? And if the comparison between a self-portrait such as Johnston's picture and the personal essay is an accurate one, what does it imply about how we might write our own essays, but also how we might read the personal essays of other people?

Frances Benjamin Johnston, *Self-Portrait*, 1896.

Inquiring into the Details

THE LITERACY NARRATIVE

Some of the great personal essays of the last 500 years were what we now call "literacy narratives," stories about how the author came to understand him or herself as a writer, reader, or speaker. Montaigne, Virginia Woolf, Fredrick Douglas, Malcom X, and others have published moving essays about how they each came to understand their relationships to language. This is an enormously useful project for you, too, because it will help you understand what might be at the root of your current beliefs about yourself as a maker and consumer of language.

Literacy narratives vary but like any other personal essay they often include stories or anecdotes that richly describe moments, scenes, or people, but these are chosen to reveal something about what has influenced how you feel about reading and writing. I wrote, for example, in "The Importance of Writing Badly" (p. 45) about Mrs. O'Neil, my seventh and eighth grade English teacher who had a fondness for the red pen and the SRA. I could have just as easily written about moments in the Highland Park Public Library, the sound of my father's typewriter in the next room, or using my first PC to compose an essay.

Literacy narratives also share with other personal essays the need to move from showing—narrating what happened—to telling—commenting on its significance, or answering the "so what?" question. It's particularly important to use this story-telling as an opportunity to reflect on how your experiences shape you *now* as a reader or writer. Specifically, how have these particular events or people in your past influenced how you think about your own relationship to language—are you a lover of words, resistant to English, a hoarder of books, a self-critical writer? How do your experiences contribute to these kinds of beliefs about yourself?

THE WRITING PROCESS

INQUIRY PROJECT: Writing a Personal Essay

Write a 1,000-word personal essay that explores some aspect of your experience. Your instructor may provide additional details. Choose your topic carefully. Because of the essay's exploratory methods, the best topics are those that you want to write about *not* because you know what you think, but because you want to *discover* what you think. The essay should have the following qualities:

- It must do more than tell a story; there must be a *purpose* behind telling the story that speaks in some way to someone else.
- It should, ultimately, answer the *So what?* question.
- Your essay should include some reflection to explain or speculate about what you understand *now* about something that you didn't understand *then*.
- It should be richly detailed. Seize opportunities to *show* what you mean, rather than simply explain it.

Thinking About Subjects

When you are assigned a personal essay, it's essential to embrace uncertainty and be willing to suspend judgment. This form of inquiry, more than any other, seems most useful when the writer has chosen a subject *because* he doesn't know what he wants to say about it. This is risky. Obviously, one of the risks when you start out with uncertainty is that you also might end up that way; your draft may just seem to go nowhere. This *is* a problem, but it often can be addressed in revision. The key to writing strong personal essays is accepting that first drafts might be real stinkers. But there's a payoff to this risk—the personal essay frequently yields surprise and discovery. You may well find out what you didn't know you knew, and that is among the greatest pleasures of a writer.

As you play with the prompts that follow, then, be particularly vigilant about pursuing subject matter that is confusing to you, that raises the hair on the back of your neck, or just makes you say to yourself, "I'm not sure what I think or feel about that."

Generating Ideas

Begin exploring possible subjects by generating material in your notebook. This should be an open-ended process, a chance to use your creative side, not worrying too much about making sense or trying to prejudge the value of the writing or the subjects you generate. In a sense, this is an invitation to play around.

One Student's Response

MARGARET'S JOURNAL: LISTING QUESTIONS

Is my cat extremely unusual or can any cat be taught to walk and be as needy and attached as her?

Does testosterone really make one more confident? Is there a correlation between high T and aggressiveness?

How did I once find Dr. Laura so compelling?

Why are women seldom loyal to each other? How are female friendships different from male ones? Can women and men be friends without an underlying sexual tension?

Listing Prompts. Lists can be rich sources of triggering topics. Let them grow freely, and when you're ready, use an item as the focus of another list or an episode of fastwriting. The following prompts should get you started.

1. Make a fast list of experiences you've had that you can't forget. Reach into all parts and times of your life.
2. Make a list of questions that have always nagged you about some of the following: school, men or women, fast food, hair, television, public restrooms, shoes, and sports.

Fastwriting Prompts. In the early stages of generating possible topics for an essay, fastwriting can be invaluable, *if* you allow yourself to write "badly." Initially, don't worry about staying focused; sometimes you find the best triggering topics by ranging freely. Once you've tentatively settled on something, use a more focused fastwrite, trying to generate information and ideas within the loose boundaries of your chosen topic. Here are some fastwriting prompts that might yield useful discoveries for a personal essay:

1. Choose an item from any one of the preceding lists as a prompt. Just start fastwriting about the item; perhaps start with a story, a scene, a situation, a description. Just follow the writing to see where it leads.

2. Most of us quietly harbor dreams—we hope to be a professional dancer, a good father, an activist, an Olympic luger, or a novelist. Begin a fastwrite in which you explore your dreams. When the writing stalls, ask yourself questions: *Where did this dream come from? Do I still believe in it? In what moments did it seem within reach? In what moments did it fade?* Plunge into those moments.

3. What was the most confusing time in your life? Choose a moment or scene that stands out in your memory from that time, and, writing in the present tense, describe what you see, hear, and do. After five minutes, skip a line and choose another moment. Then another. Make a collage.

4. What do you consider "turning points" in your life, times when you could see the end of one thing and the beginning of something else? Fastwrite about one of these for seven minutes.

Visual Prompts. Sometimes the best way to generate material is to see what we think in something other than sentences. Boxes, lines, arrows, charts, and even sketches can help us see more of the landscape of a subject, especially connections between fragments of information that aren't as obvious in prose. The clustering or mapping method is useful to many writers early in the writing process as they try to discover a topic. (See the "Inquiring into the Details" box that follows for more details on how to create a cluster.) Figure 4.2 shows my cluster from the first prompt listed here.

1. What objects would you most regret losing in a house fire? The answer would likely reveal something about your passions, your longings, even your regrets. Choose a most-treasured object as the core for a cluster. Build a web of associations from it, returning to the detail in the core whenever a strand dies out. One of the wonderful complexities of being human is that we are sometimes deeply conflicted (I'm not suggesting this is always fun). Pair two opposed feelings that you consider typical of yourself. For example, *ambivalence/commitment, fear/risk taking, lonely/sociable, beautiful/ugly, composed/flaky,* and so on. Use these paired words as a core for a cluster.

2. Draw a long line on a piece of paper in your journal. This is your life. Divide the line into segments that seem to describe what feels like distinct

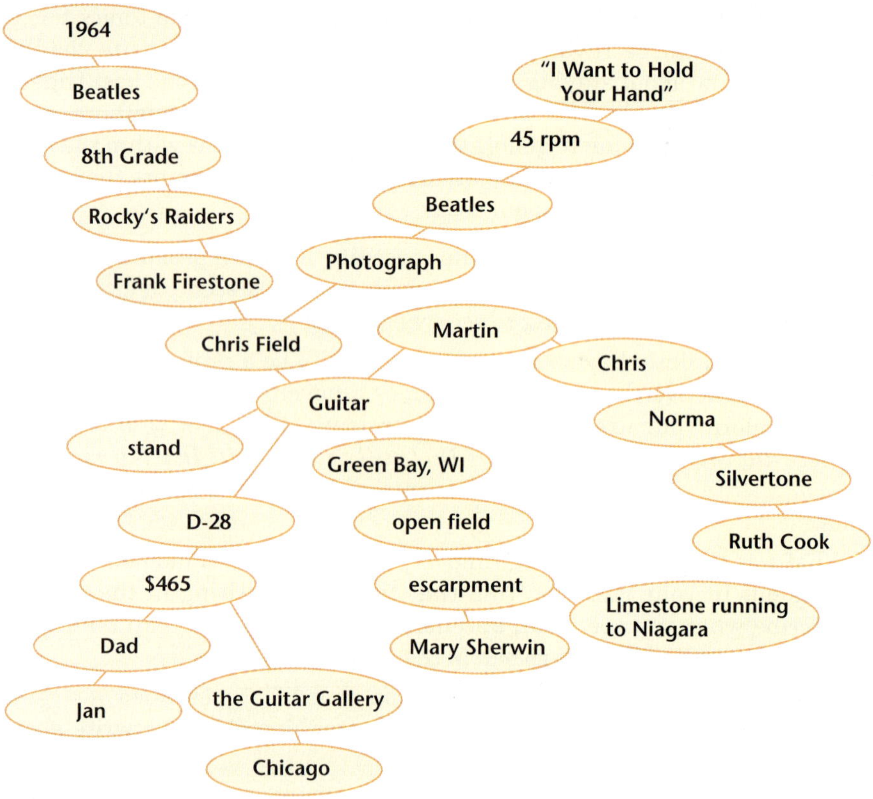

FIGURE 4.2 A cluster built around the one object I would most regret losing in a house fire: my Martin guitar.

times in your life. These may not necessarily correspond to familiar age categories like adolescence or childhood. More likely, the periods in your life will be associated with a place, a relationship, a dilemma, a job, a personal challenge, and so on, but because this is a timeline, these periods will be chronological. Examine your timeline and, as a fastwrite prompt, put two of these periods in your life together. Explore what they had in common, particularly how the earlier period might have shaped the later one. See Figure 4.3 for a sample timeline.

Research Prompts. Things we hear, see, or read can be powerful prompts for personal essays. It's tempting to believe that personal essays are always about the past, but just as often essayists are firmly rooted in the present, commenting and pondering on the confusions of contemporary life, as Naomi Shihab Nye did in "Long Overdue." In that sense, personal essayists are researchers, always

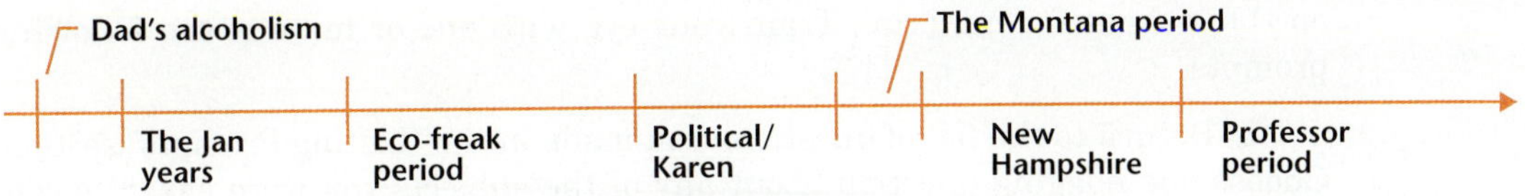

FIGURE 4.3 A sample timeline from my own life.

Inquiring into the Details

CLUSTERING OR MAPPING

One of the virtues of clustering as a method of generating information is that it defies the more linear nature of writing, putting one sentence after another in a chain of thought. When you make a cluster, there are multiple chains, each growing from a core word, phrase, or idea. In Figure 4.2, I clustered the word *guitar*. I'm not just thinking of any guitar, of course, but my 1969 Martin D-28 with Brazilian rosewood and the ding on the front. This is the one object I'd rescue from a fire.

Clusters are in code; each item in the web says more than it says, at least to me, because I'm familiar with its meaning. You don't have that kind of knowledge, obviously, so my cluster wouldn't say much to you. Each strand suggests a story, an idea, or a feeling that I might explore.

Typically, clustering is most useful at the beginning of the writing process as you test a possible subject and want to see its landscape of possibilities. I can see, for example, possible essays about not only the significance of this guitar, but essays on the eighth grade, my old friend Chris Field, and the natural history of limestone. The best clusters are richly suggestive that way, but they're only starting places for more writing. How do you cluster?

1. Begin with a blank page in your journal. Choose a core word, phrase, name, idea, detail, or question; write it in the middle of the page and circle it.
2. Relax and focus on the core word or phrase, and when you feel moved to do so, build a strand of associations from the core, circling and connecting each item. Write other details, names, dates, place names, phrases, and so on—whatever comes to mind.
3. When a strand dies out, return to the core and begin another. Keep clustering until the page looks like a web of associations. Doodle, darkening lines and circles, if that helps you relax and focus.
4. When you feel the urge to write, stop clustering and use one of the strands as a prompt for journal work.

on the lookout for material. Train your eye with one or more of the following prompts.

1. Return to the list of questions you made in the "Listing Prompts" section. Choose one nagging question about any of the subjects you were asked to consider and set aside time to explore it by carefully *observing* them. Write down exactly what you see . . . and what you think about it. (The double-entry notebook method is particularly useful for this.)

2. Newspaper "filler"—short stories often about odd or unusual things—can be a wonderful source of inspiration for personal essays. Read your local paper for a few days, clipping these brief articles. Paste them in your journal and use them as prompts for fastwriting.

3. Although the Internet offers infinite opportunities for procrastination, with some focus it can also be a great source for jump-starting ideas. What happened to your best friend from kindergarten? Type her name into the Google search engine and find out. (Be sure to put quotation marks around the person's name for a more targeted search.) Think about your favorite vacation—a search for "Grand Canyon" might help jog your memory. Or perhaps checking out "News of the Weird" on Yahoo! might remind you of your own childhood antics.

Judging What You Have

Generating may produce messy, incoherent writing that would earn you bad grades in most classes. Its virtue, however, should be obvious by now: "bad" writing gives a writer material to work with, and it's always better to work from abundance than scarcity. But if this material is going to go anywhere, it must be judged, shaped, and evaluated; the writer must emerge from particulars of his/her experience and find a vantage point to see what, if anything, those particulars add up to.

The initial challenge in producing a first draft is clarifying your topic: What are you really writing about? Later, you'll confront the *So what?* question: What are you trying to *say* about that topic? Don't reject material too soon. Suspend judgment for a bit and work through the following questions as you scrutinize the material you've collected so far in your journal.

What's Promising Material and What Isn't? A good topic for a personal essay need not be dramatic or profound; in fact, some of the most compelling essays are about quite ordinary things. But as you examine your journal writing so far, consider the following:

- **Abundance.** What subject generated the most writing? Do you sense that there is much more to write about?
- **Surprise.** What material did you find most confusing in interesting ways? *Was there something that surprised you*—perhaps a feeling you didn't

expect to feel, or a memory that seems charged, or an observation that challenged your preconceptions?

- **Confusion.** What subject raises questions you're not sure you can answer easily? The personal essay is a mode of inquiry that permits uncertainty, and even some inconclusiveness, so it lends itself to material that makes you wonder.
- **Honesty.** What subjects are you willing to write honestly about? The personal nature of the personal essay often leads us to material that may be uncomfortable or even private. However, you should not write essays that make you feel overly vulnerable or unsafe; that stuff should probably stay in your journal. Pursue subjects that you're willing to share.

Questions About Purpose and Audience. Writing should be seen in a particular situation, addressing certain subjects, and serving certain purposes for certain audiences. Knowledge about this rhetorical situation is really the only way a writer can determine what makes a piece good. With open-ended forms like the essay, however, worrying too much about purpose and audience too soon in the writing process can intrude on the development of promising subjects. The personal essay, unlike other genres, directly challenges the writer to work out his or her relationship with a subject, a process that takes place in the open, with the reader as witness. At times, it's a little like dancing nearly naked on a table in a crowded restaurant. *But initially, the essayist is the essay's most important audience.* The writer's motive is straightforward: *What do I want to understand about this that I don't fully understand now?*

The personal essay, unlike other genres, directly challenges the writer to work out his or her relationship with the subject, a process that takes place in the open, with the reader as witness.

This personal motive will guide you in choosing a topic for your draft, but before long, the rhetorical questions become more urgent. As you evaluate your journal writing and begin to draft your essay, consider these additional questions:

- Did your instructor provide guidelines for the personal essay assignment that might influence your treatment of the material? For example, did he or she specify a certain audience for this draft or a certain structure or approach for the essay? If so, will the material fit those guidelines?
- Who is your audience? If your draft will be peer reviewed, how can this subject be compelling to others in the class? Is it something they would find interesting or relevant?
- Is there a particular question that drives your exploration of this subject? Can you make the question explicit as a way of focusing your draft? For example, *Why was I relieved when my father died?* Or *Why is it true that men never ask directions, consult maps, or read instruction manuals?*

Questions for Reflection. After you've generated enough material on your topic, seize opportunities to reflect. You may do this as you're writing in your journal, thinking about your topic in the shower, or talking about it with friends. Remember that this move to reflect is an essential part of the dialectical thinking that helps writers make sense of things, going back and forth between *what happened* and *what happens,* between *showing* and *telling,* and *observations of* and *ideas about*. In the personal essay, this movement does not occur only in a writer's journal but often appears in the finished essay; in some cases, a reader can clearly see in an essay this movement between showing and telling. If you need help finding reflective distance, questions are the best way to do it. Use one or more of the following questions as prompts for thinking or writing in your journal.

- What do you understand now about this topic that you didn't fully understand when you began writing about it?
- What has surprised you most? Why?
- What seems to be the most important thing you're trying to say so far?
- Focus on how your thinking has changed about your topic. Finish this seed sentence as many times as you can in your notebook: *Once I thought* ___________, *and now I think* ___________.
- Quickly write a narrative of thought about your topic: *When I began writing about my father's alcoholism, I thought I felt relieved when he died. Then I decided that when he died some part of me died with him, and then I realized that the real truth is . . .*
- Finish this sentence in your journal: *As I look back on this, I realize that . . .* Follow that sentence with another, and another until you feel there's nothing more to say.

Writing the Sketch

It's hard to say when it's time to begin composing the draft, particularly with open-ended forms such as the personal essay. Because the essay invites writers to tackle itchy, confusing subjects, and its mode of inquiry is largely exploratory, it may seem as if you could stay in the shelter of your journal for a long time. On the

Writing with Computers

CUTTING VERSUS DELETING

Because revision is much more than tinkering with text, it often becomes necessary to remove large portions of text from drafts while revising. A good habit in these situations is to cut passages out of the draft and paste them at the end of the document or into a second document. If you decide to revisit these passages or include portions of them elsewhere in the draft, they are then easy to restore. If you delete these passages completely, they are gone forever (or will have to be retyped from hard copy or memory). Looking at passages you've removed also serves as a record of where you have gone with your thoughts, and sometimes these passages can prompt you into new and more effective directions in your main writing project.

other hand, you might be uncomfortable with all the time you're spending with "bad" writing and rush to the draft too soon, before you have enough material. Working from abundance is particularly important when you're using writing to discover, the essayist's main motive.

Before you write a full draft, you'll compose a *sketch* or two of what seems to be the most promising material. A sketch is a brief treatment—probably no more than 300 words—that is composed with a sense of audience but not necessarily a clear sense of a thesis, theme, or controlling idea (see Chapter 1). One of the ways you want to use the sketch is to try out a topic, attempting to clarify your purpose in writing about it. Later, you'll revise a sketch into a draft personal essay.

Your instructor may ask you to write several sketches using the most promising material you've developed from the prompts. *The following guidelines apply to all sketches.*

- *The sketch should have a tentative title.* This is crucial because a title can hint at a possible focus for the revision.
- *The sketch should be approximately 300 to 500 words.* The sketch is a brief look at a topic that may later be developed into a longer essay.
- *The sketch should be a relatively fast draft.* Avoid the temptation to spend a lot of time crafting your sketch. Fast drafts are easier to revise.
- *The sketch may not have a clear purpose or theme.* That's what you hope to discover by writing the sketch.
- *The sketch should have a sense of audience.* You're writing your sketch to be read by someone other than you. That means you need to explain what may not be apparent to someone who doesn't know you or hasn't had your experiences.
- *The sketch should be richly detailed.* Personal essays, especially, rely on detail to help the writer, and later, the reader, see the possible meanings of events or observations. Essayists are inductive, working from particulars to ideas. In early drafts especially, it's important to get down the details by drawing on all your senses: what exactly was the color of the wallpaper, how exactly did the beach smell at low tide, how exactly did the old man's hand feel in yours, what exactly did the immigration officer say?

STUDENT SKETCH

A hundred years ago, death was relatively common in most American communities. The infant mortality rate was high, and people—especially men—typically did not live into their seventies. In fact, the mortality rate declined an incredible 83 percent from 1920 to 1973 for those twenty-five or younger in America. Some call ours a death-free society because we are so insulated from its realities. Someone else cares for the bodies prior to cremation and burial, and when we do see the dead, they are made to look as if they are alive.

All of this may help explain why we struggle so when death visits us, as it inevitably will. The difficulty of sorting through our feelings about the loss of a family member or a friend makes it an excellent topic for a personal essay. The form encourages writers to explore ambiguities and attempt to work out mysteries. In the student sketch that follows, Lana Kuchta does just that, trying to think through the wisdom of the advice many of us have received when faced with dying relatives: to remember them as they were, avoid seeing them as they are. Like most sketches, this one doesn't arrive at an answer to the writer's questions. There is no theme or thesis yet. But it does tease out a great deal of specific information that Lana can work with later.

THE WAY I REMEMBER

Lana Kuchta

1 In the past months three people I knew fairly well have died. All of these deaths were expected to some degree because the people had terminal illnesses. This whole thing is really hard for me to grasp right now—the sheer volume of death surrounding me confuses me about how I feel about death and these friends and how I should remember them. Invariably when we talk about someone who is terminally ill, we say that we hope the person goes quickly for their sake as well as the sake of their family. After all, no one wants to have memories of a prolonged death. We want to remember the person as they were before they got sick.

2 I haven't always felt this way. For a long time after my grandpa died, I was angry that my family wouldn't let me see him in the days before his death. They had good reason for not wanting me to venture into that hospital room where death hung like pea-soup fog over his bed. I was eight months pregnant with my second son, Elliot. I was already dilated to 3.5 cm and Nora, the midwife, wanted me to wait a little longer before I had him. She felt that the stress of my grandpa's condition would send me into full-blown labor.

3 I saw my Grandpa for the last time on a Monday. He was in a lot of pain, but the doctors hadn't increased the pain medication yet. He was still himself that day. We

talked briefly about my job and the baby and Austin, my other son who wasn't quite a year old yet. It was hard for me to see him this way and as we sat silently searching for things to say I counted contractions. I know he is going to die soon; I can feel it, I hope that he will live long enough to meet the baby I am carrying. He was tired and when a nurse came to do something, I left and said I would see him in a couple of days. I didn't mean to lie about this; I really did expect that I would see him again. His condition worsened and no one would let me into his room. They told me it was better for me to remember him the way he was.

And they were right, but even if they weren't I don't think the images that would come to mind when I thought of my grandpa would be the last image I have of him in the hospital. The last image of him I like to remember is just a month or so before he went into the hospital. I am at his house for a visit. It is July in Redding, California and every day that month was over 110 degrees. My grandpa and grandma have air conditioning and it is just what my bloated pregnant body needed. We sat in their living room with the big picture window that overlooked the Sacramento River. My grandpa plays with Austin on the floor. Austin is crawling around, exploring, and pulling himself up on the furniture. Grandpa tickles him and they both laugh. Watching them play on the floor is nice, but I know that grandpa is sick again. The cancer is back and I know it even though none of us know this yet. But I am happy to be sitting in the air-conditioned house, watching grandpa play with my son. 4

I need to believe that it was better that I didn't get to see him one last time because it is all I have to hold onto now. Anything else is obviously too painful, and I realize this as I write through blurry tears that threaten to roll down my face and smear the inside of my glasses. I know my grandpa would hate this public display of emotion. He was a no bullshit kind of guy and had a very low tolerance for crying. I try to think about other things like the way he was always moving. His hands were always jingling the change in his pocket or he was drumming his fingers on some piece of furniture. He was loud and opinionated, but it was a good thing. 5

He showed that he had a passion for life and he wasn't afraid to speak up for what he believed in. 6

He was generous, but he expected you to work hard for what you had. He wouldn't just hand money over to you, but he would give you a low interest loan with easy payback terms. 7

Just as I am now glad that I didn't see him just before he died. There are things about my life since he died that I'm glad he didn't have to see. I'm glad he didn't know that my first marriage ended in a messy divorce. 8

It has been fourteen years since he died and four since my grandma died. My uncle now lives in their house on the Sacramento River. I went back to that house this summer for the first time since my grandma died. I was nervous about this. I didn't know what to expect, what I would feel, what I would say. The house was different, yet the same in so many ways. When the kids and I got into the car, 9

Austin said that it was weird being there because the house still smells the same after four years.

In the end though I am glad to have the memories of change rattling in a pocket, dirty jokes, Neapolitan ice cream, the river, the smell of cut lumber, and all the other things that remind me of him.

Moving from Sketch to Draft

A sketch is often sketchy. It's generally underdeveloped, sometimes giving the writer just the barest outline of his or her subject. But as an early draft, a sketch can be invaluable. It might hint at what the real subject is, or what questions seem to be behind your inquiry into the subject. A sketch might suggest a focus for the next draft, or simply a better lead. Learning to read your sketches for such clues takes practice.

Evaluating Your Own Sketch. Initially, you're the most important reader of your own sketches. It's likely that you're in the best position to sense the material's promise because you understand the context from which it sprang better than any reader can. What are the clues you should look for in a sketch?

1. What surprised you? Might this discovery be the focus of the draft? Chances are, if it surprised you, it will surprise your readers.
2. What is the most important line in the sketch? What makes it important? Might this line be a beginning for more fastwriting? Might it be the theme or controlling idea of the draft?
3. What scene, moment, or situation is key to the story you're telling? Could this be the lead in the draft?
4. What's your favorite part of the sketch? What would happen if you cut it?

Questions for Peer Review. If you'll be sharing your sketch with one or more of your classmates, you'll likely need the most help with clarifying your purpose and focus for a draft. It's less helpful in these early stages to receive editorial comments about sentences, especially questions about grammar and mechanics. Here are some useful questions that might guide peer responses to your personal essay sketches.

- What does the writer seem to want to say but doesn't quite say in the sketch?
- What line appears most important to the meaning of the sketch, as you understand it?
- What was most surprising about what the writer said or showed?
- What part of the story seems most important? What part might need to be told and isn't?

Methods for Peer Review of Sketches

1. Choose a partner, exchange sketches, read, and comment both in writing and through conversation.
2. Create a pile of sketches in the middle of the classroom. Everyone takes one (not his or her own, obviously), provides written comments, returns it to the pile, and takes another. Repeat this until everyone has read and commented on at least four sketches.
3. Share sketches online on the class Web site.

Reflecting on What You've Learned. Before you begin working on the draft of your personal essay, take a few minutes in your journal to think about your thinking. Finish the following sentence, and follow it in a fastwrite for at least five minutes. *The thing that struck me most about writing and sharing my sketch on ____________ was. . . .* When you finish, quickly complete the following sentences:

1. The *real* story I seem to be trying to tell is ______________.
2. So what? I'd answer that question by saying ______________.
3. The main thing I'm planning to do in the draft is ______________.

Research and Other Strategies: Gathering More Information

You may be itching to move on with the draft. That's understandable. If everything has gone well so far, then your sketch has already given you a sense of direction and some ideas about how to develop your topic. But remember the importance of that dialectical movement between sea and mountain, or collecting and composing. Now that you have a topic and a tentative sense of purpose for your personal essay, journal work can be even more valuable because it can be *more focused.* Before you begin composing the draft—or during that process—consider using the following prompts to generate more information in your notebook:

- *Explode a moment.* Choose a scene or moment in the story or stories you're telling that seems particularly important to the meaning of the essay. Re-enter that moment and fastwrite for a full seven minutes, using all your senses and as much detail as you can muster.
- *Make lists.* Brainstorm a list of details, facts, or specifics about a moment, scene, or observation. List other experiences that seem connected to this one (see the "*Cluster*" point that follows).
- *Research.* Do some quick-and-dirty research that might bring in other voices or more information that will deepen your consideration of the

topic. For example, find out exactly how long that solar eclipse was back in 1983, and whether it was in July as you seem to remember. Interview a local expert on your topic. (For more information on where to look for information, see Chapter 12, "Research Techniques.") Do some background reading.

- *Cluster.* In your journal, try to move beyond narrating a single experience and discover other experiences, moments, or scenes that might help you see important patterns. Use the preceding list of related experiences or observations and fastwrite about those, or develop a cluster that uses a key word, phrase, or theme as its core, and build a web of associations. For example, let's say your sketch is about your experience working with the poor in Chile. Have you had other encounters with extreme wealth or extreme poverty? Can you describe them? What do they reveal about your feelings or attitudes about poverty or your reactions to what happened in Chile? See Figure 4.4.

Composing the Draft

Some of my students get annoyed at all the "stuff" I encourage them to do before they begin a first draft of a personal essay. In some cases, all the journal work isn't necessary; the writer very quickly gets a strong sense of direction and feels ready to begin composing. But from the beginning I've encouraged you to gravitate toward topics that you find confusing, and with that kind of material exploratory writing is time well spent. Remember, too, that journal writing counts as writing. It not only offers the pleasures of surprise, but it can ultimately make the drafting process more efficient by generating material

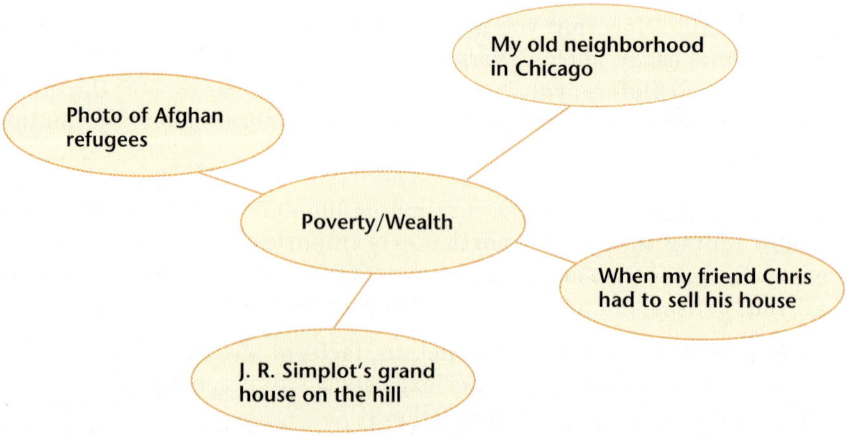

FIGURE 4.4 The start of a cluster built around Poverty/Wealth.

that you won't have to conjure up during those long, painful periods of staring at the computer screen wondering what to say next. This front-end work may also help abbreviate the end of the writing process—essentially, all this work in your journal and sketches is revision (see Chapter 14 for more on prewriting as a method of revision).

As you begin drafting, keep in mind what you've learned from your writing so far. For example:

- What is the question(s) behind your exploration of this topic?
- What do you understand now that you didn't understand fully when you started writing about it?
- How can you show *and* explain how you came to this understanding?
- Have you already written a strong first line for the draft? Can you find it somewhere in all your journal writing?

Methods of Development. How might you use some of the typical forms of development to develop your subject?

Narrative. The backbone of the personal essay is often, but not always, narrative. Remember, however, that narrative can work in an essay in at least three ways: (1) you tell an extended story of what happened, (2) you tell one or more anecdotes or brief stories, or (3) you tell the story of your thinking as you've come to understand something you didn't understand before. Often a single essay uses all three types of narrative.

When we tell a story of what happened, we naturally begin at the beginning: "I awoke startled by the unearthly buzz of the alarm clock." But sometimes beginning at the beginning is the worst place to begin. (See Chapter 14 for more about "leads.") You should explicitly or implicitly establish your focus in the first few paragraphs, and opening the essay with the first thing that happened may reveal nothing about your purpose. It just establishes that you woke up. For example, note how Anne-Marie Oomen begins "The Barn": "Barns place the farmer squarely in the middle of dirt, animals, and reverence." In a single sentence, Oomen strongly hints at her purpose: to explore how such a lowly structure can be a sacred place. Other essays, like Naomi Shihab Nye's "Long Overdue," do not state their purpose so quickly and directly. But by the end of the first two sections, we know that this is an essay about the failure of language.

Consider beginning your draft with an anecdote or the part of the story you want to tell that best establishes your purpose in the essay. If you're writing about the needless destruction of a childhood haunt by developers, then consider opening with the way the place looked *after* the bulldozers were done with it.

Naomi Shihab Nye's essay illustrates how a personal essay can stitch together not just one narrative but several stories, all of which are connected by the essay's theme or question. Notice as well how the stories defy chronology. Time in writing is nothing like real time. You can write pages about something that happened in seven minutes or cover twenty years in a paragraph. You can ignore chronology, if it serves your purpose, too. The key is to tell your story or stories in ways that emphasize what's important. Ask yourself, *What does the reader most need to know to understand my thinking and feelings about this topic? What should I show about what happened that gives a reader a clear sense of what* happens?

Using Evidence. How do you make your essay convincing, and even moving to an audience? It's in the details. This form thrives, like most literary genres, on particularity: what exactly did it look like, what exactly did she say, what exactly did it sound and smell like at that moment? Evidence that gives a personal essay authority are details that make a reader believe the writer can be trusted to observe keenly and to remember accurately. All of the professional essays in this chapter are rich in detail—there are the "stillborn calves, drowned swallows, frost-bitten kittens" in Oomen's "The Barn," and the curt monologue of the elderly theatergoer in Nye's "Long, Long Overdue," and the wilting banana leaves that curl around the coconut candy in Cofer's "One More Lesson." This focus on the particular—what it *exactly* looked like, smelled like, felt like, sounded like—makes an essay come alive for both writer and reader.

As you draft your essay, remember the subtle power of details. Tell, but always show, too.

Workshopping the Draft

If your draft is subject to peer review (see Chapter 15 for details on how to organize workshop groups), think carefully about the kind of responses you need from readers at this point in the process. In general, you should encourage comments that make you want to write again.

Reflecting on the Draft. To prepare for workshop, make an entry in your journal that explores your feelings about the draft:

- What do you think worked?
- What do you think needs work?

Following the workshop session, do a follow-up entry in your notebook that summarizes what you heard, what made sense and what didn't, and how you plan to approach the next draft. Your instructor may ask you to share this information in a cover letter submitted with the revision.

Questions for Readers. A writer can structure responses to a draft in many ways. Some of them are discussed in detail in Chapter 15, "The Writer's Workshop." The key is to find a way to get what you need *at this stage in the writing process* that will be most helpful as you revise.

There are a few questions, however, that you might pose to your group that are particularly relevant to the personal essay:

1. Is there a story I'm telling that I need to develop more? Is there a story I'm not telling that I should?
2. What do you think is the *real* story? In other words, what idea or theme lurks beneath the accounts of my experiences and observations?
3. What seems the most important detail, the one that seems to say more than it says, that *reveals* some important feeling, attitude, or idea? What detail seems less important, less revealing?
4. Do my reflective observations seem obvious or overly abstract and general? If so, what questions do you have about what I say that might direct back into the essay's details, where I'm more likely to have better insights?
5. Do I explain things that are unnecessary to explain, that are better told through *showing* rather than *telling?*

Writing with Computers

YOUR COMPUTER AS A READER

Computers can't read and enjoy writing like people. They can, however, analyze your writing in ways that people generally can't and in so doing identify issues you might not notice. For example, most word processors have a "readability calculator" as an option in the grammar and style checker. The readability calculator attempts to identify the reading level of the text. These formulas are often used to assign grade levels to books for children and teenagers. Readability calculators examine sentence length, word length, the number of sentences in a paragraph, and the average number of syllables per word and use this information to calculate a readability level. These formulas assume that longer words and sentences are more complex and more difficult to comprehend. While this assumption is simplistic and can't truly quantify the readability level of a draft, it can give writers one more way to evaluate their writing and its intended audience. Note that the grade level assigned by a readability statistic is the reading level, not the writing level. A reading level of eighth grade means that the draft requires an eighth-grade reading level.

Another feature of many word processors is the auto summarize feature. This feature analyzes the frequency of words and attempts to summarize the document. Although you probably would not want to rely on this feature to summarize important information, it can give you a glimpse into what the computer calculates as the most frequent words in a draft. You might find that you've ventured in a different direction than you originally intended, that you spent too much time on a peripheral topic, or that you repeat yourself.

Because these tools are attempts to apply mathematical formulas to a creative work, you must be the judge of what they reveal.

Revising the Draft

As I discussed earlier in the book, one of the most misunderstood aspects of revision is that you only do it at the end of the writing process. In fact, up to this point, you should have been revising your work all along, from the first few journal exercises when you chose a topic and played with possible angles on it, to the journal work you might have done to prepare to write the sketch, and then again with your efforts to turn your sketch into a more developed draft. Revision is literally "re-seeing," and every time you create the conditions that allow you to discover something new about how you see or what you think about your subject, you are, in fact, engaged in the act of revision. In a sense, then, each writing assignment you undertake is one long act of revision, from start to finish.

But once you've completed a draft, the revision process becomes more focused. You are mostly working with material that should be somewhat settled, with purposes that might be clearer, and ideas that may have more shape. At this point, the biggest temptation is to tell yourself you are largely done and what revision remains is merely a matter of "fixing things"—tinkering with sentences, correcting typos, and running a spell-checker. In the survey from Chapter 1 (see page 20), 70 percent of students admitted as much. "I usually just tidy things up" was ranked first or second by students who were asked what they do most often when they revise an academic paper.

These activities are certainly an element of revision—and an important one—but as the word revision implies, it's important to "re-see" both what you are trying to say as well as how you try to say it, even at this stage in the process. Chapter 14, "Revision Strategies," is a useful introduction to the revision process for any essay, including the personal essay. It emphasizes ways writers can break the bonds that limit their ability to find new ways of seeing the draft.

Personal essay drafts typically have some of the following problems:

- They don't answer the *So what?* question. Are you telling a story but don't help your readers understand *why* you're telling it?
- There is too much showing and not enough telling. In other words, do you *reflect* sufficiently in the draft, contributing your new understandings of what happened?
- There isn't enough detail. Because personal essays often rely heavily on narrative, they should show as well as tell. That is, help readers not only understand the significance of your experiences but in some small way experience those significant moments themselves.

Refer to Chapter 14, "Revision Strategies," for ideas addressing the problems outlined in the accompanying table and how to revise your draft following your workshop. Remember that a draft may present problems in more than one category.

GUIDE TO REVISION STRATEGIES		
Problems in the Draft (Chapter 14)	**Part**	**Page Number**
Unclear purpose ▪ Not sure what the essay is about? Fails to answer the *So what?* question?	1	603
Unclear thesis, theme, or main idea ▪ Not sure what you're trying to say?	2	609
Lack of information or development ▪ Needs more details; more showing and less telling?	3	616
Disorganized ▪ Doesn't move logically or smoothly from paragraph to paragraph?	4	620
Unclear or awkward at the level of sentences and paragraphs ▪ Seems choppy or hard to follow at the level of sentences or paragraphs?	5	626

Polishing the Draft

After you've dealt with the big issues in your draft—is it sufficiently focused, does it answer the *So what?* question, is it organized, and so on—you must deal with the smaller problems. You've carved the stone into an appealing figure but now you need to polish it. Are your paragraphs coherent? How do you manage transitions? Are your sentences fluent and concise? Are there any errors in spelling or syntax? Section 5 of Chapter 14 can help you focus on these issues.

Before you finish your draft, work through the following checklist:

- Every paragraph is about one thing.
- The transitions between paragraphs aren't abrupt.
- The length of sentences varies in each paragraph.
- Each sentence is concise. There are no unnecessary words or phrases.
- You've checked grammar, particularly for verb agreement, run-on sentences, unclear pronouns, and misused words (*there* / *their, where* / *were,* and so on). (See the handbook at the end of the book for help with these grammar issues.)
- You've run your spell-checker and proofed your paper for misspelled words.

STUDENT ESSAY

In my part of the country, the seasonal migration of field workers occurs quietly; most of us rarely notice the cars parked on the country roads and the children sitting in the shade waiting near them. We don't notice the bent backs in the fields, moving methodically from row to row. We are dimly aware, of course, that seasonal workers are key to the beet and potato harvests, but these men and women are largely invisible to us.

Julia Arredondo's essay, "Beet Field Dreams," provides a glimpse of this life. She migrated from Texas to Idaho with her family for nearly fourteen years, where they worked the fields from May to October. For many years, when assigned the ubiquitous topic "What I Did on My Summer Vacation" in school, Julia made up stories about another Julia, one with a "normal" life of picnics, barbecues, and days spent at amusement parks. In this personal essay, the Julia who migrated "like a goose" comes to terms with the truth of those summers, and what they have come to mean.

BEET FIELD DREAMS

Julia C. Arredondo

1 I was born in Welsaco, Texas and for my entire childhood I considered myself Tejana—a Texan. It was true that I didn't live my entire life—or even my childhood—in the Rio Grande Valley of Southern Texas, but El Valle was my home, where my family and I lived on our own, where I went to school, where we celebrated the major holidays—Thanksgiving, Christmas, New Year's, and everyone's birthdays. Yet the Mini-Cassia, Magic Valley, area of Southern Idaho was also my home—and in a way, not my home—as a child. My father's parents—and their parents before them—were all migrant, seasonal farm workers. This was more than a kind of tradition; it was a way of life, a way of survival, and after a time, it began to feel that it was what my family was meant to do in this world.

2 Every year from late May to August my parents worked alongside my extended family hoeing sugar beets in the fields of Burley, Rupert, Heyburn, Paul, Oakley, and Twin Falls, Idaho. It was either thinning and chopping down beets to make room for more or searching for weeds to eliminate and protect the beets. From September to late October they worked in the spud harvest. Twelve to fourteen hour days picking clots out of the clusters of potatoes that flashed before their eyes, and they worked on combines, as if that's what God had put them here to do. And so we migrated. And migrated. And migrated.

* * *

3 School usually started in early September, but by the time we returned to Texas, Alamo public schools had been running for at least a couple of months. I hated being the new kid in school every year and I especially hated it when people started asking where I'd been, why I was coming into the semester late.

It was the infamous "How I spent my summer vacation" essay assignment that would always make me lie like Pinocchio. When the essay topic was assigned, I would panic and begin to feel my heart beat faster. I couldn't tell them what I had really being doing all five months of summer. I could not help it; I'd write about a stranger's summer: picnics, vacations, amusement parks, barbecues. A family trip to Fiesta Texas was the biggest, fictional vacation my elementary mind could conjure up and I think I believed the trip myself. I raved in my essay about how we'd spent an entire week in the San Antonio amusement park, how the rides were awesome and how much fun I had had—all the while hoping, praying that no one would uncover the lies, and wishing that the teacher would never really read it. After all, they were only dreams that would never come true. I never told about the car. About the fields. Instead, I continued with the grand fabrications. 4

* * *

We slept in the car, of course. No hotels. Abandoned parking lots. Grocery store parking lots. My Dad liked to park the car somewhere where there was always a lot of light shining. One year in Moab, Utah we had a really hard time finding a resting spot. First we stopped at a store on the main road that ran through the small town; but then a police officer came around and asked us to keep on moving. He said it was illegal for people driving through to just park anywhere to sleep and pointed us toward a rest area just on the edge of Moab. We went there. Dad parked the car under the only light post in the middle of the dirt parking lot. Then, he got off the car and walked to the pay phone just out of reach of the glowing light. Only a few minutes later, a large truck roared into the empty parking lot. Men's voices shouted and hollered from within as they circled our car, picking up speed, raising up dust clouds, tying a knot in my throat. And then just like that, they were gone. My dad came back to the car, got in, and we drove off. 5

After that, we mostly slept in truck stops. They were always lit, always alive. They were twenty-four-hour oases for travelers on the go. We had bathrooms available—no matter what time my bladder decided I needed to pee. We had hot food within reach. Hot coffee. So whenever Pa wanted to wake up and drive his family on, he could have a cup. It was almost as convenient as a hotel except that we slept amongst the trucks, their thunderous vibrations never really let me sleep. We'd put towels up as curtains, to block out some of the light—noise. But sometimes when I woke up in the middle of the night, and everyone in the car was asleep, I would look out and wonder where these monsters were going and whether they were as driven as we were to move. 6

* * *

As a kid I'd wake up on most summer mornings to the sound of doors slamming shut and cool breezes of fresh morning wind sweeping into the car, making me shiver. I could feel the weight of the car shift as the grown-ups pulled their hoes from the trunk. Their voices lingered outside the vehicle for minutes as they prepared for the day's work, waiting for the first light of day to guide their strokes. 7

I'd lay still and listen as their voices became distant, then I would slowly drift back to my dreams.

8 Some mornings, when the sun wasn't quite strong enough to warm us up, my sister Debra and I would stay inside the car. I'd lounge around in the front seat—a place I hardly ever got to ride in—and impatiently wait for the adults to return to the *caheceras*. From the car they looked miniature as they moved at a hurried pace along the mile long rows. Debra and I would guess which one was Ma and which one was Pa. Sometimes we were right. Sometimes I'd drift back to sleep and miss them reaching our end of the field. I'd awake to find they were already halfway back across the field and feel my heart weigh down.

9 I was always looking for a reason to join them in their hard labor; years later when I would have to really start working I knew exactly how hard it was. Still, I'd mention to my parents how I could work too, how we'd make more money that way. I'd ask them to break a hoe in half and let me have it. They only laughed and said when the time came for me to work I wasn't going to want to, so for me to just enjoy this time.

10 Sometimes near the field there would be a farmhouse from which laughter floated down towards us. Sometimes we could spot kids that looked our age jumping on their trampoline, swimming in their pool and I'd find myself longing to be them. Normal. Playing on a lawn, instead of a field. Waking in a bed, instead of a car's backseat. Eating lunch at a table, instead of from tin foil while I sat in the dirt on the shady side of the car to avoid the hot sun.

* * *

11 When I was fourteen we finally stopped moving. Field work continued being our main source of income, but we made Idaho our permanent home. And as the years passed, returning to Texas became preposterous; we were always too afraid to fall back into the old migrating lifestyle. Yet, even today I am migrant. And it's not merely the fact that I've spent more than half my life migrating—like a goose—according to the seasons, but because it was a lifestyle that penetrates and becomes part of who I am for the rest of my life. As I grew older, I began to slowly acknowledge to others the kind of lifestyle my family lived during my childhood. Though no longer on the move, I will always be a migrant and sugar beet dreams will always haunt my sleep.

Evaluating the Essay

Discuss or write about your response to Julia Arredondo's essay using some or all of the following questions.

1. What is the essay's greatest strength? Is this something you've noticed in your own work, or the drafts of classmates?
2. Is the balance between exposition and narration, showing and telling, handled well in "Beet Field Dreams?" Does it read fairly quickly or does it drag at points?

3. The essay uses line breaks between sections. What do you think of this technique? What are its advantages and disadvantages?
4. What would you recommend to Arredondo if she were to revise "Beet Field Dreams"?

Using What You Have Learned

My students often love writing personal essays. At its best, the genre is a rare opportunity to reexamine our lives and better understand our experiences. The insights we earn are often reward enough, but what have you learned in this assignment that you might apply in other writing situations?

1. The personal essay you wrote relies heavily on narrative and personal experience. How might an ability to tell a good story, using your experiences or the experiences of others, be a useful academic skill? How might you use it to write a paper for another class?
2. The personal essay is a deeply subjective form, which would seem to put it at odds with formal academic writing, which seems to strive for "objectivity." Are they at odds?
3. Based on your experience writing a personal essay, what do you think are its most important qualities? If you were to write more personal essays, what would you strive to do next time?

Maine lobstermen heading out to sea.

Sample Student Essay: The Personal Essay

Speaking in Cycles

By Meghan Aukerbecker

I am a talker. I talk my way in to things, out of things, around things. I talk when I'm nervous or when I have something "profound" I want to say. It is the way I communicate not only *what* I want to say, but *how* I feel about the subject and *who* I feel should care about the matter. And yet, even though today I often define myself through language and my connection to it, it wasn't so long ago that talking and I were completely disengaged. You see, when I was four years old, over three years after I said my first words, I stopped talking. It wasn't like my language skills slowly petered out or like I had forgotten how to speak, it was simply that I woke up one morning and decided that I didn't want to talk anymore.

Many things could have triggered this abrupt end of my desire to communicate, and yet when you examine each separately, none seem like enough to have caused this change. Perhaps it was a combination of factors: I had recently transferred to a new school that I hated, my best friend had just started kindergarten without me, and I was tired of the negative things that occurred all too often after someone I cared about uttered unkind words to another. Perhaps that was it. Or perhaps it wasn't. I honestly may never know what was the last straw that pushed my poor little four-year-old self over the edge, but whatever it was, no amount of coaxing could get me to change my mind.

My parents took me to doctors, but they told them that there was nothing physically wrong with me and to simply wait it out. My dad tried to bribe me with cereal and cherry tomatoes, but I refused to open my mouth to say please. My mom took me to play-dates, but I was quite content to simply play with the other children without uttering a word. I didn't see anything wrong with my not talking, it was natural to me, a choice I had made, and I was quite content with the results. I still had the same connection with my peers (most of our communication was done through playing anyway!), I got out of having to answer the questions of strangers, and I could still read, write, and draw just the same as I had done before I stopped talking. So really, what else did I need in my four-year-old life? I simply was in no hurry to begin talking again.

However, many adults did not see this change in my behavior in the same way I did. My parents quickly became dissatisfied with the kind of treatment I was receiving at my preschool (I had been placed in a class for the mentally challenged) and moved me to Hoover Elementary, where I could see the tall, round Oracle buildings my mom worked at everyday. My mother had always defended me when people asked about my silence, and seeing those buildings made me believe she was right there to defend me again if anyone was to question my behavior. The teachers at Hoover had been informed of my "condition" and I was put under the care of Deirdre, a patient, caring teacher who took the time to work with me everyday. The children there were also accepting of my quietness and, in no time at all, I became best friends with Sara (a sweet, shy girl) and Analise (who I honestly cannot remember ever being quiet) and we became known as the Three Musketeers. I took part in all the organized activities: arts and crafts, story time, show-and-tell (although obviously mine was always more "showing" than "telling") and I became truly part of the group.

As time went on and more people became accustomed to me not talking, I realized that I didn't mind the silent life. I had learned how to communicate in other ways: I signed a little, motioned a lot, and often drew pictures of what I needed. I observed more, I listened better and cried less. People treated me differently, but not in a bad way. I was given more time to convey what I wanted to say and people took the time to communicate with me because they knew that if I was making this kind of effort, it had to be for something important. The questioning and coaxing of my parents and teachers became less frequent and they instead accepted and embraced my new way of communicating. I knew, however, that it still troubled them on some level even though they tried their hardest to hide it. I was confused about why my silence distressed them, why this decision that seemed so simple to me was so perplexing to others. To a four-year-old, being different isn't that big of a deal, but to the parent of that child, being different is always something that brings worry. I couldn't have that hanging over my head so slowly, very slowly, I began to speak again.

Deirdre took careful notes of my progress, writing it all down in a notebook I still have to this day. "Meghan smiled at me today," the first entry reads, and later, "she mouthed the word 'jell-o' this afternoon." At first, my speech was only the occasional whisper, and only to someone I truly trusted, but then I began to branch out and whisper to other people I met. Deirdre continued to patiently work with me, encouraged me to voice my opinions and say what I was feeling. I slowly began to interact with larger groups of people, and make more of an effort to communicate with others. Eventually, I would talk to one person at a time, which soon became two, and then whole groups of people. Within a couple months, it was hard to tell that I had ever stopped talking.

My parents were ecstatic to hear my voice again and encouraged me to talk whenever possible. Although I truly wanted to please them, I simply couldn't bring myself to talk all the time as if nothing had changed. I would often attempt to ramble on about nothing, but would find myself slowly petering out in the middle of sentences. I honestly didn't *want* to talk if I didn't have to but would rather have saved my words for when I had something important to say. However, as time went on, I slowly became more accustomed to hearing my own voice and used it with more frequency. I would say what I wanted to do, tell my parents what I had done at school, and talk with teachers and friends during various activities. I would get in to in-depth five-year-old conversations with my grandparents and yell at my best friend Tyler when he attempted to steal my favorite stuffed animal. Analise and Sara incorporated me into our Three Musketeers' songs (whereas before I had only been a back-up dancer), Deidre became an expert on the history of my favorite Littlest Pet Shop animals, and Stan-Stan the Ice Cream Man had the pleasure of hearing me debate the pros and cons of Dreamsicles and Rocketpops before I made my final decision. In short, I was talking up a storm.

and crafts, story time, show-and-tell (although obviously mine was always more "showing" than "telling") and I became truly part of the group.

As time went on and more people became accustomed to me not talking, I realized that I didn't mind the silent life. I had learned how to communicate in other ways: I signed a little, motioned a lot, and often drew pictures of what I needed. I observed more, I listened better and cried less. People treated me differently, but not in a bad way. I was given more time to convey what I wanted to say and people took the time to communicate with me because they knew that if I was making this kind of effort, it had to be for something important. The questioning and coaxing of my parents and teachers became less frequent and they instead accepted and embraced my new way of communicating. I knew, however, that it still troubled them on some level even though they tried their hardest to hide it. I was confused about why my silence distressed them, why this decision that seemed so simple to me was so perplexing to others. To a four-year-old, being different isn't that big of a deal, but to the parent of that child, being different is always something that brings worry. I couldn't have that hanging over my head so slowly, very slowly, I began to speak again.

Deirdre took careful notes of my progress, writing it all down in a notebook I still have to this day. "Meghan smiled at me today," the first entry reads, and later, "she mouthed the word 'jell-o' this afternoon." At first, my speech was only the occasional whisper, and only to someone I truly trusted, but then I began to branch out and whisper to other people I met. Deirdre continued to patiently work with me, encouraged me to voice my opinions and say what I was feeling. I slowly began to interact with larger groups of people, and make more of an effort to communicate with others. Eventually, I would talk to one person at a time, which soon became two, and then whole groups of people. Within a couple months, it was hard to tell that I had ever stopped talking.

My parents were ecstatic to hear my voice again and encouraged me to talk whenever possible. Although I truly wanted to please them, I simply couldn't bring myself to talk all the time as if nothing had changed. I would often attempt to ramble on about nothing, but would find myself slowly petering out in the middle of sentences. I honestly didn't *want* to talk if I didn't have to but would rather have saved my words for when I had something important to say. However, as time went on, I slowly became more accustomed to hearing my own voice and used it with more frequency. I would say what I wanted to do, tell my parents what I had done at school, and talk with teachers and friends during various activities. I would get in to in-depth five-year-old conversations with my grandparents and yell at my best friend Tyler when he attempted to steal my favorite stuffed animal. Analise and Sara incorporated me into our Three Musketeers' songs (whereas before I had only been a back-up dancer), Deidre became an expert on the history of my favorite Littlest Pet Shop animals, and Stan-Stan the Ice Cream Man had the pleasure of hearing me debate the pros and cons of Dreamsicles and Rocketpops before I made my final decision. In short, I was talking up a storm.

5

Writing a Profile

WRITING ABOUT PEOPLE

Some years ago, when I was writing a book on the culture of the New England lobster fishing industry, I wandered into the lighthouse keeper's house in Pemaquid Point, Maine. The lighthouse, built in 1827, was automated—like all but one lighthouse on the East Coast—but the empty keeper's house had been turned into a tiny fishing museum. I found my way there one late spring day, stepped inside, and was greeted by Abby Boynton, sitting on a folding chair working on needlepoint. I had come to look at historical objects related to lobster fishing, but instead I encountered Abby, an elderly widow whose husband, a local lobsterman, had died of cancer several years before.

We struck up a conversation, and within minutes she was leading me to the back of the museum to show me a picture book, now out of print, that documented a few days of her husband's work at the traps offshore from New Harbor, Maine. She told me the story of the New York photographer who asked her husband if he wouldn't mind company fishing that day. "He was always taking people out," she said, "so my husband said 'sure.'" That trip with the photographer led to other trips and the book that followed, *Fred Boynton, Lobsterman.* The museum copy was well thumbed and the binding was broken, but Mrs. Boynton assured me that there were still a few copies around. "I've got two copies at home," she said, "but I can't part with those. They'll be nice for the kids and the grandchildren."

Abby Boynton showed me a picture of the New Harbor house she had lived in with Fred all the years they were married. She moved three years ago because it was "too much house." As I was leaving she directed me to a model of her husband's boat, the *Dwayne B,* in a back room of the museum. It was named after their youngest son. A brass plaque on the boat model said, "In memory by his friends and fellow fishermen."

What You'll Learn in This Chapter

- How the profile and the academic case study are related.
- What distinguishes the profile from other forms.
- The importance of close observation.
- Interview techniques.
- Ways to find a profile subject who is representative of a certain group of people.
- Questions for revising a profile.

What was it like being a lobster man's wife? I asked, heading toward the sunshine. "Spent most of my time trying to keep his dinner warm," said Mrs. Boynton, resuming her post in the folding chair by the door. I glanced at the needlepoint in her lap, but couldn't read the stitched letters, which had not yet formed a word. After my fifteen minutes with Abby Boynton that seemed fitting; what didn't need a plaque or a label in this museum was the most powerful thing I found there. It occurred to me later that Abby Boynton was as bound to her husband's memory as she was to life. Only now she keeps more than his dinner warm as she waits.

This accidental interview with the lobsterman's wife reveals much more than I could explain about one aspect of community in Maine's fishing villages—the partnership between spouses who have chosen such a hard life. I can't imagine a better way to dramatize the level of devotion these marriages can demand than Abby Boynton's shrine to the memory of her husband—a worn book, a dusty model of his boat, and picture of the New Harbor home they shared. You can hear it in her voice, too, and how quickly she directs a stranger to these relics. But all of this probably doesn't need explaining; you can sense it from the vignette.

This piece could have easily continued, perhaps including information from the book *Fred Boynton, Lobsterman,* or interviews about Abby and Fred from others in New Harbor who knew them. It might have included statistics about the divorce rate among Maine fishing families, or information about the economic pressures on families during a bad fishing season—all the factors that might easily make it hard for a marriage to survive. Most of all, I might have spent more time with Abby Boynton. The result would have been a profile, not a vignette, that would put a face on the idea that lobster fishing is difficult, but for many, a good life.

MOTIVES FOR WRITING A PROFILE

E. B. White, author of the children's classics *Charlotte's Web* and *Stuart Little* and many essays for the *The New Yorker* magazine, once offered this advice: "If you want to write about mankind, write about a man." The profile is a form that accomplishes this by giving a general idea or feeling a face. Through Abby Boynton we presumably can see something about other lobstermen's wives and families. In that sense, the profile is like the personal essay—the experiences and particulars about a living subject creates, as Scott Russell Sanders once said, "a door through which [readers] might have passed." In a profile, however, the obvious subject is usually not the writer but the person he writes about.

There may be no better way of dramatizing the impact of a problem, the importance of a question, or the significance of an idea than showing how it presents itself in the life of one person.

The profile is a familiar form in the popular magazine. We can't seem to know enough about other peoples' lives. The celebrity profile is ubiquitous, but some of the best profiles are of ordinary people like Abby Boynton who are typical in some way of the people touched by the subject a writer is interested in. There may be no better way of dramatizing the impact of a problem, the importance of a question, or the significance of an idea than showing how it presents itself in the life of one person.

THE PROFILE AND ACADEMIC WRITING

While the profile may not be a common academic form, the case study is, and in a sense a profile is a form of extended case study. Almost any topic affects people's lives (if it doesn't, is it really that significant or interesting?). The profile or case study attempts to document these impacts. For example, suppose you're interested in examining the success of your university's commitment to ethnic and racial diversity—a principle the administration has publicly embraced. One way to approach the topic is to profile one international student. What has been her experience on campus? Which campus programs have proved useful? What programs are needed? The voice of your profile subject and the details of her experience would help dramatize an otherwise abstract policy debate, and the story she tells could offer a foundation from which to explore the issue.

You can write a profile in the service of an argument or as a way to explore the personal impact of an event. The profile may be part of a larger project that examines some aspect of a local culture, cultural trend, or place (see Chapter 10, "Writing an Ethnographic Essay"). It can, like good fiction, provide insight into the complexities of the human mind and soul.

More than any other form of inquiry, the profile relies on interview for information—the voice of the writer's subject should come through—as well as observation, particularly those revealing details that say something about the character or feelings of the person profiled. In some cases, these details are merely descriptive—what the subject looks like, for instance. However, telling details can often be indirect evidence of a person's character, things like the way one man stands with his feet apart and arms folded on his chest to emphasize his biceps (arrogant), how a woman carefully knots the scarf around her neck (fastidious), and so on. Writers who want to practice interview skills—a key method of collecting information in communications and the social sciences—will find the profile a useful challenge.

The profile relies on interview for information—the voice of the writer's subject should come through—as well as observation, particularly those revealing details that say something about the character or feelings of the person profiled.

FEATURES OF THE FORM

Some typical characteristics of the form include the following:

- *A profile usually provides a detailed look at one person.* The key is to decide who that person should be. The kind of profiles you'll likely write won't be of celebrities, who are inherently interesting subjects because of their fame.

Instead, you'll profile someone much more ordinary, but possibly *typical* or representative of a culture, place, situation, or topic.

- *Alone, a profile may not provide enough substantiation for an argument.* While the writer may choose a profile to dramatize a problem or support a claim, it's always dangerous to generalize from a single case, particularly if the typicality of the subject is in doubt.
- *A profile uses narrative as a method of organization.* As in the personal essay, storytelling is frequently the backbone of the profile. This may take the form of a series of anecdotes about the writer's subject, or the subject's account of an experience. Frequently, the story of the interview itself, told chronologically, is the organizing tool for the profile (see, for example, Lauren Slater's "Dr. Daedalus" later in the chapter).
- *The profile is usually written from one of two points of view—either the writer narrates in the first person or the subject is portrayed in the third person, and the writer stays out of the way.* Point of view is a crucial decision in the profile because, unlike many other forms, there are choices to make. A profile told in the first person can give an added dimension of the writer's own feelings and reactions, but risks distracting the reader from the real subject, the person being profiled. Portraying the subject in the third person loses the drama of the interaction between the writer and the person profiled, but keeps the focus on the subject.
- *Profiles go beyond mere description of subjects and reveal information about character much as a short story does, through telling details and the subject's own voice.* Like most nonfiction forms, the profile shows *and* tells. But the profile writer is more likely to use literary techniques such as telling details, dialogue, and even scenes to communicate some dominant impression or idea about the subject. Doing this well requires not only a good ear but a keen eye. Letting the subject speak for herself is particularly important, but to do this well makes special demands on the writer. (See "Inquiring into the Details: Tape Recorders" later in the chapter.)
- *A strong beginning is essential, particularly when the subject of a profile isn't famous.* We read a celebrity profile because of the fame of its subject. But when writing about ordinary people, we need to quickly give readers a reason to be interested. What about Bert, for example, makes him an interesting focus for a piece on Florida State's reputation as a party school? Within a paragraph or two, the writer tells us that Bert's a twenty-four-year-old undergraduate who mixes a drink at ten a.m. on a Tuesday, and "seemed to be vying for the honor of being the top partyer at the nation's top party school." Both pieces of information are hook enough for most readers; notice also, though, that the writer makes the case immediately that Bert, while not typical, may be representative of the extremes some students go to in order to be party animals at Florida State.

- *Scene and setting often provide useful information in a profile.* We know characters not just by what they say but what they do and where they do it. A profile often allows the reader to glimpse a subject in action in settings or situations that are revealing. For a profile of a biology professor, that might be knee-deep in a stream, sampling stoneflies.
- *The more time writers can spend with their subjects, the more revealing the profile.* The reason is obvious. You'll get to know your subject far better if you can conduct more than a single interview. It's also easier to write a profile—to write anything—when you're working from abundance rather than scarcity. The more information you have about your subject, the easier it is to focus the piece, and the more likely you are to get to the truth of things about your subject.

PROFILE

In "Thumb-Sucking Girl," a brief essay that appeared recently in the journal *Brevity*, Sonja Livingston gives us a snapshot profile. It works because the vignette is familiar—who hasn't seen a thumb-sucking child?—but Livingston's close observation makes the scene fresh and new. Among other things, profiles often require careful attention to what we see, and this isn't easy because we must actively search for particulars that are revealing, and then find the words to describe them.

While barely more than a paragraph long, "Thumb-Sucking Girl" succeeds in creating a meaningful portrait of an unnamed girl in a difficult situation. As you read it, speculate about how Livingston might have composed the piece. Other than observing carefully, what other sources of information might she have used?

THUMB-SUCKING GIRL

Sonja Livingston

Look at me. 1

At me, over here. 2

Look and shake your head all you want. At my uneven bangs, these broken-down shoes, my momma, all us kids and all our belongings shoved into just one car. Whisper and sigh all you want, because I have something better than good clothes and a permanent address. I've got my thumb. My right thumb, to be precise—and the soft pink underside of its arch. Forget that the nail on that thumb grows as smooth and flat as the inside of a seashell on account of all that sucking. Forget that my mother has tried everything (except hot pepper and mustard on my thumb, like my cousin Judith suggests, because my mother, though determined to rid me of my disgusting habit, thinks pepper and mustard too cruel for a child). Forget that I once deprived myself of the luxury of my thumb for a whole month just to show I could. 3

Forget that my teeth have begun to split down the front, that the space will stretch wide eventually, that it will ruin my permanent teeth, according to my mother. Forget all that and understand that the plug of it in my mouth is what brings me sleep, and until you've plopped a thumb into your mouth and sucked on it while using the index finger of that same hand to cradle the line of bone under your eye, to rub up and down the fleshy valley of your nose—until you have done such a thing, you know nothing of comfort.

Inquiring into the Essay

Use the four ways of inquiring to investigate your ideas about "Thumb-Sucking Girl."

1. In your notebook, play with close observation. Go somewhere—the campus library or student union, a coffee shop, a bowling alley, the hallways outside your classroom—and watch. Choose people to discreetly observe, making fast lists of details. Circle those that you believe are revealing. Which are suggestive about how your subject might feel at that moment, or what she might be thinking, or who she might be trying to be?
2. An interesting aspect of "Thumb-Sucking Girl" is its unusual point of view. This is a profile from the girl's vantage point. Explain how Livingston—or any writer who wants to write a profile this way—would need to write and research the piece.
3. When it sometimes seems that you have to write pages and pages to get a point across, a brief essay like this one can be inspiring. Evaluate the effectiveness of "Thumb-Sucking Girl" as a *meaningful* essay, despite its brevity. What evidence would you offer from the essay about how this meaningfulness is achieved in so few words?
4. Scientific investigations require close observation. Some social science research does, too. Marketing specialists spend a great deal of time documenting customer behavior. Watching carefully is an underrated skill. Assess your own observation skills. Based on Livingston's essay, what does looking closely demand?

PROFILE

One of the most memorable segments on the TV show *Seinfeld* was about the "Soup Nazi," a character inspired by the following profile. Published in *The New Yorker* by one of the staff writers, "Soup" profiles soup chef Albert Yeganeh, the tough-talking, impatient, demanding owner of a small restaurant on West Fifty-fifth Street. The force of Yeganeh's personality comes through brilliantly in this piece especially because the writer steps aside and lets the man speak for himself through extensive—and sometimes lengthy—quotations. It's hard to overstate how important it is to allow readers to hear the voices of profile subjects.

But this essay is also a great example of how important close and careful observation is to a profile. We can know people by the contexts in which they live and work, something that we could simply explain—"Yeganeh owns a soup restaurant on West Fifty-fifth Street in New York"—or describe—"The first thing you notice about it is the awning, which proclaims 'Homemade Hot, Cold, Diet Soups.'" These more specific observations bring the man's tiny world to life around him and contribute powerfully to our understanding of who he is.

Soup

Anonymous, The New Yorker

When Albert Yeganeh says "Soup is my lifeblood," he means it. And when he says 1
"I am extremely hard to please," he means that, too. Working like a demon alchemist in a tiny storefront kitchen at 259-A West Fifty-fifth Street, Mr. Yeganeh creates anywhere from eight to seventeen soups every weekday. His concoctions are so popular that a wait of half an hour at the lunchtime peak is not uncommon, although there are strict rules for conduct in line. But more on that later.

"I am psychologically kind of a health freak," Mr. Yeganeh said the other day, in a 2
lisping staccato of Armenian origin. "And I know that soup is the greatest meal in the world. It's very good for your digestive system. And I use only the best, the freshest ingredients. I am a perfectionist. When I make a clam soup, I use three different kinds of clams. Every other place uses canned clams. I'm called crazy. I am not crazy. People don't realize why I get so upset. It's because if the soup is not perfect and I'm still selling it, it's a torture. It's *my* soup, and that's why I'm so upset. First you clean and then you cook. I don't believe that ninety-nine per cent of the restaurants in New York know how to clean a tomato. I tell my crew to wash the parsley *eight* times. If they wash it five or six times, I scare them. I tell them they'll go to jail if there is sand in the parsley. One time, I found a mushroom on the floor, and I fired that guy who left it there." He spread his arms, and added, "This place is the only one like it in . . . in . . . the whole earth! One day, I hope to learn something from the other places, but so far I haven't. For example, the other day I went to a very fancy restaurant and had borscht. I had to send it back. It was *junk.* I could see all the chemicals in it. I never use chemicals. Last weekend, I had lobster bisque in Brooklyn, a very well-known place. It was *junk.* When I make a lobster bisque, I use a whole lobster. You know, I never advertise. I don't have to. All the big-shot chefs and the kings of the hotels come here to see what *I'm* doing."

As you approach Mr. Yeganeh's Soup Kitchen International from a distance, 3
the first thing you notice about it is the awning, which proclaims "Homemade Hot, Cold, Diet Soups." The second thing you notice is an aroma so delicious that it

makes you want to take a bite out of the air. The third thing you notice, in front of the kitchen, is an electric signboard that flashes, saying, "Today's Soups . . . Chicken Vegetable . . . Mexican Beef Chili . . . Cream of Watercress . . . Italian Sausage . . . Clam Bisque . . . Beef Barley . . . Due to Cold Weather . . . For Most Efficient and Fastest Service the Line Must . . . Be Kept Moving . . . Please . . . Have Your Money . . . Ready . . . Pick the Soup of Your Choice . . . Move to Your Extreme . . . Left After Ordering."

4 "I am not prejudiced against color or religion," Mr. Yeganeh told us, and he jabbed an index finger at the flashing sign. "Whoever follows that I treat very well. My regular customers don't say anything. They are very intelligent and well educated. They know I'm just trying to move the line. The New York cop is very smart—he sees everything but says nothing. But the young girl who wants to stop and tell you how nice you look and hold everyone up—*yah!*" He made a guillotining motion with his hand. "I tell you, I hate to work with the public. They treat me like a slave. My philosophy is: The customer is always wrong and I'm always right. I raised my prices to try to get rid of some of these people, but it didn't work."

5 The other day, Mr. Yeganeh was dressed in chef's whites with orange smears across his chest, which may have been some of the carrot soup cooking in a huge pot on a little stove in one corner. A three-foot-long handheld mixer from France sat on the sink, looking like an overgrown gardening tool. Mr. Yeganeh spoke to two young helpers in a twisted Armenian-Spanish barrage, then said to us, "I have no overhead, no trained waitresses, and I have the cashier here." He pointed to himself theatrically. Beside the doorway, a glass case with fresh green celery, red and yellow peppers, and purple eggplant was topped by five big gray soup urns. According to a piece of cardboard taped to the door, you can buy Mr. Yeganeh's soups in three sizes, costing from four to fifteen dollars. The order of any well-behaved customer is accompanied by little waxpaper packets of bread, fresh vegetables (such as scallions and radishes), fresh fruit (such as cherries or an orange), a chocolate mint, and a plastic spoon. No coffee, tea, or other drinks are served.

6 "I get my recipes from books and theories and my own taste," Mr. Yeganeh said. "At home, I have several hundreds of books. When I do research, I find that I don't know anything. Like cabbage is a cancer fighter, and some fish is good for your heart but some is bad. Every day, I should have one sweet, one spicy, one cream, one vegetable soup—and they *must* change, they should always taste a little different." He added that he wasn't sure how extensive his repertoire was, but that it probably includes at least eighty soups, among them African peanut butter, Greek moussaka, hamburger, Reuben, B.L.T., asparagus and caviar, Japanese shrimp miso, chicken chili, Irish corned beef and cabbage, Swiss chocolate, French calf's brain, Korean beef ball, Italian shrimp and eggplant Parmesan, buffalo, ham and egg, short rib, Russian beef Stroganoff, turkey cacciatore, and Indian mulligatawny. "The chicken and the seafood are an addiction, and when I have French garlic soup I let people have only one small container each," he said. "The doctors and nurses love that one."

7 A lunch line of thirty people stretched down the block from Mr. Yeganeh's doorway. Behind a construction worker was a man in expensive leather, who was in front

of a woman in a fur hat. Few people spoke. Most had their money out and their orders ready.

At the front of the line, a woman in a brown coat couldn't decide which soup to get and started to complain about the prices. 8

"You talk too much, dear," Mr. Yeganeh said, and motioned her to move to the left. "Next!" 9

"Just don't talk. Do what he says," a man huddled in a blue parka warned. 10

"He's downright rude," said a blond woman in a blue coat. "Even abusive. But you can't deny it, his soup is the best." 11

Inquiring into the Essay

Use the four methods of inquiry—exploring, explaining, evaluating, and reflecting—to generate a response to "Soup."

1. Use a "narrative of thought" response to explore your initial reactions to "Soup." Immediately after reading the piece, open your notebook and begin a five-minute fastwrite, starting with the following phrase: *The first thing that comes to mind after reading this essay is ______. And then . . . And then . . .* Whenever the writing stalls, seize on the phrase *and then* to get you going. Feel free, however, to digress on some aspect of the profile you want to think about through writing. After five minutes, stop and finish the following sentence: *Now that I look back on what I've said about "Soup," the thing that strikes me the most is . . .*
2. If you're profiling someone famous, you really don't have to worry much about reader interest; fame alone gives you a rhetorical advantage. But when you write about someone, like Yeganeh, who is relatively unknown, you have to "hook" your readers within the first paragraph or two, giving them a reason to read on. Explain how the writer of "Soup" attempted to do this in the first paragraph of the essay.
3. Review the essay and any writing you've done on the essay. Make a quick list of words that best describe Yeganeh. Choose one of them and, using evidence from the essay, find specific information that supports the choice. What is the strongest evidence you found that best explains the aptness of the word you chose to describe him? Evaluate the qualities of good evidence in a profile essay.
4. Go ahead and admit it. You like reading *People* occasionally (or maybe often). It's the first magazine I pick up in the doctor's waiting room. Reflect for a moment on what you find so appealing about reading profiles of celebrities. Now consider how you felt about reading "Soup." Were your motives and responses the same? How would you distinguish between a *People* piece on Nicole Kidman and the *New Yorker* profile of Albert Yeganeh?

PROFILE

It's good to remember that plastic surgeons do more than nose jobs and face lifts. They rebuild our bodies after accidents, restoring severely damaged fingers and faces, saving us from the loss of the familiar. Perhaps more than any other physicians, plastic surgeons are guided by cultural standards that dictate what looks "right." This may be why the plastic surgeon profiled in Lauren Slater's "Dr. Daedalus" is so disturbing; he dares to imagine breaking the rules. Dr. Rosen is less interested in what looks good than what might work better. Why settle for "normal" ears when they can be "beefed up" so we can have the "range of an owl"? And why not wings? Might we learn to fly like angels?

The profile you are about to read is excerpted from a longer piece that appeared in *Harper's* in 2001. It's a good contrast to the previous essay, "Soup," because the writer chooses to be part of this essay, referring to her own feelings and reactions to her subject and what he says. Slater uses the story of getting to know Dr. Rosen as the narrative backbone of the piece. The choice to do this has its advantages, and principal among them is that telling the story of meeting and getting to know your profile subject is an easy way to organize the material. But there are risks, too. Does the writer get in the way because she makes herself a subject of the profile, too?

DR. DAEDALUS

Lauren Slater

Part I: Beautiful People

1 Joe Rosen, plastic surgeon at the renowned Dartmouth-Hitchcock Medical Center, and by any account an odd man, has a cold. But then again, he isn't sure it's a cold. "It could be anthrax," he says as he hurries to the car, beeper beeping, sleet sleeting, for it's a freezing New England midwinter day when all the world is white. Joe Rosen's nose is running, his throat is raw, and he's being called into the ER because some guy made meat out of his forefinger and a beautiful teenager split her fine forehead open on the windshield of her SUV. It seems unfair, he says, all these calls coming in on a Sunday, especially because he's sick and he isn't sure whether it's the flu or the first subtle signs of a biological attack. "Are you serious?" I say to him. Joe Rosen is smart. He graduated cum laude from Cornell and got a medical degree from Stanford in 1978. And we're in his car now, speeding toward the hospital where he reconstructs faces, appends limbs, puffs and preens the female form. "You really wonder," I say, "if your cold is a sign of a terrorist attack?"

2 Joe Rosen, a respected and controversial plastic surgeon, wonders a lot of things, some of them directly related to his field, others not. Joe Rosen wonders, for instance, whether Osama bin Laden introduced the West Nile virus to this country. Joe Rosen wonders how much bandwidth it would take to make virtual-reality contact lenses available for all. Joe Rosen wonders why both his ex-wife and his current wife are

artists, and what that says about his deeper interests. Joe Rosen also wonders why we insist on the kinds of conservative medical restraints that prevent him from deploying some of his most creative visions: wings for human beings; cochlear implants to enhance hearing, beefing up our boring ears and giving us the range of an owl; super-duper delicate rods to jazz up our vision—binocular, beautiful—so that we could see for many miles and into depths as well. Joe Rosen has ideas: implants for this, implants for that, gadgets, gears, discs, buttons, sculpting soft cartilage that would enable us, as humans, to cross the frontiers of our own flesh and emerge as something altogether . . . what? Something other.

And we're in the car now, speeding on slick roads toward the hospital, beeper beeping, sleet sleeting, passing cute country houses with gingerbread trim, dollops of smoke hanging above bright brick chimneys; his New Hampshire town looks so sweet. We pull into the medical center. Even this has a slight country flair to it, with gingham curtains hanging in the rows of windows. We skid. Rosen says, "One time I was in my Ford Explorer with my daughter, Sam. We rolled, and the next thing I knew we were on the side of the highway, hanging upside down like bats." He laughs. 3

We go in. I am excited, nervous, running by his bulky side with my tape recorder to his mouth. A resident in paper boots comes up to us. He eyes the tape recorder, and Rosen beams. Rosen is a man who enjoys attention, credentials. A few days ago he boasted to me. "You shouldn't have any trouble with the PR people in this hospital. I've had three documentaries made of me here already." 4

"Can I see them?" I asked. 5

"I don't know," Rosen answered, suddenly scratching his nose very fast. "I guess I'm not sure where I put them," and something about his voice, or his nose, made me wonder whether the documentaries were just a tall tale. 6

Now the resident rushes up to us, peers at the tape recorder, peers at me. "They're doing a story on me," Rosen says. "For *Harper's*." 7

"Joe is a crazy man, a nutcase," the resident announces, but there's affection in his voice. 8

"Why the beeps?" Rosen asks. 9

"This guy, he was working in his shop, got his finger caught in an electric planer. . . . The finger's hamburger," the resident says. "It's just hamburger." 10

We go to the carpenter's cubicle. He's a man with a burly beard and sawdust-caked boots. He lies too big for the ER bed, his dripping finger held high in the air and splinted. It does look like hamburger. 11

I watch Rosen approach the bed, the wound. Rosen is a largish man, with a curly head of hair, wearing a Nordstrom wool coat and a cashmere scarf. As a plastic surgeon, he thinks grand thoughts but traffics mostly in the mundane. He has had over thirty papers published, most of them with titles like "Reconstructive Flap Surgery" or "Rhinoplasty for the Adolescent." He is known among his colleagues only secondarily for his epic ideas; his respect in the field is rooted largely in his impeccable surgical skill with all the toughest cases: shotgunned faces, smashed hands. 12

"How ya doin'?" Rosen says now to the carpenter. The carpenter doesn't answer. He just stares at his mashed finger, held high in the splint. 13

14 Rosen speaks softly, gently. He puts his hand on the woodworker's dusty shoulder. "Looks bad," he says, and he says this with a kind of simplicity—or is it empathy?—that makes me listen. The patient nods. "I need my finger," he says, and his voice sounds tight with tears. "I need it for the work I do."

15 Rosen nods. His tipsiness, his grandiosity, seem to just go away. He stands close to the man. "Look," he says, "I'm not going to do anything fancy right now, okay? I'll just have my guys sew it up, and we'll try to let nature take its course. I think that's the best thing, right now. To let nature take its course."

16 The carpenter nods. Rosen has said nothing really reassuring, but his tone is soothing, his voice rhythmic, a series of stitches that promises to knit the broken together.

17 We leave the carpenter. Down the hall, the teenage beauty lies in still more serious condition, the rent in her forehead so deep we can see, it seems, the barest haze of her brain.

18 "God," whispers Rosen as we enter the room. "I dislike foreheads. They get infected so easily."

19 He touches the girl. "You'll be fine," he says. "We're not going to do anything fancy here. Just sew you up and let nature take its course."

20 I think these are odd, certainly unexpected words coming from a man who seems so relentlessly anti-nature, so visionary and futuristic in his interests. But then again, Rosen himself is odd, a series of swerves, a topsy-turvy, upside-down, smoke-and-mirrors sort of surgeon, hanging in his curious cave, a black bat.

21 "I like this hospital," Rosen announces to me as we leave the girl's room. "I like its MRI machines." He pauses.

22 "I should show you a real marvel," he suddenly says. He looks around him. A nurse rushes by, little dots of blood on her snowy smock. "Come," Rosen says.

23 We ride the elevator up. The doors whisper open. Outside, the sleet has turned to snow, falling fast and furious. The floor we're on is ominously quiet, as though there are no patients here, or as though we're in a morgue. Rosen is ghoulish and I am suddenly scared. I don't know him really. I met him at a medical-ethics convention at which he discussed teaching *Frankenstein* to his residents and elaborated, with a little light in his eye, on the inherent beauty in hybrids and chimeras, if only we could learn to see them that way. "Why do we only value the average?" he'd asked the audience. "Why are plastic surgeons dedicated only to restoring our current notions of the conventional, as opposed to letting people explore, if they want, what the possibilities are?"

24 Rosen went on to explain other things at that conference. It was hard for me to follow his train of thought. He vacillates between speaking clearly, almost epically, to mumbling and zigzagging and scratching his nose. At this conference he kangaroo-leapt from subject to subject: the army, biowarfare, chefs with motorized fingers that could whip eggs, noses that doubled as flashlights, soldiers with sonar, the ocean, the monsters, the marvels. He is a man of breadth but not necessarily depth. "According to medieval man," Rosen said to the convention, finally coming clear, "a monster is someone born with congenital deformities. A marvel," he explained, "is a person with animal parts—say, a tail or wings." He went on to show us pictures, a turn-of-the-century newborn hand with

syphilitic sores all over it, the fingers webbed in a way that might have been beautiful but not to me, the pearly skin stretched to nylon netting in the crotch of each crooked digit.

25 And the floor we're on now is ominously quiet, except for a hiss somewhere, maybe some snake somewhere, with a human head. We walk for what seems a long time. My tape recorder sucks up the silence.

26 Rosen turns, suddenly, and with a flourish parts the curtains of a cubicle. Before me, standing as though he were waiting for our arrival, is a man, a real man, with a face beyond description. "Sweeny," Rosen says, gesturing toward the man, "has cancer of the face. It ate through his sinus cavities, so I scraped off his face, took off his tummy fat, and made a kind of, well, a new face for him out of the stomach. Sweeny, you look good!" Rosen says.

27 Sweeny, his new face, or his old stomach, oozing and swollen from this recent, radical surgery, nods. He looks miserable. The belly-face sags, the lips wizened and puckered like an anus, the eyes in their hills of fat darting fast and frightened.

28 "What about my nose," Sweeny says, and then I notice: Sweeny has no nose. The cancer ate that along with the cheeks, etc. This is just awful. "That comes next. We'll use what's left of your forehead." A minute later, Rosen turns to me and observes that pretty soon women will be able to use their buttocks for breast implants. "Where there's fat," Rosen says, "there are possibilities."

Inquiring into the Essay

Use the four methods of inquiry to think about "Dr. Daedalus."

1. Profiles aren't just about a person. The writer deliberately selects a person because he or she stands in for certain ideas, questions, or problems. In "Dr. Daedalus," Lauren Slater writes that Joe Rosen "wonders why we insist on the kinds of conservative medical restraints that prevent him from deploying some of his most creative visions: wings for human beings; cochlear implants to enhance hearing . . . super-duper delicate rods to jazz up our vision. . . ." He asks later in the essay, "Why do we only value the average?" What do you think of these medical restraints? Are they wise? Is what Rosen proposes daring and imaginative or somehow immoral or unethical? Fastwrite openly for five minutes, exploring your own thoughts about these questions. Begin by writing to yourself about what you would surgically change, if you could, about your own body, and what you might want to change about the way you look that you believe is going too far. Why?
2. If you've ever seen the movie *The Elephant Man,* then the closing anecdote about Sweeny is especially painful. How are we to respond to Sweeny—with pity or disgust? Explain how you felt Slater handled her own response to Sweeny. How does his story influence your thinking about the questions the profile raises about the possibilities of plastic surgery?

3. Does this essay evaluate the questions Rosen raises? What is Slater's argument?
4. Profiles tell true stories about someone. Short stories that focus on a single character are fiction. Does that make a difference in how you read them?

PROFILE

Joe Cool, aka Lonnie Beasley, worked in the produce department at Kroger, and he was the emcee of overstock. "Hey folks," he said on the store PA, "this is Joe Cool and my manager's jumpin' all over me 'cause I done stacked too many beans out there . . . So, please—come on over and buy some of these beans so I can get my manager off my back." The following profile of Beasley was originally published in the *Journal of Management Inquiry*. It is a work of academic scholarship, even if it doesn't read like one.

The discipline of business and economics, like many academic fields, is finding that this kind of alternative scholarship offers knowledge that traditional forms of research lack. For example, one business scholar who reviewed "Learning about Work from Joe Cool" wrote that "this story represents a more holistic view of work . . . than is usually the case in studies of organizational behavior." Another wrote that this profile is "powerful in reminding us that the analysis of work is ultimately etched in the life experiences of workers." The chance to look into the life of someone like Beasley, these scholars argue, provides knowledge that traditional quantitative research does not.

Learning About Work from Joe Cool

Gib Akin

1 The announcement over the supermarket PA system cut through the anonymous burble of shopping talk: "Hey folks, this is Joe Cool and my manager's jumpin' all over me 'cause I done stacked too many beans out here. Old Joe won't be COOOOL no more if he don't get these things movin'. So, please—come on over and buy some of these beans so I can get my manager off my back. And while you're here we've got a great buy on California navel oranges."

2 Here's Joe Cool himself: slim, angular, small turned-up nose on a face that is slightly dished, older than what you would expect from the name. But that's part of what makes him cool, acting so youthful, even at 55, and sporting an intensely white beard. The hair is striking in its contrasting black, and is parted in the middle, with a wing-like sweep back over each temple, plastered flat. It gives him an old fashioned look, like your jolly barkeep from the 1890s. A name tag on his denim apron makes it official that he really is Joe Cool. He's constant motion and constant talk, moving produce, keeping the customers, especially women customers, happy.

3 Lonnie Beasley became Joe Cool in the Kroger produce department, first only behind the scenes and then out front with the customers. He started produce work in

1971 and by 1975 his coworkers had begun to corroborate the Joe Cool persona. They gave him a pair of sunglasses to emulate the Peanuts cartoon showing Snoopy as Joe Cool. Stickers of the cartoon character began appearing on his locker, as well as near the water fountain and the time clock. The back room was becoming Joe Cool's domain. The work there was physically demanding, and all were amazed at Lonnie's youthful strength and endurance—lifting, unloading trucks, and stacking and moving large four-wheeled carts of produce.

But the idea that Lonnie was cool came mainly from his constant joking, talking, 4
and relentlessly youthful attitude. "He would say anything." The mostly younger coworkers liked it that someone older could be like them, always fooling around, not serious, "a nut." But he also retained his seniority, and was paternal as well. He helped everybody. Susan Marsh remembers that "he always made me feel like a daughter he hadn't seen in quite a while." (She didn't know the circumstances that give her simile its keenness.)

And, he rode a motorcycle to work, the crash helmet worn for protection also 5
creating his nineteenth-century hairdo. He didn't ride a mean machine as an aging outlaw biker, but a friendly, playful one as the fresh-air kid. That was really cool. He had a sly affection for the slightly wild image of a motorcyclist, even though he claimed he started riding motorcylces because of the good gas mileage.

When the store moved to a new location, a system of weighing and pricing pro- 6
duce in the section rather than at the register was started, and Lonnie was given the "out front" job as scale man. That's when grocery shoppers got to meet Joe Cool. Donald Linke, who also worked in produce and like Lonnie had come from the other store, now made an "official" name tag that read JOE COOL.

From his new job out front, Lonnie also became the idol of the airwaves. When 7
he got on the PA system to announce some special promotion, people in the store would be quiet so they could hear what Joe Cool was going to say. On one Fourth of July holiday, the store manager, in response to running out the year before, had overstocked hamburger and hot dog rolls. As the day wore on and there were mountains of unsold buns remaining, Lonnie gave the play-by-play: "Folks, the manager has gone crazy, flipped his lid, gone bananas. He's giving away rolls, two for the price of one." And ten minutes later, "He's getting worse, now the poor fool has gone completely over the edge. He's giving four for the price of one. Y'all better get over here and stop this before we have to carry him off." As people arrived, Lonnie would load their baskets and whisk them off. What to do with all the buns? Nobody worried; it was Joe Cool.

Someone said to the manager, "Do you hear what that guy is saying about you?" 8

"Don't bother me none. Them rolls are moving aren't they?" 9

Lonnie was especially attentive to the ladies. He claimed that his beard had turned 10
white as a result of all the smooching he had done (wink, touch your shoulder). Women shoppers always knew that both they and their vegetables were beautiful. Having been raised on a farm and always having his own garden even when living in town, Lonnie knew about produce and would help women pick the best vegetables and then advise on preparation.

11 Attention to women was also about kids. Kids loved Joe Cool and would have their mothers take them to see him.

12 The grocery store job was a second one, even though for most of the time it was a 40-hour-a-week commitment, a full-time job in its own right. Lonnie had always been a two-job man. "I guess working is just my thing." He had worked as a salesman at Sears and drove a Yellow cab as a second job. He sold life insurance as a first job and sold tires at the B. F. Goodrich store as a second. In 1971, he joined the University of Virginia police department working the graveyard shift and soon after began working days at the supermarket.

13 The police job had a lot of the same opportunities to help people. Lonnie claimed only 30 percent was crime fighting, and 70 percent was helping people and doing PR. And especially with University police, you got to deal with better people. Still, the people in produce were an antidote to some of the unfixable unhappiness he saw as a police officer.

14 Coworkers at the store would wonder how, and why, he would do it. "How much sleep you get?"

15 "Three or four hours."

16 "You call that living?"

17 "Depends on your aim."

18 Lonnie had two aims in work. One was simple, conventional, economic, and easy to talk about. Lonnie described himself as a depression baby, born in 1931. His parents separated when he was five, and his mother carried him back to the country where her people were. They never had anything but always worked to pay their way. You didn't want to owe anything or anybody. And what you did was work.

19 He had always wanted to go back to the country, and the work earnings eventually allowed the purchase of a house and seven acres—not really a farm, but a place that could be lived on farm-like. In an open, ramshackle barn, is stored his second motorcycle, a blue 500cc Yamaha that replaced the Honda 350 he started with in 1976. They look faded and scrawny next to his current ride, a huge Honda Gold Wing with a sidecar. There's also a little-used RV. Three old cars live on the acreage, only three of many projects in various states of completion.

20 Depression babies, who never had anything, don't throw things away. Lonnie and Nancy's house was full of things collected deliberately or just impossible to part with. And they all had stories connected with them. Lonnie told the stories while Nancy listened. She sometimes interjected to show physical traces of the story, a photo, a card, a toy, a piece of clothing. (There was quite a collection of icons of the Snoopy Joe Cool character, modeled in banks, T-shirts, soap, a radio.) In retrieving one thing, something else always surfaced, and that kicked off another story. It wasn't having the things themselves, it was that they privided a kind of archaeology, the shards in which their life was encoded, an aid to the remembering and telling that make things real.

21 The accumulation has now attained some sort of critical mass so that there is not the same need to work so much. (Nancy, who Lonnie always calls "Mamma" or "doll," has never worked.) Part of the fullness has been achieved by inheriting some money,

primarily from Nancy's side of the family. The farmers who were her kin may have lived poorly, but in the end their land had substantial cash value, which helped Lonnie and Nancy finally have something.

The other aim of Lonnie's work was less conventional and harder to tell. 22

Lonnie and Nancy referred to their son, James Irvin, as the achievement of their life. 23
He was born in 1954, two years after they were married. At the age of two, James Irvin was taken sick with encephalitis and spent the rest of his life in need of special care. He died in a hospital in Lynchburg, 60 miles away from his family, in 1976. While he was alive, Lonnie, always devoted to helping people, couldn't really help as he would have liked.

During the time when James Irvin was alive and after his death, work was a form 24
of therapy. "Cheaper than a psychiatrist," Lonnie claimed. It was a way to keep busy, a way to keep from worrying himself into the hospital.

Nancy quietly did most of the direct care giving, while Lonnie, feeling more and 25
more distressed, took a second job and spent more time working. A friend admonished Nancy that Lonnie was running away and not helping. But Nancy, uncharacteristically, stood up strong, defending that Lonnie was doing his part by working to pay the bills, doing what he could do in his own way for James Irvin.

When his son died, Lonnie cried, but he kept on working. 26

Lonnie also couldn't help his daughter as he would have liked. Born seven years 27
after James Irvin and named Nancy like her mother, she always knew her dad was cool. What was really cool was being delivered to school by taxi, a regular treat when Lonnie worked a second job as a driver for Yellow Cab. She recalled motorcycle trips to visit relatives in the Tidewater and that her dad would do anything to help someone in need, including her and her stricken brother.

The younger Nancy was married before finishing high school. Her dad didn't 28
exactly approve ("I may be Joe Cool, but I'm a square"). He remained supportive of her, nevertheless. Nancy and her husband had a daughter, but soon separated, and Nancy went to California—a place that for Lonnie was mysterious and dangerous, a place that changed people and made his daughter into someone he didn't know. He worried that she was drawn to men who were bad for her. But he was still there for her, even helping her move back to California after some time back at home. When she left with "her fellah" (Lonnie still can't say the name of the man he so disliked), Nancy's daughter Amber stayed with her grandparents.

Later, Lonnie and Nancy sued for custody of Amber, who was living with them. 29
At the time, the younger Nancy was angry that her parents were trying to take her daughter away. She now sees it differently, that Lonnie had to make this arrangement to be able to get Amber into school and to be able to provide medical care. Her reframing keeps alive the father she knows as helping people, as being supportive of her even if not approving.

When the younger Nancy's "fellah" was killed in an accident, Lonnie paid for the 30
funeral and helped Nancy get resettled. And Nancy, exactly as her father would have done, managed the pain and confusion by going to work. Employed as a receptionist at a psychiatric hospital, she was back at her job the next day. When a fellow

employee, surprised that she was working so soon after the loss, asked what she was doing there, she replied, "To keep from going crazy. And if I do go crazy here you can just put me in one of the rooms down the hall." Work as therapy seemed to be an idea with genetic connections.

31 Lonnie doesn't like to talk about these times. It's as if he doesn't know how, that there is no understandable face to put on it, no way to make anyone happy. It's not like what he could do at work.

32 There is less pain now, and there are fewer bills to pay. Lonnie wants to spend time with Amber. And with the two Nancys. Be at home more. Lonnie is so social at work you might expect him in retirement to want to be around other people. He's a self-declared "people person," but that doesn't mean just being social: it means being personal. Sociability covers much of the pain that comes from not being able to help, to make someone else happy. There's less of that now, so there isn't as much need for work as therapy.

33 When an early leave plan was offered by the grocery company in late 1986, Joe Cool could retire. He still worked the graveyard shift as a university police officer, but spent more time at home with Amber and Nancy, his wife of 41 years and a "right cute chick" he still likes to do things for.

34 On a recent Sunday, as Lonnie, Amber, and the two Nancys were strolling the local shopping mall, they were approached by a young mother. "Aren't you Joe Cool? I want you to say hello to my son."

Inquiring into the Essay

Once again, use the four methods of inquiry to investigate your thoughts and feelings about Akin's profile of "Learning about Work from Joe Cool."

1. Academic reviews of this essay suggest that this kind of scholarship offers us knowledge of subjects that traditional academic research does not. In your notebook, explore that idea. Take three minutes to make a fast list in response to this question: *What does knowing Joe Cool through this profile tell me about the nature of some workers and workplaces?*
2. Choose one or more of the segments in this essay—the sections separated by white space—and explain its purpose. What particular knowledge about workers or workplaces does the segment seem to offer? Why was it included?
3. Evaluate the effectiveness of "Joe Cool" as research. Do you agree that this kind of research—informal case studies that read like stories—make a valuable contribution to our knowledge of a subject? What are their strengths and weaknesses?
4. Reflect on what you would do if you were Gib Akin, the author of this story, charged with writing a profile of Joe Cool. What parts of the process would you enjoy? What parts would you find hard? As you consider writing your own profile of somebody, do you anticipate any personal challenges?

Seeing the Form

Roy Takeno Reading Paper in Front of Office by Ansel Adams

The photographer and the painter who are after a truthful portrait of someone confront the same problem as the writer: How can you possibly capture the complexity of a human being in a single image or on a few pages? The answer, of course, is that you can't. The best you can do is find, in the moment when you press the shutter release, a picture that says something more. A good photographic portrait, like a good written profile, reveals some aspect of who the subjects are, creates some particular impression, or, as in this photograph by Ansel Adams, uses the portrait to comment not just on the subject but a larger problem.

Ansel Adams, *Roy Takeno Reading Paper in Front of Office*, 1943. (Library of Congress Prints and Photographs Division.)

In 1943, Adams, best known for his landscape photographs, took more than 200 photographs at the Manzanar War Relocation Center in California, one of a number of internment camps created by the U.S. government to detain Japanese Americans during World War II. Look closely at Adams's picture of Roy Takeno. If this were a written profile about the man, what would be an idea around which the profile is organized?

THE WRITING PROCESS

INQUIRY PROJECT: Representative Profile

Write a 1,000- to 1,200-word profile of someone who strikes you as representative, in some ways, of a larger group. For example, write a profile of your neighbor, the Harley Davidson aficionado, because he seems typical, in some ways, of bikers. Profile a nurse because that's a profession you're interested in. Write about an African American student on your predominantly white campus to discover what of his or her experience might represent the experience of other minority students there. Your instructor may give you additional instructions.

Work toward a profile that has the following qualities:

- It is ultimately organized around ways your profile seems representative or typical of the larger group to which your subject belongs.
- The profile includes at least three anecdotes, or little stories, that help reveal this theme.
- You bring in the voice of your subject through selective quotations.
- The end of the essay circles back to the beginning.

Thinking About Subjects

Sometimes you don't choose the subject; he or she chooses you. That was frequently my experience when I researched my book on lobsters—as I traveled and talked to people about the subject I was researching, I found fascinating people whose experience, like Abby Boynton's, would powerfully reveal some aspect of lobstering that seemed important. One way to find suitable profile subjects, therefore, is simply to look for them in the course of doing your research. Who have you read or heard about or perhaps met who might provide a useful focus for a subject in which you're interested?

On the other hand, you might have an idea of who you'd like to profile now, someone you know or would like to know. But if you'd like to play around with some ideas, the following prompts should help. As always, keep generating ideas until you feel you have some potentially promising material.

Generating Ideas

Play with possible subjects, withholding judgment for the moment about what might be a good one. Again, as in the previous chapter, don't let your critical side stifle your creative side. At this point in the process, you can let yourself explore freely.

Listing Prompts. To select a topic within which you'd like to find someone to profile, try the following:

1. Who have you known whom you can't forget? Make a fast list of memorable individuals from each period of your life.

2. Make a quick list of issues or controversies in the local community—or on campus—that people talk about or that have gotten your attention. Choose one of the controversies that interests you, and try the first two steps in the "Research Prompts" section that follows.

3. Make a fast list of careers that interest you. Choose one of these and profile someone who is involved in that profession.

4. Develop a "snapshot profile." Go to a public place—a café, the campus library, a fast-food restaurant—and observe people. Choose someone whom you can discreetly observe for at least ten minutes. Generate a list of observations of that person, double-entry style, in your notebook, using the left-facing page. Concentrate on particulars. This is key. Don't just note, "He is sitting there"; observe *how* he is sitting: "He is sitting there with his left leg crossed over his right, and an untied shoelace dangles from his brown leather shoe that jiggles with nervous energy." Make this list as long as you can.

One Student's Response

JENNIFER'S JOURNAL

LIST OF OBSERVATIONS: CELL PHONE SALESWOMAN

blonde and brown streaked hair
straight to shoulders
black cotton sweater
low cut green patterned blouse
long fingernails, painted white
pecks at computer keys carefully
cell phone to ear
performs one-handed: writing form, pecking at computer, opening boxes

silver watch
"hey you" to girlfriend passing by
black nametag
Kimberly
eyebrows rise when smiles
"Get the only RAZR that's got it all"
looks into eyes of customer when talking
takes long strides when walking
black pants
black shoes, low heels

SNAPSHOT PROFILE

CELL PHONE SALESWOMAN

Kimberly does her job one-handed because the other hand is always holding a cell phone to her ear. Selling cell phones obviously means using cell phones while you sell them. She is young, perhaps 22, and has long nails that are carefully enameled in white. These present problems when she types on the computer, slowing down her hunting and pecking considerably, a process that is performed, as always, with her right hand, since the left holds the cell phone to her ear. Kimberly works at a Verizon wireless counter that is a kind of island in the middle of the mall, and she moves effortlessly in the small square area behind the counter that she shares with two other salespeople. They share a private joke, and she smiles, and when she does one of her eyebrows lifts. This is not freak accident. It happens again and again, and makes her seem skeptical. She unfolds a large brochure showing the company's national service area—accomplished once more single handedly—and points with a long white fingernail at something. The customer nods. Kimberly smiles, and the eyebrow lifts once again.

Fastwriting Prompts. Fastwriting is a great way to loosen up your creative side and at the same time generate raw material. Here are a few prompts to get you writing:

1. Choose a name from the first list you generated earlier—who have you known whom you can't forget? Choose someone you find interesting for some reason. Perhaps it's a grandfather who tells stories about the war, or an old friend who now works at the Museum of Sex in New York City (yes, there really is one). Maybe your friend's mother is a writer who is on the verge of publishing her first book of poems and you wonder what it feels like. Write the person's name at the top of a journal page. Begin a fastwrite in which you describe in detail the scene or situation in which you last saw and talked to your subject. Follow the writing from there.

2. Think of one word that best describes the character or personality of a subject you might profile. Arrogant? Generous? Selfless? Narcissistic? Put that word at the top of a journal page and create two scenes describing that person that *show* that word. For a challenge, don't mention the word at all in your scenes.

3. Review the data you collected for your "snapshot profile" under Listing Prompt 4, especially noting those that are suggestive in some way about your subject and how exactly you see her. On the right-facing page of your notebook, compose a fat paragraph that uses the best evidence you collected, all working toward some dominant impression or idea about your subject that you'd like to communicate to a reader. Use this material as the basis for a short vignette like "Thumb-Sucking Girl."

Visual Prompts. Maps, clusters, lines and arrows, charts, and even sketches can help us piece together subjects in ways that writing sometimes cannot. Consider the following options:

1. Put the name of a possible profile subject in the center of a cluster. Build a web of associations for five minutes, and then begin fastwriting when you feel the urge.

2. Go through old photographs for ideas about profile subjects; this might be especially useful for reminding yourself of family and friends who might be good subjects.

Research Prompts. It is impossible to write a profile without conducting research of some sort, if not in the library or online, then in the field with one's subject. Doing some research up front, then, can be a useful way to find a subject to write about.

1. Return to the list you generated earlier in the "Listing Prompts" section. Choose a controversy in the community or on campus as the focus for your profile. Check the community and campus newspapers to discover who has been active as advocates on the issue, or who has been impacted by it. Is any one person suitable for a profile?

2. Discuss your topic with your friends or people in your class. Who do they know that would be good as a profile subject?

3. On the Internet, search the archives of the local newspaper to find the names of potential profile subjects on an issue or controversy in which you're interested.

4. If you have a career interest, a profile of a working member of the profession can be compelling. Call the state professional association for suggestions about how to find an interview subject, or ask friends and family for suggestions.

One Student's Response

BRUCE'S JOURNAL

RESEARCH ON LIST OF ISSUES

ISSUE	INTERVIEW SUBJECTS
Recall	Margaret the storekeeper, Mayor Coles
Owyhee's wilderness	Congressperson Simpson, Pat Ford
Migrant workers	Miguel Gomez, Rep. Bieter
Foothills preservation	Jack Coulter, Mayor, Nancy Maynard

Judging What You Have

You should have a considerable body of material to work with. It may not be coherent at this point, but again it's always better to work from abundance than from scarcity. Your job now is to use your critical side to judge, shape, and evaluate this material.

What's Promising Material and What Isn't? Let's look critically at the material you've generated. How will you choose the best profile subject? Consider the following criteria:

- *Accessibility.* You're interested in the experience of death row inmates at the supermaximum prison in the next county. An obvious choice of subject is the guy recently convicted of a local rape and murder who was sentenced last week to the death penalty. Can you get to talk to him? Probably not. His attorneys may be preparing an appeal, or your request for an interview might be one of many, most of which come from news organizations. If you could talk to him, would there be sufficient time for the interview? The greatest subject in the world is no good to you if he or she is inaccessible.
- *Background.* Lacking time to spend with an interview subject, writers often look for information that may already exist: perhaps an article or two, a diary, a cigar box full of old pictures. This background information can provide extremely useful material to supplement what the writer gets in a face-to-face interview. Might there be such information on a possible subject?
- *Typicality.* Is the subject representative in some way of an aspect of a topic you'd like to investigate? Every human being is unique, obviously, but we all occupy certain categories of human experience. I've been interviewed, for example, as an English professor, a book author, and an expert on the methods of dispatching lobsters. Am I typical of each category? Gee, I don't like to think so, but some of my experiences are typical.
- *Extremity.* On the other hand, you may look for a subject who represents not the norm in a category of experience but an extreme. Bert, a Florida

State undergraduate, was a great subject for a piece on the nation's top party school not because he represented the norm of male party animals but because he was so radically committed to that lifestyle. Bert isn't typical, in that sense, but rather a dramatic example of how out of hand things can become.

- *Spontaneity.* Profiles of politicians and celebrities are particularly challenging because they have learned to "manage" an interview. That is, they've developed the skills to control the course of an interview, ensuring that what they plan to say gets said and little more. Less experienced subjects, the kind you are most likely to profile, often have appeal because they *aren't* practiced at talking about themselves. There's freshness and even naiveté sometimes about what they say and how they say it that makes profiles particularly compelling.
- *Quotability.* This doesn't necessarily mean articulateness. I remember a devastating profile some years ago of the New York socialite Cornelia Guest. Her remarkable inarticulateness at expressing her personal values and commitments to charities were quotable *because* they were so goofy. The reader's dominant impression of Guest from the piece was that she was a complete airhead. On the other hand, the people you may least expect to be articulate about their experiences can just blow you away. Sometimes you simply can't know how quotable a subject might be until the interview. But if you do know beforehand that someone speaks in an interesting way, you may have a great profile subject.
- *Willingness.* I put this last for a reason. Most of us assume that people resist the kind of interviews a profile demands. A few profile subjects may, at first, resist the *idea* of being interviewed, but in reality people simply love to talk about themselves. An interview gives a subject a willing listener; how often do we enjoy the undivided attention of someone who is vitally interested in what we have to say about ourselves? A profile subject may have concerns—perhaps discomfort with what they might reveal about themselves, or initial distrust of the interviewer, who may be a stranger—but by and large it's hard to find an unwilling subject.

Questions About Audience and Purpose. As always, profile writing begins with a personal motivation. Is there something you think you can learn from your subject, perhaps something about an aspect of the world you are interested in, or something about the human spirit? By interviewing someone else is it possible to even learn something about yourself? You might also begin with a simpler, less grand, but no less important motive: Is there something this subject knows or feels that should be documented and preserved? This is one reason we interview and profile family members and friends, but personal motive is not enough reason to write a profile—the piece must hold interest for readers who may not immediately share your fascination with Uncle Leopold's account of his marriage to Aunt Edna. As always, the *So what?* question lurks in the background.

The profile can, like good fiction, provide insight into the complexities of the human mind and soul.

As you evaluate the material you've generated, consider some of the following purposes that transcend your personal ones.

- *Which possible profile subject best fits the details of the assignment?* Your instructor may have provided guidance on how to approach the profile, including suggestions about choices of a profile subject or things to consider about audience. Which subject seems to best fit these guidelines?
- *Does this profile subject help illuminate an idea, issue, or controversy that might interest some of your readers?* Remember the *Migrant Mother?* That portrait pointed to larger social issues. Lauren Slater's profile of Dr. Rosen in "Dr. Daedalus" is not about just the plastic surgeon but also the ethics of tampering with the human form.
- *Does a profile subject provide a focus on an interesting bit of history?* One way to write a focused treatment of a larger historical event or story is to find someone who lived it. If you want to write, for example, about the internment of the Japanese during World War II, the particulars of Kaz Kasamoto's experience as a child in one of the camps will give readers a dramatic glimpse at this sad piece of American history.
- *Does a profile subject represent a "type" of person that might interest readers?* Perhaps you're interested in the culture of sorority life on your campus and you have a willing subject who has belonged to Kappa Kappa Gamma for the last three years. Or perhaps you want to become a registered labor and delivery nurse. A profile of a working obstetric nurse will not only teach you something about your career choice but convince others that such a job is interesting, demanding, or not for them.
- *Is the profile subject an interesting character?* Don't be fooled. Even so-called ordinary people can be fascinating if you can get them to let their masks slip a little. But what makes a subject inherently interesting even if, for example, the person isn't a "type," didn't experience a bit of history, or can't represent an issue or idea? In a word, *surprise.* What often makes profile subjects interesting is that they shatter our assumptions about people and how they are in the world—a ninety-year-old man who still hikes fourteen-thousand-foot peaks, a fourteen-year-old college student, a therapist with marital problems, a lesbian activist in rural Mississippi, the president of an antifraternity fraternity. We are all composed of contradictions like these, but some are more surprising than others.
- *Who is your audience?* A key factor in any writing situation is audience. Who are you writing for in this assignment and which possible profile subjects would that audience find most compelling?

Interviewing

His interview subjects sometimes see John McPhee, one of the great profile writers, as "thick-witted." At times McPhee seems to ask the same questions over and over, and he frequently seems to possess only the most basic information about his subjects. According to William Howarth, when McPhee "conducts an interview he tries to be as blank as his notebook pages, totally devoid of preconceptions." His theory is that unless his interview subjects "feel superior or equal to their interviewer" they won't talk as freely or at length. McPhee never uses a tape recorder, but jots down spare notes in a notebook—these are the telling details and facts that reveal his subject's character.

McPhee is what some have called an *immersion journalist,* someone who spends substantial time with his subjects, getting to know them more intimately. This is the best basis for writing a profile because it generates enough information to get closer to the truth about the subject. But it's also a difficult approach for student writers who rarely have that time to spend; that's why the availability of background information on the person you hope to profile can be so useful. Still, this general principle still stands: *the more time you can spend talking with your interview subject, the better the profile will be.* If at all possible, then, plan on requesting more than a single time to talk, or at least an extended time—perhaps an hour or more—if only one meeting is possible.

You can find more information about interviewing techniques in Chapter 12, "Research Techniques," but the following tips should help you start developing a plan for your interviews.

Making Contact. I'm a fairly shy guy. In fact, when I began writing nonfiction articles many years ago the worst part of the work was calling people to ask for their time to do an interview. These conversations almost always ended well for a simple reason—people love to talk about themselves. That's hardly surprising. After all, how often do we enjoy for more than a few minutes the undivided attention of someone who appears fascinated by everything we say, and even writes some of it down? E-mail has made the process of contacting an interview subject less intimidating, although it's not a totally satisfactory substitute for a phone conversation.

Asking a family member or friend to be an interview subject is easy, but how do you ask a stranger? You start by introducing yourself and straightforwardly describing the profile assignment, including your feeling that the subject would be a great focus for your piece. You must be prepared to answer the almost inevitable follow-up question: "Well, gee, I'm flattered. But what is it about me that you find interesting?" Here's where McPhee's elementary knowledge is crucial: Although you need to know only a very little about your interview subject, you must know enough to say, for instance, that you're aware of his role in a bit of history or his involvement in a local issue, or recognize him as being knowledgeable about a topic you find of interest.

What you want from this initial contact is time. The conventional interview—when you sit across from your informant asking questions and writing down answers—can be very useful, but it may be more productive if you can spend time *doing* something with your profile subject that relates to the reason you've chosen him. For example, if you are profiling a conservative activist, spend an hour watching him work the telephone, lining up people for the meeting at city hall. Your interview with a homeless woman could take place during lunch at the local shelter. *Seeing* your subject in a meaningful situation can generate far more information than the conventional interview. Imagine what those situations might be.

What do you do if your subject doesn't want to be interviewed? In that unlikely event, you're permitted to ask why. If your reassurances aren't sufficient to change the person's mind, then you need to find another subject.

Conducting the Interview. You've arranged a time and place for an initial conversation. Should you prepare questions? Sure, but be prepared to ignore them. Interviews rarely go as planned, and if they do, they are often disappointing. An interview is a *conversation,* and these are best when they head in unexpected directions. Go with the flow in the initial interview; if you need to ask informational questions, you can save them for the next time.

Certain generic questions can reveal things about a subject's character. These are more *open-ended questions* that often lead in surprising and interesting directions. Some of these open-ended questions include the following:

- In all your experience with ________, what has most surprised you?
- What has been the most difficult aspect of your work?
- If you had the chance to change something about how you approached ________, what would it be?
- Can you remember a significant moment in your work on ________? Is there an experience with ________ that stands out in your mind?
- What do you think is the most common misconception about ________? Why?
- What are significant trends in ________?
- Who or what has most influenced you? Who are your heroes?
- If you had to summarize the most important thing you've learned about ________, what would you say? What is the most important thing that people should know or understand?

Note taking during an interview is a challenge. A popular method is to use a tape recorder (see "Inquiring into the Details: Tape Recorders"), but even if you do it's essential to take handwritten notes as well. While the tape recorder will capture the voice of your subject, it will not collect the essential details of the scene. You have to do that. Jot down any facts, details, phrases, mannerisms, or even personal reactions you have during the interview. This is crucial. Don't worry if these notes are fragmentary. Immediately after you conclude the interview you can write out a fuller account, using the fragments as prompts.

Inquiring into the Details

TAPE RECORDERS

There are advantages and disadvantages to using a tape recorder to record your interview. If you record you will have a complete account of your conversation, which can free you up to take notes on your subject's mannerisms, environment, and such. When recording you might also feel more able to participate in the conversation if you aren't obsessed with transcribing your subject's words. However, many people are unsettled by the recorders, feeling unable to speak freely or to open up with a machine recording their every "um" or pause. Ultimately you'll decide which approach you think is best, but if you use a tape recorder, here are some tips:

- Practice at home first. Set up the tape recorder and make sure you have fresh batteries as well as an extension cord. Be sure to have extra tapes. Label your tape with the name of the subject and date of your interview. Then turn on the machine and record a few minutes of testing. When you finally meet with your subject your machine should be absolutely ready to go, with a minimum of fiddling.
- Ask your interview subject if you can use the recorder. If the answer is no, don't record.
- If possible, place the recorder somewhere unobtrusive (but not too far away—you still want it to pick up the conversation).
- No matter what, take notes as if the recorder isn't on. The tape recorder should be your backup, not your primary source of information. (In my experience, technology often fails when it is most needed. Therefore the recorder may record your test conversation perfectly but fail when you are in the actual interview.)
- Once you get home, transcribing your conversation may reveal ideas, themes, and quotes you don't remember. Transcribing is incredibly time consuming, but can be well worth the effort.

While my students have used the double-entry journal effectively as a note-taking format for profiles, putting the observed information and quotations on the left page and personal responses on the right, I'm keen on those pocket-sized memo books. They're incredibly unobtrusive and easy to carry and they force you to be spare. I especially like the ease with which I can take the memo pad out and put it away, at times using it to signal to my subject that I'm more—or less—interested in something he's saying.

Listening and Watching. The art of interviewing relies, more than anything else, on the craft of listening. Few of us are good listeners, which is why profile writing can be so hard. First you must control your anxiety about getting things down, asking the next question, and making your subject relaxed. Only then can you give your interview subject your full attention. Novice interviewers should remember that the quality of the conversation matters more than anything else, including careful note taking and asking clever questions. You can always call back to check your facts or prompt your subject to repeat something memorable. E-mail can be a useful follow-up method for such things.

What makes a good conversation? When it generates the kind of information that will help you write the profile, including the following:

- *Stories.* Interesting stories and anecdotes help you build a narrative backbone to your essay.
- *Memorable quotations.* A typical interview produces only a handful of these, so don't desperately write down everything a subject says. Wait until you hear something that is nicely put or distinctive, particularly quotes that reveal something about your subject's character.
- *Background information.* This can be in the form of stories, but might also be basic but essential information such as your subject's age, place of birth, and history of involvement in relevant jobs or issues.
- *Feeling.* A good conversation is an honest one in which the subject is willing to let the mask slip to reveal the face sweating underneath. Be alert to those moments of feeling when your subject seems to be revealing herself—what *really* matters to her, what might be hard, where she finds joy.

Moments of honesty are often signaled by body language. I once interviewed a New Hampshire lobsterman, and after a long day of setting traps with him I offhandedly asked whether he hoped his sons and daughters would go into the business. He had spent most of the day talking about how much he loved the independent lifestyle, and so when he didn't reply immediately to my question I paid attention. I noticed him looking at his hands, roughened by saltwater and toughened by the thick plastic line he roped to the traps. "Too much work for what they get out of it," he said suddenly. The response surprised me, and I think I would have missed it if I hadn't noticed him looking at his hands. Mannerisms can be revealing, but so can the things a profile subject surrounds himself with—the books on the bookshelf, the type of car he drives, or the style of his house. Collect these observations as you would any other kind of evidence—scrupulously and with care.

INTERVIEW NOTES

Below are interview notes that Margaret Parker took in preparation for writing the powerful profile "Medical Student," which appears at the end of this chapter. As you read her notes, imagine the kinds of questions she had to ask to produce this kind of specific information about her subject, JD. Note the care Parker takes to get the facts straight, as well as her work to create a story through scenes and characterizations.

Your interview notes are the main source of information for your profile. If they're skimpy—brief or vague—you can't possibly write a profile that brings your subject to life.

Selected Interview Notes: "Medical Student"

Margaret Parker

"Oh my God JD you look so . . . together!"

Day begins at 3:30 a.m and ends at 8:30. Every fifth day "On-Call," goes to bed around nine in the student call room, divided by a sheet, sleeps in scrubs and sweat-shirt and thick socks because it's freezing, around midnight a trauma comes in and have to do surgery. Then back to work the next day at 5:00 a.m, start with rounds and quizzed at 6:30 by residents.

Notice how careful the writer is to collect specific details—exact times, descriptions, and so on.

110 hr/week is average . . . 120 hrs one week because she had call three times.

Operating Room (OR) environment—everything is sterile, only see eyes of people, must keep hands between waist and shoulders at all times, if not, the OR nurses scream at you and you have go leave and rescrub, shames, OR nurses like Nazis, her first week she was screamed at constantly, you just don't realize how hard it is to keep hands in place and the terror of getting yelled at. Just trying to please and doing really menial tasks like holding retractors or skin and muscle back so that the surgeon can do his thing, back spasms, very exhausting for five or eight hours, terrified to move. Med students are everybody's peon, the OR nurses are the worst . . .

The Worst Day

In her notes, the writer integrates quotations within the overall narrative. She organizes her notes by roughly following the story she wants to tell. This often isn't possible because you don't yet know the story when you interview.

Supposed to be there at 5:00 for rounds, and meet with residents at 6:30 for the residents, her alarms didn't go off and the clock read 5:45. It takes forty-five minutes to drive from her apartment to Olympia Fields hospital, arrives at 6:27, "peeing my pants," Kelley—a short mall rat junior high looking girl, starts screaming at all of them, she asks JD a question and she doesn't know it, she walks away and the team is angry with JD. She scrubs in for the surgery, a cholecystectomy of a 16 yr. old girl, expected to last two hours, hands drop below the waist slightly and the OR nurse screams "I don't believe this crap, Student, you better go rescrub," the attending with open contempt in his eyes, the resident satisfied smirk barely detectable below the mask, holds the camera in the stomach for hours, the surgery starts to go badly, it is apparent it will take much longer than two hours, drags into its fourth hour, struggle to keep still, back spasms, "Wrong Godamn direction!", everybody in shock, the camera is still in the girl's stomach, nobody moves to do anything, then he gets a hold of himself and resumes, it goes on, terrified, trying not to shake, part of her wants to walk out, screw him, she didn't sign up for this, paying 30 grand a year to be shaken and terrorized by psychopaths, but she stays, five hours the surgery is over, "God walks out," Kelly comes up and says, "Oh my God JD, don't worry about it, he's a jerk," and for a second these words are gratefully received, felt like an abused woman wanted to get in a car wreck so she wouldn't have to go, cried the whole way home, calculating the hours till she has to go back

Here the writer breaks with the narrative to get down descriptions of other characters.

The Team

Ryan—top of his class, wanted to do surgery but after the first week decided on Family UP practice or ER, counseled each other every day, go and hid and bitch

Keith "Special K"—disorder, you name it he's got it, OCD, super book smart but no social skills, disappears for hours, she tried to follow him but he lost her, then her friend Bernie called and swore that he saw him on campus, a good 45 minutes away, "Where the f—k is Keith," SD had to take over his surgeries because certain nurses wouldn't work with him, he touched his head and was generally unresponsive to their abuse, yet they wouldn't tell him, "SD tell him to put on his scrubs, tell him to go away," every night nightmares

An extended quotation. These help the reader really hear your subject's voice, and they can be quite revealing. They're also hard to get without a tape recorder or excellent note-taking skills.

Kelly—"so bipolar," seems like your chatty mall rat friend but then she turns into a demon

Trauma was better, the people were nicer, she was more valued, did useful things like chest compressions, took patient histories so they read her notes, Wendy Marshall the head honcho—British, teacher in every aspect, 'Pump-firing away of questions . . .'

"I have always wanted to be a doctor, and I couldn't really explain why. It was kind of a joke during my medical school interviews, because they always ask you, why do you want to be a doctor? And I'd reply with the generic, I wanna help people. But I guess now I think that I really like talking to people, and maybe in medicine I can help them. I think talking is the most important way to help sick people, not the real medicine that they teach you in school. People have such absolute faith in their doctor, and I love that feeling, that people confide in me."

Writing the Sketch

When you think you've collected enough information about your profile subject from interviews, observations, and background research, compose a 500-word typewritten sketch. The sketch is a brief treatment of a promising subject that may lack a clear sense of purpose but does not lack specific information. For your profile sketch, your instructor will tell you which of the following elements you should incorporate:

- At least two potentially revealing anecdotes or brief stories about your profile subject.
- At least two strong quotations from your subject.
- A title.

- A paragraph of background information, including your informant's age, a physical description, and perhaps relevant job or personal history.
- A strong lead (perhaps one of the anecdotes) and an ending that somehow returns to the beginning.

Moving from Sketch to Draft

A sketch is generally underdeveloped, sometimes giving the writer just the barest outline of his subject. But as an early draft, a sketch can be invaluable. It might hint at what the "real" subject is, or what questions seem to be behind your inquiry into the subject. A sketch might suggest a focus for the next draft, or simply a better lead. Here are some tips for finding clues in your sketch about directions you might go in the next draft.

Evaluating Your Own Sketch. It might seem like an impossible task to capture in a couple pages the complexity of the person you interviewed or observed the other day. You must begin evaluating your sketch with more reasonable ambitions. It *is* impossible to capture the whole person, but what you are working toward in your profile is to capture an *aspect* of that person, some particular quality that stands out. That quality may be an impression you're trying to create—for example, this is an incredibly selfless individual—or it might be the particular contribution your subject is making to a controversy, an argument or an idea. Read your sketch, then, paying attention to one or both of those purposes:

1. *Dominant impression.* What feeling or personality trait do I want to communicate about my profile subject? Can I name it? Is there evidence in the sketch that points to this?
2. *Role.* What exactly am I trying to show—or might I show in the next draft—about my subject's participation in an idea, an issue, or an event?

Questions for Peer Review. Peer review of sketches can help writers clarify purpose. You've already done some thinking about that; now ask readers for help. You might pose the following questions:

- If you were to use one word to describe your main impression of the person I profiled, what would it be?
- What evidence would you point to in the sketch that contributes to that impression?
- Did you find my portrait sympathetic or critical?
- In a sentence, what seems to be my subject's main point of view, attitude, or belief?
- What one detail—a fact, observation, description, or quotation—struck you as most revealing? What did it reveal?
- What would you like to know more about in the next draft?
- After reading the draft, what did you come to understand about the type of person profiled that you didn't know when you began the draft?

Methods for Peer Review of Sketches

1. Choose a partner, exchange sketches, and read and comment both in writing and through conversation.
2. Create a pile of sketches in the middle of the classroom. Everyone takes one (not his or her own, obviously), provides written comments, returns it to the pile, and takes another. Repeat this until everyone has read and commented on at least four sketches
3. Share sketches online on the class Web site.

Reflecting on What You've Learned. Before you begin composing the next draft, make a journal entry that explores your thinking about the sketch and everything you heard. Begin an entry with the prompt, *Based on what I've learned so far about my profile subject, the main thing I seem to be trying to show is* _________.

Follow this prompt, continuing to reflect on what your intentions might be in the next draft. When the writing stalls, skip a line and make a quick list: *The three things I heard during peer review that I want to remember are: (1)* _________*; (2)* _________*; and (3)* _________.

Research and Other Strategies: Gathering More Information

If you emerged from the experience of writing and sharing your sketch with a stronger sense of purpose, then you're close to being ready to draft. If you didn't, return to your notes or share your sketch with a few more readers. In either case, you'll probably need to collect more information before you begin the draft. Most important, plan another interview with your subject. This one will likely be quite different; now that you have a clearer purpose for your profile, your questions will be directed at getting the information you need to more fully develop your piece. For example, suppose you were profiling a student activist who is working on behalf of local migrant farm workers. Peer review of your sketch helped clarify your intentions—you'd like to show how instrumental student leaders like your profile subject were in the struggle last year to guarantee a minimum wage for migrant workers. In a follow-up interview, you'd likely ask that question directly: How important *were* student activists in that legislative battle? Your questions also might inspire your subject to tell stories about key moments in that struggle, particularly if they highlight the effectiveness of young activists. Can you see how useful a follow-up interview can be once you've determined your purpose? It's likely to generate invaluable information that could well be key to the success of the profile.

You might consider other sources of information as well:

- Interview people who know your profile subject.
- If your subject is a public figure, do library or Web research for background.

- Do background research on your profile subject. Find out more about what they do or where they do it. Find out how they fit into a larger context. If you're writing about a nurse-midwife, find out how many are working in the state and what their licensing requirements might be.

The quotes and information you gather can be used in your profile, usually with attribution. Research the idea, issue, or event, if any, that provides the context for your profile.

Composing the Draft

If you haven't collected enough information, you'll run aground pretty quickly in the draft. One of the signs of not enough information include using everything you've gathered about your profile subject, including information that may not be relevant to your purpose. Alternatively, you might simply write short, failing to meet the page length requirement. If you encounter these obstacles, return to the generating exercises earlier in the chapter or the tips listed previously.

If you're confident that you're working from abundance, consider beginning the drafting process by writing multiple leads. For example, work toward three one-paragraph beginnings—perhaps each focused on a different anecdote—and decide which one seems to point the draft in the direction you want it to go and is most likely to capture your readers. Once you've chosen a lead, follow it. You'll likely find that the leads you didn't use find a place for themselves somewhere else in the draft.

Writing with Computers

TIPS FOR REVISION

From a practical standpoint, revising your drafts on a computer can be easier than doing so on paper. You can copy, paste, delete, and insert new text into the draft on a computer with a mouse click or a few simple keystrokes. As you work through multiple drafts, though, you should save each draft as a separate file. For ease in identification, number or insert the date of composition into each file name (for example, "draft3.doc" or "draft07-14.doc"). Saving copies of each draft allows you (and potentially others, including your instructor) to evaluate your progress from one draft to the next. It also gives you the option of picking up again from an earlier draft if you find that your later drafts have moved in a direction that ultimately proves unrewarding. You should also print out and keep hard copies of each draft. Why? Your computer may seem completely reliable, but it takes only one bad experience to prove that it's not. Hard copies can be scanned or retyped, potentially saving you from having to start over. Also, when it comes time to read back over your drafts, the printed page is usually easier on the eyes than a computer screen.

Methods of Development. You can pursue various strategies to develop your profile.

Narrative. The profile form often relies on narrative. It can do this in several ways; perhaps the most familiar is that the piece tells the story of the writer's encounter with her subject. For example, Lauren Slater's profile of plastic surgeon Joe Rosen is organized around an evening she spent with him at the hospital. Her account includes her reactions to what he was saying and doing. Profile writers are often drawn to the first-person account—my day with my subject—which is obviously a convenient structure if that matches the experience of the interviewer. However, consider whether a first-person point of view interrupts the narrative too much and interferes with the reader's view of the profile subject. After all, the writer isn't the subject of a profile.

Known to Unknown. If your profile subject is a public figure and your motive is to reveal a less well-known aspect of your subject's life or work, beginning the essay with information that first seems to confirm public perceptions but then promises to challenge them—in other words, moving from what's known to what's less known—can be an effective way to structure the profile. This method of development is quite common for celebrity profiles.

Using Evidence. The most authoritative information in a profile is the voice of your subject. It is also the information that will be most heavily scrutinized by the subject herself: "Did I really say that?" Readers of the profile often believe that the subject's voice is the most authentic information because it is less mediated by the writer, an assumption that isn't always accurate. After all, unless quotations come directly from the tape recorder, interviewers must rely on their note-taking skill. Even with a recorded transcription, writers commonly tidy up bad grammar and remove irrelevant utterances such as "uh" and "um."

A profile writer must also establish his authority by giving readers a sense that he is a keen and careful observer; he does so by carefully using not just quotation but detail, description, and research. Consider how the author of "Soup" did this when profiling restaurant owner Albert Yeganeh.

Workshopping the Draft

If your draft is subject to peer review (see Chapter 15 for details on how to organize workshop groups), think carefully about the kind of responses you need from readers at this point in the process. The following questions might help you prepare.

Reflecting on the Draft. As you prepare your draft for peer review, think about what you most need in a response. Are you reasonably confident that the purpose and focus of your profile is clear? Or are you feeling anxious about how well you managed to pull it all together? Your initial feelings about the draft will be a factor in the kind of response you request from your group.

- Make a journal entry in which you reflect in a five-minute fastwrite about how you feel about the draft. What worked? What needs work?
- If the writing stalls, consider this question: *If I could change the process of writing this draft, from initially generating a subject to write about to this first draft, what would I change?* Follow this with a fastwrite until you have nothing more to say.

Questions for Readers. As you prepare for peer review, certain questions are also particularly useful to consider when drafting profiles. Pose to your group any of these that seem relevant to your draft or possible plans for revision.

1. What dominant impression did the draft create of its subject? What words would you use to describe that impression?
2. In a sentence or two, what does the draft seem to be *saying* about its subject?
3. Does the end strain to return to the beginning, or does it give the profile a sense of wholeness or unity?
4. What is the strongest/weakest quote? What is the strongest/weakest anecdote?
5. What do you want to know about the profile subject that the draft doesn't say?
6. Did you find this person interesting? Why or why not?
7. Did you learn anything about this type of person?

Revising the Draft

As I discussed earlier in the book, one of the most misunderstood aspects of revision is that you only do it at the end of the writing process. In fact, up to this point, you should have been revising your work all along, from the first few journal exercises when you chose a topic and played with possible angles on it, to the journal work you might have done to prepare to write the sketch, and then again with your efforts to turn your sketch into a more developed draft. Revision is literally "re-seeing," and every time you create the conditions that allow you to discover something new about how you see or what you think about your subject, you are, in fact, engaged in the act of revision. In a sense, then, each writing assignment you undertake is one long act of revision, from start to finish.

But once you've completed a draft, the revision process becomes more focused. You are mostly working with material that should be somewhat settled, with purposes that might be clearer, and ideas that may have more shape. At this point, the biggest temptation is tell yourself you are largely done and what revision remains is merely a matter of "fixing things"—tinkering with sentences, correcting typos, and running a spell-checker. In the survey from Chapter 1 (see page 20), 70 percent of students admitted as much. "I usually just tidy things up" was ranked first or second by students who were asked what they do most often when they revise an academic paper.

These activities are certainly an element of revision—and an important one—but as the word revision implies, it's important to "re-see" both what you are trying to say as well as how you try to say it, even at this stage in the process. Chapter 14, "Revision Strategies," is a useful introduction to the revision process for any essay, including the profile. It emphasizes ways writers can break the bonds that limit their ability to find new ways of seeing the draft.

Profiles typically have some of the following problems, most of which can be addressed by selecting appropriate revision strategies, or by repeating some of the earlier steps in this chapter.

- The draft lacks a single coherent theme, or dominant impression. Is your profile organized from beginning to end around one main thing you're trying to say about your subject?
- The theme or dominant impression is obvious but isn't developed with enough specific information. Do you need to do another interview?
- You find your subject interesting, but you haven't given your readers enough reason to agree. Does your lead make a strong enough case? Is there another story you should tell?

Refer to Chapter 14, "Revision Strategies," for ideas on how to revise your draft following your workshop. Use the accompanying table as a guide to the appropriate revision strategies for your draft, and remember that a draft may present problems in more than one category.

Polishing the Draft. After you've dealt with the big issues in your draft—is it sufficiently focused, does it answer the *So what?* question, is it organized, and so on—you must deal with the smaller problems. You've carved the stone into an appealing figure but now you need to polish it. Are your paragraphs coherent? How do you manage transitions? Are your sentences fluent and concise? Are there any errors in spelling or syntax? Section 5 of Chapter 14 can help you focus on these issues.

Before you finish your draft, work through the following checklist:

- Every paragraph is about one thing.
- The transitions between paragraphs aren't abrupt.
- The length of sentences varies in each paragraph.
- Each sentence is concise. There are no unnecessary words or phrases.
- You've checked grammar, particularly verb agreement, run-on sentences, unclear pronouns, and misused words (*there/their, where/were,* and so on). (See the handbook at the end of the book for help with these grammar issues.)
- You've run your spell-checker and proofed your paper for misspelled words.

GUIDE TO REVISION STRATEGIES		
Problems in the Draft (Chapter 14)	**Part**	**Page Number**
Unclear purpose ▪ Not sure what the essay is about? Fails to answer the *So what?* question?	1	603
Unclear thesis, theme, or main idea ▪ Not sure what you're trying to say?	2	609
Lack of information or development ▪ Needs more details; more showing and less telling?	3	616
Disorganized ▪ Doesn't move logically or smoothly from paragraph to paragraph?	4	620
Unclear or awkward at the level of sentences and paragraphs ▪ Seems choppy or hard to follow at the level of sentences or paragraphs?	5	626

STUDENT ESSAY

What impresses me most about the following profile is the way that Margaret Parker managed to write in a style that captures the intensity of her subject's experience during a single day as a medical student. The piece has a breathless, panicked quality that wonderfully matches the writer's purpose in the profile. The essay is also richly detailed, keeping our attention riveted on the subject throughout. An amazing thing about this is that Parker didn't actually witness the story she writes about; all of the material was gathered from her interviews (see "Selected Interview Notes: 'Medical Student,' " earlier in the chapter). Can you imagine what questions she must have asked to be able to write these scenes?

Medical Student

Margaret Parker

The Worst Day

1 Something is terribly wrong. For starters, she feels almost rested. The deep black pitch of the room has begun to soften into the gray light of dawn. JD's stomach plummets as she sees the glaring red numbers on her alarm clock.

2 *5:45 a.m. Ohmygodohmygodohmygod . . .*

3 She swears she set the alarm for 3:30 the night before, but it didn't go off. Rounds start at 6:30, but she's supposed to arrive at Olympia Fields Hospital by 5:00 a.m. to examine all her patients and prepare for the resident's inquisition at 6:30. There's no time to brush her teeth, eat, drink, think; she throws on some clothes, dives into her car and screams obscenities in the air throughout the frantic forty-five-minute drive. By some miracle she makes it to the hospital by 6:27. Ryan and Keith, the other third-year medical students on her surgery rotation team, cast disapproving glances tinged with terror in her direction.

4 Chief Resident Kelly saunters up to the students; even at this ungodly hour she is bright-eyed and menacing, ready for the kill. She assesses each of them with a consciously intimidating drawn-out glare, and once again displaying an uncanny instinct for sensing weakness in her prey, zones her attention on JD.

5 "Hey Student, tell me about Mrs. Gomez's labs."

6 The collective fear of the group is palpable. JD bites the bullet and replies the unthinkable, "I don't know."

7 Rage and disgust wash over Kelly's face. "You're all so pathetic," she says, and then turns and walks away. Rounds end early this morning; they have all failed.

8 Ryan won't even look at her he's so furious and even Keith snorts angrily and stomps off. If Keith thinks you're a loser, you know it must be true. The residents call him "Special K" because he suffers from obsessive-compulsive disorder and just about every other mental illness you can imagine. He hasn't been able to adapt to the turbo-intense lifestyle of the general surgery rotation. He'll show up to his scheduled surgery without his scrubs, ask the same question repeatedly, or simply disappear for hours at a time. On any other day the "team screw-up" award would invariably go to him, but on this hellish morning, JD has emerged the winner.

9 But there's no time to dwell. She has to go to the pre-op room and scrub in for surgery. This morning she will assist Dr. Donnelly, Chief Attending Surgeon, Kelly, and an OR nurse in the cholecystectomy of a sixteen-year-old girl. Donnelly isn't too worried about it; he told the girl's parents it would take two hours, max.

10 All scrubbed in and donning a surgical mask, cap, and scrubs, JD marches into the OR room where the others are already waiting for her. For just a split second, her hands fall below her waist, and she immediately corrects her stance and looks around to make sure no one has seen her slip. The OR nurse is fuming in her direction. It amazes JD how much emotion a person can express when half of her face is covered with a mask.

11 "Student get the hell outta here and rescrub! Jesus!" she booms throughout the room. Donnelly and Kelly roll their eyes and share a moment of mutual disgust.

12 JD can't believe she did this again, and on this morning of all mornings. Her first week of surgery was pure torture as she was constantly being thrown out of the OR for allowing her hands to drift out of the sacred "waist to shoulders" zone, but she's a sharp girl, and their scare tactics had effectively beat it into her. But her tardiness this morning has frazzled her nerves, and she's not herself.

She sucks in a deep breath, closes her eyes, and reenters the OR to begin the surgery. Donnelly has her position a long probe with a tiny camera attached to it into the patient's stomach so he can view what he is doing on a TV monitor. She must hold this position in complete stillness for the entire surgery. 13

The two-hour mark passes, and it becomes clear to all that the procedure is not going well. Donnelly starts swearing and muttering under his mask, and the tension in the room rises. Three and a half hours. Donnelly is seething; he just can't seem to get it right. He snaps at JD to turn the camera at a different angle; she does this. He barks at her to turn it again, just slightly to the right, and she complies. 14

Then he snaps. 15

"Student you've got it the wrong goddamn way!" he snarls at her, grabbing her arm and painfully bearing his fingers into her. He loses it, starts shaking her violently in spite of the instrument she is still holding inside the patient's stomach. Kelly and the nurse stare dumbly at them both. 16

Donnelly stops shaking her, composes himself and turns his focus back on the patient. The others emerge from their stupor and do the same. JD is dumbfounded. Should she leave, walk out? If she had an ounce of self-respect left she would. Who does this guy think he is? But she knows if she leaves, he'll fail her, and she's worked way too hard to fail now. 17

After five hours, the surgery is a success. Donnelly closes the patient up, and with the air of a god, swaggers out of the OR. Once he's outside and well out of earshot, Kelly whispers to JD conspiratorially: "Oh my God JD, don't worry about it . . . he's such a jerk." 18

For a split second, JD's eyes water over and she is touched by this rare display of kindness from the girl she calls "the demon." But it doesn't last. It dawns on her that Kelly hadn't said a word to Donnelly; she'd let him take it all out on the medical student to save her own ass. 19

Thank God for Ryan. He doesn't hold a grudge from this morning; he can't afford to. JD and Ryan barely knew each other before this rotation began, but war has a way of bonding soldiers together. They spend the hours between surgery and rounds seeking out hiding places in the hospital where they spew out all the crap they've had to deal with that day. As they whisper in a janitor's closet, a voice sounds over the hospital intercom: "Surgery extern report to OR-3, surgery extern, report to OR-3." 20

"Why do they call us 'externs'? That makes it sound like we get to go home," she laughs. 21

"Doesn't 'Special K' have surgery in 3 today?" Ryan asks. 22

"Oh crap," JD says. She knows what this means. There's a certain OR nurse who refuses to work with Keith. He simply lacks the Pavlovian response mechanism that allows creatures to learn from negative feedback; no matter how much she screams at him, he continues to touch his head in the OR and let his arms droop to his sides. But no one will tell Keith that he's been banned. Instead they page JD to fill in for him and leave Keith clueless. 23

JD jogs over to OR-3 where Keith is purposefully scrubbing in. As usual, no one
24 has told him. The OR nurse approaches JD. "Student, tell him he can't scrub in."

"Uh, Keith," she says, "why don't you go check on your patients' labs or something."

25 Keith looks crushed as the situation sinks in. He knows he is failing, and every
26 day he seems more and more unstable. He mutters some obscenity and storms off. JD
scrubs in for another five-hour procedure.

It's 8:00, almost time to go home. She's had nothing to eat or drink all day.
27 Surgeons severely limit their intake of liquids because they cannot under any
circumstances leave the OR to use the bathroom. Her urine is bloody from dehydration. After evening rounds are over, she slugs into the locker room to change back into her normal clothes. Keith is standing there, perfectly still, wearing ridiculously skin-tight scrubs.

28 "JD," he says in a faraway voice without looking at her, "do you have any trauma
scissors?"

29 "Sure," she says. "Why?"

30 "These scrubs are so tight," he says. "I don't know how I ever got into them.
Could you cut them off of me?"

31 JD ponders this for a moment, wondering if he has finally lost it completely.

32 "Sure, Keith." She starts at his feet and cuts a sliver all the way up to his neckline.
He peels them off like skin and stands before her in his boxers. An eerie, uncomfortable silence lingers between them. She gathers her things and leaves.

33 JD climbs into her car and starts the drive home. She starts crying, and soon her
whole body is heaving with sobs. As she drives on the busy Chicago streets, the thought that's been pestering her mind like a virus since she began the surgery rotation returns to her. She fantasizes about swerving off the road—oh, not to die, really, just to be injured enough to not have to go back to that hellhole tomorrow. She doesn't want to be a doctor anymore, not if this is what it is really like. If she weren't $75,000 in debt, she would drop out right now and never look back. It's almost 9:00. In six and a half hours it will all begin again.

Evaluating the Essay

1. How does Margaret Parker craft the essay to give it the panicked, breathless feeling that contributes so much to her overall profile of JD? What does she do at the sentence and paragraph level that gives it those qualities?
2. "Medical Student" focuses on a single day. In what other ways might you use time to help you organize and focus a profile?
3. Like many profiles, "Medical Student" focuses on a single person as part of an effort to give the reader a glimpse at a category of people (med students) or experiences (internships at hospitals). Is there a danger of overgeneralizing from a specific case? How do writers avoid that?
4. If the essay were to continue, what else would you want to know or see about JD and the life she leads?

Using What You Have Learned

You've read published profiles and one written by a student. You've also had the chance to write your own. What have you learned about the profile genre of writing and how might you use this in other writing situations?

1. What are the ethical obligations of writers to their profile subjects? For example, do you think it should be standard practice for subjects to approve profiles before they're published? What is reasonable for a profile subject to expect from a writer?
2. While a profile isn't an academic form, can you imagine how you might use some of the methods and approaches you tried here in papers for other classes?
3. A profile of one person who is representative of a larger social group is decidedly unscientific. It just isn't possible to make scientifically reliable generalizations about the group from a single case. Then what good is a profile?

French movie poster for *Amelie.*

A Stetson and a Smile

"Karl Tyler Chevrolet" reads the bold print on the plaque across the room. The fine print is much harder to read, but it seems irrelevant in light of the countless other awards and certificates surrounding it, all of them presented to the same organization. An expansive oak desk sprawls out in front of me, organized but full, with a lot of work piled on top of it. Western artwork dots the office, including a three foot bronze statue of a cowboy on a bronco, and a painting, mediocre at best hanging above me. I find myself relieved that I don't have to stare at it. I can only guess it has some personal meaning, like the numerous photos scattered about the brightly lit office.

A simple "Hello" breaks my concentration as Karl walks into the room. If you didn't already know him, his unsuspecting demeanor wouldn't lead you to guess he is the guy who belongs in this office. He is tall, always standing straight, with a firm handshake, and even firmer eye contact. The smile is always genuine, and a burgeoning beard spackles his face, as it always does when hunting season comes around. It has got a little more color than the rest of his hair, but the majority of it is gray. He is only now starting to show his age. The belt buckle is hard to miss, as are the Wranglers and boots. It is not the attire you would expect for the guy who belongs in this office. He is obviously as comfortable in the saddle as he is in the boardroom.

The sign outside the window says "Chevrolet" in big but simple letters, and I am reminded that he has three other offices just like this, at his dealerships throughout Idaho and Montana, as well as a massive cattle operation in Idaho. It is an impressive and intimidating thought. As his voicemail blinks an urgent red light at him, and his inbox spills over onto his desk, his attention turns to me.

"How's school?' he asks. I find myself grateful that he can take the time to sit down and talk to one of his 200-some employees like this. It is not what you would expect of the guy in this office. The interview quickly faded into nostalgic conversation.

Tyler grew up in exceptionally modest surroundings in eastern Idaho, and his great spiral upwards is something of a classic American success story. He came to love the cowboy lifestyle of his childhood, and it is a passion of his to this day, but he got his start in the car business washing cars at Wally Orvik Chevrolet in Moscow, Idaho in 1967. He worked his way up through the following years, trying his hand at sales, management, and all the facets of dealership business before finally becoming the owner of an Oldsmobile store in Colville, Washington in 1984. Only two years later he relocated to Missoula, where he opened Karl Tyler Chevrolet. It would become the flagship store of his Rocky Mountain auto empire.

Tyler's modest beginnings have created a policy of always putting the customer first. He embraces their role in his success. This conviction runs far and deep throughout his business. It transcends any policy or business model, and is simply habit for him and his employees. "Do the right thing now and it will pay great dividends down the road," he says matter-of-factly. Apparently, he is right. In any given month, this store can outsell all the other GM stores in Montana combined. It is not what you would expect of somebody in a business with such a notorious reputation for exploiting customers.

"There's nobody else like him in the car business," says Pete Kelly, an employee of 21 years. "He would never, ever take anything from anyone." Kelly says in reference to the industry's bad reputation. Perhaps the only thing more important to Tyler's business than his customers, are his employees. And there are over two hundred of them. Kelly is a perfect example of how Tyler's respect for an employee has created insurmountable loyalty. "I've never considered leaving, simply because of the man in charge," Kelly continues. The list of employees who have worked for Tyler's organization for ten years or more exceeds fifteen, and it grows every year.

"He leads by example. It's inspiring," says Jason Nordberg, a 17 year veteran and general manager of the Missoula store. When asked about Tyler, Nordberg, oddly enough, has a prepared list of words describing his boss which sitting under a pile of papers on his desk. It is almost as if he is tired of answering inquiries about the man. "Unselfish, commitment, loyalty," he reads, "work ethic, honesty, integrity…' The list goes on. Nordberg started as a part-time employee, while attending classes at the University of Montana, and through Tyler's stewardship, has grown to become the second in command. In talking with Tyler, it becomes obvious that he relishes the opportunity to form a bond with his employees, and hopes they treat their job not only as a paycheck, but a springboard to any thing they may aspire to. Several previous employees of the dealership have moved on to be successful in numerous other capacities. As our conversation draws to a conclusion, I cannot help but be inspired.

The simplicity of his style is remarkable. He speaks not in condescending proverbs or in academic run-ons, but in sagacious common sense. This unusually personal approach is what separates Tyler from his colleagues in the auto industry. "Always answer your phone," he says, "you never know who it could be." To this day he has customers from his Colville, Washington store calling to give him their business, and the wake of his loyalty is only spreading further. "Now if you'll excuse me, I have to go haul some cows," he says placing his black Stetson over his brow. I find myself again alone in his office.

As I step out into the showroom, an interesting juxtaposition is laid out before me in the small herd of elk mounts reflecting off the sparkling black sheen of a new Corvette. The scene perfectly illustrates Tyler's western charm and approach to business. There is a definite bustle about the cavernous room, with chuckles in the distance and employees' dogs wandering freely about. There is a small log cabin in the corner selling Wrangler's, and the tantalizing aroma of freshly popped pop corn mixes with the unmistakable scent of un-purchased tires. A quick stroll around the building will convince you that his approach is working.

The sign at Wally Orvik Chevrolet now has Karl Tyler's name on it, and just up the road from Leadore, Idaho, the gates to the KCK Angus ranch loom large over a tract of land extending from horizon to horizon. It is easy to imagine Mr. Tyler passing through these gates with a tip of his hat to the western sky and a smile on his face, because he knows he will sell cars 'till the cows come home. But these people don't come to buy cars from Chevrolet, they come to buy cars from Karl Tyler.

Using What You Have Learned

1. Think about the proposal draft you've written, and all those that you've read, both in this chapter and in your workshop group. Spend one minute answering, in writing, the following question: *What do you need to know to write an effective proposal?*
2. Draw a line down the middle of the page of your journal. Compare the proposal with another genre of writing you've tried in this book, looking specifically at the following:
   - degree of difficulty (which was harder, and why?)
   - audience awareness (when and how much did you consider who you were writing for?)
   - level of discovery (how much did you learn about your subject, or about yourself?)
   - application to other situations (how much and what might you use from this form of writing and apply in other writing situations?)
3. What approaches or ideas will you borrow from proposal writing that you can apply to other forms of writing and other writing situations? Can you imagine revising an essay you've already written in another genre using what you've learned here?

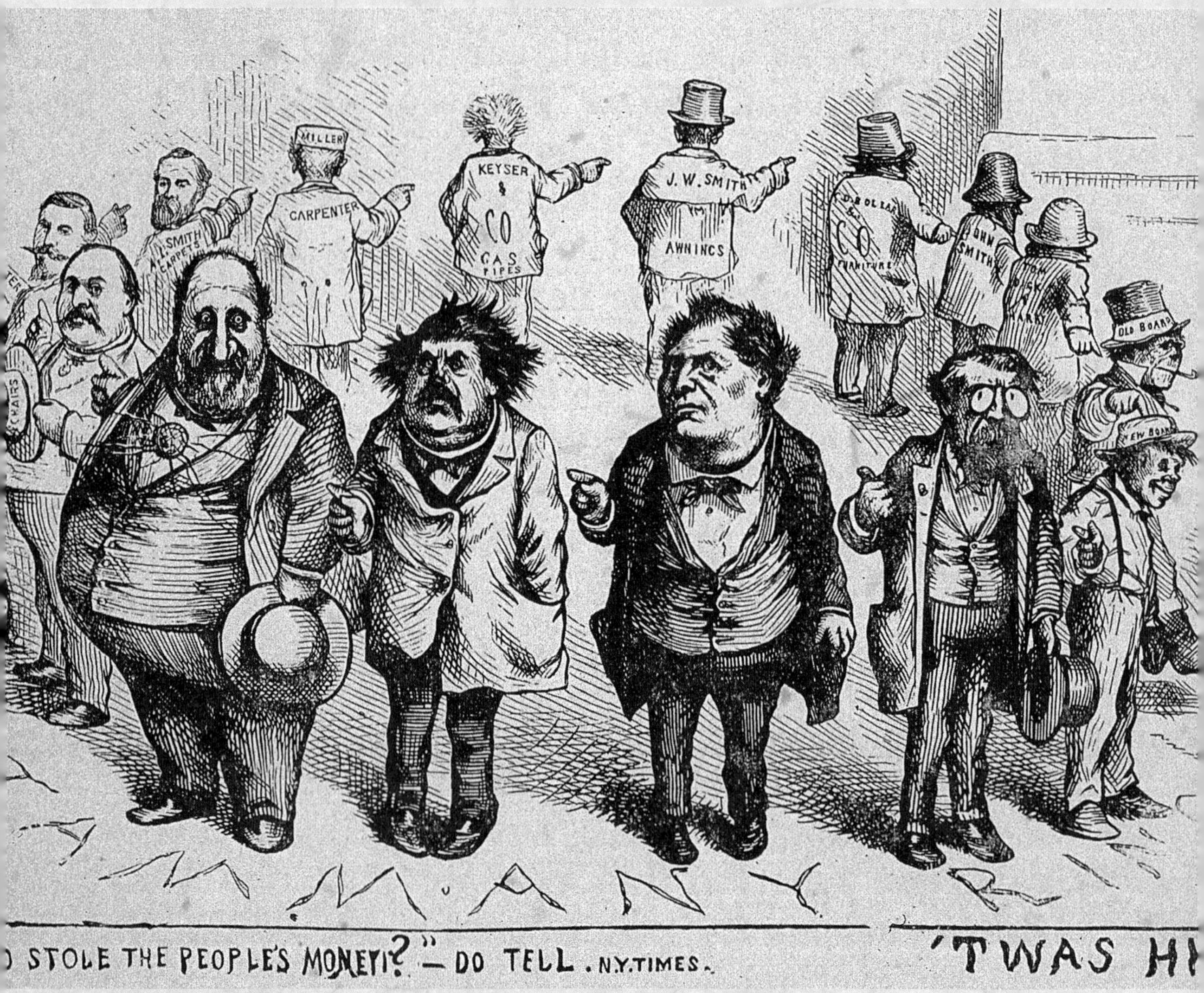

Tammany, a political machine that dominated New York City politics for nearly a hundred years, is lampooned here in an 1871 cartoon by Thomas Nast. The head of Tammany at the time was the corrupt William "Boss" Tweed. Testifying to the power of visual argument exemplified by Nash's cartoon, Tweed reportedly said "I don't care what the newspapers publish about me—most of my constituents can't read anyway. But them dam' pictures!—everybody can read them."

8

Writing an Argument

WRITING TO PERSUADE PEOPLE

Where I live, public arguments about wolf reintroduction, saving salmon, growing property taxes, and the need for a local community college are waged on the editorial pages of the local newspaper, *The Idaho Statesman*. The paper's editorials and so-called op-ed articles (short persuasive essays that are literally on the opposite page from editorials) present usually well-reasoned arguments of 250 to 600 words, but the real slugfest takes place in the letters to the editor. Reading letters to the editor is a form of recreation here. One correspondent complained a few years ago that the song "Rain, Rain, Go Away" was objectionable because it made her children dislike precipitation. Another letter writer, an angry animal rights activist, is a regular who always generates heated rebuttals here in cattle country. Last week, she railed about the evils of "Rocky Mountain oysters" (fried cattle testicles), which were served up at the Eagle Fire Department fund-raiser. I can't wait to see the responses to that one.

Letters to the editor, while an important opinion forum, frequently feature great examples of flawed arguments, including logical fallacies, poor reasoning, and a pitiful lack of audience awareness. In the hands of a good writer, however, a short persuasive essay like the op-ed can move people to think and act. It is a genre that attracts some of the best nonfiction writers in the country—Ellen Goodman, George Will, Bob Greene, Anna Quindlen, and others—but op-ed essays are also written by anyone with an idea about a public problem. Across the United States, newspapers and magazines publish the opinion pieces of ordinary citizens, and these essays are among our liveliest forums for public debate.

What You'll Learn in This Chapter

- New ways to understand the purpose of argument.
- Some differences between formal and informal arguments.
- The basic argument strategies most writers use.
- How to map an argument.
- How to avoid common logical fallacies.
- Revision strategies to fine-tune your argument.

While we often think of persuasive writing as stiff and formal, the op-ed essay is usually lively and engaging. Here's a sample of some opening lines from published op-ed pieces:

> Many of the hundreds of thousands of Hispanic demonstrators who poured out into the streets on Monday may not know much English, but they've learned the language of American politics: Flags. Tons of flags. And make them American.
>
> —"Immigrants Must Choose," Charles Krauthammer

> Maybe it was at the moment I found myself on my knees in my bathrobe, carefully prying tiny shards of paper out of the immobilized teeth of the shredder, that it finally hit me: The shredder had a paper jam. I had an info jam.
>
> —"C'mon, America, Fire Up Those Shredders," Lisa Johnston

> On the premise that spring is too beautiful for a depressing topic like Iraq, I thought I'd take up a fun subject—global warming.
>
> —"Global Warming: What Me Worry?" Molly Ivins

Persuasive essays like the op-ed are a great way to participate in public debates that affect your campus and community, and even your nation.

While these essays are often informal, they are still persuasive forms, and as you'll see later, they often employ the same methods of more formal arguments. However, unlike formal arguments—the kind you might write in a logic or philosophy course—persuasive essays of this kind have a much larger audience, and they are a great way to participate in public debates that affect your campus and community, and even your nation. In this chapter, you'll learn how to use some principles of argument to write persuasive essays like the op-ed that will give voice to things you care about, and that will increase the likelihood that voice will be heard.

Getting into Arguments

In 1990, the book *You Just Don't Understand* became a runaway best-seller. Written by Deborah Tannen, a linguistics professor, the book analyzed the range of ways in which men and women struggle to communicate with each other. *You Just Don't Understand* made its author famous, and before long she was on the talk show circuit and the subject of newspaper profiles. Despite the many benefits of this exposure, Tannen became increasingly disturbed by how some of the TV shows were orchestrated. Some producers "insisted on setting up a television show as a fight," pitting Tannen against the host or another guest. Newspaper reporters aggressively pursued Tannen's colleagues trying to get them to criticize the book, and some in her discipline obliged, often misrepresenting her work. This experience inspired her 1997 book, *The Argument Culture,* in which she claims that the pervasive "adversarial spirit" in American culture subverts cooperation and community, and reduces complex issues to opposing sides. "Approaching situations like warriors in battle," Tannen writes, "leads to the assumption that intellectual inquiry, too, is a game of attack, counterattack, and self-defense."

Tannen doesn't believe that arguments are things to be avoided, but maintains that there are other ways of approaching subjects that deserve more attention. While this seems like a reasonable position, it's hard to avoid the feeling that being a good debater is what counts most in academia. Yet is argument really "war"?

It sometimes seems that way. It certainly *felt* that way to me at the dinner table those many years ago when I'd walk away from an argument with my dad and feel angry and defeated. Yet my mom's side of the family is Italian American, and my best friends growing up came from predominantly Jewish households. In many of my relatives' and friends' homes, arguments were commonplace, raised voices the norm. At times I would find this upsetting, and wonder, "Why can't these people just get along?" But they often *were* getting along because argument and conflict in some cultures is an expression of commitment and caring. For example, Deborah Tannen notes that in many western European countries "agreement is deemed boring." I've often admired, for example, the French and Italian passion for national politics and their eagerness to share political views with each other, particularly disagreements. On the other hand, what Tannen calls "cultures of harmony," such as those of Japan and China, view open conflict and disagreement as a threat to the group. That does not mean that people always agree, but arguing is indirect, and sometimes undetectable to Western ears.

Obviously, culture influences our response to argument. In the United States, by and large, we argue a lot and in the open. We are a litigious society, and even children in the schoolyard threaten to "sue" each other. Combat metaphors are among the most common ways of talking about conflict—we attempt to "win" an argument, "find more ammunition" to support our position, "leap into the fray," or "attack" our opponent's position. It's hard for the gun-shy among us to feel comfortable participating in such verbal combat, one reason why some of my students retreat into silence when class discussion becomes the least bit combative.

For many of us, then, argument in civic and private discourse is bound by our *feelings* about argument—how comfortable we are with conflict, how confident we are in our ability to say what we think, and how strongly we feel about our opinions. These feelings are complicated by our beliefs about the purpose of argument. Sorting through these beliefs can help us discover new, perhaps more productive ways of approaching argument. Does argument make you uncomfortable? What do you consider a "good" argument? What is a "bad" argument?

Argument and Inquiry

There's often a tension between argument and inquiry. Most people see argument as a closed process—you already have strong opinions about something and therefore the task is to find support for existing beliefs (see Figure 8.1). In contrast, inquiry is an open-ended process. Your motive is not necessarily to simply reinforce existing opinions but to test your ideas against evidence or discover new ways of thinking about a topic.

Yet argument is an essential part of inquiry. When scientists seek to understand something about the way the world works, they often begin with a hypothesis—for

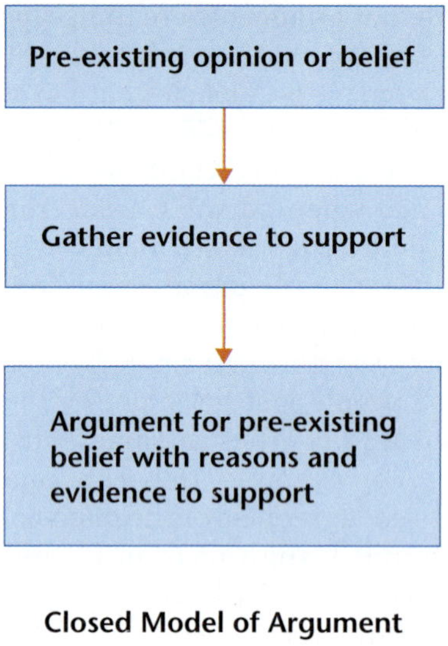

FIGURE 8.1 Many people consider argument to be a closed process like this model.

example, *the rate at which glaciers are melting in the Chilean Andes cannot be explained by natural cycles of atmospheric warming and cooling.* They then design an experiment to collect data that is meant to determine the truth of the hypothesis. That evidence may lead them in several directions: to believe the original hypothesis is true or false, or to consider yet another hypothesis that better explains the results (see Figure 8.2).

Argument can be a similar process of discovery—only instead of proposing hypotheses, you're making claims, testing their truth against what you learn from your research, observations, interviews, and experience.

Argument is also useful when you move from the initial open-ended investigation of your subject, discover what you think about it, and then want to convince others that your ideas are valid.

In the first case, you begin with a belief (hypothesis) and use the process of argument to reinforce the belief, revise it, or abandon it altogether. In the second case, you begin the process with no opinion about your subject, explore the issue to discover what you believe, and then build a case for it.

Making Claims

Arguments make claims, or assertions about which reasonable people might disagree. Argument expert Richard Fulkerson suggests that a claim (or *proposition,* to use his term) is a statement in which the response "I disagree" or "I agree" is a sensible reply. For example, "I have a headache" is a statement but not a claim because it would be goofy to agree or disagree with it.

Obviously, we make claims all the time: "Robert is a narcissist." "That textbook is boring." "Osama bin Laden misread the Qur'an." It is human nature to make

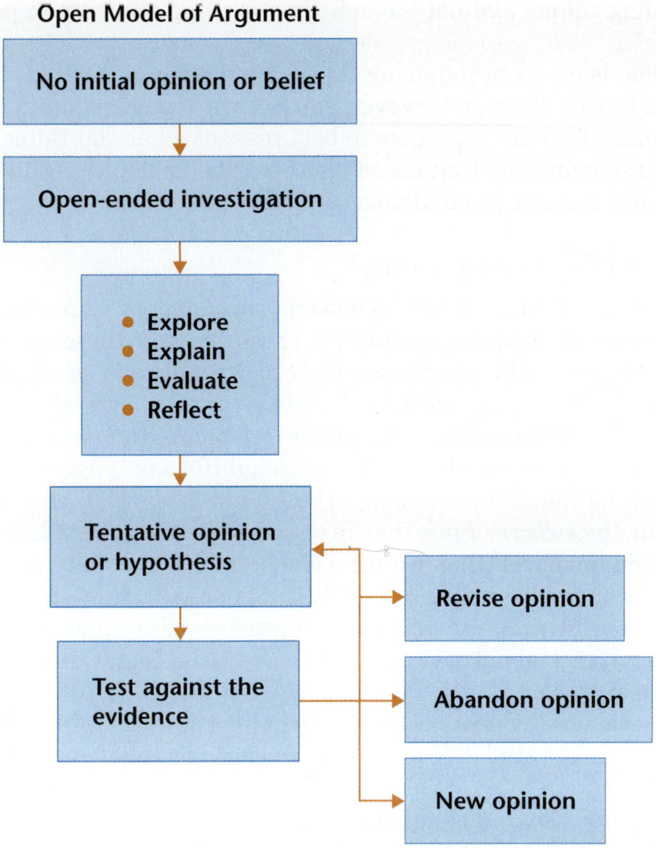

FIGURE 8.2 Inquiry-based argumentation favors the open process modeled here.

judgments, interpretations, and assertions about the people, things, and events that swirl around us. Since the beginning of this book, you have been encouraged to use evaluation as a way of inquiring as you responded to readings, images, your own work, and the work of others, asking questions such as, *What's my take on this? What do I find convincing? Do I see things any differently?* We usually describe this as the process of forming opinions.

But we rarely examine the *assumptions* or *reasons* that lurk behind these opinions or claims, those often shadowy ideas that provide the platform from which we make our assertions about the way things are. For example, if Robert is a narcissist, what does the speaker assume are the behaviors that qualify for such a label? In other words, what *definition* of narcissism seems to provide the basis for the claim about poor Robert? If bin Laden "misreads" the Qur'an, what does that assume about the "proper" reading of that holy text?

One way to discover these assumptions is to use the word *because* before or after the claim. For example, "That textbook is boring *because* it spends too much time explaining things and not enough time inviting students to participate in the learning."

Evaluation is a way of inquiring that is fundamental to all kinds of persuasive writing. In this chapter, however, you'll learn to use evaluation along with other techniques for analyzing how to best present what you think. You'll learn to *build* an argument. And that doesn't necessarily mean picking a side and then developing your case, as you'll discover in the next section.

Two Sides to Every Argument?

TV talk shows stage "discussions" between proponents of diametrically opposed positions. Academic debating teams pit those for and those against. We are nurtured on language like *win* or *lose, right* and *wrong,* and *either/or.* It's tempting to see the world this way, as neatly divided into truth and falsehood, light and dark. Reducing issues to two sides simplifies the choices. But one of the things that literature—and all art—teaches us is the delightful and nagging complexity of things. By inclination and upbringing, Huck Finn is a racist, and there's plenty of evidence in *Huckleberry Finn* that his treatment of Jim confirms it. Yet there are moments in the novel when we see a transcendent humanity in Huck, and we can see that he may be a racist, *but* . . . It is this qualification—this modest word *but*—that trips us up in the steady march toward certainty. Rather than *either/or,* can it be *both/and*? Instead of two sides to every issue, might there be thirteen?

Here's an example:

One side: General education requirements are a waste of time because they are often irrelevant to students' major goal in getting a college education—getting a good job.

The other side: General education requirements are invaluable because they prepare students to be enlightened citizens, more fully prepared to participate in democratic culture.

It's easy to imagine a debate between people who hold these positions, and it wouldn't be uninteresting. But it *would* be misleading to think that these are the only two possible positions on general education requirements in American universities. One of the reasons why people are drawn to arguing is that it can be a method of discovery, and one of the most useful discoveries is some side to the story that doesn't fall neatly into the usual opposed positions. The route to these discoveries is twofold: *initially withholding judgment* and *asking questions.*

For instance, what might be goals of a university education other than helping students get a good job and making them enlightened citizens? Is it possible that a university can do both? Are general education courses the only route to enlightenment? Are there certain situations in which the vocational motives of students are inappropriate? Are there certain contexts—say, certain students at particular schools at a particular point in their education—when general education requirements might be waived or modified?

All of these questions, and more, tend to unravel the two sides of the argument and expose them for what they often are: *starting points* for an inquiry into the question, *What good are general education requirements?*

To argue well is an act of imagination, not a picking of sides.

In presenting their arguments, then, the best argument essays make a clear claim, but they do it by bowing respectfully to the complexity of the subject, examining it from a variety of perspectives, not just two opposing poles. And you will come to appreciate that wonderful complexity by keeping an open mind.

MOTIVES FOR WRITING AN ARGUMENT

Classical rhetoricians like Plato, Aristotle, and Cicero had a great deal to say about how to argue well, and while their focus was largely on public speaking, their ideas are foundational for a modern understanding of argument. For Aristotle, there were three arenas for persuasion—before the courts, before legislators and others who make public policy, and at social occasions. The purpose of each varied. For example, court arguments involved defending or accusing someone, or arguing about past events; the purpose of legislative persuasion was to exhort or dissuade about a future action; and persuasion at social occasions focused on praise or blame, or arguments about the present.

Of course, there are plenty of other reasons to argue. In academic writing, the purpose of argument is usually to establish the truth of something. Modern advertising, the most common medium of modern persuasion, attempts to influence people's behaviors. Generally speaking, you can distinguish between these two purposes—to establish the validity of a certain way of seeing things and the desire to move people to action—but because the persuasive essay you will be writing in this chapter can do both, we won't make much of the distinction between these two purposes here.

Whatever its purpose, people often have quite strong feelings about arguing. Some of these feelings may originate, like mine, in negative experiences with a parent or other adult who seemed condescending when we expressed naive or poorly developed opinions. Some scholars maintain that *agonistic* forms of argument, or those that seem to emphasize the contest between ideas and those who hold them, are particularly masculine approaches because they focus on power rather than cooperation, and proclaiming rather than listening. Yet some people have always loved arguing. My father did, and not just because he was confident in the game; my father genuinely enjoyed matching wits and logic, looking for faulty reasoning or indefensible claims.

Arguing is a civic duty. In fact, it is an essential activity in any democratic culture, and it's certainly a major element of academic discourse; academic argument is one of the key means of making new knowledge. Argument is also commonplace in relationships. Who hasn't argued with a spouse, a partner, a friend? In fact, one Web site on the Internet sponsored by the magazine *Psychology Today,* http://psychologytoday.psychtests.com/tests/arguing_style_r_access.html, offers an arguing style test that analyzes how constructive you are in dealing with relationship conflicts. Therapists and counselors share the conviction that arguing is a natural part of intimate relationships and that much more harm can come from *avoiding* conflict rather than facing it. It's all in *how* you do it, they say.

Knowing how to argue well has practical value, even if you don't become a lawyer. It might help you make the best case to a local legislator to support the bill providing tuition relief to students, or even bargaining with the used-car dealer for a better price on that black convertible Mazda Miata. Understanding argument helps you find the flaws in *other people's* arguments as well. Knowing how to analyze an argument gives me a language to talk about the flawed arguments in the letters to the editor in *The Idaho Statesman,* and it also helps me thoughtfully and critically read articles and essays that make claims.

Finally, the most important motive behind writing and studying argument is that you care about something. Throughout this book, I've argued that the personal motive for writing is the most powerful one of all; in this case, you're passionate about a question or an issue, and building a written argument channels that passion into prose that can make a difference.

THE ARGUMENT AND ACADEMIC WRITING

Argumentative writing is one of the most common of all academic forms. One reason for this is that the ability to argue well requires some command of subject matter. But there is another motive for mastering argument in academic settings, however, and it has less to do with proving that you know your stuff. Argument is really about trying to get at the truth.

This is an open-ended as well as a closed process; it involves suspending judgment *and* coming to conclusions, hearing what has already been said *and* discovering what you think. Dialectical thinking—a process you've applied to all kinds of writing in *The Curious Writer,* from the personal essay to the proposal—is just as useful in crafting an argument. It will help you discover what you think, consider other points of view, and shape your work so it's convincing to others. The dialectical process, along with those habits of mind central to academic inquiry—particularly suspending judgment and tolerating ambiguity—will help you as a writer get to the truth of things as you see it.

Argument is an essential activity in any democratic culture, and it's certainly a major element of academic discourse; academic argument is one of the key means of making new knowledge.

In college, the audiences for your arguments are often your instructors. As experts in a particular discipline, professors argue all the time. They're not simply trying to be contrary but trying to get at the truth. Arguing is the main way that the academic community makes knowledge.

Notice I used the word *make.* While it often seems that the facts we take for granted are immutable truths—as enduring as the granite peaks I can see through my office window—things aren't often that way at all. Our knowledge of things—how the planet was formed, the best ways to save endangered species, the meaning of a classic novel, how to avoid athletic injuries—are all ideas that are *contested.* They are less mountains than the glaciers that carved them, and in some cases the sudden earthquakes that bring them down. The primary tool for shaping and even changing what we know is argument.

Richard Fulkerson writes that he "wants students to see argument in a larger, less militant, and more comprehensive context—one in which the goal is not victory, but a good decision, one in which all arguers are at risk of needing to alter their views, one in which a participant takes seriously and fairly the views different from his or her own." This is how I'd like you to approach argument within the persuasive essay. This form will challenge you to make arguments that might be convincing to a range of readers, including those who might not agree with your claims. The argument essay is also an invitation to consider how you feel about local issues and controversies as well as national or even international debates that might have some effect on how you live.

FEATURES OF THE FORM

Generally speaking, persuasive writing can take many forms. Indeed, reviews and proposals, two essays addressed earlier in this book, both represent different types of persuasive writing. The argument essay we are covering in this chapter, however, more obviously embodies persuasive writing than either of these two other forms. This essay typically makes explicit claims and backs them up with hard evidence. It also employs the well-established rhetorical devices and the reasoning of formal argumentation in the effort to sway readers to its point of view. However, unlike more formal academic papers, the argument you'll be writing in this chapter is intended for a more general audience. It's the kind of piece you might see in your local newspaper, or in a magazine. *Newsweek*'s "My Turn" column is an excellent example. (See Figure 8.3 for a comparison of argument essays.)

Rhetorical Context	Academic Argument Essay	Informal Argument Essay
Audience	Academic discourse community	Publication's readers
Speaker	You as a member of above	You as an authority on subject
Purpose	To demonstrate your authority	To make something happen
Subject	Of academic interest	Of community interest
Voice	Conventional, academic	Personal, informed
Research	Always	Usually
Citations	Yes	No
Length	Varies, usually 8–25 pages	Varies, usually 500–1,000 words
How to read	Slowly, thoughtfully	Rapidly, mining for meaning

FIGURE 8.3 A comparison of academic and informal argument. (Devan Cook, Boise State University.)

Here are some the features of the informal argument essay:

- *Op-ed essays are often relatively brief treatments of a topic.* Readers of newspapers and many magazines read fast. They want to quickly get the gist of an essay or article and move on to the next story. In addition, space is often limited, particularly in newspapers. As a result, the op-ed or opinion piece rarely exceeds 1,000 words, or about four double-spaced manuscript pages. Longer arguments may be harder to write because you have to provide deeper analysis of your key claims and more evidence, but don't underestimate the difficulty of writing persuasive essays like the op-ed. They must be concise, direct, and well-crafted.
- *Subject matter often focuses on issues of public concern.* The magazines and newspapers that publish argument essays typically report on news, events, or issues that might affect a lot of people. Not surprisingly, then, writers of these essays are keen observers of public debates and controversies. While a nationally syndicated essayist such as George Will may write about the federal budget deficit or the need for more troops in Iraq, a locally grounded writer may focus on an issue affecting a university campus, city hall, or state government, although sometimes writers find a local angle on a national controversy.
- *An op-ed piece has a central claim or proposition.* Sometimes we also call this a *thesis,* a term that's a holdover from the scientific terminology that dominated American scholarship from the end of the nineteenth century. Classical arguments, the kind many of us wrote in high school, usually state this central claim or thesis in the introduction. But many arguments, particularly op-ed essays that rely on narrative structure or explore the answer to a question or problem, may feature the thesis in the middle or at the end of the essay.
- *The central claim is based on one or more premises or assumptions.* You already know something about this from the discussion earlier in the chapter. Basically, a premise suggests that something is true *because* of something else; it expresses the relationship between *what* you claim and *why* you believe that claim to be true. This is discussed at greater length later in the chapter.
- *The op-ed essay relies on evidence that a general audience will believe.* All arguments should use evidence appropriate for a particular audience. Academic writers in marine biology, for example, rely on data collected in the field and analyzed statistically because this kind of evidence is most persuasive to other marine biologists. Anecdotes or personal observation alone simply won't cut it in the *Journal of Marine Biology.* But the persuasive essay's more general audience finds a greater range of evidence convincing, including personal experience and observation. Writers of persuasive essays are likely to do the kind of research you

use to write research papers—digging up statistics, facts, and quotations on a topic.

- *Op-ed essays sometimes invite or encourage a response.* Earlier I noted a broad distinction between the purposes of argument: (1) to establish the validity of a writer's way of seeing what's true and (2) to move or persuade an audience to act a certain way. The second purpose is most obvious in the advertisement, which is a visual argument that asks viewers to *do* something—buy a Jeep or change toilet bowl cleaners. But op-ed essays sometimes ask for or imply a course of action readers should take. An op-ed piece might attempt to change the views and behaviors of political leaders, or influence how people vote for them. It might urge support for a school bond issue, or encourage fellow students to protest against the elimination of an academic program. But even academic articles invite reader response in several ways: they encourage other scholars to examine some part of the question that wasn't addressed by the present research, or they offer claims that can be contested in other articles. Put simply, most argumentative forms are out to change people's behavior and attitudes.
- *Readers won't respond unless they know what's at stake.* An essential element of argument is establishing why a certain action, policy, or idea *matters.* How will opposition to the administration's strip-mining policies in West Virginia and Kentucky make a difference in the quality of life in those states, but even more important, why should someone in Boise, Idaho, care? The best arguments are built to carefully establish, sometimes in quite practical terms, how a certain action, belief, or idea might make a difference in the lives of those who are the argument's audience.

ARGUMENT

Ellen Goodman, whose op-ed essays appear in more than 375 newspapers nationwide, often writes about the intersection between public events and her personal life, and the following essay, "Getting Real in the Classroom," is no exception. While her essay, like many, is sparked by the release of a new public report—in this case on the challenges boys face in the classroom—she finally bends her discussion towards her own grandchildren. What Goodman concludes from watching her granddaughter, 4, and grandson, 3, is that "differences among boys and among girls are greater than the differences between boys and girls." A sharply honed line like that is typical of Goodman's writing. But so is the clarity of her reasoning. In the essay that follows, notice how much time she takes to come to conclusions about the issue. Along the way, she assembles evidence that unravels the argument that there is a "boy crisis" in schools, preparing us for her argument that the underperformance of boys is not really the problem.

Getting Real in the Classroom

Ellen Goodman

1 Too bad the study came out during summer vacation. We tend to forget whatever we learned by the time school rolls around again. But there's something worth retaining over the long, lazy days: The "boy crisis" in education is not what it was cranked up to be.

2 Let's go to the videotape. The first salvo in the battle of the classroom sexes probably came six years ago with the publication of "The War Against Boys." Christina Hoff Sommers's screen opened with the dire warning: "It's a bad time to be a boy in America."

3 Since then, things have gone from "bad" to worse. We've had documentaries and cover stories, psychologists and sociologists, scholars and ideologues offering a horror story of boys in academic free-fall.

4 On the seesaw of this school playground, the message is that as girls went up, boys went down. The social changes that were good for the goose were bad for the gander. The common wisdom is that boys have fallen behind. Behind girls.

5 The causes and cures for the boy crisis are all over the map. The problem is either feminism that demonizes boyishness, or sexism that boxes boys in. It's either nature that hard-wires the boy brain to learn differently, or nurture that creates what has been called a "biologically disrespectful model of education." It's that boys need more discipline, or less.

6 Last December, Doug Anglin, a senior from Milton High School in Massachusetts, filed a lawsuit claiming sex discrimination in the whole system. "If you sit down, follow orders and listen to what they say, you'll do well and get good grades," he complained. "Men naturally rebel against this." (Where? In the Army?)

7 Now a Washington think tank, the Education Sector, has performed a crisis intervention. "The real story," it reports, "is not bad news about boys doing worse; it's good news about girls doing better." Using data from the National Assessment of Educational Progress—a.k.a. "the nation's report card"—the report found that girls score higher in reading and writing and boys score higher in math and science. But girls are closing the math gap faster than boys are closing the writing gap. It turns out that boys aren't doing worse in school. They are doing better than ever. But girls—with apologies to the grammar police—are doing more better.

8 In college, too, more men than ever are enrolling, but at a slower pace than women. Women do get 57 percent of the bachelor's degrees—including a large number of older women returning to school—but the gap at traditional four-year colleges is much less and, let us remember, boys are still a majority in the Ivy League.

9 The "boy crisis" isn't exactly a myth, says Sara Mead, author of the report. It's a "some boys crisis." Race and class are the real issues. In Boston, for example, 100 white males graduate for every 104 white females. But 100 black males graduate for 139 black females. "It's sexier to think about gender," says Mead. "It's something people like debating." Americans, she fears, "have gotten used to thinking poor and minority students do poorly in school. Whereas if you hear that boys are doing worse, it's startling." Especially to the middle-class object of this anxiety attack.

As the besotted grandmother of a 4-year-old girl and a 3-year-old boy, I'm not about to deny gender differences. Moreover, I'm uneasy about the massive drugging of little boys for whatever is labeled attention deficit disorder. And we know too little about the different pace of development or the meaning of new brain research. I also worry that something in the culture is teaching poor Hispanic and African-American boys that being smart isn't masculine. Remember when being smart wasn't feminine? Is that message percolating up through the boy culture? 10

But in the same grandmother role, I see that differences among boys and among girls are greater than differences between boys and girls. And I don't think the "boy crisis" should let us stop worrying about why girls lose their interest in math or why women with those bachelor's degrees still earn less than their male counterparts. 11

Last week, there was some good news from New York, a city with a high school graduation rate of only 58 percent. The 15 small schools started in the city in an experiment posted a graduation rate of 73 percent. Could size and personal attention matter more than gender? 12

The battle of the sexy ideas is a distraction from the struggle for the minds of the younger generation. We need to worry more about children one by one. And less about whether boys are losing their place at the head of the class. 13

Inquiring into the Essay

Explore, explain, evaluate, and reflect about "Getting Real in the Classroom."

1. The performance of boys versus girls in school is a topic you already know something about, though you probably haven't thought about it much. After all, you're either a boy or girl and you've spent years in school. In your journal, explore your own experience of the ways you've noticed gender matters in school. As a boy, or as a girl, were you discouraged from doing or achieving something academically? Were there ever moments that you felt being one sex or the other gave you certain advantages or disadvantages? Fastwrite about this. If you can, begin with a story. At the end of five to seven minutes, skip a line, and compose an answer to this question: *Based on your experience in school, how would you respond to the claim that boys in school are falling behind partly because girls are advancing?*
2. Analyze Goodman's argument and explain two things: her main claim(s) and the premises or assumptions behind it (them). To refresh your memory about these terms and what they mean, consult "Features of the Form" earlier in the chapter. What basic argument strategies does Goodman seem to use? (See the "Inquiring into the Details: Some Basic Argument Strategies" box.)
3. A critic of Goodman's argument here might claim that she's being hypocritical. When girls were academically behind, the women's movement made much about how gender was a factor in their performance. Teachers, for example, were said to discourage girls from pursuing science

while encouraging boys. Now Goodman is too quick to dismiss arguments that gender is a factor in boys' scholastic performance, and that seems unfair. How would you evaluate this claim?

4. Do at least one more full reading of the essay, from beginning to end. While you do, pay attention to what you notice in the essay while rereading it that you didn't really notice in earlier readings. How does your own opinion about an author's argument influence the way you reread it? Do you read more selectively? Does the rereading reinforce what you already think or challenge it in some way?

Inquiring into the Details

SOME BASIC ARGUMENT STRATEGIES

- **Argument from Generalization:** What I've seen or observed of a particular group is true of the group as a whole. *Risk: Are you sure that what you've observed is typical of the larger population?*
- **Argument from Analogy:** If it is true in one situation it's likely true in another similar situation. *Risk: Are the situations* really *similar?*
- **Argument from Cause:** If one thing always seems present with something else, then one probably causes the other. *Risk: Is cause and effect* really *the relationship between the two things?*
- **Argument from Authority:** If an expert said it, it's true. *Risk: Is the expertise of the authority* really *relevant to the question at issue?*
- **Argument from Principle:** This general principle (which most of us agree with) applies in this case. *Risk: Is there* really *agreement on the rightness of the principle, and does it actually apply in this specific context?*

Adapted from Richard Fulkerson, *Teaching the Argument in Writing*. Urbana, IL: National Council of Teachers of English, 1996.

ARGUMENT

With grace and intelligence, conservative columnist George F. Will writes about a range of topics from the federal budget to baseball. In this essay, Will strikes close to home for me—and possibly for you, too—when he sharply criticizes writing instruction in the United States, an approach he calls the "growth model," one that Will argues offers no "defensible standards" for good writing and emphasizes the "undirected flowering of the student's personality." He bemoans the absence of instruction in grammar and style.

You are the students Will is talking about in this op-ed essay. Does he accurately describe your experience in this and other writing classes? For example, do you also sense that process matters more than content in composition? Do you agree with Will's basic premise that students graduating from high school are "functionally illiterate"?

THE "GROWTH MODEL" AND THE GROWTH OF ILLITERACY

George F. Will

Summertime, and the living is easy. Schools are empty, so the damage has stopped. During this seasonal respite from the education system's subtraction from national literacy, consider why America may be graduating from its high schools its first generation worse educated than the generation that came before. Particularly, why is it common for high school graduates to be functionally illiterate, uncertain when reading, and incapable of writing even a moderately complicated paragraph? 1

Heather Mac Donald knows one reason: More and more schools refuse, on the basis of various political and ethical and intellectual theories, to teach writing. Her essay, "Why Johnny Can't Write," in the summer 1995 issue of *The Public Interest* quarterly, is a hair-raising peek into what she calls "one overlooked corner of the academic madhouse." 2

Mac Donald, a contributing editor of the Manhattan Institute's *City Journal*, explains how the teaching of writing has been shaped by "an indigestible stew of 1960s liberationist zeal, 1970s deconstructionist nihilism, and 1980s multicultural proselytizing." Indeed many teachers now consider the traditional idea of teaching to be intellectually suspect and morally offensive because it is tainted by the authoritarian idea that there are defensible standards and by the inegalitarian idea that some people do things better than others. 3

At a 1966 conference organized by the Modern Language Association and the National Conference of Teachers of English, the "transmission model" of teaching composition was rejected in favor of the "growth model." The idea of transmitting skills and standards was inherently threatening to the values of that decade—spontaneity, authenticity, sincerity, equality, and self-esteem. Education in the new era of enlightenment was to be not a matter of putting things into students—least of all putting in anything that suggested a hierarchy of achievement—but of letting things out. Nothing must interfere with the natural, undirected flowering of the student's personality. One interference would be a teacher cast as an authority figure rather than in the role of supportive, nurturing friend. 4

The "growth model" was, Mac Donald notes, impeccably liberationist: Who was to judge anyone else's "growth"? And that model "celebrated inarticulateness and error as proof of authenticity." This was convenient for evolving racial policies. In 1966 the City University of New York began the first academic affirmative action program. Open admissions would soon follow, as would the idea that it is cultural imperialism to deny full legitimacy to anything called "Black English." Simultaneously came the idea that demands for literacy oppress the masses and condition them to accept the coercion of capitalism. 5

"Process" became more important than content in composition. Students would "build community" as they taught each other. A reactionary emphasis on the individual was replaced by a progressive emphasis on the collectivity. But, says Mac Donald, 6 there have been difficulties: "Students who have been told in their writing class to let their deepest selves loose on the page and not worry about syntax, logic, or form have trouble adjusting to other classes." Thus a student at St. Anselm's College complains that in her humanities class, "I have to remember a certain format and I have to back up every general statement with specific examples."

7 Academic fads have followed hard upon one another, all supplying reasons why it is unnecessary—no, antisocial—to teach grammar and style. The deconstructionists preached that language is of incurably indeterminate meaning. The multiculturalists, who preach the centrality of identity politics in every endeavor, argue that the rules of language are permeated by the values of the dominant class that makes society's rules and also makes victims. Mac Donald says, "The multicultural writing classroom is a workshop on racial and sexual oppression. Rather than studying possessive pronouns, students are learning how language silences women and blacks."

8 As student writing grows worse, Mac Donald notes, the academic jargon used to rationalize the decline grows more pompous. For example, a professor explains that "postprocess, postcognitive theory . . . represents literacy as an ideological arena and composing as a cultural activity by which writers position and reposition themselves in relation to their own and others' subjectivities, discourses, practices, and institutions."

9 Nowadays the mere mention of "remedial" courses is coming to be considered insensitive about "diversity," and especially insulting and unfair to students from American "cultures" where "orality" is dominant. So at some colleges remedial courses are now called ESD courses—English as a Second Dialect.

10 The smugly self-absorbed professoriate that perpetrates all this academic malpractice is often tenured and always comfortable. The students on the receiving end are always cheated and often unemployable. It is summertime, and the nation is rightly uneasy about autumn.

INQUIRING INTO THE ESSAY

Use the four methods of inquiry to think about Will's essay.

1. For five minutes, fastwrite about your own experience with writing instruction by telling the story of the teacher or teachers that had the most impact on how you think about yourself as a writer and reader.
2. Describe the argument that Will makes in this essay. Begin with a summary of one of his basic claims, then a reason behind the claim, and then list the evidence he offers to support them both. Compare these with other students in the class and analyze the effectiveness of Will's argument. What are the strongest elements of his argument? The weakest?
3. Compose a 250-word letter to the editor that responds in some way to Will's article.

4. Reflect on your own experiences in this composition course. Would Will be scornful of this course—and perhaps this text—and its approach to teaching writing? What have been the most and least effective approaches to teaching reading and writing that you've experienced in high school, or perhaps even in this class?

ARGUMENT

When Erin Aubry Kaplan was hired by *The Los Angeles Times* to be one of their regular columnists, it was a historic move; unlike most other major metropolitan newspapers, the *Times* had never employed an African American op-ed writer. While her work often focuses on issues of race, a relevant topic in such a diverse city as Los Angeles, Kaplan has also written on the arts, parenting, and other topics. Her early personal essay, "Blue Like Me," on race and depression, won Kaplan an award for literary journalism, and she was runner-up recently for Los Angeles Columnist of the Year.

In the essay that follows, Kaplan writes about the "politics of hair." She condemns the move by some corporations and even black colleges to enforce bans on certain kinds of hairstyles, especially those like dreadlocks and braids, that these institutions see as "threatening." The essay is built on a number of assumptions, one of which is that there is, in fact, a "politics of hair," particularly for African Americans, and that this is closely tied to feelings about racial identity. Do you share this assumption?

Still Trying to Kick the Kink

Erin Aubry Kaplan

When I was young, one of the first things I learned about myself was that I had "good" hair. It was curly and close enough to the texture of a white person's hair to not need pressing, hot-combing, greasing or some other method of straightening that extremely curly black hair—also known as kinky or "bad" hair—needed before it could venture out in public. Yet even my hair was not quite good enough. 1

Every Sunday my mother washed it, set it on rollers the size of frozen orange-juice cans and put me under a hairdryer for a couple of hours. When it was over, I had the ultimate "do"—smooth and swingy, with none of the wayward curl or frizz that would have confirmed my blackness as much as the Marlo Thomas look cleverly denied it. 2

I eventually learned early that this "denial" look was the ideal for black girls and women, and though I had to do less denying than most, I was not exempt. I also learned that good hair on black people was considered good for reasons much deeper than convenience—it connoted assimilation, sophistication, intelligence, refinement, success. Even when I jettisoned the whole hair ritual and got a short, punky cut, I did it more to reject the limitations of an old paradigm than to celebrate a new one. 3

I might have saved my protest. Denial is still at the core of black hair fashion, which in turn is at the still-unstable core of black identity and acceptability in the United States 4 in 2006. Although braids, dreadlocks and other natural black hairstyles have become more visible, perms, weaves and extensions for black women have become ubiquitous.

5 In short, the debate about the best choices for "black hair," always charged, is flaring up again. A Louisiana sheriff said last week that anyone on the streets in dreadlocks "can expect to be getting a visit from a sheriff's deputy" because a murder suspect answering that description remained at large. In April, Susan L. Taylor, the iconic editorial director of *Essence* magazine, canceled a campus speech when she discovered the college forbids its students to wear "unusual" hairstyles—including braids, which are Taylor's signature look. This was noteworthy because the college was Hampton University, one of the nation's oldest historically black campuses. Then it was discovered that *Black Enterprise* magazine had a similar ban for student interns.

6 The message is clear. If blacks want to have a chance in the increasingly unforgiving corporate world, they will have to shave off their edges—starting with their hair. To Taylor and to many others, including me, such a message implies a false choice between assimilation and self-affirmation. What looks like practicality is, in fact, more denial.

7 What's troubling is that, by being forced to change their hair, black people once again are being forced to shoulder the burden of proof: We're not as fearsome as we look. It's up to us to mitigate our dark skin and ethnic features by framing them with hair that's as neat and unethnic as possible.

8 That the requirement comes from black institutions only makes it more disturbing. Yes, they are inherently conservative institutions, but they understand the political significance of hair. They should know that this is not the same as a dress code that calls for a suit and tie (understandable), or a Cosby-like antipathy toward trendy, sloppy, vaguely criminal black fashion such as baggy pants or expensive sneakers (understandable, but misplaced).

9 Unlike any of those looks, braids and other natural styles have long been associated with socially conscious and self-confident black people, the kind who would fit nicely in corporate settings that like to say diversity is a priority. But companies tend not to hire them, and black people with those hairstyles tend to gravitate toward work that's necessarily non-corporate. Yet surely we have all earned the right to wear our hair as we please. The freedom we're still working toward is supposed to be aesthetic as well as economic.

10 Mablean Ephriam, the black TV judge from Fox's popular "Divorce Court"—who says she lost her contract this year partly because of irreconcilable hair differences with the company—perhaps said it best in a contentious parting statement that concluded with a quote from Maya Angelou: "And still I rise." I trust she meant her hair.

Inquiring into the Essay

Explore, explain, evaluate, and reflect on Kaplan's essay.

1. You don't have to be an African American to feel that there are social meanings to certain hairstyles. Explore your own experience with this. Tell yourself a story about a time in your life when you were most interested in what your hair said about you, or when you witnessed the effects of the "politics of hair." Fastwrite for five minutes in your notebook, and

then skip a line, and compose an answer to the following question: *Based on your experience, would you agree with the assumption that there is a "politics of hair," and that this is something worth being concerned about?*

2. In the beginning of the essay, Kaplan concedes that there was a time when she engaged in the "denial look," or styling her hair to present a muted racial identity. How does this concession affect the persuasiveness of her essay? Explain what impact a writer's concession that she might be a part of the problem she's discussing has on the strength of her argument. When might such concessions be unnecessary?
3. I mentioned earlier that one assumption behind this essay is that hairstyles do have political and social meanings. Evaluate Kaplan's argument by identifying other assumptions on which her essay rests. Are there any of these that most readers might not necessarily agree with? Should these, if any, have been explicitly discussed to make her argument more persuasive?
4. If you're not African American or a minority of any kind, reading an essay like this one can be challenging because it might feel presumptuous to believe that you truly understand the Other's experience. Did you feel this way reading Kaplan's essay? How does one bridge this gap when encountering readings from writers of other races or other cultures?

Seeing the Form

THE "IMAGETEXT" AS ARGUMENT

While model Kate Moss is likely disturbed by the appropriation of her image by advocates in the pro-anorexia ("pro-ana") movement, Moss's picture along with those of other celebrities such as Calista Flockhart, Mary-Kate Olsen, and Keira Knightley appear as "thinspiration" on Web sites that argue that eating disorders are a "lifestyle choice," not a disease. Some of these images (though not this one) are digitally altered to make the models seem even thinner than they really are. In a recent article on the "imagetexts" used by these controversial Web sites, Robin Jensen observes that images rarely argue in isolation, a phenomenon that is particularly relevant to the Web, which often combines pictures and verbal texts. Jensen notes that when pictures like this one of Kate Moss are given a new "visual frame," quite different from the one originally intended, the meaning of the picture can be manipulated. Imagine, for instance, that the Kate Moss photograph appeared in a "thinspiration" gallery of celebrity photographs on a "pro-ana" Web site, and included the following caption: "Maintaining a weight that is 15 percent below your expected body weight fits the criteria for anorexia, so most models, according to medical standards, fit into the categeory of being anorexic." Analyze this "imagetext" rhetorically. How does this picture of Moss combined with the caption serve the purpose of the "pro-ana" movement? What message is it meant to convey and is it persuasive to its intended audience?

Kate Moss in ultra-thin pose.

THE WRITING PROCESS

INQUIRY PROJECT: Writing an Argument

Now that you've explored various approaches to persuasion and argument, try your hand at writing an argument essay. Remember that these are brief (700- to 1,000-word) essays meant for a general audience. Imagine, for example, that you're writing an op-ed piece for the campus newspaper, the local daily, or *The New York Times.* Your essay should be lively and logical, with a strong personal voice, and also have the following features:

- It focuses implicitly or explicitly on a question. This is always the starting point for inquiry in any genre. In an argumentative essay, you are providing evidence to support a particular answer to this question.
- The essay makes clear premises and claims, including one central claim around which the draft is organized. In other words, *the essay should be clear about what it is asking its readers to do or to believe.*
- It provides specific and appropriate evidence in support of the claims, including research when relevant.
- The essay should address one or more of the counterarguments offered by those who take a different position from yours.

Thinking About Subjects

If you haven't yet figured out a way to make your composition instructor's eyes roll, announce that you want to write an argument essay on gun control. Gun control, abortion rights, and other hot-button public controversies often make the list of banned topics for student essays. This is not because they aren't important public debates. Instead, the problem is much more that the writer has likely already made up his mind and sees the chance to ascend a soapbox. In addition, polarized debates produce such a mass of information that it's difficult for a writer to locate some territory in the topic that isn't already filled with voices repeating the same things to each other. There is so much background noise that it's almost impossible to hear yourself think.

Now, I have my own favorite soapboxes; people with strong convictions do. But as you think about subjects for your essay, consider that the soapbox may not be the best vantage point for practicing dialectical thinking. If you've already made up your mind, will you be open to discovery? If you just want to line up ducks—assembling evidence to support an unwavering belief—will you be encouraged to think deeply or differently? Will you be inclined to filter the voices you hear rather than consider a range of points of view?

The best persuasive essays often emerge from the kind of open-ended inquiry that you might have used writing the personal essay. What do you want to understand better? What issue or question makes you wonder? What controversies are you and your friends talking about? Be alert to possible subjects that you might write about *not* because you already know what you think, but because you want to find out. Or consider a subject that you might have feelings about but feel uninformed, lacking the knowledge to know exactly what you think.

The best argument essays make a clear claim, but they do it by bowing respectfully to the complexity of the subject, examining it from a variety of perspectives, not just two opposing poles.

Generating Ideas

Begin exploring possible subjects for an argument essay by generating material in your notebook. This should be an open-ended process, a chance to use your creative side without worrying too much about making sense or trying to prejudge the value of the writing or the subjects you generate. In a sense, this is an invitation to play around. Later, you can judge the material you've generated and choose a topic that interests you.

Listing Prompts. Lists can be rich sources of triggering topics. Let them grow freely, and when you're ready, use an item as the focus of another list or an episode of fastwriting. The following prompts should get you started.

1. In your journal, make a quick list of issues that have provoked disagreements between groups of people in your hometown or local community.

2. Make a quick list of issues that have provoked disagreements on your college's campus.

3. Make another list of issues that have created controversy between groups of people in your state.

4. Think about issues—local, statewide, regional, national, or even international—that have touched your life, or could affect you in some way in the following areas: environmental, health care, civil rights, business, education, crime, or sports. Make a quick list of questions within these areas you wonder about. For example, *Will there be enough drinking water in my well if the valley continues to develop at this rate?* Or *Will I be able to afford to send my children to the state college in twelve years?* Or *Do new domestic antiterrorism rules threaten my privacy when I'm online?* Or *Will I benefit from affirmative action laws when I apply to law school?*

5. Jot down a list of the classes you're taking this semester. Then make a quick list of topics that prompt disagreements among people in the field that you're studying. For example, in your political science class, did you learn that there are debates about the usefulness of the electoral college? In your biology class, have you discussed global warming? In your women's studies class, did you read about Title 9 and how it affects female athletes?

Fastwriting Prompts. Remember, fastwriting is a great way to stimulate creative thinking. Turn off your critical side and let yourself write "badly." Don't worry too much about what you're going to say before you say it. Write fast, letting language lead for a change.

1. Write for five minutes beginning with one of the questions you raised in Question 4 in the "Listing Prompts" section. Think through writing about when you first began to be concerned about the question, how you think it might affect you, and what you currently understand are the key questions this issue raises. Do you have tentative feelings or beliefs about it?

2. In a seven-minute fastwrite, explore the differences between your beliefs and the beliefs of your parents. Tell yourself the story of how your own beliefs about some question evolved, perhaps moving away from your parents' position. Can you imagine the argument you might make to help them understand your point of view?

3. Choose an item from any of the lists you generated in the "Listing Prompts" section as a starting place for a fastwrite. Explore what you understand about the issue, what are the key questions, and how you feel about it at the moment.

One Student's Response

BEN'S JOURNAL

FASTWRITE

WHY DO STUDENTS SEEM SO APATHETIC ABOUT POLITICS?

We're in the midst of presidential elections and I can't seem to get anyone interested in talking about it. I wonder why that is? Are college students more cynical about politics and politicians than other groups? It seems like it to me. I can think of a few reasons right off the bat. First, college students are mostly young (though certainly not all at this school) so they don't have the habit of going to the polls. Whenever a generation loses the habit of voting, I'll bet the next generation is even more likely to be apathetic. I also think my generation has seen so few effective politicians. My dad talks about being inspired by the likes of JFK but I can't think of too many national politicians that have inspired me as much as JFK inspired him. I also wonder if there is that basic sense of powerlessness. We just don't feel like much of anything makes a difference. I wonder if that is also reflected in volunteerism. Do students volunteer less than they used to? Have to check on that. I guess I just find politics kind of interesting. I wonder why? Hmmm . . . I think it had something to do with my Dad. But I guess I also have this basic belief in voting as an important part of being a citizen. Seems like one of the best ways to be patriotic . . .

Visual Prompts. Sometimes the best way to generate material is to see what we think represented in something other than sentences. Boxes, lines, webs, clusters, arrows, charts, and even pictures and sketches can help us see more of the landscape of a subject, especially connections between fragments of information that aren't as obvious in prose.

Find an advertisement, poster, or other image with a persuasive purpose and create an argument map (see Figure 8.4, which maps the Guess.com ad on page 290). Choose an image that bothers you for some reason. By visually graphing its implicit argument, you might discover ways to offer a critique or a counterargument in your own essay. Use the first box of the argument map to summarize the main claim of the image you've selected. In the next box, list the (often implicit) reasons or premises behind the claim. Use the word *because* to tease this out. In the next box put the two together, creating a premise and a claim, and then follow this up by listing the evidence the image provides to support the premises and claim. Now use your map to generate a list of quick responses to some of the following questions: *Do you agree with the claim? Do you agree with the premises? Which seems most suspect? Why? What might be a more truthful claim? What might be more accurate premises? Is this an argument you've seen elsewhere? Do the claims and premises represent a way of seeing the world typical of a particular social group? How would you redesign the ad to make it more truthful? What is your argument against this argument?* Use the lists and fastwrites generated from analyzing your argument map to develop an argument of your own.

Research Prompts. By definition, argument essays deal with subjects in which people beyond the writer have a stake. And one of the best ways to collect ideas about such issues is to do a little quick and dirty research. Try some of the following research prompts:

1. Spend a few days reading the letters to the editor in your local paper. What issue has people riled up locally? Is there one that you find particularly interesting?

2. Do a Web search to find op-ed essays written by one or more of the following national columnists: Ellen Goodman, Cal Thomas, George Will, David Broder,

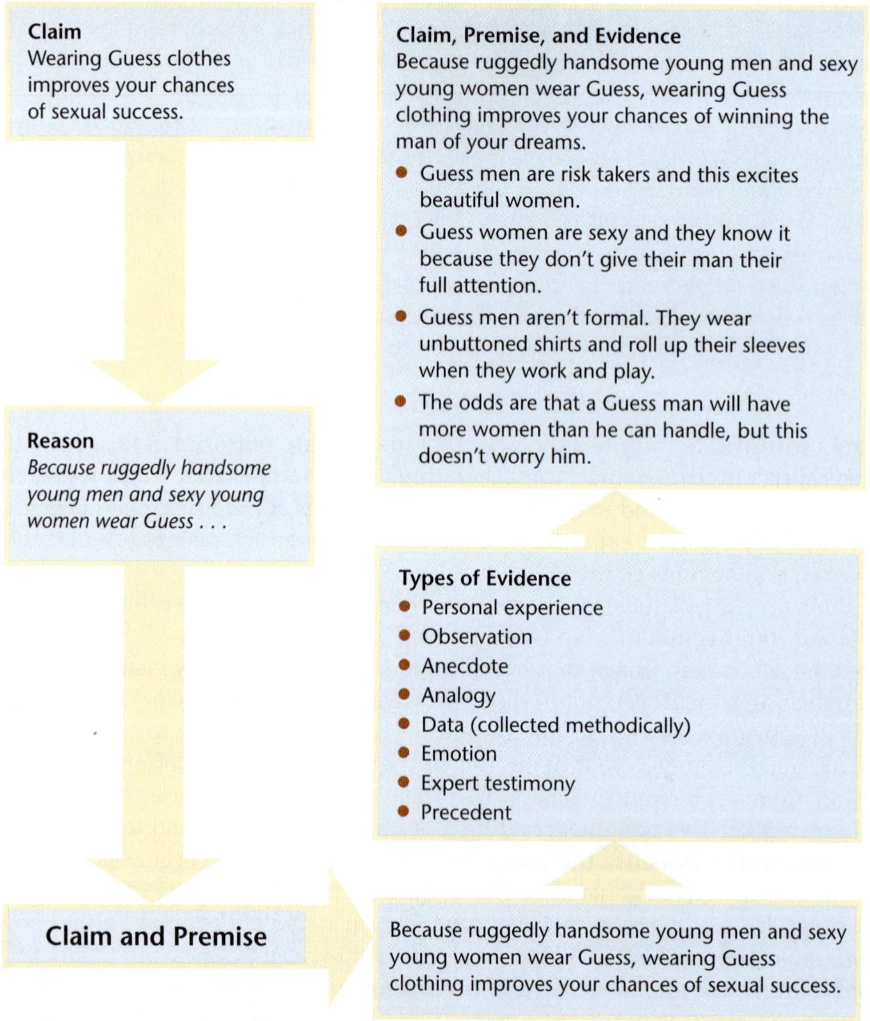

FIGURE 8.4 An argument map (see page 300 for Guess.com ad).

Nat Hentoff, Mary McGrory, Molly Ivins, Bob Herbert, or Clarence Page. Read their work with an eye toward topics that interest you.

3. Do a Google search on terms or phrases on an issue that interests you, such as "global warming Greenland glaciers" or "pro-anorexia Web sites." Did you produce any results that make you curious, or make you feel something about the issue, one way or another?

4. Interview people you know—on campus or off—about the public issues that they care most about.

Writing with Computers

ARGUMENTS ON THE INTERNET

The Internet is a repository of ideas. It is almost always useful to make the Internet a first stop when starting a new writing project in order to determine what others think or believe about a topic. Web sites of organizations reveal how organized cooperative groups treat an issue, Web pages or Web logs (blogs) show the thoughts of individuals, and discussion boards and comments to blog postings can show how multiple people negotiate and debate a topic. Unlike traditional publications, such as books and journals, many of the arguments found on the Internet have not been evaluated or screened by editors. Remember, anyone with a computer and Internet connection can publish ideas and arguments on the Internet. This dynamic gives almost everyone equal access to share beliefs and arguments. This means that new and innovative ideas are often found alongside shallow and unsupported arguments. Always evaluate arguments found on the Internet with a critical viewpoint. If possible, try to validate them with traditional sources.

Judging What You Have

Shift back to your more critical mind and sift through the material you generated. Did you discover a topic that might be interesting for your argument essay? Did you stumble over some interesting questions you'd like to explore further? Did anything you wrote or read make you *feel* something? Evaluate the raw material in your journal and keep the following things in mind as you zero in on a topic for your argument essay.

What's Promising Material and What Isn't? Let's take a critical look at the subjects you've generated so far; what promising topics might be lurking there for an argumentative essay? Consider some of the following as you make your choice.

- *Interest.* This almost goes without saying. But you were warned earlier about seizing on a topic if you already have strong convictions about it. Do you already know what you think? If so, why not choose a topic that initially invites more open-ended inquiry? On the other hand, it matters a lot whether you *care.* What topic might touch your life in some way? Do you have some kind of stake in how the questions are answered?
- *Brevity.* One of the most common flaws of student drafts in all genres is that they attempt to cover too much territory. A more *limited* look at a larger landscape is always best. Because these argument essays are brief, consider topics that you can do justice to in less than a thousand words. As you review potential topics for your essay, can you see how some aspect of a larger question can be addressed by asking a smaller question? For example, the topic of spending on athletic programs at American universities relative to spending

on academic programs raises this obvious question: *Is too much spent on sports?* It's not very difficult to see how this large question can be focused for an effective argument. For example, *Does Boise State University spend too much on its athletic programs and too little on its academic ones?* You can't write a short piece about the negative impact of affirmative action policies on the nation's colleges and universities, but you can write a brief op-ed about the specific impacts on your school.

- *Disagreement.* A topic lends itself to argumentative writing if it leads to disagreement among reasonable people. *Is smoking bad for your health?* was once a question that was debatable, but now pretty much everyone concedes that this question has been answered. *Did the Holocaust really happen?* is a question that only blockheads debate. But the question, *What are the motives of people who deny the Holocaust?* is a question that would generate a range of views.
- *Information.* Is sufficient information available on the topic for you to make a reasonable judgment about what is true? Is it accessible? One great advantage of choosing a local question as the focus for an argumentative essay is that often the people are close by and the relevant information can easily be had. It's also essential that you can obtain information from more than just a single viewpoint on the question.
- *Question.* What makes a topic arguable is that it raises questions to which there are multiple answers. Which of them makes the most sense is at issue. But some questions are merely informational. For example, *How do greenhouse gases contribute to global warming?* is a question that will likely lead to explanations rather than argument. On the other hand, *Is the U.S. rejection of the Kyoto accords on global warming a responsible policy?* is an arguable, rather than informational, question.

Questions About Audience and Purpose. Persuasive writing is a very audience-oriented form. *To whom* you make your case in an argument matters a lot in *how* you make it, but audience also matters in *whether* one topic is a better choice for an essay than another topic. The op-ed essay is written for a more general audience. Your readers are unlikely to be experts on your topic, and they are likely to read your essay quickly rather than slowly and thoughtfully. What does this imply about the best subjects?

- *Do your readers have a stake in the question you're answering?* The word *stake* can be broadly considered. For example, a topic may directly affect the readers of your essay; say you're writing for fellow college students on your campus, all of whom pay tuition, and your topic addresses whether a 12 percent hike in fees is justified. Sometimes, however, you choose a topic because readers need to know that they *do* have a stake in how a question is answered. For instance, the argument that new antiterrorist rules threaten online privacy is something you believe your readers, most of whom surf the Web, should consider.

- *Can you identify what your readers might already believe?* One of the key strategies of persuasion is to find ways to link the values and attitudes of your audience with the position you're encouraging them to believe. Does your potential topic lend itself to this kind of analysis?
- *Is your purpose not only to inform readers but also to encourage them to believe or do something?* As you know by now, one of the things that distinguishes argument essays such as the op-ed piece from other forms of writing is the writer's intention to change his or her audience. Frequently this purpose is quite explicit and even behavioral: vote a certain way, support a certain policy, or *don't* do something like buy a gas-guzzling SUV. Other times, persuasive writing attempts to persuade readers to believe something that may lead to some kind of behavior.

Research Considerations. So you want to look into the controversy over oil drilling in the Arctic National Wildlife Refuge? Your gut reaction is against proposals that would allow oil companies to drill test wells. It seems to be a real can of worms—if you allow testing and then there's momentum for full-scale development, you wonder if the environmental risks will be worth the gain in oil. But you really don't know very much. What are the risks? Is there a significant promise of oil production? How might it affect your region, your state, or the prices at your local Chevron? This is a big subject, of course, and there is lots of information out there. Where do you begin?

Maybe you believe you already know a lot about your topic—you've had enough experience and observations, or perhaps read enough to feel pretty well informed. But if you took my advice to choose a topic about which you might *feel* something but not really know what you *think,* then once you have selected your topic your next step in the process is to collect information.

While writing this argument essay does involve some research, it isn't exactly a research paper. A research paper is a much more extended treatment of a topic that relies on more detailed and scholarly information than is usually needed for an argument essay. In Chapter 12, you'll find information on research strategies that will help you with this project, especially how to conduct effective Internet searches and how to evaluate the sources you find. The section on library research, particularly key references, may also be valuable.

But for the purpose of this essay, you can have a more modest research agenda, and that's when the Web can be especially useful. Because many of the topics ripe for a good argument essay are current, a major source of information will be publications such as newspapers and magazines. As more of these print sources have gone online, the Web has become a central source for topical information. It's a great place to start learning about your topic, but there are hazards. First, the Web can be a trap. Searching and surfing can suck up an enormous amount of time; it can easily become obsessive—"I need just a few more sources and then I'll quit"—or even worse, digressive—"Gee, I just stumbled on a game site . . . it's got Super Mahjongg!" Either of these can become an excuse not to write. The other hazard is the reliability of information on the Web, which is uneven (see "Evaluating Web Sources" in Chapter 12).

Address these pitfalls by making your Web research efficient. Magazines and newspapers are key sources for op-ed essays, and they're likely the best place to begin looking for background information. National issues such as oil drilling in the Arctic National Wildlife Refuge are addressed by national newspapers, which are usually reliable sources of information. Search sites such as *The New York Times* or *The Washington Post* for information on your topic if you think that it might have garnered national attention. In addition, the useful site at http://www.refdesk.com/paper.html lists links for newspapers by state and around the world.

Magazines online are good sources as well, but access to their archives may be limited to subscribers. The university library is useful because it not only subscribes to many magazines but allows you to search them; you may be able retrieve full articles electronically or read them on microfilm. Access to your college's database of magazines is likely online, too, so check the library Web site for more information.

A general search engine such as http://www.google.com will help you find newspapers, magazines, Web sites, and other online publications for background on your topic. Be ready for an avalanche, however. For example, a Google search on the Arctic National Wildlife Refuge turned up nearly 3,000 links.

If you're writing about a campus or community issue, the Web can still be useful, particularly if your campus or local newspapers have sites. State and local governments also post information on the Web (for information on sites, visit State and Local Governments on the Net at http://www.statelocalgov.net/index.cfm). But campus and local issues often call for a different kind of research: basic footwork. The best way to become knowledgeable is to talk to people who are affected by the topic, perhaps people you've identified with particular points of view about it or even other students in your class who may have some knowledge. The local public library, as well as the campus library, can be a valuable source of information on local issues as well.

Narrowing the Question. I've been vaguely aware of the crisis in Medicaid funding—federal health care support for the poor—but the issue really came home when officials told Dorothy Misner, a ninety-two-year-old woman in nearby Nampa, that she would have to gum her food because the state refused to pay for dentures. Probably the best way to make a larger controversy a manageable writing topic is to find a local angle. In this case, for example, the larger question—*Should the national Medicaid program do more to support the poor without health insurance?*—becomes a much narrower question: *Is the state's Medicaid program failing people like Dorothy Misner?* Whenever possible, make big issues smaller by finding some connection to the local.

That isn't always possible, however. Unless you live in Alaska, for instance, the debate over development of the Arctic National Wildlife Refuge is hard to cut as a local issue. Then it becomes important to find a narrower question, something that may not be possible until after you've done a little research. For example, the question, *Should the Arctic National Wildlife Refuge be open to oil development?* could be narrowed by asking, *Are oil company claims about the potential of recoverable oil in the refuge reasonable?*

Another way to narrow the focus of an argument is to find a useful case study, anecdote, or example that somehow typifies some aspect of the issue you want to examine. Suppose you want to write about the impact of oil development on native subsistence hunting in the wildlife refuge. The story of one family, or one local native community's reliance on the nearby caribou population, can anchor an extended discussion of the risks oil development poses to people like them.

Finally, do what journalists do: peg your essay to a recent event related to the issue you're writing about. George Will's approach to many of his op-ed essays is to use a newly released study, report, academic article, or interview with an expert as the anchor for his piece. He then takes off on his own from there. Other events might include a relevant hearing, a protest, a court decision, a crime, an accident, and so on.

Writing the Sketch

Now draft a sketch of roughly 500 to 600 words with the following elements:

- It has a tentative title.
- It makes at least one claim and offers several reasons that support the claim.
- It presents and analyzes at least one contrasting point of view.
- The sketch includes specific evidence to support (or possibly complicate) the reasons offered in support of the claim, including *at least* several of the following: an anecdote or story, a personal observation, data, an analogy, a case study, expert testimony, other relevant quotations from people involved, or a precedent.

STUDENT SKETCH

Inspiring young voters isn't easy. In my own classes, I almost never hear younger students talk casually about elections. On the rare occasions that I actually see a button on a backpack for one candidate or another, I'm always a little surprised. Are young voters apathetic? And if they are, what should be done about it? Those were Ben Bloom's questions, both of which arose from a fastwrite. Here is his sketch on the topic. Where should he go from here? What should he research before the next draft? What should he consider that he doesn't consider here?

How to Really Rock the Vote

Ben Bloom

1 MTV sponsors "Rock the Vote." Presidential candidates swing through college campuses wearing blue jeans and going tieless. There's even an organization called "Kid's Vote" that tries to get high school students involved in the political process. It's pretty clear that student vote matters but are these efforts paying off?

2 It doesn't seem so. On my own campus, fewer than a few hundred students vote in the annual elections for the Student Senate. I can't even get my roommate to talk about the Presidential election, much less who's running for student body president.

3 What seems typical is the following comment from a college-age columnist: "On the issue of voter apathy, I look at myself first. I'm not even registered to vote, which is as apathetic as it gets. I do, however, educate myself about presidential candidates and their proposed policies—I just never have thought my one, lonesome vote could matter. I've neglected registering because it has never seemed logical to inconvenience myself, through the registration process, only to give another drop of water to an ocean (to add one vote to millions)."

4 "Never seemed logical to inconvenience" yourself to participate in the most basic part of the democratic process? Has it gotten this bad?

5 The student journalist above was responding to a survey that came out two years ago from a group called Project Vote Smart. It found what I suspected from my own experiences: young voters are staying away from the polls.

6 According to the study, there has been a decline in the numbers of 18- to 25-year-olds voting by 13% over the last twenty-five years. Actually, I think the situation is worse than that. The main reason they cite is that young people don't think their votes make a difference.

7 What should be done about this? How can we convince young voters to believe in the power of their vote? Are organizations like "Rock the Vote" or "Project Vote Smart" going to convince students like the guy who finds voting "inconvenient" that it's worth the effort?

8 In my opinion, celebrities and rock stars won't make a difference. The key is for political candidates to find a way to talk about issues so that young voters overcome their apathy and actually *feel* something. In the sixties, it was the draft. I'm not sure what the issues with emotional impact are these days. But the people who want students to vote have got to find them.

Moving from Sketch to Draft

A sketch is often sketchy. It's generally underdeveloped, sometimes giving the writer just the barest outline of his subject. But as an early draft, a sketch can be invaluable. It might hint at what the real subject is, or what questions seem to be behind your inquiry into the subject. A sketch might suggest a focus for the next draft, or simply a better lead. Here are some tips for finding clues in your sketch about directions you might go in the next draft.

Evaluating Your Own Sketch. You've read and written about an issue you care about. Now for the really hard part: getting out of your own head and into the heads of your potential readers, who may not care as much as you do. At least not yet. Successful persuasion fundamentally depends on giving an audience the right reasons to agree with you, and these are likely both logical and emotional, involving both *logos* and *pathos* (see the "Inquiring into the Details: *Ethos, Pathos,* and *Logos* and the Rhetorical Situation" box).

Another element of argument is the way the writer comes across to readers—his or her *ethos.* What's the ethos of your sketch? How might you be perceived by a stranger reading the sketch? Is your tone appealing, or might it be slightly off-putting? Do you successfully establish your authority to speak on this issue, or do you sense that the persona you project in the sketch is unconvincing, perhaps too emotional or not appearing fair?

Inquiring into the Details

Ethos, Pathos, and *Logos* and the Rhetorical Situation

Persuasion theory may have begun with Aristotle's *Rhetoric,* but modern communication researchers have made it a science. Still, Aristotle and other classical rhetors laid the foundation for the study of persuasion. One of Aristotle's most important contributions to our understanding of argument is shown in Figure 8.5, a variation of the rhetorical triangle you learned about in the beginning of the book.

Each of these terms—*ethos, logos,* and *pathos*—represents different kinds of persuasive appeals. *Ethos* refers to the character of the speaker (or writer), and how he or she comes across to the audience. *Logos* is the logic and methods of reason used to make an argument. *Pathos* is an appeal to the audience's (or reader's) emotion.

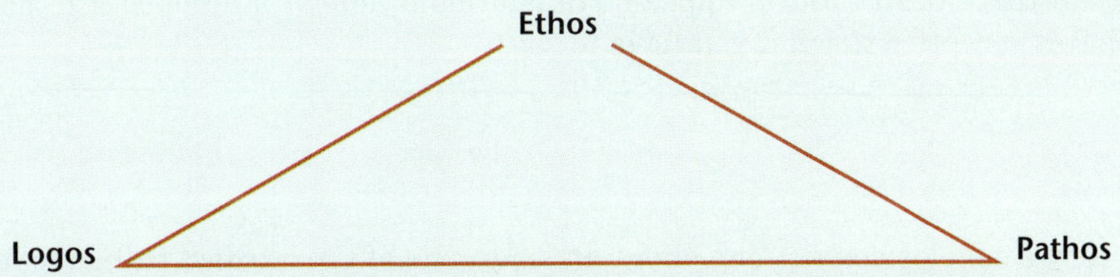

FIGURE 8.5 Aristotle's rhetorical triangle.

Disposition of Audience	*Ethos*	*Pathos*	*Logos*
Resistant	Most important	Least important	Most important
Neutral	Important	Important	Important
Receptive	Least important	Most important	Least important

FIGURE 8.6 Audience and the balance of ethos, logos, and pathos.

All arguments are an artful combination of *ethos, logos,* and *pathos*. As always, what is the most effective combination depends on the rhetorical situation. One way of analyzing a situation is to consider the initial disposition of the audience. Figure 8.6 broadly describes the balance between Aristotle's three categories of appeals in the three most common rhetorical situations: when an audience is resistant to what you're trying to say, neutral about it, or receptive. For instance, direct-mail marketers, particularly those trying to raise money for nonprofit groups and political causes, make a living buying and cultivating lists of people who might be receptive to their messages. Direct-mail letters, therefore, are strong on emotional appeals (*pathos*): The humane society will include photographs of a sad-looking abandoned puppy, a conservative political action group will raise fears about threats to "family values," and so on. There's no need to spend a great deal reasoning (*logos*) with an audience that already agrees with your message. Move them with emotion!

In contrast, resistant audiences immediately suspect the credibility of speakers or writers (*ethos*), and so their challenge is to establish some common ground with their audiences. Emotional appeals will be unlikely to move this audience, at least initially.

Neutral audiences may be difficult to gauge. Sometimes an emotional appeal will spark their interest. Sometimes a well-reasoned argument (*logos*) will move them, and sometimes a neutral audience will be persuaded by the credibility of the speaker. Frequently, a careful combination of all three of Aristotle's appeals transforms a neutral audience into one that is receptive to what you have to say.

As we develop convictions about an issue, one of the hardest things to manage in early argument drafts is creating a persuasive persona *(ethos)*. Another is finding ways to establish connections with our audience; this connection is not just between writers and readers but creating some common ground between readers and *the topic.* There are many ways to do this, including the following:

1. Connecting your readers' prior beliefs or values with your position on the topic.
2. Establishing that readers have a *stake,* perhaps even a personal one, in how the question you've raised is answered; this may be self-interest, but it may also be emotional (remember the advertiser's strategy).
3. Highlighting the common experiences readers may have had with the topic and offering your claim as a useful way of understanding that experience.

As you look over your sketch, evaluate how well you create this common ground between your topic and your intended audience. Might you revise it by exploiting one or more of the strategies listed here?

Finally, is there enough evidence to support the reasons you've provided to support your claims? Initial drafts commonly lack enough specifics. Do you see places in the sketch that could be developed with specific information in the next draft?

Questions for Peer Review. Because the argument essay is such an audience-oriented form, these initial peer reviews of your sketch are invaluable in helping you get your bearings. Much of what you might have felt about how you managed the ethos and connections with readers can be confirmed or challenged by this first public reading. Ask your workshop group some of the following questions:

- How is the *ethos* of the sketch? Do I come across in the sketch as an advocate for my position? For example, am I *passionate, preachy, reasonable, one-sided, sympathetic, overbearing, intimate, detached, objective, subjective, uncaring, empathetic, humorous, serious, angry, mellow, contemptuous, approachable, patronizing, respectful, thoughtful, presumptuous, fair,* or *judgmental?*
- In your own words, what do you think was my central claim?
- Which reasons did you find most convincing? Which were least convincing?
- What do you think was the best evidence I offered in support of my reasons? Where exactly did you feel that you needed more evidence?
- What were the stated or unstated "warrants" behind the claims? What do you need to assume is true to believe in their validity (see "Inquiring into the Details: Using Toulmin to Analyze Arguments")?

Reflecting on What You've Learned. Spend a few minutes following your peer review workshop to generate a list of everything you heard, and then begin a five-minute fastwrite that explores your reaction to these suggestions and your tentative plan for revision. In particular, what will you change? What will you add, and what will you cut in the next draft? What problems were raised that

Guess.com advertisement—a not too subtle yet insidiously persuasive form of visual argument.

you don't yet know how to solve? What problems *weren't* raised that you expected might be? Do you still need to worry about them? End your fastwrite by writing about what you understand now about your topic, and your initial beliefs about it, that you didn't fully understand when you began writing about it.

Research and Other Strategies: Gathering More Information

Here's a mortifying thought: You've completely changed your mind about what you think about your topic and what you want to say in your argument. That's unsettling, but it's also a sign that you're willing to allow things to get a bit messy before they get sorted out. This is good because it's much more likely to result in an essay that gets at the truth of what you feel than if you doggedly stick to a particular point of view, come what may. If you *have* changed your mind, you have a lot of collecting to do. Return to the Web sites of current publications and search for information that might be relevant to your emerging idea.

Another research strategy can be helpful whether you change your mind or not: the interview. People who are somehow involved in your topic are among the best sources of new information and lively material. An interview can provide ideas about what else you should read or who else you might talk to, and it can be a source of quotations, anecdotes, and even case studies that will make the next draft of your argument essay much more interesting. After all, what makes an issue matter is how it affects people. Have you sufficiently dramatized those effects?

Inquiring into the Details

USING TOULMIN TO ANALYZE ARGUMENTS

Stephen Toulmin, an English philosopher, has had an enormous influence on how argument is analyzed and taught. He proposes that most arguments, no matter what the subject or discipline, include *claims, evidence, warrants,* and *backing.* You're likely familiar with at least two of these terms: claims and evidence.

But the most penetrating aspect of Toulmin's approach is the idea that *warrants*—assumptions about the way things are—are key to the logical relationship between evidence and claims. For example, my friend and colleague, Dr. Michelle Payne, asks students to make claims about what type of person she is based on the contents of her handbag. What does the fact that she has three credit cards say about her? Some students say she probably has a lot of money, while others suggest the opposite—that she must carry a lot of debt. Michelle prompts students to state the warrants by asking, *What do you need to believe is true if your claims from the evidence are valid? Backing* is evidence that supports a warrant. For those who claim that the number of Michelle's credit cards is evidence that she might struggle with debt, the warrant is clear: One has to believe that there is a relationship between the numbers of credit cards and debt—the more you have, the more you spend beyond your means. A quick search on the Web uncovered backing for such a warrant. Apparently consumer debt and numbers of cards *are* related, making the original claim more convincing.

Warrants are either stated or unstated. Typically, writers or speakers who believe that their audience shares the assumptions behind their warrants don't explicitly discuss them. Advertisers are expert at this. While it seems logically silly to accept the warrant in a Guess ad that wearing their jeans will help guarantee sexual and social success, we tend not to question the assumption. If we did, we might demand backing: do habitual Guess jeans wearers who are single spend fewer Saturday nights at home alone than those of us who wear Levis?

Can you see how this method allows you to analyze the effectiveness of all kinds of arguments—including visual arguments—particularly by trying to tease out the warrants behind the claims? Toulmin can also help you generate information that will help you write an argument more effectively by challenging you to state your warrants and provide backing when necessary.

Suppose you read a recent poll that considerably more people today believe in the possibility that someone can start poor and get rich in America than they did in 1983. Of the many possible claims that might arise from this evidence, Figure 8.7 presents two: more people believe that the U.S. is the land of opportunity, or Americans apparently choose to ignore the widening gap between rich and poor in this country. In other words, we are either inspired optimists or complete dupes. If you ask yourself what you have to assume is true for each claim to be valid you'll surface some warrants that might be worth questioning. I've listed one warrant for each claim in Figure 8.7.

The effectiveness of arguments rise and fall with the persuasiveness of their warrants. If you think the warrants behind your claim might not reflect assumptions that readers share, then finding backing for your warrants is an important research strategy. Do you think warrant #2 below needs backing?

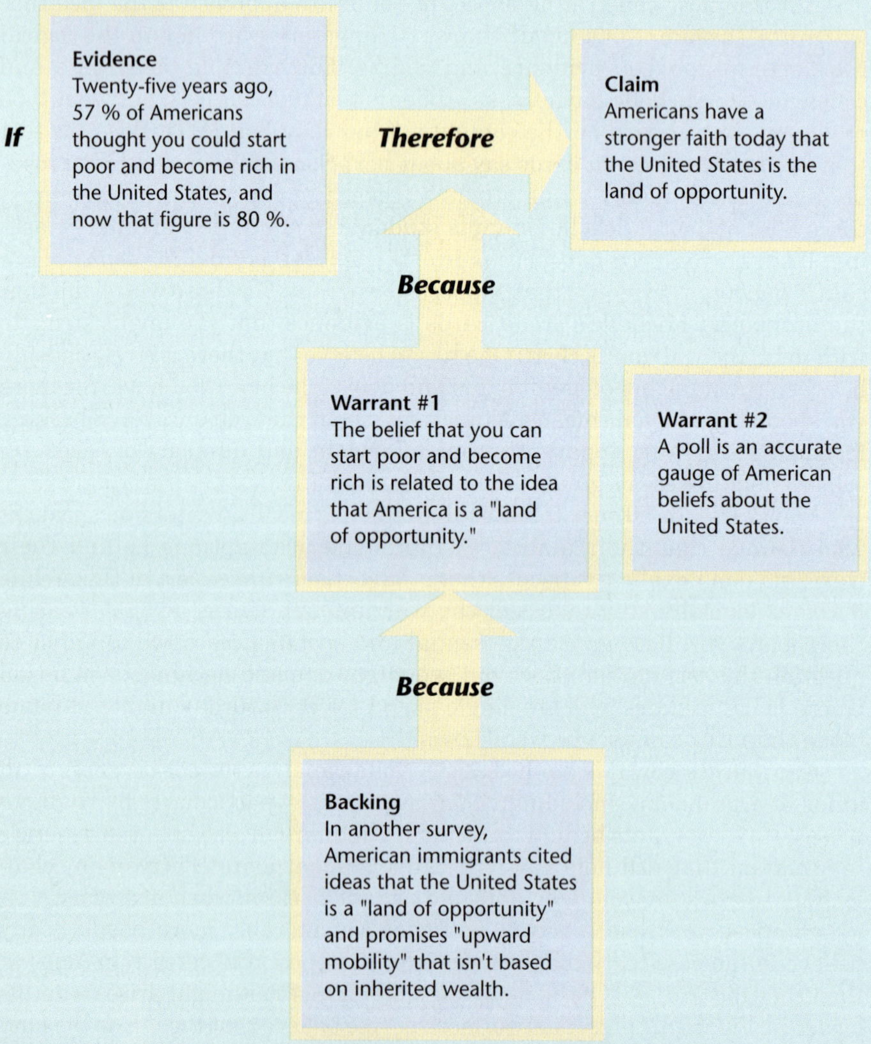

FIGURE 8.7 You can use the Toulmin model to guide your research efforts when you revise.

For more information on face-to-face interviewing, see Chapter 5, "Writing a Profile," as well as Chapter 12, "Research Techniques." The Internet can also be a source for interview material. Look for e-mail links to the authors of useful documents you found on the Web and write them with a few questions. Interest groups, newsgroups, or electronic mailing lists on the Web can also provide the voices and perspectives of people with something to say on your topic. Remember to ask permission to quote them if you decide to use something in your draft. For leads on finding Web discussion groups on your topic, visit the following sites:

- **Google Groups,** http://groups.google.com, allows you to search for online discussion groups on virtually any topic.
- **Yahoo Groups** offers a similar service, allowing you to search for groups by keyword. Find it at http://groups.yahoo.com.
- **Catalist,** the official catalog of electronic mailing lists, http://www.lsoft.com/lists/listref.html, has a database of about 15,000 discussion groups.

One of the most useful things you can do to prepare for the draft is to spend forty-five minutes at the campus library searching for new information on your topic. Consider expanding your search from current newspapers and periodicals to books or government publications (see Chapter 12 for more information about searching for government documents). In addition you can refer to almanacs such as *Infoplease* (http://www.infoplease.com) and the *CIA World Factbook* (http://www.odci.gov/cia/publications/factbook/) and statistical information available from sources such as the U.S. Census Bureau's *American Fact Finder* (http://factfinder.census.gov/home/saff/main.html?_lang = en), which is a wonderful resource that draws on the agency's massive database of information on U.S. trends.

Composing the Draft

As always, it's best to work from abundance rather than scarcity. If you don't have enough evidence to support your argument, find more. But if you're feeling reasonably well prepared to develop your argument essay from a sketch (or proposal) to a longer draft, then begin by crafting a strong lead. There are so many ways to begin an essay like this one; which is best? As always, think of a beginning that not only might interest your readers in your topic but hints at or states your purpose in writing about it. Through tone, your beginning also establishes your relationship with your readers. Here's instructor Andrew Merton's lead in "The Guys Are Dumbing Down," a piece that argues that students' baseball caps in class indicate something other than studiousness.

> Here is the big social note from the campus of the University of New Hampshire, where I teach: Dumbing down is in. For guys.

Merton's tone is a strong element of this lead. He begins casually—"Here is the big social note . . ."—suggesting some friendly, almost chatty relationship with his readers. This lead also does what many argument essay beginnings do: it states the writer's main claim. You may assume it is always required to state your thesis in your introduction, but this isn't true at all. Some argument essays, especially op-ed pieces, have a delayed thesis, in which the writer works methodically toward his or her point. Which approach should you use in your draft? In part, that depends on your method of development.

Methods of Development. What are some of the ways you might organize the next draft?

Narrative. Telling a story is an underrated way of developing an argument. One of my favorite persuasive essays is George Orwell's "A Hanging," a piece most don't consider a persuasive essay at all. Orwell's essay is his eyewitness account of a man who is hanged at a squalid prison in colonial Burma. "A Hanging" argues against capital punishment by focusing on about eight minutes of the event—the most dramatic eight minutes obviously—and only in the middle does Orwell break with his story to state his position on the issue. The story is so compelling it's hard to even notice that Orwell is trying to persuade the reader to believe something. Can you imagine a way to turn your topic into an extended story, perhaps by focusing on the experience of a particular person or group of people, in a particular place, at a particular time? Somehow the story must, like Orwell's, be logically linked to your claim; obviously, just any old story won't do.

There are other ways to use narrative, too. Anecdotes, or brief stories used to illustrate an idea or a problem, are frequently used in argument essays. One effective way to begin your essay might be to tell a story that highlights the problem you're writing about or the question you're posing.

Question to Answer. Almost all writing is an attempt to answer a question. In the personal essay and other open forms of inquiry, the writer may never arrive at a definite answer, but an argument essay usually offers an answer. An obvious method of development, therefore, is to begin your essay by raising the question and end it by offering your answer. This can work in a number of ways. For example, an Ellen Goodman essay on recent proposals to bring back publicly funded single-sex schools is organized around what she thinks are some of the key questions this raises. She asks those questions throughout her essay, and answers each before moving on to the next. Following a beginning that provides some background on the proposal, Goodman asks, *How did we get here?* She then explains the "odd coalition" that supports the proposal, describes their arguments and methodically rebuts them. By the middle of her essay, Goodman asks a second question, *Can you have separate but equal schools?* The remainder of her piece examines the answer to this question, and by the end she arrives at her main claim: The solution to poor schools is not an end to coeducation but innovation in teaching.

Are there several key questions around which you might organize your draft, leading, as Goodman does, to your central claim at the end?

Problem to Solution. This is a variation on the question-to-answer structure. But it might be a particularly useful organization strategy if you're writing about a topic readers may know very little about. In that case, you might need to spend as much time establishing what exactly the problem is—explaining what makes it a problem and why the reader should care about it—as you do offering your particular solution. That's what George Will did earlier in the chapter in his argument on the failure of writing instruction. He spent a fair amount of time explaining what he believed were the indefensible current theories of teaching students to write, ideas most of his readers would know little about.

Effect to Cause or Cause to Effect. At the heart of some arguments is the *relationship* between two things, and often what is at issue is pinpointing the real causes for certain undesirable effects. Once these causes are identified, then the best solutions can be offered. Sadly, we know the effects of terrorism, but what are its causes? If you argue, as some do, that Islamic radicalism arose in response to U.S. policies toward Israel and the Palestinians, then the solution offered might be a shift in foreign policy. The international debate over global warming, for some participants, is really an argument about causes and effects. If you don't believe, for example, that U.S. contributions to atmospheric carbon dioxide in the next ten years will match contributions from the developing world, then the U.S. refusal to sign the Kyoto treaty—one proposed solution—may not matter that much. Some arguments like these can be organized simply around an examination of causes and effects.

Combining Approaches. As you think about how you might organize your first draft, you don't necessarily have to choose between narrative, problem-to-solution, or cause-to-effect structures. In fact, most often they are used together. We can easily see that in Erin Aubry Kaplan's essay earlier in the chapter on the politics of hair. The piece begins with a narrative account of her hair straightening efforts as a child, and then shifts to an exploration how recent events highlight a return to the "denial" look in African American hairstyle.

Using Evidence. All writing relies on evidence, usually some specific information in relationships with general ideas (see the "Inquiring into the Details: What Evidence Can Do" box.) Evidence in an argumentative essay often has a *particular* relationship to ideas; most often it is offered to support ideas the writer wants the reader to believe. What *kind* of evidence to include is a rhetorical question. To whom are you writing, and what kind of evidence will they be more likely to believe? Generally speaking, the narrower and more specialized the audience, the more particular they will be about the types of evidence they'll find convincing.

For example, as you write more academic papers in your chosen major, the types of evidence that will help you make a persuasive argument will be more and more prescribed by the field. In the natural sciences, the results of quantitative studies count more than case studies; in the humanities, primary texts count more than secondary ones. The important thing for this argument essay, which you're writing for a more general audience, is that you attempt to *vary* your evidence. Rather than relying exclusively on anecdotes, include some quotes from an expert as well.

Inquiring into the Details

WHAT EVIDENCE CAN DO

Usually we think of using evidence only to support an idea or claim we're making. But evidence can be used in other ways, too. For example, it can do the following:

- *support* an idea, observation, or assertion
- *refute* or challenge a claim with which you disagree
- *show* that a seemingly simple assertion, problem, or idea is really more complex
- *complicate* or even contradict an earlier point you've made
- *contrast* two or more ways of seeing the same thing
- *test* an idea, hypothesis, or theory

Workshopping the Draft

If your draft is subject to peer review, see Chapter 15 for details on how to organize workshop groups and decide on how your group can help you. The following journal activities and questions should help you make the most of your opportunity to get peer feedback on your work in progress.

Reflecting on the Draft. After you've finished the draft, prepare for peer review by making a journal entry that explores your experience writing the essay.

- What proved hardest?
- What most surprised you about the process?
- What did you find particularly gratifying? What was especially frustrating?
- How did your process for writing this type of essay differ from writing the personal essay or some other form?
- If you were going to start all over again, what would you do differently?

Discuss the insights that might have emerged from this open-ended writing in class or in your workshop group. After your draft has been discussed, make some notes in your journal in response to the following questions:

- What most surprised you about your group's response to your essay?
- What did you hear that most made you want to write again?
- What specifically do you think you need to do in the next draft?

Questions for Readers. Here are some questions that might prompt members of your workshop group to offer helpful advice on your argument draft.

1. What was the most interesting part of the draft? What was the least interesting?

2. What did you believe about my topic before you read the draft? What did you believe after you read it?
3. What reason most strongly supported my main point? What reason seemed the weakest?
4. What was the most convincing evidence I offered? What was the least convincing?

Inquiring into the Details

COMMON LOGICAL FALLACIES

An important way to evaluate the soundness of an argument is to examine its logic and, in particular, look for so-called logical fallacies that may lead writers' reasoning astray. Aristotle was one of the first to point out many of these, and a quick search on the Web using the term "logical fallacies" will reveal dozens and dozens of them that plague public argument. Many of them have indecipherable Latin names, testifying to their ancient origins.

Here are ten of the most common logical fallacies. I think they cover about 90 percent of the ways in which writers stumble when making an argument.

1. **Hasty generalization:** We're naturally judgmental creatures. For example, we frequently make a judgment about someone after just meeting them. Or we conclude that a class is useless after attending a single session. All of these are generalizations based on insufficient evidence. Hasty generalizations *might* be true—the class might turn out to be useless—but you should always be wary of them.

2. **Ad hominem:** When arguments turn into shouting matches, they almost inevitably get personal. Shifting away from the substance of an argument to attack the person making it, either subtly or explicitly, is another common logical fallacy. It's also, at times, hard to resist.

3. **Appeal to authority:** We all know that finding support for a claim from an expert is a smart move in many arguments. But sometimes it's a faulty move because the authority we cite isn't really an expert on the subject. A more common fallacy, however, is when we cite an expert to support a claim without acknowledging that many experts disagree on the point.

4. **Straw man:** One of the sneakiest ways to sidetrack reason in an argument is to misrepresent or ignore the actual position of an opponent. For example, one way I might criticize George Will's earlier essay on writing instruction is to point out that he conveniently misrepresents the actual goals and practices of what he calls the "growth model" of teaching writing. Therefore he creates a "straw man" that is easy to knock down. When writing critically about the ideas of another, we must always be careful to represent those ideas as accurately as we can.

5. **False analogy:** Analogies can be powerful comparisons in argument. But they can also lead us astray when the analogy simply doesn't hold. Are A and B *really* similar situations? For example, when a critic of higher education argues that a public university is like a business and should be run like one, are the two really analogous? Fundamentally, one is nonprofit and the other is designed to make money. Is this a really useful comparison?

6. **Post hoc or false cause:** Just because one thing follows another doesn't necessarily mean one *causes* the other. It might be coincidence, or the cause might be something else entirely. For example, if you're really keen on arguing that losing the football coach was the cause of the team's losing record, you might link the two. And it's possible that you're right, but it's also just as possible that the injury to the quarterback was one of the real reasons.

7. **Appeal to popularity:** In a country obsessed by polls and rankings, it's not hard to understand the appeal of reasoning that argues that because it's popular it must be good or true. Advertisers are particularly fond of this fallacy, arguing that because their brand is most popular it must be best. In fact, this might not be the case at all. The majority can be wrong.

8. **Slippery slope:** I love the name of this one because it so aptly describes what can happen when reasoning loses its footing. You might start out reasonably enough, arguing, for example, that a gun control law restricts the rights of some citizens to have access to certain weapons, but pretty soon you start sliding toward conclusions that simply don't follow, such as that a gun control law is the beginning of the end of gun ownership in the country. Now you might really believe this, but logic isn't the route to get there.

9. **Either/or fallacy:** In a black-and-white world, something is right or wrong, true or false, good or bad. But ours is a colorful world with many shades. For instance, while it might be emotionally satisfying to say that opponents of the war in Iraq must not support the troops there, it is also possible that the war's opponents are against the war *because* they're concerned about the lives of American service people. Rather than *either/or* it might be *both/and.* We see this fallacy often in arguments that suggest that there are only two choices and each are opposites.

10. **Begging the question:** This one is also called circular reasoning because it assumes the truth of the arguer's conclusion without bothering to prove it. An obvious example of this would be to say that a law protecting people from Internet spam is good because it's a law, and laws should be obeyed. But *why* is it a good law?

Revising the Draft

As I discussed earlier in the book, one of the most common misconceptions about revision is that you do it only at the end of the writing process. In fact, up to this point, you should have been revising your work all along, from the first few journal exercises when you chose a topic and played with possible angles on it, to the journal work you might have done to prepare to write the sketch, and then again with your efforts to turn your sketch into a more developed draft. Revision is literally "re-seeing," and every time you create the conditions that allow you to discover something new about how you see or what you think about your subject, you are, in fact, engaged in the act of revision. In a sense, then, each writing assignment you undertake is one long act of revision, from start to finish.

But once you've completed a draft, the revision process becomes more focused. You are mostly working with material that should be somewhat settled, with purposes that might be clearer, and ideas that may have more shape. At this point, the biggest temptation is to tell yourself you are largely done and what revision remains is merely a matter of "fixing things"—tinkering with sentences, correcting typos, and running a spell-checker. In the survey from Chapter 1 (see page 20), 70 percent of students admitted as much. "I usually just tidy things up" was ranked first or second by students who were asked what they do most often when they revise an academic paper.

These activities are certainly an element of revision—and important ones—but as the word *revision* implies, it's important to "re-see" both what you are trying to say and how you try to say it, even at this stage in the process. Chapter 14, "Revision Strategies," is a useful introduction to the revision process for any essay, including the argument essay. It emphasizes ways writers can break the bonds that limit their ability to find new ways of seeing the draft.

Draft argument essays have some typical problems at this stage in the process. Do any of these apply to yours?

- Is your central claim or thesis stated clearly?
- Do you employ any logical fallacies? See "Inquiring into the Details: Common Logical Fallacies."
- Do you have sufficient evidence or information to make your assertions convincing? Do you need to gather more facts?
- Have you considered any counterarguments in your essay? This is especially important if you think the audience for your essay might not be inclined to initially agree with your position.
- Have you clearly established what stake your readers have in the issue you're writing about?
- Does the draft use *pathos, logos,* and *ethos* effectively? (See Figure 8.6.)

Chapter 14, "Revision Strategies," can help you address most of these problems. Refer to the following table to find specific strategies for ideas on how to revise your draft following your workshop. Remember that a draft may present problems in more than one category.

GUIDE TO REVISION STRATEGIES

Problems in the Draft (Chapter 14)	Part	Page Number
Unclear purpose ■ Not sure what the paper is about?	1	603
Unclear thesis, theme, or main idea ■ Not sure what you're trying to say?	2	609
Lack of information or development ■ Need more convincing evidence? Need to check for logical fallacies?	3	616
Disorganized ■ Doesn't move logically or smoothly from paragraph to paragraph?	4	620
Unclear or awkward at the level of sentences and paragraphs ■ Seems choppy or hard to follow at the level of sentences or paragraphs?	5	626

Polishing the Draft

After you've dealt with the big issues in your draft—is it sufficiently focused, does it answer the *So what?* question, is it well organized, and so on—you must deal with the smaller problems. You've carved the stone into an appealing figure but now you need to polish it. Are your paragraphs coherent? How do you manage transitions? Are your sentences fluent and concise? Are there any errors in spelling or syntax? Section 5 of Chapter 14 can help you focus on these issues.

Before you finish your draft, work through the following checklist:

- Every paragraph is about one thing.
- The transitions between paragraphs aren't abrupt.
- The length of sentences varies in each paragraph.
- Each sentence is concise. There are no unnecessary words or phrases.
- You've checked grammar, particularly verb agreement, run-on sentences, unclear pronouns, and misused words (*there/their, where/were,* and so on). (See of the handbook at the back of the book for help with these grammar issues.)
- You've run your spell-checker and proofed your paper for misspelled words.

STUDENT ESSAY

Many Americans are fond of talking about our country's native people in the past tense. We admire the tribal cultures as they existed a century or two ago, and borrow freely from them, engaging in "vision quests" and drumming circles. We feel the tug of nostalgia for these lost tribes, and yes, guilt for the sad history of relations between the mostly white immigrants who dispossessed the tribes and the Indian people who were confined to reservations. It's convenient to assume that the problems were in the past because contemporary Native Americans are largely invisible to us—except if you happen to drive through a reservation as Kelly Sundberg would on her way to visit friends at a nearby university.

Confronting Native Americans in the present tense forced Kelly to examine her own prejudices, and in the essay that follows she argues that the route to understanding begins at school.

I Am Not a Savage

Kelly Sundberg

1 Salmon, Idaho, is named after the river that runs through it, a river that is filled with turbulent whitewater punctuated by deep and calm pools and shallow riffles. In the spring, I have looked into these riffles and seen waves of silver and red moving gently just underneath the surface of the water.

2 We call them "reds"—spawning salmon. Nowadays, they are diminished in numbers, but at one time the river was full of them, and full of abundance as well for the Lemhi Indians who once lived on the banks. For the Lemhi, the salmon was not solely for sustenance, but also an integral part of their culture and spirituality.

3 Today there are few "reds" and almost no Lemhi left in the valley.

4 The initial influx of Mormon settlers followed by migrations of Californians and Midwesterners forced Native Americans out of the valley. Still, upon entering the Salmon city limits from Highway 28, a large sign proclaims, "Welcome to Salmon, Idaho. Birthplace of Sacagawea!" In a time when anything related to Lewis and Clark means profit, the city of Salmon, my hometown, has now chosen to capitalize on this marketable heritage, even though they once ignored it or treated it derisively.

5 My high school mascot is the "Salmon Savage." The marquee in front of the school has a picture with an Indian warrior on it, and when the football team scores a touchdown a white girl wearing war paint and a "made in China" headdress will ride a horse around the track in celebration.

6 I never questioned the integrity or intent of these symbols until I was a sophomore at the school. For Civil Rights Day, the school invited Rosa Abrahamson, a Lemhi Indian, to speak to the students. She cried as she spoke about the injustice of the name "savage." "My people are not savages," she said. "We are peaceful and do

not take pride in that name." When she finished speaking the applause was polite but subdued.

7 The next speaker was a rancher named Bud, who lit into a tirade about the government subsidizing "lazy Indians." As he finished with fists raised into the air, he was greeted by a standing ovation. For the first time in my life, I felt ashamed to be a part of the community.

8 It wasn't that those of us in the gym had consciously made the decision to be racist. It was simply ignorance. Despite the history of the Lemhi in the valley, our ideas of their culture are shaped from drives through the reservation on the way to campus visits at the University of Idaho. Our perceptions were safely gleaned from inside of an automobile and never involved real interaction with Native Americans.

9 Once, when asked to write our opinions about reservations in a U.S. government class, I wrote that I thought the government was making it "too easy on the Native Americans and they had become apathetic and unmotivated because of subsidies."

10 I got a better glimpse at my Lemhi neighbors recently reading Sherman Alexie's novel The Lone Ranger and Tonto Fistfight in Heaven. Alexie, a member of the Spokane/Coeur d'Alene tribes, conveys the opposition between contemporary and traditional Native American culture. His characters are torn and struggle to reconcile the two: "At the halfway point of any drunken night, there is a moment when an Indian realizes he cannot turn back toward tradition and that he has no map to guide him toward the future."

11 My own community struggles to reconcile two conflicting ideas as well—we embrace the symbols of savagery to inspire the football team, yet in order to make a profit we proudly claim Sacagawea as one of our own. Still, when the Lemhi wanted to build a school near Sacagawea's birthplace, the county refused to sell them the land, claiming it would become a "mini-reservation."

12 Ironically, Salmon shares more than it cares to admit with its neighbors on the reservation. Poverty, alcoholism, and depression are a way of life for many Salmon residents. Yet the perception in the community is that an alcoholic white man is somehow superior to a "drunk Indian."

13 In Salmon, all students are required to take an Idaho history class, yet this class makes almost no mention of Native American history in the valley. None of the readings in Advanced Placement English classes are by Native American authors, and government classes don't address Native American issues at all.

14 Is it any wonder that racism persists?

15 The local school system needs to lead. English teachers should require readings by authors like Alexie, they should provide field trips to local and national archeological sites, and they should bring in Native American interpreters to speak about local history. By letting go of negative and outdated ideas, the city of Salmon and the Lemhi can take the first step toward healing.

Evaluating the Essay

Discuss or write about your responses to Kelly Sundberg's essay using some or all of the following questions:

1. What is the thesis of the essay? Where in the piece is it most clearly stated?
2. Refer to the box that lists ten common logical fallacies and reread Sundberg's essay. Do you suspect there are any logical fallacies in "I Am Not a Savage"?
3. Consider the *ethos* of this essay. How does the writer come across? Is her persona effective?
4. What do you think is the most effective paragraph in the essay? Why? What is the least effective?

Using What You Have Learned

You've read published op-ed essays and a student draft. You've also worked on your own argument essay, a genre that may be new to you. Take a moment to consider how you might use what you've learned.

1. Reflect on how your thinking about argument and argumentative writing may have changed because of the reading and writing in this chapter by finishing the following sentence in your journal at least four times: *Before I began this chapter I thought ________, but now I think ________.*
2. The personal essay (discussed in Chapter 4) and the argument essay might seem at first to be fundamentally different kinds of writing. Do you see any connections between the two genres now?
3. Examine the letters to the editor or the editorial in your local newspaper. How do you read these pages differently after studying and writing an argument? Clip a letter or editorial that might best demonstrate what you've learned.

The poet Grace Butcher, pictured here at a reading in Ohio, sometimes writes about crows, which are quite ordinary birds, unless they fly through the imagination of a writer like Butcher. The best literature often finds the extraordinary significance in familiar things.

Part Three
INQUIRING DEEPER

At the heart of academic inquiry is the ongoing conversations between people who share an interest in something. As researchers, we listen in on those conversations to discover what has already been said, and then look for ways to add something new—a different interpretation, an alternative argument, a fresh finding, a new perspective.

11

Writing a Research Essay

WRITING WITH RESEARCH

Let's be honest. Most students hate writing research papers. There are exceptions, of course, and these are invariably students who see in a research-based essay the same thing they see in other writing they enjoy: an opportunity to discover something new and share it with someone else. In contrast, students who dislike research-based writing usually share the following assumptions:

- Whenever "facts" are required in a paper, the writing is generally boring.
- The research paper is a unique genre of writing, different from other forms, with its own special rules.
- No matter what the instructor says, the student's own opinions aren't really very important in a research paper.

With these assumptions in mind, I should clarify a few things now about the research essay. The most important is this: *The research essay shares qualities with all of the inquiry projects you've written to this point, whether it's a profile, a proposal, or a personal essay. In fact, the research essay is a natural extension of all of these other essays.* Research is something writers naturally do whenever they have questions they can't answer on their own. This was made clear in earlier chapters of *The Curious Writer.* Indeed, every inquiry project in this book emphasizes the importance of research *throughout* the writing process.

However, the research essay does present a few differences: First, the research essay may be the most thoroughly documented of the essays you've written so far, and it may be the one that is most likely to require scholarly sources such as journal articles and academic books. It's also likely to be a project that takes more time to do, and may be the

What You'll Learn in This Chapter

- How to apply what you've learned about writing shorter inquiry-based papers to an extended research project.
- Which beliefs about research you may want to "unlearn."
- How to distinguish between academic research genres.
- Techniques for reading academic articles.
- How to discover a "researchable" question.
- How to focus your essay.

Research is something writers naturally do whenever they have questions they can't answer on their own.

longest essay you're assigned, ranging from eight to twenty pages. A writing project with such an extended process of inquiry is more complicated to manage—it has more steps, you have more information to organize, and it's often harder to figure out what you want to say. For all of these reasons, the research essay is a form of inquiry that deserves special attention.

Still, research is hardly something alien to you. You've written research essays before, and although you probably don't consider yourself a researcher, for most of us research is a daily affair, whether looking up the details on new laptop computers in order to buy the right one or hunting for a new apartment in a highly competitive real estate market. Finally, research need not be boring at all. On the contrary, reading, observing, and interviewing can crack open worlds of study you never imagined.

RESEARCH ESSAYS VERSUS RESEARCH PAPERS

Broadly speaking, there are two approaches to academic research. The more traditional approach, the research *paper*, involves using research to make an extended argument about something in an effort to prove a claim. This may be an argument the writer knew he wanted to make even before he started the research. Or the project may have begun with a question that drove a process of inquiry and resulted in an answer the writer wants to prove.

Less common, but also used in some disciplines, is the research *essay*. The motive for writing a research essay, at least initially, is not *to prove* but *to discover*. Usually writers of research essays begin with a genuine desire to find out what they think about their subjects, or they might have a theory they want to test against the evidence they collect through research. For instance, a researcher might ask this: Have teenage courtship rituals changed since the eighties and, if so, how have the changes influenced relationships? A research essay on that topic may not be framed as an argument but instead narrate the process of investigating the question. It might describe some of the current findings on dating patterns, providing analysis on which of these seem most persuasive. A research essay might also *end* with a tentative thesis, rather than begin with one as research papers often do.

Each of these—the research essay and research paper—are perfectly valid forms and they share many qualities, but the research essay is much more likely to encourage the habits of mind that encourage genuine inquiry, including suspending judgment, beginning with questions not answers, and accepting ambiguity as a natural part of the process. You can apply these intellectual practices to either form of research, and you've applied them already to many writing assignments in this book. That's why I give the research essay so much attention in this chapter. Keep in mind, though, that the traditional argumentative research paper is an important academic form, and that the most versatile writers recognize that composing is often both a chance to discover *and* to prove.

In the three professional readings that follow in this chapter, you'll get a chance to see the range of approaches to research writing, from the informal and undocumented researched essay to the formal research paper. All of these readings focus on a single subject—courtship and sexuality on the American college campus—which will help you appreciate how the different forms of research writing offer different ways of examining a subject.

The research essay is much more likely to encourage the habits of mind that encourage genuine inquiry, including suspending judgment, beginning with questions not answers, and accepting ambiguity as a natural part of the process.

MOTIVES FOR WRITING A RESEARCH ESSAY

I was in the market for a new guitar, and for several weeks I'd been studying back issues of an acoustic guitar magazine, searching the Web for guitar makers, and talking to people who play. My process was driven by particular questions I had: *What are the best tone woods for a classical guitar? What are the various models and how much do they cost? What are the sound qualities to consider when selecting an instrument?* While I probably would never write an essay using my research, the stakes were rather high. I was likely to spend a lot of money on a guitar and I didn't want to make a mistake.

Although everyday research may not be as methodical as academic research, both approaches employ many of the same skills and share the same motive: curiosity. Sometimes this curiosity is intellectual interest—What are the origins of radical Islam?—and sometimes it's in response to a need for information: What is the best-quality acoustic guitar? Either way, the process begins as all inquiry projects do, with a question.

Not just any question will do. It has to be one that will drive the process for the few weeks it takes for you to learn about your topic and know enough to discover your own ideas about it. For example, the question, "Is Elvis dead?" will take about a second to answer: Yes, the King is dead. Why people keep asking that particular question is much more interesting and a more researchable question that just might work for an extended investigation. But whatever question you ask, it must be interesting to *you.*

Academic researchers *always* ask questions that interest them; curiosity is the most important motive. It should be for you, too. The essential thing you must learn about research writing is how to craft a good question that makes you wonder enough to live with the question long enough for you to write on it. This takes more skill than you might imagine, but once you know how to ask researchable questions, you'll be much more likely to see research writing the way your professors do—an opportunity for discovery.

THE RESEARCH ESSAY AND ACADEMIC WRITING

The research paper is a fixture in high school courses, usually lodged in the junior or senior English class and advertised as preparation for The College Research Paper. (Even my nine-year-old daughter wrote research papers.) Research-based writing assignments are probably among the most common in college, across the curriculum. In fact, at my own university almost three-quarters of the faculty surveyed said they assign an "academic paper that requires research." That's one reason you're writing a research essay in your composition class—to help prepare you to write papers in other courses.

These writing assignments can take a number of forms, including term papers, proposals, literature reviews, abstracts, and reports. But they all demand facility with finding information in the library, on the Web, or in the field; the skills to evaluate the information you have uncovered; and the ability to *use* that information appropriately and purposefully. Because research writing involves dealing with all of these things—something like a novice juggler trying to keep five balls in the air—even talented writers can see their prose fall apart when trying to communicate their findings. Additionally, the writers' beliefs and assumptions may make it harder to get the work done, and their beliefs and assumptions may even be misleading, if not downright wrong.

Some years ago, I surveyed about 250 first-year writing students about the research paper assignment, and at least 60 percent of them shared the following beliefs:

- "I have to be objective."
- "I have to know my thesis before I start."
- "I need to follow a formal structure."
- "I can't use I."

There is an element of truth to each of these, but each of these beliefs *works against* a genuine understanding of what it means to do academic research. Then what *is* the nature of academic research and the research essay?

FEATURES OF THE FORM

There's quite a range of research-based writing. Nearly every assignment you've done so far in *The Curious Writer* might be considered research based; reading, interviewing, and observing could be an element of any of the inquiry projects you've attempted using this book. But the research essay has a few distinctive features:

- *Academic research is driven by questions, not answers.* Most scholarship begins with a question about something: What is the impact of congressional redistricting on representation of minorities? What are the various ways the river might be understood symbolically in *Huckleberry Finn?* What is the distribution of bracken fern in a mature upland forest? What are the rhetorical strategies of pro-anorexia groups on the Web? Researchers begin with a question, not an answer, and although they may hypothesize, researchers are always prepared to be proved wrong. Framing the question is a crucial and often difficult part of the process.

- *The question is put in the context of what has already been said.* You're interested in whether so-called relational aggression between girls might be present in your niece's second-grade classroom. That's a great research question. What have others already said about it? How might the answers to your question contribute to the ongoing conversation about how young girls treat each other? This often means that you will need to become familiar with the published conversation about your topic, a step in the research process called a literature review (see Appendix B for details about literature reviews).
- *Source material is used in the service of what writers are trying to say about their topics.* Research essays are not like encyclopedia entries or the research reports you may have written in high school. They do not merely present information gathered from source material. Instead, they actively *use* the information to explore or answer questions or to test the truth of an idea or thesis. In this sense, the research essay is very much like the other kinds of essays you have written so far.
- *Sources that contributed to a writer's thinking are formally given credit.* The larger purpose of academic inquiry is to make new knowledge, to contribute in some way to what people understand about how the world works. This always involves standing on the shoulders of others who have already said something about your topic, and this is something that you acknowledge explicitly through citation. While citation has all sorts of conventions, and yes, it can be a pain, the acknowledgment of your sources is both a gracious gesture and a source of authority for you—it indicates that you're party to the ongoing conversation about your topic. Accurately acknowledging your sources is also an ethical obligation that all good researchers take seriously.
- *Most research essays have a clearly stated thesis.* Like a long train, research essays carry a lot of freight and they must stay on track. One way to do this is to clearly organize the information you gather around an explicit focusing question. This question should lead readers to some answers, particularly one main idea, claim, or thesis that seems most persuasive to the writer. While some formal research papers state this thesis in the introduction, research essays typically have a "delayed" thesis that may be stated somewhere near the end.
- *Research essays typically use four sources of information.* Nonfiction writing draws on four sources of information: memory or experience, observation, interviews, and reading. It's not unusual to read a personal essay that relies solely on the writer's memory of an experience as a source of information. A profile might use two or three sources, including observation and interview. But a research essay may draw information from *all four* sources. Writers cast as wide a net as possible to discover the answers to their questions.

UNDOCUMENTED RESEARCH ESSAY

College students don't date anymore; they "hook up" or get committed to an "ultra-serious" relationship. At least that was the conclusion of a controversial study of 1,000 college women across the United States conducted by the Independent Women's Forum, a part of the conservative Institute for American Values (IAV). The 2001 project found that 40 percent of women surveyed reported that they had "hooked up" with a partner at least once and 10 percent had done it more than six times.

"Hooking up," as you probably know, is an intimate encounter between people who likely know each other but don't consider themselves committed. Hooking up often involves alcohol.

The study's release caused a storm of commentary from students, political and cultural commentators, and college administrators. In the brief essay that follows, a staff writer from *The Christian Century* magazine uses the release of the IAV study to explore the demise of "courtship rituals" that lead to marriage. Like a lot of articles for a general audience, "Courting Confusion" does not rely heavily on academic sources nor are the few sources it uses documented with citations; this essay is an informal researched essay, the kind that journalists and opinion writers publish.

COURTING CONFUSION

Christian Century Magazine

1 The word *courtship* and the idea of it—a prescribed process of getting to know someone in preparation for marriage—is virtually archaic. The courting rituals that members of the baby-boom generation still enacted or endured have largely disappeared. Young people no longer live with expectations about male initiative and female reticence. When they arrive at college, they often find coed dorms, perhaps even coed bathrooms, which offer a simulated experience of familial intimacy. In this scene, the rituals of dating are as antiquated as chaperones or calling cards.

2 The dissolution of many of the older rituals was no doubt a necessary step toward egalitarian relationships. But some observers have suggested that young people today suffer from the lack of any tradition for channeling and reflecting on erotic desires. Amy and Leon Kass, drawing on years of teaching at the University of Chicago, recently suggested that "there are no socially prescribed forms of conduct that help guide young men and women in the direction of matrimony." People still make it to the altar, the Kasses noted, but it's almost by accident; they have no compass to direct them. (The popularity of Ellen Fein and Sherrie Schneider's 1995 book *The Rules* indicates there is a felt need for such a compass, though the book merely recommends, rather cynically, that some of the old gender dichotomies are strategically useful for women.)

3 A recent study by the Institute for American Values offers some confirmation of the Kasses' judgment. In surveying college women's attitudes toward sex and marriage, researchers

encountered repeated references to men and women "hooking up"—a distinctive new social form, though really more of an antiform. The researchers developed this consensus definition of the "hook-up": it can involve a range of sexual activities, from kissing to intercourse; is usually engaged in when both parties are drinking or drunk; may or may not be repeated with the same partner; and is understood by both parties to involve no emotional commitment or even affection. "Hook-ups usually occur between people who do not know one another well, with little if any expectation that either person will follow through and try to continue the relationship," says the IAV report released last month (see **www.americanvalues.org**). According to the survey, 40 percent of college women have hooked up at least once, and 10 percent more than six times.

Though less than half of students are engaging in the practice, and though hooking up is 4
hardly a brand-new phenomenon on campuses, the prominence of the hook-up in these women's lives is a sign of an impoverished social scene—impoverished socially, romantically and even erotically. The IAV report includes some poignant remarks by young woman about their confusion in the aftermath of hooking up. Though they know that a hook-up entails no emotional attachment, they still worry about how to act afterward, not knowing how the young man will respond or whether the relationship will continue in any way. (The survey doesn't report how the young men feel.) Especially poignant are the women who upbraid themselves for caring this much. A generation ago, these young women probably would have felt a little guilty about the sex; now they feel a little guilty about the residual commitment.

The IAV report suggests that colleges offer unprecedented opportunities to hang out casu- 5
ally with the opposite sex, along with the freedom for some couples to bond intensely—living, eating and sleeping together at an early age—but they do not offer many options in between. There are few chances to explore deeper relationships in a safe and measured way, and with a sense of shared and legitimate expectations.

The old courtship rituals cannot and should not be retrieved. But perhaps, in light of 6
reports like this one, it's time to give thought to some new rituals.

Inquiring into the Essay

Explore, explain, evaluate, and reflect on "Courting Confusion."

1. The author of "Courting Confusion" writes that college life provides "unprecedented opportunities" to spend time with the "opposite sex," including the chance to have sex with little commitment. But the cost of this, the essay argues, is there are "few chances to explore deeper relationships in a safe and measured way." Fastwrite in your journal for seven minutes about your own ideas about this. Spend half the time playing the "believing game" and half the time the "doubting game."
2. Find the report on which this essay was based on the Web by visiting the following site: http://www.americanvalues.org/html/r-hooking_up.html. Browse the report, "Hooking Up, Hanging Out and Hoping for Mr. Right: College Women on Mating and Dating Today," and summarize in a tight paragraph what you believe are its most significant findings.

3. What's your evaluation of the argument in "Courting Confusion" that there is a need for new "courtship rituals"? If you agree or disagree, what reasons would you offer as a basis for your position?
4. This is an undocumented essay; that is, it doesn't include any in-text citations or a bibliography. Reflect on why the author was or was not justified in using this strategy for this essay.

DOCUMENTED RESEARCH ESSAY

When I went to college in the seventies, dating was dead but "hooking up," at least in its current meaning, was not all that common. Though the "sexual revolution" of the sixties still resonated on campuses thirty years ago, people generally were still interested in commitment when they sought intimacy. However, I dated in high school, as did most of my friends. There were dances, dinners, movies, and concerts, all occasions that demanded dates. I imagine that it's hard for my younger students today to picture the dating scene, which is why the following academic essay, excerpted from the book *From Front Porch to Back Seat: Courtship in the Twentieth Century*, is so illuminating.

Using the popular magazines of the day as sources, Beth Bailey describes the rise of dating as a social ritual in the 1940s and 1950s. This historical context is useful when considering the argument in the preceding reading, "Courting Confusion," that we need new rituals like dating that stop way short of "hooking up."

While "The Worth of a Date," unlike some research essays, makes an argument from the outset, it is a less formal treatment of its subject and taps largely popular sources rather than academic ones. Notice, however, that it is a scholarly essay that includes citations and references. Unlike the preceding essay, "The Worth of a Date" is intended for other academics, but it's written to be accessible to nonspecialists, too.

The Worth of a Date

Beth Bailey

1 Before the sexual revolution of the 1960s provided juicier material, *Esquire* was fond of running cartoons featuring a short, elderly, and paunchy millionaire escorting a tall, enormous-breasted young showgirl through opulent settings. The captions didn't really matter. The cartoons worked best subtextually, and all contained variations on the same theme: money and sex; the coupling of wallet and bosom.

2 It is easy, today, to center on the objectification of woman represented by the showgirl, a caricature stripped to her essentials: legs, breasts, and greed. She is clearly a commodity, purchased by man's wealth. But the man, too, is objectified. His value to her lies only in what he can buy. He is interchangeable with any other well-stuffed wallet. Their relationship is obviously mutually exploitative: the man is as much a commodity to the woman as she is a commodity to him.

The millionaire and the showgirl are a long way from our image of young love, but this mass-produced image can illustrate some of the values inherent in the American dating system. In courtship, no less than in the culture at large, we find America's "culture of consumption"—a way of seeing that encourages the paired acts of consumption and commodification. 3

The culture of consumption, as Jackson Lears and Richard Wrightman Fox describe it in a book of that title, is not simply the system of values underlying a consumer economy or a society "saturated by mass-produced and mass-marketed goods." It is also "an ethic, a standard of living, and a power structure" that centers on consumption, in which "individuals have been invited to seek commodities as keys to personal welfare . . . even to conceive of their own selves as commodities" (Wrightman and Lears ix–xvii). And, I might add, to transform personal relationships into commodities. 4

In dating, American young people sought their "personal welfare" through dates (and later through steadies), as commodities that afforded public validation of popularity, of belonging, of success. Whether or not one liked the date (person), the date (event) was valuable, a necessary commodity in youth culture. As commodities, dates (events) were valued differentially by the level of consumption they entailed—in short, by their cost. The date (person) could also become a commodity. In this system, men and women often defined themselves and each other as commodities, the woman valued by the level of consumption she could demand (how much she was "worth"), and the man by the level of consumption he could provide. 5

The particular form the American dating system took as it emerged in the early twentieth century was determined, in large part, by the new centrality of money in the act of courtship. As "going somewhere" became the thing to do, the man had to spend money to provide entertainment, refreshments, and transportation for the couple. Gradually, as dating became the dominant form of courtship, participants and observers recognized how important money had become. In general, dates had come to be defined by the fact that they cost money. Over and over in the national media, women and men, girls and boys, advisers and experts insisted on this definition of dating. Money was central: a date took place when a couple "went out" and spent money. 6

All the polls and columns and books on dating in the second third of the twentieth century made abundantly clear that American youth did not consider spending time with a member of the opposite sex the same as dating. In almost all instances, a date centered around an act of consumption: going out for dinner or a Coke, seeing a movie, buying access to some form of entertainment. Of course, the emphasis was not on unbridled consumption. The act had to take place within certain limits and according to many conventions, one of the most important being that the man pay the woman's way. 7

The "sub-deb" adviser for the *Ladies' Home Journal* shows the extent of these implicit definitions of a date in a 1944 column. She tells the story of a young girl—about fourteen—who is "fed up" because she can't get a date. The girl, as the author describes her, has a good social life—lots of friends, including boys who like her well enough to meet her and sit beside her at the movies. The adviser does not give the obvious moral. Instead of pointing out that this sub-deb should concentrate on enjoying the movie and the boy's company, she approvingly recounts the girl's "plan": she will concentrate on "Pete," the "likeliest one" (note that she does not say "the one she likes best"). "When he sits by me in the movies," the girl says, "I'm going to pretend he paid my way in. I'm going to play-act it's a real date" (Woodward 8). The only thing lacking, evidently, is knowledge that the boy *paid* for her. 8

9 A real girl, Margaret Graves of St. Louis, had a similar opinion on the subject. Writing to *Senior Scholastic* in 1951, she said, "If a girl has to pay her own way [on a date], she might as well go alone or with girl friends" (Head 24). To her, the date was not the event, was not the companionship, was not even being *seen* with the boy. A date meant being paid for. And boys agreed. A *Senior Scholastic* poll on dating found that while 90 percent of the girls questioned would agree to "occasionally," if reluctantly, share expenses, 50 percent of the boys strenuously objected to the idea. "If a boy is financially embarrassed," one boy wrote, "he shouldn't date" (Head 24) . . .

10 This concern with being seen is crucial, for it relates to the role of the date in youth culture . . . [D]ates often functioned in youth culture as tools for acquiring popularity—much as did clothes, cars, and other consumer goods. But a date that had no independent content, that was only a marker for popularity, had no meaning if no one knew about it. The date had to be public.

11 The boy who longed for a date, as Margaret Mead noted in the 1940s, was not longing for a girl, much less for a relationship with a particular girl (Mead 145). He desired to be in the public situation that defined a date: he desired to *have* a date, and he desired for others to see that he had a date. This sort of date, "had" and displayed, is itself a commodity . . .

12 Of course, some dates were prized more than others. Teen advice books warned girls to be understanding and hospitable to the boy who was occasionally low on funds, but not to let him get in the habit of hanging around their living rooms with no "real" dates in exchange. And real dates, the public culture of dating constantly emphasized, were expensive and flamboyant. While most polls discovered that teens' usual dates were for a movie and a snack, the magazines that conducted these polls frequently described the unusual dates—the "ideal" dates—in loving detail . . . .

13 The high school prom, the biggest social event of the year, represented the "ideal" date to most students. Proms were, of course, something more than special dates. They were a kind of rite of passage that transformed boys and girls into young men and women; they were occasions for magical extravagance. They required elegant evening attire and transportation, and included postprom entertainment at the fanciest night spot the area offered. . . .

14 Proms offered high school students not only a taste of the "ideal" extravagant dates otherwise largely denied them (at least until they were older) but also a forum for social competition. The first level of competition was simply rating a bid or getting a date; the next was getting the "right" date. Beyond these basics, proms stressed competition through material goods. With all (who qualified) brought together, it was easy to compare dresses, to see who rated an orchid and who just a gardenia, to rank postprom destinations and modes of transportation. The pressure could be intense, and during the Depression years of the 1930s, Chicago high school principals frequently cancelled school proms because they feared the many students who couldn't afford them would be "psychologically wounded" by that failure (Gutowski 256). . . .

15 In college, the pressure was more consistent. College students didn't have to contend with only one prom or ideal date a year, but with a whole succession of extravagant events. College football weekends were glamorized by a wide range of national magazines as one dizzy succession of brunches and lunches and dances and dinners—at a cost to men, *Good Housekeeping* estimated in 1953, of about $83 a weekend (Frey 225). *Mademoiselle*, in its 1954 college issue,

showed the pressure for expensive dates by defining "*Quiet Evening*" as "Any nocturnal date that results in a heightened feeling of well being and costs less than $5" (Frey 309). The previous year *Good Housekeeping* had published results of an informal survey of the cost of college "big" dates. Average outlays for one date ranged from a low of $25 in Boston and Dallas to a high of $35 in St. Louis. Paducah, Kentucky, with a population of 35,000, came in just about average at $30 (Frey 224). . . .

Flowers, both in college and outside, exemplify the dating system's emphasis on competing through consumption. Almost every description of a "big date," from the 1920's through the 1950's, features the kind of corsage the girl or woman wears, and sample budgets for major dates allot anywhere from $2 to $10 for corsages (Frey 225). These flowers were not private gifts—cut flowers for the woman's dressing table—but public symbols. They said, for the man, "See what I can afford," and for the woman, "See how much I'm worth." The girl who said she could buy her own Cokes understood that in the dating competition the companionship of a Coke date couldn't match the symbolic importance of flowers on a big date. . . . 16

In quite literal terms, women gauged their own value in dating by how much money men spent on them. . . . In this system, that the man pay for the date was crucial. Beyond that, the more he spent—publicly—the better. 17

Works Cited

Frey, Richard L. "The High Cost of Dating." *Good Housekeeping* Aug. 1953: 224–309.

Gutowski, Thomas. "The High School as Adolescent-Raising Institution: An Inner History of Chicago Public Secondary Education, 1856–1940." Diss. of Chicago, 1978.

Head, Gay. "Boy Dates Girl Jam Session." *Senior Scholastic* 11 Apr. 1951: 24.

Mead, Margaret. "The Male and Female." *Ladies' Home Journal* Sept. 1949: 145.

Woodward, Elizabeth. "The Sub-Deb: I'm Fed Up." *Ladies' Home Journal* Jan. 1944: 2.

Wrightman, Richard Fox, and T. J. Jackson Lears, eds. *The Culture of Consumption*. New York: Pantheon, 1983.

INQUIRING INTO THE ESSAY

Use the ways of inquiring—exploring, explaining, evaluating, and reflecting—to discover what you think about "The Worth of a Date."

1. Historical research such as "The Worth of a Date" is a frame through which we can see the present, in this case specifically the ways that social rituals such as dating have changed. As soon as you finish the essay, try to use the frame that Bailey provides as a way to look at your own experience. In your journal, write for five full minutes, using the reading as a prompt. Begin by exploring what struck you most by this description of dating in the 1930s through 1950s, especially when compared with your own experiences in the present.

2. Define the term *social ritual* in your own words. Explain how the dating scene fifty years ago described in this essay does or does not meet your definition. Return to the argument in the previous reading, "Courting Confusion." Do you think there is a need for new social rituals?
3. The argument in "The Worth of a Date" is implied by its title. Do you find the idea that dating was "commodified" persuasive? Even more important, is such a claim relevant?
4. Some years ago, a writer used the term *presentism* to describe how modern readers often unfairly apply contemporary moral standards and values to historical events. It wouldn't be hard to do the same thing here. Reflect on how a modern researcher can avoid being blinded by presentism.

Inquiring into the Details

READING ACADEMIC RESEARCH ESSAYS

Just as reading a poem demands some different reading strategies than reading an essay, making sense of academic writing presents its own peculiar challenges. Here are some tips for picking your way through an academic journal article.

- Pay particular attention to the *justification* for why this research question is worthy of study. Do you understand how it extends existing scholarship on the topic?
- Imagine an artichoke. You have to work your way through the leaves to get to the heart, the best part. In a journal article, this is the main argument, thesis, finding, or claim. You will find this in a range of locations—sometimes it's stated in an "abstract" (if there is one), at the end of an introduction or literature review, or even at the very end of the article.
- You don't have to understand all the jargon, just enough that you understand the research question and the conclusions.
- You're probably not in a position to evaluate the methods used, but make an effort to identify and understand them.
- When doing your own research, pay attention to names of people who are cited often. These are often people who have said the most in the ongoing conversation about the topic.
- Carefully consider how the author qualifies his or her conclusions. This often mutes the significance of the findings and helps you understand how seriously to take them.

DOCUMENTED RESEARCH PAPER

Though the following academic paper, published in the *Journal of Sex Research,* was originally written as an undergraduate honors thesis, chances are that, unless you're going on to graduate school, you won't write a paper that will end up in a scholarly journal. But depending on the field you choose, you will be expected to think and write like the author of this essay. That means that you must learn to ask researchable questions that somehow extend or challenge what has already been said by others on your topic. It also means that you will collect and analyze evidence of some kind to test your hunches. And above all, being an academic researcher means you explore topics that genuinely interest you and might make a difference to others.

"Pluralistic Ignorance and Hooking Up" does all of these things. Tracy Lambert and her coauthors take an idea that has been around for a while and wonder whether it might apply to hooking up behaviors on her college campus. She suspects that something called "pluralistic ignorance," or the sense that what makes you feel uncomfortable probably doesn't bother other people nearly as much, strongly operates among men and women who hook up. With the help of her professors, Tracy designs a study to test the hypothesis.

Like most social science research, this paper follows a prescribed format: introduction (literature review and purpose of the study), methods, results, and discussion. At first, these conventions might seem alien to you (see "Inquiring into the Details: Reading Academic Research Essays"), but once you get used to navigating academic discourse, a whole new world of information opens.

Pluralistic Ignorance and Hooking Up

Tracy Lambert, Arnold Kahn, and Kevin Apple

"Hooking up"—when two people agree to engage in sexual behavior for which there is no future commitment—has become popular on college compuses. In this study we examined the extent to which pluralistic ignorance affects hooking up. One hundred thirty-six female and 128 male college students answered questions regarding their own comfort and their perceived peers' comfort in engaging in a variety of sexual behaviors while hooking up. We hypothesized and found that both women and men rated their peers as being more comfortable engaging in these behaviors than they rated themselves. Men expressed more comfort than did women in engaging in these behaviors, and both sexes overestimated the other gender's comfort with hooking up behaviors. Pluralistic ignorance appears to apply to hooking up on college campuses, and we explore some potential consequences of pluralistic ignorance in this context.

Although one-night stands and uncommitted sexual behaviors are not a recent phenomenon, past research has focused on personality traits, attitudes, and individual differences in willingness to engage in such behaviors (e.g., Gerrard, 1980; Gerrard & Gibbons, 1982; Simpson & Gangestad, 1991; Snyder, Simpson, & Gangestad, 1986). The tacit assumption in this past research was that sexual behaviors within a committed and loving relationship were unproblematic, but that unloving, uncommitted sexual relations had to be explained. 1

However, today on college campuses across the United States what was once viewed as problematic has now become normative, and students refer to this process as "hooking up."

2 Hooking up occurs when two people who are casual acquaintances or who have just met that evening at a bar or party agree to engage in some forms of sexual behavior for which there will likely be no future commitment (Boswell & Spade, 1996; Kahn et al., 2000; Paul, McManus, & Hayes, 2000). The couple typically does not communicate what sexual behaviors they will or will not engage in, and frequently both parties have been drinking alcohol (Kahn et al., 2000; Paul et al., 2000). Paul et al. (2000) found that 78% of women and men on the campus being studied had engaged in hooking up at least once. In the Kahn et al. (2000) sample of college students, 86% of the women and 88% of the men indicated they had hooked up. Almost one half (47%) of the men and one third of the women in the Paul et al. sample engaged in sexual intercourse during the hookup, and Kahn et al. found that their sample believed petting below the waist, oral sex, and sexual intercourse occurred with some regularity in the process of hooking up.

3 *Pluralistic ignorance*, a concept first coined by Floyd Allport (1924, 1933), exists when, within a group of individuals, each person believes his or her private attitudes, beliefs, or judgments are discrepant from the norm displayed by the public behavior of others. Therefore, each group member, wishing to be seen as a desirable member of the group, publicly conforms to the norm, each believing he or she is the only one in the group experiencing conflict between his or her private attitude and his or her public behavior. Group members believe that most others in their group, especially those who are popular and opinion leaders (Katz & Lazarsfeld, 1955), actually endorse the norm and want to behave that way, while they themselves privately feel they are going along with the norm because of a desire to fit in with the group and exemplify the norm (Prentice & Miller, 1993, 1996). In this study we examined the extent to which pluralistic ignorance might be related to U.S. college students' comfort levels with sexual behaviors involved in hooking up. Consistent with the premise of pluralistic ignorance, we hypothesized that college students would perceive others as having a greater comfort level engaging in a variety of sexual behaviors than they themselves would have.

4 Prentice and Miller (1993) demonstrated pluralistic ignorance among college students in the area of alcohol consumption. On a campus where heavy alcohol use was the perceived norm, Prentice and Miller found that students estimated both the average student and their friends to have less discomfort with the level of alcohol consumption on campus than they reported for themselves. Furthermore, for male but not female students, they found greater consistency between respondents' comfort levels with alcohol consumption and the perceived norm and between respondents' reported drinking levels and the perceived norm at the end of the semester than at the beginning of the semester. Although correlational in nature, these results suggest that over time, male students may have changed their attitudes and behaviors to bring them more in line with the perceived norm. Perkins and Berkowitz (1986) reported similar findings with regard to the discrepancy between college students' own comfort with the amount of drinking at the university and what they estimated to be the general campus attitude.

5 Although pluralistic ignorance was originally conceptualized as a discrepancy between public behavior and private beliefs (Miller & McFarland, 1987), others have used the concept to refer to situations in which there is not direct evidence of behavioral similarity (e.g., Fields & Schuman, 1976; O'Gorman & Garry, 1976). More recently, Cohen and Shotland (1996)

invoked the concept of pluralistic ignorance in a variety of dating situations for which public scrutiny was absent. They found that both men and women believed that the average other person of their sex had more liberal sexual expectations than they set for themselves, both sexes believing the average other person of their sex would expect sexual intercourse much sooner in a relationship than they themselves would expect it. When asked whether a same-sex peer would expect to have sexual intercourse with a person with whom they were emotionally involved but for whom they felt no physical attraction, both men and women believed the average man and woman would expect sexual intercourse, while only approximately 50% of the participants would expect sex themselves in such a relationship, and an even smaller percentage reported having had sex in such a relationship. Finally, when there was neither emotional nor physical attraction to a partner, few women or men expected that they would have sexual intercourse with the partner, but believed the average man and woman would indeed expect sexual intercourse.

Pluralistic ignorance might have consequences when beliefs about the norm condone intimate sexual behaviors. In the process of hooking up, pluralistic ignorance may lead one or both sexual partners to act according to the perceived norm rather than to their own convictions. There is a large literature showing that men have more liberal attitudes towards sexual behaviors and expect sexual intercourse sooner in a relationship than do women (Cohen & Shotland, 1996; Knox & Wilson, 1981; Oliver & Hyde, 1993) and that men are much more receptive than are women to offers of sexual intercourse (Clark & Hatfield, 1989). Byers and Lewis (1988) found that disagreements among dating partners on the desired level of sexual behavior was almost always in the direction of the male partner wanting a higher level of sexual intimacy than that desired by the female partner. Thus, it is possible that many men go into hooking-up situations hoping to engage in more intimate sexual behaviors than are desired by their female partners. Because men are expected to initiate sexual activity (DeLamater, 1987; Peplau & Gordon, 1985), it is possible that in the process of hooking up, some women will experience unwanted sexual advances and possibly even sexual assault or rape. 6

In their research on hooking up, Kahn et al. (2000) asked 92 female and 50 male college students if they had ever had a "really terrible hooking up experience." Nearly one half of the women (42%) and the men (46%) indicated they had had such an experience. A "terrible experience" for the men was usually due to the women wanting a relationship or to the use of too much alcohol or drugs; none mentioned pressure to go further than they desired. However, nearly one half of the women (48.3%) who reported having a terrible hooking-up experience indicated that they were pressured to go further than they had wanted to go. They gave responses such as "I hooked up with a guy who didn't understand the meaning of 'no'" and "I didn't want to—he did—he wouldn't back off." These women may have experienced sexual assault during a hook up but did not label their experiences as such because they believed the behaviors to be normative. In addition, 10.3% of the women and 11.1% of the men in this sample said the hook up was terrible because they had gone too far without mentioning pressure from their partner. Going too far might have been the consequence of pluralistic ignorance, conforming to a presumed norm. 7

The present study sought to extend the findings of Cohen and Shotland (1996), which were restricted to expectations of sexual intercourse in dating situations, to the area of hooking up. Further, we wanted to examine whether pluralistic ignorance occurred with other sexual behaviors besides sexual intercourse. Based on the research on pluralistic ignorance and gender differences in expected sexual behaviors, we hypothesized that both male and female students would see other 8 students as more comfortable with various hooking-up behaviors than they were themselves. Although we expected individuals would vary in their own comfort levels with various hooking-up behaviors, we expected they would believe other students to be uniformly more comfortable engaging in those behaviors than they were themselves. Furthermore, consistent with previous literature, we hypothesized that men would be significantly more comfortable than women with engaging in all hooking-up behaviors. Finally, we hypothesized that due to pluralistic ignorance, both women and men would overestimate the other gender's comfort with all hooking-up behaviors.

Method

Participants

9 One hundred seventy-five female and 152 male undergraduate students from a mid-sized residential southeastern public university that has few nontraditional students served as participants for the study. The convenience sample represented a moderately even distribution of year in school: for first years, $n = 79$ (41 females, 38 males); for sophomores, $n = 70$ (37 females, 33 males); for juniors, $n = 84$ (45 females, 39 males); and for seniors, $n = 93$ (52 females, 41 males). A female experimenter approached students as they entered the university library and asked them to volunteer to answer some questions about hooking up and sexual behaviors as part of her senior honors project. She approached other students in their residence halls. No differences appeared between these two samples for any of the dependent measures. Analyses concerning pluralistic ignorance and comfort with hooking up are based on the data from 136 women (77.7%) and 128 men (84.2%) who indicated that they had hooked up.

Materials and Procedure

10 The questionnaire consisted of questions developed by the authors to examine student attitudes toward hooking up. On the first page, students read that the investigator was interested in "students' attitudes and behaviors with regard to dating and 'hooking up,'" and hooking up was defined as "a sexual encounter between two people who may or may not know each other well, but who usually are *not* seriously dating." Participants also signed an informed consent form, which indicated all information would be anonymous and confidential. To insure anonymity and encourage honest responding, the only demographic information obtained was the participants' year in school. We made no attempt to determine sexual orientation or marital status: however, on this residential campus the overwhelming majority of students come to the university directly from high school, identify themselves as heterosexual, and have never been married (James Madison University Office of Institutional Research, 2001–2002). Participants were told they were not required to complete the survey if they became uncomfortable.

11 Students who said they had hooked up were instructed to continue to the next page. We constructed 11-point scales modeled after those used by Prentice and Miller (1993) on which 3 points were labeled: 1 = *very uncomfortable*, 6 = *neutral*, and 11 = *very comfortable*. Participants responded to the question "How comfortable are you with the amount of hooking up that goes on at [school name]?" They then responded to the question "How comfortable are you with engaging in the following activities during a hook up?" with regard to "petting above the waist," "petting below the waist," "oral sex," and "sexual intercourse." Participants used the

same scales in response to the questions "How comfortable do you think the *average female* student is with the amount of hooking up that goes on at [school name]?" and "How comfortable do you think the *average female* student is with engaging in the following activities during a hook up?" Finally, they responded to the questions "How comfortable do you think the *average male* student is with the amount of hooking up that goes on at [school name]?" and "How comfortable do you think the *average male* student is with engaging in the following activities during a hook up?"

Students who indicated that they had never hooked up were asked to skip to a different page of the survey, which contained questions regarding why they did not hook up and whether or not they believed that there was a relationship between hooking up and sexual assault. This part of the questionnaire was included so that all participants would work on the survey for approximately the same amount of time without knowing who had or had not hooked up. 12

Participants completed the questionnaire privately, usually within a short distance of the researcher. Those participating at the library placed their completed questionnaires in a large box, and those participating in their residence hall placed completed questionaires in a large envelope. When they were finished, participants were encouraged to ask questions and discuss the questionnaire with the researcher, who provided them with a debriefing statement and a list of campus resources for sexual assault. 13

Results

We tested the hypothesis that students would experience pluralistic ignorance regarding hooking up with a 2 (Gender) X 2 (Target: self or other) ANOVA, with target as a within-subjects variable. As hypothesized, participants demonstrated pluralistic ignorance by evaluating their own comfort level with the amount of hooking up. $M = 7.08$, $SD = 2.31$, significantly lower than their estimate of a same-sex peer's comfort level, $M = 7.75$, $SD = 2.08$, $F\ (1.262) = 24.24$, $p < .0001$, partial $\eta^2 = .085$. Participants believed that other college students were more comfortable with the amount of hooking up than were they. This main effect of target was qualified by a significant gender by target interaction, $F\ (1, 262) = 7.55$, partial $\eta^2 = .028$, $p < .01$. Both men and women showed the same pattern of overestimating their peers' comfort levels: however, the pattern was more pronounced among the male students (9.01_{peer} vs. 7.95_{self}), $t\ (127) = 4.68$, $p < .0001$, $d = .502$, than among the female students (6.57_{peer} vs. 6.26_{self}), $t\ (135) = 1.85$, $p < .05$, one-tailed, $d = .185$. Table 11.1 presents these means and standard deviations. 14

Table 11.1. Ratings of Own and Average Same-Sex Student's Comfort With Hooking Up

Measure	Self: M (*SD*)	Average student: M (*SD*)
Women	6.26 (1.79)	6.57 (1.63)
Men	7.95 (2.48)	9.01 (1.74)

Note. Ratings were made on 11-point scales (1 = *not at all comfortable* and 11 = *very comfortable*).

Table 11.2. Ratings of Men's and Women's Own Comfort With Hooking-Up Behaviors

	Men: M (*SD*)	Women: M (*SD*)
Petting above the waist	9.12 (2.47)	7.29 (2.68)
Petting below the waist	8.42 (2.60)	5.13 (2.73)
Oral sex	7.56 (3.05)	3.49 (2.63)
Sexual intercourse	5.65 (3.57)	2.15 (2.31)

15 A dependent t test for equality of variances revealed that participants showed significantly less variability in their ratings of peer comfort level in hooking up than in their ratings of peer comfort level in hooking up than in their self-ratings. $t\ (262) = 1.96, p < .05$, one-tailed. When rating their own comfort levels, the standard deviation in participants' responses was 2.31. However, the standard deviation significantly decreased to 2.08 when participants estimated their peers' comfort with hooking up. This decrease in variability when estimating others' comfort provides some evidence for an illusion of universality. That is, participants showed greater uniformity in their beliefs about others' comfort levels compared to their own actual comfort levels.

16 We used multivariate analysis of variance (MANOVA) to examine the hypothesis regarding men's and women's own comfort levels with various sexual behaviors, with participant gender as the between-subjects variable. Men reported significantly greater comfort with these behaviors than did women. $F\ (4.259) = 35.17, p < .0001$, partial $\eta^2 = .352$. Table 11.2 shows that men's greater comfort occurred with all four hooking-up behaviors.

17 We tested the hypothesis that both men and women would overestimate the other gender's comfort with hooking-up behaviors using two separate MANOVAS. The first examined the men's estimates of the average woman's comfort, and the second examined the women's estimates of the average man's comfort. To evaluate the accuracy of these estimates, the comfort estimates were compared with the means of the actual comfort

Table 11.3. Differences Between Each Gender's Own Comfort Level With Hooking-Up Behaviors and Estimates of the Other Gender's Comfort Levels

	Women's estimate of men: M (*SD*)	Men's actual comfort level: M (*SD*)	Men's estimate of women: M (*SD*)	Women's actual comfort level: M (*SD*)
Petting above the waist	9.80 (1.45)	9.12 (2.47)	7.73 (1.92)	7.29 (2.68)
Petting below the waist	9.30 (1.67)	8.42 (2.60)	6.38 (2.07)	5.13 (2.73)
Oral sex	8.61 (1.93)	7.56 (3.04)	5.49 (2.19)	3.49 (2.62)
Sexual intercourse	7.62 (2.24)	5.65 (3.57)	4.28 (2.36)	2.15 (2.31)

ratings of these hooking-up behaviors. Both the men, $F\ (4, 259) = 7.82$, $p < .0001$, partial $\eta^2 = .108$, and the women, $F\ (4, 259) = 16.25$, $p < .0001$, partial $\eta^2 = .201$, significantly overestimated the other gender's actual comfort levels with various hooking-up behaviors. As shown in Table 11.3, this overestimation occurred for both sexes on each of the four hooking-up behaviors.

Discussion

Cohen and Shotland (1996) found evidence of pluralistic ignorance regarding expectations of sexual intercourse on a date. The current research extended these findings to other sexual behaviors, and did so in the context of hooking up. We found that both women and men reported less comfort with their perceived norm of hooking up than they believed was experienced by their same-sex peers, with men showing a greater difference between self- and peer-ratings than women. In addition, both men and women believed members of the other gender experienced greater comfort with hooking-up behaviors than members of the other gender actually reported. Men were less comfortable with engaging in hooking-up behaviors than women believed them to be, and women were less comfortable with engaging in hooking-up behaviors than men believed them to be. These findings appear to be due to pluralistic ignorance: Hooking up has become the norm for heterosexual sexual relationships on this campus, and since the great majority of students do in fact hook up, it appears that most students believe that others are comfortable—more comfortable than they are themselves—with engaging in a variety of uncommitted sexual behaviors. It is likely that most students believe others engage in these hooking-up behaviors primarily because they enjoy doing so, while they see themselves engaging in these behaviors primarily due to peer pressure. 18

Consistent with other pluralistic ignorance research (e.g., Prentice & Miller, 1993), this study showed evidence of an illusion of universality. The students failed to appreciate the extent to which others have different comfort levels with hooking-up behaviors. That is, students wrongly assumed that the attitudes of others about hooking up were more homogenous than they actually were. 19

Similar to other researchers (Cohen & Shotland, 1996; Knox & Wilson, 1981; Oliver & Hyde, 1993), we found that men expressed greater comfort than did women with sexually intimate hooking-up behaviors. In the context of hooking up, this could lead to serious consequences. Our study suggests that men believe women are more comfortable engaging in these behaviors than in fact they are, and also that women believe other women are more comfortable engaging in these behaviors than they are themselves. As a consequence, some men may pressure women to engage in intimate sexual behaviors, and some women may engage in these behaviors or resist only weakly because they believe they are unique in feeling discomfort about engaging in them. In this context it is possible for a woman to experience sexual assault but not interpret the behavior as such, believing it to be normative behavior with which her peers are comfortable. 20

"Most of Us" is a campaign implemented on many college campuses in an attempt to reveal pluralistic ignorance about alcohol consumption among college students (DeJong & 21

Langford, 2002; Haines, 1998). The campaign is based on providing students with statistical evidence about actual student attitudes and behaviors regarding alcohol consumption. The goal of the campaign is to show that pluralistic ignorance exists regarding college students' heavy alcohol consumption, and that most students prefer to drink less than what is commonly perceived to be the norm. Considering the results of this study, we propose that a similar campaign highlighting students' beliefs about and comfort levels with sexual behaviors while hooking up might help reduce pluralistic ignorance about hooking up.

Tracy A. Lambert is now at the University of Georgia.

This paper is based on an honors thesis by the first author under the direction of the second author. We wish to thank Steven Wise for his statistical assistance.

Address correspondence to Arnold S. Kahn, School of Psychology, MSC 7401, James Madison University, Harrisonburg, VA 22807: e-mail: **kahnas@jmu.edu**.

References

Allport, F. H. (1924). *Social psychology*. Boston: Houghton Mifflin.

Allport, F. H. (1933). *Institutional behavior*. Chapel Hill: University of North Carolina Press.

Boswell, A., & Spade, J. (1996). Fraternities and collegiate rape culture. *Gender and Society, 10*, 133–147.

Byers, S., & Lewis, K. (1988). Dating couples' disagreements over the desired level of sexual intimacy. *The Journal of Sex Research, 24*, 15–29.

Clark, R. D., & Hatfield, E. (1989). Gender differences in receptivity to sexual offers. *Journal of Psychology and Human Sexuality, 2*, 39–55.

Cohen, L. L., & Shotland, R. L. (1996). Timing of first sexual intercourse in a relationship: Expectation, experiences, and perceptions of others. *The Journal of Sex Research, 33*, 291–299.

DeJong, W., & Langford, L. A. (2002). Typology for campus-based alcohol prevention: Moving toward environmental management strategies. *Journal of Studies on Alcohol Supplement, 14*, 140–147.

DeLamater, J. (1987). Gender differences in sexual scenarios. In K. Kelley (Ed.), *Females, males, and sexuality* (pp. 127–139). Albany, NY: SUNY Press.

Fields, J. M., & Schuman, H. (1976). Public beliefs and the beliefs of the public. *Public Opinion Quarterly, 40*, 427–448.

Gerrard, M. (1980). Sex guilt and attitudes towards sex in sexually active and inactive female college students. *Journal of Personality Assessment, 44*, 258–261.

Gerrard, M., & Gibbons, F. X. (1982). Sexual experience, sex guilt, and sexual moral reasoning. *Journal of Personality, 50*, 345–359.

Haines, M. (1998). Social norms: A wellness model for health promotion in higher education. *Wellness Management, 14*(4), 1–8.

James Madison University Office of Institutional Research. (2001–2002). Retrieved February 22, 2003, from **http://www.jmu.edu/instresrch/statsum/2001_02/2001-02toc.htm**

Kahn, A. S., Fricker, K., Hoffman, J., Lambert, T., Tripp, M., Childress. K., et al. (2000, August). Hooking up: Dangerous new dating methods? In A. S. Kahn (Chair), *Sex, unwanted sex, and sexual assault on college campuses*. Symposium conducted at the annual meeting of the American Psychological Association, Washington, DC.

Katz, E., & Lazarsfeld, P. F. (1955). *Personal influence: The part played by people in the flow of mass communication*. Glencoe, IL: Free Press.

Knox, D., & Wilson, K. (1981). Dating behaviors of university students. *Family Relations, 30*, 255–258.

Miller, T. D., & McFarland, C. (1987). Pluralistic ignorance: When similarity is interpreted as dissimilarity. *Journal of Personality and Social Psychology, 53*, 298–305.

O'Gorman, H. J., & Garry, S. L. (1976). Pluralistic ignorance: A replication and extension, *Public Opinion Quarterly, 40*, 449–458.

Oliver, M. B., & Hyde, J. S. (1993). Gender differences in sexuality: A meta-analysis. *Psychological Bulletin, 114*, 129–151.

Paul, E. L., McManus, B., & Hayes, A. (2000). "Hookups": Characteristics and correlates of college students' spontaneous and anonymous sexual experiences. *The Journal of Sex Research, 37*, 76–88.

Peplau, L. A., & Gordon, S. L. (1985). Women and men in love: Gender differences in close heterosexual relationships. In V. E. O'Leary, R. K. Unger, & B. S. Wallston (Eds.), *Women, gender, and social psychology* (pp. 257–292). Hillsdale, NJ: Lawrence Erlbaum Associates.

Perkins, H. W., & Berkowitz, A. D. (1986). Perceiving the community norms of alcohol use among students: Some research implications for campus alcohol education programming. *International Journal of the Addictions, 21*, 961–976.

Prentice, D. A., & Miller, D. T. (1993). Pluralistic ignorance and alcohol use on campus: Some consequences of misperceiving the social norm. *Journal of Personality and Social Psychology, 64*, 243–256.

Prentice, D. A., & Miller, D. T. (1996). Pluralistic ignorance and the perpetuation of social norms by unwitting actors. In M. P. Zanna (Ed.), *Advances in experimental social psychology* (Vol. 28, pp. 161–209). San Diego, CA: Academic Press.

Simpson, J. A., & Gangestad, S. W. (1991). Individual differences sociosexuality: Evidence for convergent and discriminant validity. *Journal of Personality and Social Psychology, 60*, 870–883.

Snyder, M., Simpson, J. A., & Gangestad, S. (1986). Personality and sexual relations. *Journal of Personality and Social Psychology, 51*, 181–190.

Manuscript accepted August 21, 2002

Inquiring into the Essay

Use all four ways of inquiring to think about your reaction to this essay.

1. If true, the idea of "pluralistic ignorance"—that we consistently behave in ways that make us uncomfortable because we want to conform to the norm—is pretty disturbing because it implies that we internalize a certain kind of social control over our behavior that may not be in response to something real. For instance, this study suggests that for women especially, hooking up might not feel right but they do it anyway because

they don't think others feel as they do. Explore this in your own life. Fastwrite about whether "pluralistic ignorance" makes sense to you, and bend the writing, if you can, toward a story that might reveal your own experience with the idea.

2. Using different-color highlighters or pens, identify some of the following elements of an academic paper: review of the literature, hypothesis, purpose of the study, interpretation of data, and assertion about the significance of the findings.
3. Are the findings of this study credible? Based on your own experience and observations, how would you evaluate them? If you were going to suggest an area for further research, what might that be?
4. A common and perfectly understandable response to an initial encounter with academic discourse like this is to find it utterly boring. Why is this so? If it is important to learn to get past this initial response to do serious research, what strategies would you use?

SEEING THE FORM

IDAHO STATE PENITENTIARY, WOMEN'S PRISON

I took the accompanying picture on a ridge overlooking the valley where I live. It includes a lot of visual information: long shots of the city of Boise, the university, the state penitentiary, and in the far distance, the Owyhee range, which is currently being considered for wilderness designation. But do you really get a good look at any of these subjects? I don't think so, which is why I don't think much of the photograph. My brother, a professional photographer, would probably consider this shot a throwaway—a kind of photographic "prewriting" activity that might help him discover the visual subject he *really* wants to work with.

At the bottom middle of the photograph is a small building surrounded by high stone walls. This was the women's prison, which was built in the 1920s. It's a fascinating place both visually and historically, and so I "revised" my photographic project to focus on the women's prison rather than attempting to capture the valley. I took a slew of shots of the women's prison, including the two pictures shown here—one of a small cell with the light streaming through the tiny window and another of a rusting iron door. They are hardly masterpieces, but I do like them a lot better than the landscape shot. Do you agree? If so, why?

If the process of taking these pictures is a good analogy for the process of writing research essays, what do the comparisons between the landscape shot and the women's prison photographs suggest to you about the qualities of a good paper? What do they imply about the research process?

▪ THE WRITING PROCESS ▪

INQUIRY PROJECT: Write a Research Essay

Develop a 2,000- to 3,000-word research essay on a topic of your choice. (Your instructor may present some broad subjects or other limitations on topic choice.) The most important quality of this research essay is that it be organized around your own questions or ideas about the topic; it should be an *essay,* not a *report.* The research question should also have a sufficiently narrow focus. Don't look at the entire landscape of a topic but focus instead on a specific feature in that landscape. Your essay should also do the following:

- Be based on a "researchable" question.
- Have a central thesis or claim that represents your answer to the question you pose, even if it's tentative.
- Use appropriate and relevant sources based on your own experiences, observations, interviews, and reading, or all four sources of information.
- Be cited using the conventions recommended by your instructor.
- Be written for an audience of peers rather than experts on the topic.

Thinking About Subjects

"The death of curiosity," writes one educator, "may begin sometime in the second grade." After that the "system takes over" and it's "time to get efficient and serious," preparing for a career. Whatever the reason for it, the diminished sense of wonder seems most poignant whenever I talk to my students about research writing. In a way, it's no big surprise. Too often, research papers have been exercises in drudgery. But even when students choose their own topics for their investigations, they are initially quite sure that the whole enterprise is *not* about surprise and discovery. A few even sigh and suggest that I should just tell them what to write about. "That would be easier," they say.

Begin thinking about subjects for your research essay by remembering that the best reason to investigate something is because you genuinely wonder about it. Let curiosity lead you through the library's heavy glass doors, or into the far reaches of cyberspace, or perhaps to the office of an expert on your topic in a nearby campus building. In many cases, the best subjects grow from your own experiences and observations. Ask yourself, *What have I seen or experienced or heard about that raises questions that research might help answer?*

Approaching your research project this way is exactly the impulse that might have motivated you to write a personal essay on growing up with an autistic sibling or a persuasive essay on the downside of recruiting NCAA athletes at your school. It's the same motive that inspires all genuine inquiry: *How do I feel about this? What do I think about this? What do I want to know?*

Generating Ideas

Use your notebook to generate some material. As in previous inquiry projects, at this stage don't prejudge anything you come up with. Let yourself play around with possibilities.

Listing Prompts. Lists can be rich sources of triggering topics. Let them grow freely, and when you're ready, use an item as the focus of another list or an episode of fastwriting. The following prompts should get you started.

1. Inventory your interests by creating five separate lists on a page of your notebook. Choose among the following words as a general category for each of the five lists you will create: Places, Trends, Things, Technologies, People, Controversies, History, Jobs, Habits, Hobbies. In each of the five categories you chose, brainstorm a list of words or phrases that come to mind when you think about *what you know and what you might want to know.* For example, under Places I would put "Florence pigeons" because I want to know more about their impact on Renaissance buildings. Under Hobbies, I would put fly fishing because that's something I know about. Spend about fifteen minutes building these lists.

2. Look over your lists and ask yourself, *Are there research topics implied by a few of the items on these lists?* In other words, what here raises questions that more research might answer? What is it about this item that I wonder about?

3. Finally, choose a promising item from one of the lists and generate questions about it that you'd love to have answered. Perhaps you already know something about the topic but would like to learn more. Don't worry yet whether all the questions are great.

Fastwriting Prompts. Remember, fastwriting is a great way to stimulate creative thinking. Turn off your critical side and let yourself write "badly."

1. Choose an item from your lists and use it as a prompt for a seven-minute fastwrite. Begin by telling yourself the story of when, where, and why you first got interested in the subject. When the writing stalls, write the following phrase, and follow it for as long as you can: *Among the things I most want to learn about this are . . .*

2. Get a copy of the daily newspaper. Read it quickly and then clip any articles that make you think or feel something, even if you can't quite say much more about your reaction. Choose one article and glue it into your notebook. Just below,

ONE STUDENT'S RESPONSE

JULIAN'S JOURNAL

TOPIC: JAZZ

My dad was into jazz. Would listen to it all night long after working all day long. He listened to all kinds of jazz—Bird, Miles Davis, Billy Holiday, Monk. It took me years to really appreciate the music but now it's my favorite kind. **Among the things I most want to learn about** jazz is its connection to African music and slave songs. It makes me wonder whether the uniqueness of jazz, its spontaneity especially, has something to do with the hymns and spirituals of the slaves. **Among the other things I want to learn** is whether jazz was accepted in the early days. I seem to remember my dad saying that the . . .

use the article as a prompt for a "narrative of thought" response. Begin this way: *When I first read this article, I thought (or felt) . . . And then I thought . . . And then . . .* If the writing takes off in another direction, let it. End by finishing the following sentence: *When I first started thinking about this, I thought* ________, *but now I think* ________.

Visual Prompts. Sometimes the best way to generate material is to see what we think represented in something other than sentences. Boxes, lines, webs, clusters, arrows, charts, and even sketches can help us to see more of the landscape of a subject, especially connections among fragments of information that aren't as obvious in prose.

1. Cluster the phrase, *I'm really curious about* . . . Put the phrase in the center of a blank page and build a web of associations, each of which might begin with the word *why.* Explore your curiosity about things in your personal life, in the community, in the region, the state, the country, the world.

2. Do an image search using Google on some person, place, thing, or event that interests you (see the accompanying photo). Might one of the pictures you find be the focus of an investigation? Who *was* that guy? What was going on when this happened? Why did it happen?

Research Prompts. Do some research before you begin your research? Absolutely. By exploring what others have said or done or wondered about, you might discover an interest in something you wouldn't have otherwise considered.

1. Surf the Net, perhaps beginning with a subject directory such as The Virtual Library (http://vlib.org). Start by clicking on a subject area that interests you. Keep following the links as you branch more deeply into the subcategories and subdisciplines of that area of knowledge. Look for specific subject areas that intrigue you. For example, you might have begun in the broad subject of history,

A Google image search on the "Harlem Renaissance" produced this 1936 painting, *Aspiration* by Aaron Douglas. The image depicts one reason for the African American artistic renaissance in many American cities back then—the migration of blacks from the South to places such as New York and Chicago. The image suggests a great focus for an investigation of the Harlem Renaissance: Why did this migration occur?

clicked the link for medieval history (maybe you've always wondered what was dark about the Dark Ages), and ended up reading some fascinating articles on the home life of medieval women. Does it raise some questions you'd like to explore?

2. Study the local newspaper. Devote some time to reading the local paper to discover a local controversy that intrigues you. Say there was an article on the impact of Title IX on the university's athletic department, and you wonder, *Is the elimination of the men's wrestling team really the result of shifts in funding to women's sports?* Or perhaps there's a letter to the editor about the condition of housing for migrant workers in the valley. Are things really that bad?

Judging What You Have

The great thing about simply generating material is that you can turn off your critical mind and simply muck about all sorts of possible topics for your essay. But as always, the process depends on taking a more analytical look at whether you've discovered anything genuinely useful. Remember your goal at this stage: You want to identify a possible topic—and maybe, if you're lucky, a research question—that will move your investigation forward in the next few days. The following suggestions should help.

What's Promising Material and What Isn't? Deciding what a good research topic is mostly depends on one simple thing: Do you have a researchable *question?* The topic itself may not be the problem at all. Wondering whether Elvis is really dead isn't really a very good research question because the answer is pretty simple—yep. But wondering why certain people keep asking the question in the first place—why there's a need to maintain the fiction that the King is still around—is an excellent opening question for a research project. I've read riveting books on the most common subjects—salt, for example—that succeeded because the writer found interesting questions to ask about them. This, by the way, is the key to writing strong research papers about assigned topics. Virtually any topic can be interesting to you if you find the question that makes you wonder.

Is It a Researchable Question? What is a researchable question? I've already mentioned the most important characteristic: *the question interests you.* But there some other things to consider as well:

- *Is it the right size?* As illustrated in the earlier "Seeing the Form" feature, the quickest way to make any research project unmanageable is to ask a really, really big question: What were the causes of the Gulf War? Why is there racism in America? At the other extreme is the question that is so limited, so small in scope, that it isn't enough to carry the weight of your investigation, but this is rarely a problem. The key is to find an opening question that isn't too broad and isn't too narrow, one that allows you *to exclude* aspects of the topic because they aren't relevant.
- *Has something already been said about it?* In other words, is information available that *is* relevant to the question you're asking? Have experts and others addressed the question in some way, perhaps indirectly or in other contexts? This may be hard to know until you look.
- *Does it raise more questions?* Some questions have pretty simple answers. For example, wondering why the sky is blue might be an interesting question but it probably won't sustain any kind of extended inquiry because the reasons for blue skies are well known. A better research question raises more questions the more you think about it, or seems to lead to controversies, debates, or disagreements among knowledgeable people.
- *Does it matter?* It might matter to you, and it needs to. But the best research questions should be potentially interesting and relevant to other people, too. Doing research on how to deal with your messy boyfriend, for example, may not matter really to anyone but you. But it really depends on how you frame the research question. Do men and women in this culture

see domestic spaces differently, use them for different reasons, and talk about them in different ways? That's probably too big a research question, but it certainly transcends your personal problem to address questions many of us find interesting and relevant to our lives.

Questions About Audience and Purpose. The best motive for writing a research essay about a particular topic is the same reason you might want to write about anything—it makes you curious. It could interest you for any number of reasons. Perhaps you want to research an illness because your mother has it; maybe you're an engineering major and you're interested in the early history of the computer; maybe you're a hunter and want to know the impact of gray wolf reintroduction on the elk herd; or maybe you're a single parent interested in the impact of divorce on very young children.

Your personal interests will help you choose a topic, but the question behind your investigation—what I call the tentative focusing question—will also be influenced by some of the conventions of academic research, things I already mentioned as qualities of a researchable question and the interests of your audience. In many cases, we write research papers for an audience of one—the instructor—someone who is likely to know more about the subject you're writing about than you will, even after you've done your research. For this assignment, however, you'll be writing for a larger, less specialized audience—your peers and your instructor in this class. Learning to write about complex or technical subjects for a more general audience is enormously valuable, not only because you have to write papers in future classes. Much of the research-based writing you'll do after college will demand the ability to write clearly for readers who are less knowledgeable than you about a subject.

Practically speaking, then, this means choosing a topic that might interest other nonexperts. It also means choosing a good question to guide your investigation, one that people other than you might want to know the answer to. You can get some direction on this in class; also see the "Inquiring into the Details: Finding the Focusing Question" box.

Inquiring into the Details

FINDING THE FOCUSING QUESTION

Once you tentatively settle on a topic, you're ready to do this in-class exercise. It should help you find questions that will help you focus your project.

1. Each student will take a piece a paper or a large piece of newsprint and post it on the wall. (In computer labs, students can use a word-processing program and move from station to station in the steps that follow.)
2. Write your topic at the very top of the paper (for instance, hybrid cars).

3. Take a few minutes to briefly describe why you chose the topic.

4. Spend five minutes to briefly list what you know about your topic already (for instance, any surprising facts or statistics, the extent of the problem, important people or institutions involved, key schools of thought, common misconceptions, important trends, and controversies).

5. Now spend fifteen or twenty minutes brainstorming a list of questions about your topic that you'd love to learn the answers to. Make the list as long as you can.

6. Look around the room. You'll see a gallery of topics and questions on the walls. Now you can help each other. Move around the room, reviewing the topics and questions other students have generated. For each topic posted on the wall, do two things: Check the *one* question on the list you find most interesting, and add a question *you* would like answered about that topic.

7. Now you have long lists of questions about your topic. Is there one that you think might be researchable, using the criteria for such questions? Which questions seem to generate the most interest in the class? Do any of those interest you, too?

8. Pick one question from the list that could be your initial focusing question. Remember, you can change it later.

One Student's Response

JULIAN'S JOURNAL

FINDING THE FOCUSING QUESTION

1. The Blues
2. Chose this topic because I've listened to jazz and blues since I was a kid, but never really understood its origins.
3. Some famous blues singers: Robert Johnson, Blind Lemon Jefferson . . . Some qualities of blues: appeals more to the heart than the head, has a characteristic "bluesy" sound, early music in the south . . .
4. Questions:

   What's the relationship between blues and jazz?

   Who was the most influential blues musician in the early days?

   How is African music part of the blues?

   Did only blacks listen to blues in the beginning?

   How does the blues vary by region?

Writing the Sketch

The sketch for your research essay will be a little different from those you've written earlier. Rather than writing a "sketchy" draft of a possible essay, you'll develop a project narrative, one that summarizes your working knowledge of the topic and how your thinking about it has evolved so far. A working knowledge of your topic is achieved when you have enough information to be able to talk about it for five minutes without repeating yourself. You develop a working knowledge by conducting basic research on the Web and at the university library. (See Chapter 12 for details on how to develop working knowledge of a topic.)

Once you are ready, your sketch should have the following features:

- The title should be the tentative focusing question you've chosen on your topic.
- The sketch itself should tell the story of your thinking about that question and topic from the beginning until now.
- This narrative of thought should discuss the ways in which your working knowledge of the topic has changed the way you think about it.
- The sketch should be about 500 words.
- Information, ideas, or quotations you borrow from outside sources should be cited. (See the "MLA Documentation Guidelines" and "APA Documentation Guidelines" sections in Chapter 13.)

STUDENT SKETCH

It was spring and Amy Garrett-Brown began to imagine shorts and bathing suits, but then she took a look at her skin in the mirror. She looked pale and pasty. Wouldn't a nice tan be good about now? But would she be compromising her health for vanity, she wondered? Suddenly, Garrett had a research topic and an opening question. Here's her sketch on the topic.

WHY DO PEOPLE TAN?

Amy Garrett-Brown

This started as a simple question spurred by one of my occasional "people are so stupid" rants. I wondered who was to blame for this, who made it cool for white people to be tan? It seems completely asinine on the surface to waste money and time on a prepaid tan that will only result in prematurely leathered and wrinkled skin and a much higher risk of developing melanoma or other skin cancers. And then I looked down at my arms and noticed that I've managed to build up a decent tan this summer myself, not via lightbulb technology, but the old fashioned way, by playing in the sun. Hmmm . . . am I a hypocrite? 1

2 I wondered about that. As I researched sunbathing and the like I came across an interesting article in *The Atlanta Journal-Constitution* titled "The Rural South These Days Has More Tanning Salons Than John Deeres" by Rheta Grimsley Johnson. Johnson summarizes her point with a quote from E. B. White, "I am fascinated by the anatomy of decline . . . by the spectacle of people passively accepting a degenerating process which is against their own interests." She then explains, "He was writing about the redesign of the automobile—longer and lower with bigger fenders. He also objected to replacing the car window crank with a lazy push-button. If he could see us now, jumping into our foreign cars and speeding down to the tanning bed and nail art salon. Lost, buffed souls" (M1).

3 It struck me as I read the last lines of this sardonic critique of society that I don't necessarily wonder why people tan, but why they completely gyp themselves of the pleasures of the sun to be rewarded with a battle with cancer at worst and saggy skin at best. It seems like everyone wants to feel active, even if they aren't.

4 In a survey conducted by *Seventeen* magazine, "2/3 of the teens say they look better with a tan and feel healthier, more sophisticated and 50% say they looked more athletic" (qtd. in "Sun Tanning"). Somehow it seems that society has missed the forest for the trees. A nice tan once meant you spent your days on the beach playing volleyball and swimming, hiking in the mountains or riding a horse, riding a bike around town or jogging in the afternoons; it was usually accompanied by fit and trim bodies and healthy smiles. Now it means you spent $45 a month building a base tan.

5 But somehow the message isn't translating. People still feel healthy with a bastardized tan? So there must be something more to it all. Is the fashion industry that powerful? In her fashion column Patricia McLaughlin puts the fascination with a tan into perspective.

> White people have it tough. At least the pale ones, whose skin is really a mottled, unappetizing grayish-yellowish-pinkish off-white threaded with blue veins. Once, amazing as it may seem, it was actually cool to have skin this color. Then Coco Chanel came home with a tan from a cruise on the Duke of Westminster's yacht, and ever since, white people have preferred to be a biscuity golden color. (02)

6 So maybe that's it, people just like the way it looks to be tan. I know I feel better about putting on a bathing suit if I'm not so starkly white that I worry about blinding young children. I also know that it just feels good to be in the sun. The warm rays beating down on my back and shoulders as I work outdoors or go for a hike seem therapeutic and natural.

7 But the health industry sure doesn't like to condone it. In an article by Alexandra Greeley titled "No Tan Is a Safe Tan," she presents her case against spending time in the sun and especially tanning with facts and statistics, but I couldn't help but wonder if she ever has any fun after reading the closing lines to her article. "In the end, there really is nothing new under the sun, except that perhaps more people are staying out of it, heeding medical warnings such as Bergstresser's: 'Less sun is better. No sun is best of all' " (15).

8 I disagree. But I'm no expert, so I sought proof of my hunch that the sun is really our friend and found it. Of course, I'm not condoning the 1976 "Savage Tan" or complete ignorance of the dangers of a depleted ozone and proof that severe sunburns lead to cancers, but I think there must be some middle ground.

Works Cited

Greeley, Alexandra. "No Tan Is a Safe Tan." *Nutrition Health Review: The Consumer's Medical Journal* 59 (Summer 1991): 14–15.

Johnson, Rheta Grimsley. "The Rural South These Days Has More Tanning Salons Than John Deeres." *The Atlanta Journal-Constitution* 23 Apr. 2000, home ed.: M1.

McLaughlin, Patricia. "Dying for a Tan This Summer?" *St. Louis Post-Dispatch* 15 June 1995: 02.

"Sun Tanning." *Cool Nurse 2000–2003* 18 June 2003.

Moving from Sketch to Draft

Your sketch may not really be an early draft of the essay you'll write later. It's probably more of a record of your thinking about your topic, perhaps leading you to a clearer idea about the best focusing question and perhaps a stronger sense of what you might want to say in the draft. Your sketch also gives you a chance to share what you've discovered so far with others in your class, but not in the usual way. Rather than workshopping your sketch you'll use it to develop a brief presentation.

Evaluating Your Own Sketch. Follow the road map of the thinking present in your sketch to get a clearer sense of where you want to go in the draft.

1. What seemed to be the turning point in your own thinking about the topic? What caused it?
2. Is the focusing question you wrote at the beginning of the sketch still the right title? Does that question need to be revised or do you need to write a new one?
3. Based on what you know now, how would you answer the question you're asking?

Questions for Peer Review. Rather than workshopping your sketch, you will use it as the basis for a brief class presentation. Following a press conference format, you will speak for about five to ten minutes, highlighting some or all the following:

- What focusing question did you start with? What question do you want to ask now?
- What is the most surprising thing you've learned so far?
- What do experts on the topic debate about?
- What are the most common misconceptions about the topic?
- What story can you tell about the topic—a case study, a telling event, a profile of the person involved?

Try to make this presentation lively and interesting. Your purpose, in part, is to get a sense of potential reader interest in your topic and the question you're pursuing. Students listening to the presentations should be encouraged to ask questions about what you've said—or haven't said. They also might have some suggestions of questions about your topic you hadn't considered, or tips on where to search for more information. Allow another five to ten minutes for this question and answer session.

Reflecting on What You've Learned. Spend a few minutes following your presentation generating a list of everything you heard, and then begin a five-minute fastwrite that explores your reaction to these questions and suggestions and your tentative plan for revision. Did the class have a lot of questions about your topic following the presentation? What seems to have most piqued their interest? What questions or controversies seem to ignite the most discussion? What did the discussion suggest might be new avenues for research? End your fastwrite by writing about what you understand now about your topic and your initial beliefs about it that you didn't fully understand when you began writing about it.

Research and Other Strategies: Gathering More Information

Writing a draft will require more than a working knowledge of your topic. Now you'll need to develop a deep knowledge, one that will give you enough of a grasp of the subject to know some or all of the following things about it:

- Which other writers and researchers have addressed the question you're interested in, and what have they already said about it?
- Which sources did you find particularly persuasive?
- How did those sources influence the way you think about your topic?

Acquiring such an understanding of your topic will require that you cast a wider net for information by using more advanced references, and moving beyond a few general sources to many varied and specialized sources. See Chapter 12 to learn how to systematically find additional sources on the Internet and in the campus library that will help you develop deep knowledge of your subject.

One technique that was introduced to you earlier in *The Curious Writer*—the double-entry journal—will be more crucial now. (Check out alternatives to the double-entry journal in Chapter 12.) You must do some writing *as you research* because not only will it help you figure out what you think about the things you find, but it will also actually get you started on writing your draft. I know this is a tough sell. What you really want to do is simply to print out copies of Web pages, collect books and articles, and put the library photocopier or printer to work. To imagine spending time writing about a promising article at this stage in the process, rather than simply collecting as many sources as you can, might seem like a waste of time. But consider this: By writing about important sources *as you encounter them* you're essentially beginning to write your paper. You'll be able to use some of what you write in the draft, but more important, you'll be able to use some of what *you thought,* the most important part of any research essay.

Composing the Draft

Sara was a compulsive collector of information. She researched and researched, collecting more books and articles and Web sources until the desk in her apartment looked like a miniature version of downtown Chicago—towering piles of paper and books everywhere. She never felt as if she knew enough to begin writing her essay, and would only begin drafting when forced to—the paper was due tomorrow. Neal figured he could find most of what he needed pretty quickly on the Internet. He printed out a few articles and Web pages and felt confident he could write his paper using those. He didn't feel pressured to begin writing until the due date loomed. When Neal started writing and realized that he probably wouldn't be able to get the required page length, he widened the margins.

Sara and Neal obviously use different strategies for getting to the draft. Sara relies on accumulating great quantities of information, trusting that aggressively collecting sources will make the writing easier—the main source of anxiety for her—although she probably doesn't really believe that. On the other hand, Neal suffers from overconfidence. He figures he can make do with a few sources and doesn't look around much. Both Neal and Sara do what research paper writers have done forever: wait until the last minute. Neither of these writers will be happy with the result.

It's easy to avoid this situation if you begin the draft after you've accomplished the following:

- *You've done some writing before you start writing.* In other words, have you exploited the double-entry journal or an alternative note-taking method to both collect useful information and to explore your reaction to what it says?
- *You are working from abundance (but not overabundance).* Neal is much more typical than Sara. He is trying to compose his draft by drawing from a nearly empty well. Almost any writing—and particularly research writing—depends on working from abundance. You need to collect more information than you can use. But not too much. Don't let endless collecting become an avoidance tactic.
- *Your focusing question has helped you* exclude *information.* A good focusing question is a guide. It will help you see the relevance of certain portions of the sources you've collected and give you reason to ignore the rest. If you sense that this is happening consistently as you review your sources, you're probably ready to write.
- *You have a tentative idea about what you think.* By now, you know enough about your topic to have some feelings or ideas about a possible answer to the question behind your investigation. Remember the draft may make you change your mind—that's fine—but begin composing with at least a tentative point of view.

Methods of Development. The research essay is more likely than the previous essays to combine a range of methods of development. You can see that already from the professional essays earlier in this chapter. However, here are some more typical designs for research essays:

Narrative. We don't usually associate narrative structure with research papers, but research-based writing tells stories all the time. Perhaps one of the most common techniques is use of the case study, which can be an excellent way to begin your paper. Case studies or anecdotes about people involved or affected by a topic often bring that topic to life by moving it closer to the everyday *lives* of people. But narrative is also used as the backbone of a research essay. Sometimes an essay tells the story of what the writer wanted to know and what she found out, a kind of narrative of thought. The sketch you wrote earlier is an early project narrative that established your initial focusing question and some tentative clues about where it might lead. This structure could easily be imported into the final draft of your research essay, only it will be more developed and more insightful.

Question to Answer. Because much of the research process is devoted to developing a good question to drive the inquiry, it makes sense to consider organizing your essay around what that question is, where it came from, and what has already been said about it, and then reporting what you've discovered about possible answers to the question that triggered the investigation. A lot of formal academic research is organized this way, although there might be an added section about the methods the investigator chose to try to seek the answers.

Known to Unknown. This is a variation on the question-to-answer structure that might be particularly useful if you're writing about a complex topic about which much remains unknown. Your research might have led to the discovery that the question you're interested in is a question that has very speculative or limited answers. For example, Andy was writing about the use of psychiatric medicine such as antidepressants and antipsychotics on children because his family physician had recommended them for one of his own kids. Andy quickly discovered that this was a relatively new use for such drugs and that much mystery surrounded both the diagnosis and treatment of children with emotional problems. It became clear that the purpose of his essay was not to offer a definitive answer to his question, but to suggest areas that still needed further study.

Using Evidence. While every discipline has its own ideas about what counts as good research evidence, the research essay is a less specialized form with a more general audience. Therefore, the rules of evidence for a research essay aren't nearly as strict as they might be, say, in an academic article in psychology or biology. But that's not to say that anything goes. Research writing obviously depends mainly on sources outside the writer—published materials, interviews with people involved in the topic, and observations in the field—but the writer's personal experience can count if it's relevant. In some cases, you may want to cite your own experience as evidence that either supports or contradicts a claim made by someone else, but your experience alone probably isn't sufficient evidence. Find other voices that confirm it.

Not all outside sources are equally convincing either. Figure 11.1 suggests a hierarchy that is one way of evaluating how "authoritative" a source might be. Notice that, generally speaking, the more specialized a publication's audience, the more likely the information in it will be valued. For example, an article on dream interpretation in the *Journal of American Psychology* is considered more authoritative than an article on the same subject in *Ladies' Home Journal*. The reasons for this are pretty obvious: When you write for experts in the field you better know what you're talking about.

Research writing obviously depends mainly on sources outside the writer . . . but the writer's personal experience can count if it's relevant.

Finally, an important way to write authoritatively using outside sources is not only to use the right sources but to cite them carefully. It's crucial that you acknowledge those whose ideas have helped you see more deeply into your topic. In your draft, acknowledge your sources in two ways:

1. Mention them in your essay using attribution tags, such as *according to Jones . . .* or *Hill argues that . . .* or *Baraka said . . .*
2. Cite borrowed information, quotations, and ideas using MLA or APA conventions. (See the "MLA Documentation Guidelines" and "APA Documentation Guidelines" sections in Chapter 13.)

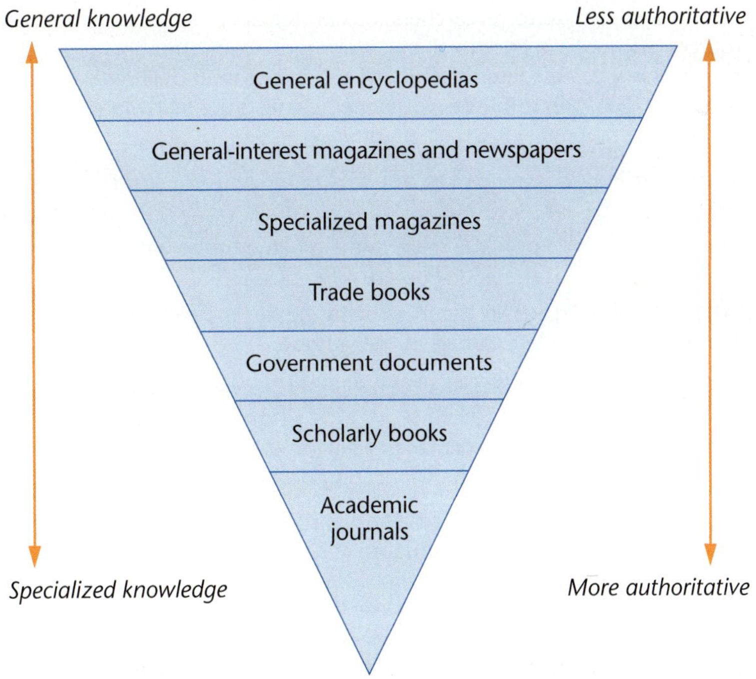

FIGURE 11.1 A hierarchy of sources places the most credible at the bottom of an inverted pyramid. For academic research, these are usually articles and books that are reviewed by other experts before they're published.

Workshopping the Draft

Share your research essay in a small group workshop before you begin your final revision. Because of the length of these essays you might want to allow more time for these discussions, or encourage group members to read the drafts before the group meets. Your instructor might also put you in smaller groups.

Reflecting on the Draft. A draft is a thing the wind blows through. That might be especially true of the full first draft of your research essay. After all, this project involved juggling a lot more than most other inquiry projects—controlling information and the ideas of a wide variety of sources, the challenge of trying to surround that outside material with your own ideas, worries about following citation conventions, and the struggle not to let the whole project get away from your own purposes and questions. Spend a little time reflecting on how all this went.

Writing with Computers

FINDING DOCUMENTATION INFORMATION FOR ONLINE SOURCES

Unlike book and periodical publishing, Web publishing has few standards. This oversight presents a challenge to researchers looking for documentation information for online sources. Rather than finding all of the appropriate information at one location, it may be necessary to navigate throughout a Web site to find all of the documentation information. For Web resources you generally need the following:

1. **Author Name:** Many Web pages do not attribute authorship, but if the page you are viewing does, make sure you record the author's name.
2. **Web Address:** The full Web address of the page you are using is needed. It is not sufficient to provide only the main domain name to the whole site. You must give the complete URL for the page you are referencing.
3. **Title of Web Site:** This is generally on the home page, but might also be found in the title bar (top left corner) of the window.
4. **Dates:** Record the date you visited the page and also the date of its last update if it can be found.
5. **The Sponsoring Organization:** Many sites are operated by larger organizations. If this is the case, record the sponsoring organization's name.

Researchers should be in the habit of recording this information immediately. Online resources change, move, and disappear all the time. Copying and pasting the information into a separate word processor file is a quick way to archive this information in your own notes. Some Web browser add-on programs allow you to click a button to "archive" the page and make notes about the date you viewed the page, its URL, and any other notes you wish to include. But even if you have this type of software you will still need to identify the other documentation elements if they are not contained on the specific page you are viewing.

Even though it may be difficult to uncover complete source information for an online resource, most reliable resources will make it available somewhere on the Web site. The less information you can find on the site, the more suspicious you should be of the source's credibility.

In your notebook or on a separate piece of paper you'll attach to the draft when you hand it in, answer the following questions:

- What's the most important thing you learned about your topic after the research and writing you've just completed? Is this important understanding obvious in the draft?
- Choose two paragraphs that incorporate outside sources—one that you think is written pretty well, and another less well. What differences do you notice between the two? Can you identify at least one problem you need to work on in the next draft that will help you improve the way you integrate sources?
- What was your focusing question? How does the draft attempt to answer it?

Questions for Readers. Make sure that you have some specific questions you'd like to ask your workshop group about how the draft is working. Here are some others:

1. In your own words, what do you think is the main thing I'm trying to say in the draft? Where in the draft do you think I say it?
2. What was the most interesting part of the essay? What was the least interesting? Why?
3. After you read the first few paragraphs, did you have a clear sense of what my focusing question was?
4. Did any part of the draft seem to drift away from that focus?
5. Where do I need more information or more evidence?

Revising the Draft

As I discussed earlier in the book, one of the most common misconceptions about revision is that you do it only at the end of the writing process. In fact, up to this point, you should have been revising your work all along, from the first few journal exercises when you chose a topic and played with possible angles on it, to the journal work you might have done to prepare to write the sketch, and then again with your efforts to turn your sketch into a more developed draft. Revision is literally "re-seeing," and every time you create the conditions that allow you to discover something new about how you see or what you think about your subject, you are, in fact, engaged in the act of revision. In a sense, then, each writing assignment you undertake is one long act of revision, from start to finish.

But once you've completed a draft, the revision process becomes more focused. You are mostly working with material that should be somewhat settled, with purposes that might be clearer, and ideas that may have more shape. At this point, the biggest temptation is to tell yourself you are largely done and what revision remains is merely a matter of "fixing things"—tinkering with sentences, correcting typos, and running a spell-checker. In the survey from Chapter 1 (see page 20), 70 percent of students admitted as much. "I usually just tidy things up" was ranked first or second by students who were asked what they do most often when they revise an academic paper.

These activities are certainly an element of revision—and important ones—but as the word *revision* implies, it's important to "re-see" both what you are trying to say and how you try to say it, even at this stage in the process. Chapter 14, "Revision Strategies," is a useful introduction to the revision process for any essay, including the research essay. It emphasizes ways writers can break the bonds that limit their ability to find new ways of seeing the draft.

As you plan for revision, do any of the following problems typical of research essay drafts apply to yours?

- Is the essay sufficiently focused? Remember the photography metaphor from the "Seeing the Form" feature (page 450): you want to take closer pictures rather than landscape shots of your subject. Having too broad a focus is a particularly troublesome issue with research-based writing. You can fix this by refining your question and narrowing the scope of your project.
- Did you collect enough information? Drafts that work from scarcity typically run short, have too broad a focus, or suffer from vagueness. The solution? Go back to the library or the Web and collect more information.
- Is the essay organized around your research question from beginning to end? Do any paragraphs or passages strike off in irrelevant directions?
- Does the draft say too much? Remember that a strong research essay not only asks an interesting question about a topic but explicitly states what the writer thinks is the best answer, even if it's speculative. Is this thesis clear?

Refer to Chapter 14, "Revision Strategies," for ideas on how to revise your draft following your workshop. In particular, it would probably be useful to check your draft for logical fallacies, using the table on page 307. Because one of the challenges of a longer essay with sources is organizing all that information, consider some of the structure exercises in Chapter 14, particularly Revision Strategy 14.17, "The Frankenstein Draft." Use the following table to find other appropriate revision strategies. Remember that a draft may present problems in more than one category.

GUIDE TO REVISION STRATEGIES

Problems in the Draft (Chapter 14)	Part	Page Number
Unclear purpose ▪ Not sure what the paper is about?	1	603
Unclear thesis, theme, or main idea ▪ Not sure what you're trying to say?	2	609
Lack of information or development ▪ Need more convincing evidence? Need to check for logical fallacies?	3	616
Disorganized ▪ Doesn't move logically or smoothly from paragraph to paragraph?	4	620
Unclear or awkward at the level of sentences and paragraphs ▪ Seems choppy or hard to follow at the level of sentences or paragraphs?	5	626

Polishing the Draft

After you've addressed the more global problems in your draft, you should focus on more local matters, such as how effectively you integrate and cite sources, how successfully you've organized your paragraphs, and whether you've written the draft in a clear, lively style. Don't forget to use the handbook at the back of the book to help you with any grammatical and stylistic questions you might have; also use the guide to MLA or APA citations in Chapter 13 to check how well you've followed those conventions.

Before you finish your draft, work through the following checklist:

- Every paragraph is about one thing.
- The transitions between paragraphs aren't abrupt.
- The length of sentences varies in each paragraph.
- Each sentence is concise. There are no unnecessary words or phrases.
- You've checked grammar, particularly verb agreement, run-on sentences, unclear pronouns, and misused words (*there/their, where/were,* and so on).
- You've run your spell-checker and proofed your paper for misspelled words.
- You've double-checked your citations and Works Cited or References page to ensure that the formatting is correct.

STUDENT ESSAY

Gordon Seirup's essay "College Dating", which is formatted according to MLA documentation guidelines, is a great finale to this chapter's readings on the "hooking up" phenomenon on American college campuses. I like this essay because Seirup takes control of the information he gathered in his Web research by finding—and naming—the patterns he saw in college dating and using them to organize his essay. He does a great job of tapping a variety of sources and bringing in the voices of other students and experts who have something relevant to say. Also notice how well these quotations are embedded in Gordon's own prose.

Like any work, "College Dating" could be an even stronger essay. While the essay employs evidence from some of the professional readings in this chapter, most of these sources Seirup cites consist of informal quotations taken from the online versions of college newspapers and lack the authority of formal print sources. Though the research question is clear, Gordon's essay also isn't explicitly organized around a specific claim that arises from his research. What thesis about college romance would you advance after reading the essay?

Gordon E. Seirup

Professor Ballenger

English 101

6 October 2006

College Dating

First there was the passing notes, hand holding, and name-calling of middle school. Then you survived your first heartbreak when your high school sweetheart decided it would be best to "just be friends." Now swept away in college life you hardly take the time to step back and ask yourself, "What am I doing here? Whose bed did I just wake up in, and how the hell did I get here?!" If you have not yet taken the time to ponder what it is you plan to do with the so-called best four years of your life, besides studying and eating dorm food, perhaps it is about time you did. What do you want to be accomplishing in these prime dating years? More importantly, is that what you are accomplishing? In short, my purpose is to discuss the question: "What role should dating play in college students' lives?" 1

Seirup 2

2 One might also think that college students, being in the midst of their own dating lives, would be able to define dating, be familiar with their intentions, and have a strong concept of where the decisions about dating they make today will take them tomorrow. Surprisingly, of the students I spoke with here informally on the Colorado State University campus, none would have met that standard. All hesitated when asked to simply "define dating." Once done struggling through that answer, they were asked, "In your opinion, what is the purpose of dating in college?" These students' answers ranged from "getting laid!" to "discover more about yourself through others" to "find the person you want to marry" to "I have no clue." Clearly, the college masses are blissfully unaware of exactly what it is they are doing when they are in pursuit of relationships.

3 First, what is dating? For purposes of this analysis, dating is defined as seeing someone socially in a one-on-one setting. Other terms used within the following pages are "hooking up" and "courtship," defined as noncommittal sexual acts and nonserial exclusive dating with the intention of marriage, respectively. What I mean by "nonserial" dating is that when you choose to date someone, it is your every

intention to marry them. While this may not work out, and lead you to enter this process again, each person you choose to date is sincerely meant to be your spouse. In this way, while you may court more than one person, it isn't your intention to do so. Now, with these terms clearly defined, we may delve into just what the various opinions are as to the purpose of dating.

4 I have defined five major approaches based on their common purpose, values, and motivations, in addition to their general line of reasoning: Casual Dating, Exclusive Dating, Courting, Cannot Date, and Hooking Up. Naturally, each of these groups is mainly composed of college students.

5 Casual dating is a concept that got its best reputation during the American 1950s, although Beth Bailey notes that "between 1890 and 1925, dating--in practice and in name--had gradually, almost imperceptibly, become a universal custom in America" (19). The emergence of public dating rituals coincided with the emergence of mass media, especially TV and magazines that made dating a feature of the typical American romance (Bailey 9). Casual dating was modeled on popular TV shows, and analyzed in mostly women's magazines--where to go, how much to spend, when to allow a first kiss. A major

Seirup 4

motive for dating was, according to Bailey, public competition to spend the most, choose the best partner, and so on.

6 However, dating these days is much less ritualized. Rather than focusing on public display, these days casual daters value meeting new people, discovering and/or reinventing who you are as a person, and enjoying yourself. The original scenario for casual dating typically went something like this: Guy meets a Girl, decides he would like to see her socially, and asks her to join him at the diner for hamburgers and a shared milkshake. If this date goes well, they may see each other again. After about three dates there is a good chance Guy would be graced with a goodnight kiss.

7 These dates do not imply exclusivity or any concrete commitment at all. They are designed for our subjects to enjoy each other's company. While social enjoyment is the driving force behind the Casual Dating approach, there are two other important aspects: meeting new people and discovering yourself. By the simple act of participating in these dates, each party naturally learns more about themselves through their interaction. "Dating one-on-one gives you a chance to become comfortable with new people," says Julie

Seirup 5

Baugher, Georgetown University's premier relationship columnist (Baugher, "'Rules'").

The key to developing sufficient attachment for a couple to want to date multiple times is that elusive quality called "chemistry." One study which attempted to pin down exactly what college students mean by chemistry suggested that it involves similarity of interests and backgrounds, as well as "reciprocity," or the feeling that both partners are giving something to each other (Peretti and Abplanalp 5). 8

But chemistry isn't necessarily a scarce phenomenon, and it's possible to find it with more than one person. According to Lee Ann Hamilton, a health educator at the University of Arizona, "College is the time to re-invent yourself and try new things; many people don't want to be tied down" (qtd. in Hill). It is very important to keep in mind that not being "tied down," as Ms. Hamilton put it, is a fundamental aspect of the Casual Dating approach. 9

Columnist Julie Baugher has laid out some guidelines helpful to circumventing our typical defensive maneuvers when it comes to dating. (It may be useful to remember these next time you are asked out for a date.) "Don't think

Seirup 6

about whether you want to Date him with an uppercase 'D' (meaning exclusive dating). Don't conclude that he isn't 'Your type.' Don't assume this is the beginning of a long-term relationship that you're not ready for" (Baugher, "Dating"). With this agreement of casual interaction, one may date as many people as there are nights available in the week, so long as all parties involved know the arrangement.

10 Similar to the Casual Dating approach is the Exclusive Dating approach. Both value dating as an activity for social enjoyment, as well as self-education. Exclusive dating may be thought of as the "next step" from casual dating, and indeed commonly tends to grow out of casual dating. When exclusively dating, you are not only learning more about yourself, but also consciously aware of what you are learning about your partner. Which characteristics can you see yourself living with for the rest of your life? Which make you want to run away and never date again? "Through several short-term relationships, students can find personalities with which they are most compatible," claims Matt West, a writer at the University of Virginia. "Relationships at this age allow you to explore what you

Seirup 7

like and don't like in a partner," agrees Mary Anne Knapp, a clinical social worker. Through a series of exclusive relationships, one forms a model of the ideal spouse (qtd. in Pleiss).

However, here is the crucial detail for this approach: 11
This model of spousal qualifications and fleeting thoughts of marriage are solely a mental exercise. Marriage is not a goal of the exclusive dating approach. Exclusively dating college students are aware of their proximity to marriage; however, they are not going to let that detail dominate their lives. The goal is gaining knowledge. This distinction is memorably worded by Jennifer Graham, a senior staff writer at Stanford University: "I think I'm going to put marriage on the backburner and, at least for the time being, refrain from appraising my peers' credentials for parenthood. There's no need to sap all the joy from life." Don't misinterpret Graham as saying she wishes to ignore completely her peers' credentials for parenthood; rather it is at which stage in the dating process they come into play that is important. When making the choice of whether or not to date someone, these marriage-related thoughts are minimally important. However, while in the relationship, it

Seirup 8

would be wise to take note of these credentials so that when you are shopping for a spouse you know what you are looking for.

12 To add to the strength of the Exclusive Dating approach, there is expert testimony. Clinical social worker Mary Anne Knapp says these exclusive relationships are healthy and "serve more of a purpose than just having a permanent date every Friday night" since "having a supportive partner, someone who knows you and is on your side, is good for a positive outlook on life" (qtd. in Pleiss 1).

13 The Courting approach states that dating should play no role in the lives of college students. In essence, supporters believe in a return to the practice of courtship rather than dating, and thus hold marriage absolutely paramount. Furthermore, proponents argue, this courtship would best take place after college. This is the only approach in which it may be said that the majority of the members fall into a distinct group of students. In general, students who advocate the Courting approach share strong religious backgrounds, and actively use their faith to both justify their opinion and denounce others'. In fact, the approach is as

Seirup 9

much their adamant opposition to dating as it is their support of courtship, saying casual dating is "a bankrupt convention . . . a training ground for divorce [and] . . . a cheap imitation of the love and intimacy of a real marriage." Furthermore, they believe that the practice of casual dating is futile: "If the couple never intends to get married in the first place, then breaking up is a foregone conclusion, and their relationship is doomed" (Jensen).

Advocates of this approach value the unique bonds that are formed between husband and wife as well as purity upon entering marriage. Courtship "is the only way to date with true love, respect and honesty because it is rooted in a desire to take the relationship to its complete and glorious fulfillment" (Jensen). Those seeking courtship seek others who seek the same. This reason is rooted in the principle that if you have kept pure in pursuit of marriage, you should expect the same of your to-be spouse--though today this makes for a slim selection. "It's hard enough to meet somebody who doesn't have a past relationship that is like a skeleton in her closet," says Matt Sweet, finance major at the University of Virginia (qtd. in Jensen). According to those who take the 14

Courting approach, if college students were to adopt their strategy, this problem would cease to be.

15 Both a wholehearted commitment to a relationship that will lead to marriage and the best possible education while in college are also views of the proponents of the Courting approach. A great deal of value is placed on the concept of college students being just that--students. Their primary job at this stage in life is to pursue the best education possible and, while involved in this pursuit, they have neither the time nor energy to responsibly court a spouse. Therefore, it is best for people to engage in courtship only after they have graduated from college and adequately settled into their careers.

16 Another approach that calls for dating to play no role in the lives of college students is the Cannot Date approach. Rather than opposing the concept of dating, these students have tried to date, or at least wanted to, but deemed it to be impossible. Like the Courting approach, these students value their standing as students and hold education as a very high priority. Students are practically overwhelmed with balancing their schedules as is, before the addition of a dating relationship. This approach is

Seirup 11

aptly described by a student at the University of Arizona: "While pursuing a double major, interning, working, maintaining a social life and attending school full time," Danielle Demizjian, a business economics and finance senior, finds "exclusive dating too much of a commitment" (qtd. in Hill). This is a common complaint among college students. Despite their desire to date, exclusively or casually, there just does not seem to be the time, though time alone is not the only issue. For those students advanced in their time management skills, the emotional burden may be too great. Jaime Dutton, a sophomore at Johns Hopkins University, says, "It's hard enough to have fun here with all the work you have to do, [and] there's no reason to have the extra drama in your life" (qtd. in Saxe). Nicole Kucewitz, a writer for the Rocky Mountain Collegian, agrees: "Relationships take time and patience, and in college, both of these can be very limited."

Finally, there is the Hooking Up approach. This last 17
group also does not date, but rather has an alternate social structure to replace traditional dating. Their philosophy: at the college level, formally dating is unnecessary. For social activities, in contrast with the one-on-one date,

groups are ideal. As for sexual needs, noncommittal hooking up is not only acceptable, it's preferred. Common values amongst this group include enjoying yourself socially with friends, casually fulfilling sexual needs, and avoiding commitment. This "new age" form of dating is the solution that has flourished as a result of the gripes of the Cannot Date approach.

18 Many of the students who fall into this approach see the dating arena as split into two distinct portions: "People are either single or practically married" (Burney). Hence, here is the solution for those people who wish to, for the most part, retain their single status, while still satisfying their social and sexual needs, all the while avoiding the "marriage-type" exclusive relationship. Dan, a student at Duke University, puts it this way: "In the real world, there is an expectation that after the third date, you might get a hookup. At Duke, there is the expectation that after the third hookup, you might get a date" (qtd. in Beckett). So perhaps once college students reach the "real world" this approach will fade away, nevertheless, as for the role of dating while in college; this approach holds the largest number of students.

Seirup 13

One appealing aspect to Hooking Up is the avoidance of complication when compared to exclusive dating or even casual dating. With this approach, future hookup partners spend time in groups and get to know each other in a friendlier context first. In this way a lot of the awkward chesslike strategies common to the predate period are circumvented. Or even simpler, the story goes like this: "Now all a guy in a decent fraternity has to do to hookup on a Saturday night is to sit on the couch long enough at a party. It's slow at first, but eventually a girl will plop herself down beside him, they'll sit there drinking, he'll make a joke, she'll laugh, their eyes will meet, sparks will fly, and the mission is accomplished. And you want me to tell this guy to call a girl, spend $100 on dinner and hope for a goodnight kiss" (Beckett)? This trend is perpetuated by "the beds [being] short walks from the parties. This increases the likelihood of the drunken hookup, while simultaneously decreasing the frequency of actual dates," according to Tom Burney, a columnist and student at Duke University (qtd. in Beckett). 19

With this tendency to go from partying to hooking up, a critic may be quick to draw the conclusion that alcohol 20 is the driving force behind this approach. On the contrary, this is a premeditated method of pursuing the attractive sex by getting to know them as friends (at least superficially) first. David Brunkow, computer science major at Colorado State University, attests to this: "Most of the people I've been with were already my friends. . . It's so much easier that way. You already know they're a good person and that they're not going to screw you over. Also, if things don't work out, you don't lose your friend" (qtd. in Borra).

21 The concept of non-random hooking up is reinforced by research. According to Paul and Hayes, the best hookups were more likely to be prefaced by hanging out, flirting, mutual attraction, and talking. The worst hookups often resulted from a friend's instigation (Paul and Hayes 648).

22 Of the five categories I've offered to describe college dating, Hooking Up is both the most common and the most controversial. In a recent study, three quarters of students interviewed reported that they had hooked up at least once and at least a third said this involved sex with a stranger or a new acquaintance (Paul, McManus, and Hayes 84). Students who choose Hooking Up may not believe that

Seirup 15

there are other, socially sanctioned choices, as this paper suggests. Do participants think Hooking Up is a good thing? One would assume so since it's so popular these days. But there is some evidence that the practice is driven by "pluralistic ignorance" or the mistaken assumption that their discomfort with the behavior is unique. This is particularly true of women (Lambert, Kahn, and Apple 132), a situation which could lead to abuses.

While no one approach is clearly ideal for all 23
students, there seems to be one to suit everyone, despite a wide range of personal beliefs. Casual Dating, Exclusive Dating, Courting, Cannot Date, and Hooking Up represent distinct alternatives to college students, difficult choices that add to the complexities, both academic and non-academic, that college students find themselves caught up in every day. But it's crucial that students at least be aware that there are choices to make.

Seirup 16

Works Cited

Bailey, Beth. "The Worth of a Date." From Front Porch to Back Seat: Courtship in Twentieth-Century America. 1998. Baltimore: John Hopkins University Press.

Baugher, Julia. "Dating with a Lower Case 'd.'" Hoya 4 Oct. 2002. 8 Oct. 2003 <http://www.thehoya.com/viewpoint/100402/vie2.cfm>.

Baugher, Julia. "'Rules' Teach Ladies Tricks to Winning Love." Hoya 15 Nov. 2002. 7 Oct. 2003 <http://www.thehoya.com/guide/111502/guide9.cfm>.

Beckett, Whitney. "What Lies Between the Hookup and Marriage?" Chronicle 5 Sept. 2003. 13 Oct. 2003 <http://newsdirectory.com/go/?f=&r=nc&u=chronicle.duke.edu>.

Borra, Jessup. "The 'He-Said-She-Said' on Dating." Rocky Mountain Collegian 17 Oct. 2002. 19 Oct. 2003 <http://www.collegian.com/media/storage/paper864/news/2002/10/17/Verve/The-heSaidSheSaid.On.Dating-1700491.shtml?norewrite200608281352&sourcedomain=www.collegian.com>.

Burney, T. "Dating Sea Nuggets." Chronicle 26 Mar. 2003. 13 Oct. 2003 <http://newsdirectory.eom/go/?f=&r=ne&u=chronicle.duke.edu>.

Graham, Jennifer. "Graduation Time: Cap and Gown or Wedding Gown?" Stanford Daily 17 July 2003. 13 Oct. 2003 <http://newsdirectory.com/go/?f=&r=ea&u=daily.stanford.org>.

Hill, Tessa. "UA students Have Lost That Lovin' Feeling." Arizona Daily Wildcat 30 Jan. 2003. 8 Oct. 2003 <http://wc.arizona.edu/papers/96/85/01_1.html>.

Jensen, Mark. "A Return to Courtship." Cavalier Daily 26 Apr. 2002. 19 Oct. 2003 <http://www.cavalierdaily.com/CVArticle.asp?ID=12358&pid=868>.

Kucewicz, Nicole. "Ins and Outs of the College Dating Game: Fun or Forever?" Rocky Mountain Collegian 15 Aug. 2001. 19 Oct. 2003 <http://www.collegian.com/vnews/display.v/ART/2001/08/15/3d78c7cd538ef?in_archive>1>.

Lambert, Tracy, Arnold Kahn, and Kevin Apple. "Pluralistic Ignorance and Hooking." Journal of Sex Research 40.2 (2003): 129-33.

Paul, Elizabeth, Brian McManus, and Allison Hayes. "Hookups: Characteristics and Correlates of College Students' Spontaneous and Anonymous Sexual Experiences." Journal of Sex Research 37.1 (2000): 76-88.

Paul, Elizabeth, and Kristen Hayes. "The Casualities of Casual Sex: A Qualitative Exploration of the

Seirup 18

Phenomenology of College Student Hookups." Journal of Social and Personal Relationships 19 (2002): 639-61.

Peretti, Peter, and Richard Abplanalp, Jr. "Chemistry in the College Dating Process: Structure and Function." Social Behavior and Personality 32.2 (2004): 147-54.

Pleiss, Carissa. "Couples Can Offer Support, Comfort." Collegian 11 Feb. 2003. 17 Oct. 2003 <http://www.collegian.psu.edu/archive/2003/02/02-11-03tdc/02-11-03dscihealth-02.asp>.

Saxe, Lindsay. "Books before Relationships?" Johns Hopkins News-Letter 28 Mar. 2003. 8 Oct. 2003 <http://www.jhunewsletter.com/vnews/display.v/ART/2003/03/28/3e83a90c940a0?inarchive=1>.

West, Matt. "Steering Clear of Marriage until after College." Cavalier Daily 26 Apr. 2001. 19 Oct. 2005 <http://www.cavalierdaily.com/CVArticle.asp?1D=8570&pid=726>.

EVALUATING THE ESSAY

1. Choose a page of Seirup's research essay, and using a highlighter, mark every line or passage in which he actually *does* something with information rather than simply explain or report what he found. In other words, where does he interpret, argue, analyze, assert, speculate, or evaluate? How much of the page is covered with color? Do the same thing with your

own essay draft. Do you do more than report? Do you control information as well as Seirup did here?

2. Using Seirup's essay as a model, identify at least one question you have about the proper way to cite sources in a research essay.
3. If you were going to suggest that the writer revise "College Dating" around a particular assertion or thesis, what would it be? After reading the essay, what are your conclusions about the dating scene at American universities?
4. Identify at least two places where you might use other information from the professional readings in this chapter in "College Dating." Exactly what information would you use? How would you cite it?

Using What You Have Learned

You've been involved in writing your own research essay and reading published and student essays that use research. What have you learned about the research process and the research essay that you can apply in other writing situations?

1. Explore how your thinking about research writing might have changed by completing the following sentence at least five times in your journal: *Before I worked through this chapter I thought writing research essays involved __________, but now I think __________.*
2. In this chapter you were introduced to a range of research-based work, from an undocumented essay to a formal academic paper. How will you use your understanding of academic research genres to prepare to write a research paper for another class? What information will you want to know before you start?
3. Writers of any academic essay must come across as an authority of sorts—credible and persuasive voices on whatever topics they choose to write about. This is particularly important in research-based writing. How exactly do you establish this authority?

The cavernous stacks in the library at Trinity College, Dublin. This may seem a daunting place to find a book, but in a library human knowledge is organized, evaluated, and cataloged. In contrast, the Internet is a great sea of information that can be a navigator's nightmare.

Sample Student Essay: The Research Essay

The following introductions show four different versions Patrick Gibbons created while working on his essay, "Catharsis."

Introduction #1 (Essay Sketch)

In a world already overstuffed with tragic events and shattered individuals, what draws a person to pay for something that just mirrors the sadness that they already feel? Why do people go to sad movies, why do you listen to a sad song when you yourself are already sad? The entertainment industry has made fortunes on sad songs and sadder movies, why in a industry that was created to escape reality do people want to escape to a even more undesirable one?

Introduction #2 (First Essay Draft)

The complex human machine contains many paradoxes. The most basic goals for people to live by are deceptively simple; maximize the good and minimize the bad. However, throughout life, it is far from difficult to avoid the devastating reality of it, and the inherent sadness and hardship that so many have to endure. So in order to step back from this reality, people throughout history have looked to be entertained. Whatever media chosen to employ, it makes no difference, only that it serves as that much needed distraction.

Introduction #3 (Second Essay Draft)

What lies behind someone's motivation towards a given alternative? The most basic goals for people to live by seem deceptively simple; maximize the good and minimize the bad. However, throughout life, it is hardly difficult to avoid the devastating reality of it, and the inherent sadness and hardship that so many have to endure. So in order to step back from reality, people throughout history have looked to be entertained. It makes no difference the genre of media chosen to employ, only that it serves as that much needed distraction.

Introduction #4 (Portfolio Draft)

The reality of life is rarely what you wish it to be. Life hands out failure, loss, and heartbreak like a roulette wheel, spinning wildly away any perception of control you think you may have over it. So, nearly as far back as the written word, people have looked for entertainment to give them relief from this reality, and to immerse themselves into a simpler, more constructed world.

Research Techniques

12

What You'll Learn in This Chapter

- How librarians organize knowledge.
- How to use library and Internet sources to develop a working knowledge of your topic.
- How to craft the best search terms for the library and the Internet.
- How to use more advanced research strategies to build on your working knowledge and develop a deep knowledge of your topic.
- How to evaluate sources and decide what you should use in your writing and what you should ignore.
- Methods of note taking that promote a conversation with sources.
- Techniques for developing surveys and conducting interviews.

METHODS OF COLLECTING

One sure sign that research is an integral part of our everyday lives is the fact that Google, the name of an Internet search engine, is now a verb. Someone can say, "I Googled it" or "I Googled that" and there's a good chance someone else will respond, "Oh really? What did you find?" The Internet makes research easy. It's even fun sometimes. This is a far cry from the experience many of us have had doing academic research at the library, wandering through the stacks trying to find a book that's supposed to be but isn't there, or impatiently waiting in line to commandeer the one photocopy machine on the fifth floor, wondering whether that pocketful of change will be enough to copy Chapter 10 of *The Dreaming Brain.*

But I can also remember moments as a college student—well before the Web—when I hunkered down until midnight in a study carrel in the campus library, reading my way through articles and books that opened doors on the subject I was researching. On rare occasions, I was even blinded by the light that suddenly poured in. Research is a process that, like writing, can be filled with discovery. And it should be, particularly if you've found questions that really interest you about your subject and you don't have to spend too much time learning the technicalities of how to find what you need.

This chapter should help you know everything you need to know about finding what you need in the university library and on the Web. It is particularly useful for collecting information for research essays, but research is a source of information that can make *any* essay stronger. Every assignment in *The Curious Writer,* therefore, includes suggestions for research as you're searching for a topic and writing your draft. Research also can be an especially useful revision strategy for any essay.

Use this chapter much as you would a toolbox—a handy collection of tips and research tools that you can use for any assignment. Refer to it whenever you discover a topic that raises questions that research can help answer, or whenever it would be helpful to hear what other people say about the things you're thinking about.

RESEARCH IN THE ELECTRONIC AGE

The problem used to be not finding enough information on a research topic. Now, according to some librarians, students are so swamped with information that they pretty much print out the first few things they find and rush off to write their papers. "Google has won," lament some librarians. Like any other technological advance, the wide availability of electronic databases is a mixed blessing. On the one hand, these databases are really wonderful. They are searchable not only from the library reference room but also from the comfort of students' own computers in their dorms or apartments. They allow researchers to search twenty years or more of journals and magazines in seconds, something that took hours and hours in the old days when bound indexes were all that was available.

The downside of the Internet and electronic databases is that student researchers can quickly produce such long lists of possible sources that they simply skim off the top, going for the first few that offer full-text versions and ignoring the rest, many of which might be better. The companies that create and sell databases to your university library are aware of this fondness for full-text articles, so they keep adding more and more. This isn't a bad thing, necessarily, except that there is little thought about which sources would be most valuable to academic researchers. In fact, the more useful sources, often articles from the most important journals in a discipline, are still least likely to be served up as full-text articles. The buffet of electronic information is heavy on high-calorie, low-protein offerings, stuff that satisfies your immediate cravings but leaves you hungry later.

This is especially true of the Web. About 80 percent of the Web is dominated by commercial sites. These are great if you're trying to get the best price on an answering machine, but commercial sites usually don't have much value for academic research. Even if you do weed through the dot-com offerings after a Google search, you shouldn't feel at all confident that your search has been comprehensive. Although Google and Yahoo! are remarkable search engines, they don't actually search the entire World Wide Web. What they search is their *own* databases of Web pages, and while these can be quite substantial, they're only a very small fraction of what's out there. In fact, some experts believe that most of the Internet is invisible to conventional search engines. That doesn't mean that this information, much of which is quite useful for academic research, is completely inaccessible; you just have to know how to find it.

Research is easier, faster, and, at times, more pleasant in the electronic age. But it demands new electronic literacies.

Research is easier, faster, and, at times, more pleasant in the electronic age. But it demands new *electronic literacies* that include knowledge about how to exploit the technology to find relevant information and new ways of thinking about how to evaluate and analyze what you find.

Magic Words That Open Doors

One of the key electronic literacies is something that seems so simple you might wonder why I bring it up first: *the words you choose to search for information.* Consider that in 1850 the Harvard library, the first academic library in the nation, had only 84,200 volumes, and many of those were kept behind locked cabinets. To search these stacks, a student would plead with a librarian for a look. Today, my own university's library has more than a half million books and access to millions more through interlibrary loan. In addition, it has tens of thousands of periodicals on microfilm, and access to millions more through electronic databases. Then there's the World Wide Web; it's impossible to know its actual size, but the number of pages is certainly in the billions. All this information can make a researcher giddy, except for this: How do you find your needle in that gargantuan haystack?

In 1850, the Harvard librarian was familiar with the books in the stacks and could lead you to what you wanted. Today, librarians must trust in the language systems and codes they've created to organize knowledge; to find anything, you have to know those language systems. And while information on the Web isn't nearly as organized as it is in the library—for one thing, there isn't any librarian in charge, although there are some Internet directories that librarians maintain—the software that searches the Web also uses a language logic. Using it well means the difference between getting 1 million "hits" on a topic search, which you will never be able to read through, or getting 300 hits, many of which will be relevant to your topic.

How Librarians Organize Books

The Dewey decimal system and the Library of Congress system are the two systems for classifying books. Dewey decimal is what your hometown library uses; Library of Congress is the approach used in the university library. How much do you need to know about a system for shelving books? Not a whole lot, except that you should be familiar with its logic because it will save you time. The key thing to understand is that the letters on the spines of books actually mean something about the structure of knowledge. In the accompanying Library of Congress system table, you'll note that each letter suggests a division of human knowledge; you'll never memorize this, but it does help you to know, for instance, that when you're browsing books in the B's you're in the world of psychological knowledge.

LIBRARY OF CONGRESS SYSTEM

ORGANIZATION OF BOOKS BY LETTER

A General Works
B Philosophy, Psychology, Religion
C Auxiliary Sciences of History
D History: General and Europe
E History: America
F History: America
G Geography, Anthropology, Recreation
H Social Sciences
J Political Sciences
K Law
L Education
M Music
N Fine Arts
P Language and Literature
Q Science
R Medicine
S Agriculture
T Technology
U Military Science
Y Naval Science
Z Library Science and Reference

These letters, used in combination with other letters and numbers, make up the call numbers that will help you locate a book in the library. For instance, suppose you're looking for a book about study habits, and your library's book search tool lists a book called *What You Need to Know about Developing Study Skills, Taking Notes and Tests, Using Dictionaries and Libraries* (see Figure 12.1). The call number is LB2395.C65 1991. What may seem like just a bunch of letters and numbers actually gives a lot of information about the book, including the body of knowledge from which it came, when it was published, and the first letter of the author's last name.

But you want to find it. Your library will place books on specific floors or areas of your library according to the first one or two call letters. There should be an index of these locations on the wall. Once you've generally located the book using the letters on the first line (e.g., LB), the second line (e.g., 2395) tells you where it is in relation to the books next to it (see Figure 12.2 and Figure 12.3).

Library of Congress Subject Headings

The *Library of Congress Subject Headings* (*LCSH*) conveniently lists the words that librarians use to index information. This underappreciated and much ignored multivolume book is the key to efficiently finding what you're looking for when using electronic indexes. It holds the magic words to successful searches. For example, if you are writing about the history of arm wrestling you could simply type in *arm wrestling, history* as a subject search in your library's online search form. You might come up with something, but if you turned up nothing, might you give up on the topic? The *LCSH* can help out because it suggests a broader term (BT) for *arm wrestling, history* that might produce some results: *sports records.* Would that have occurred to you on your own? Here's another example: My student Gracie's topic is bipolar disorder. Without checking the

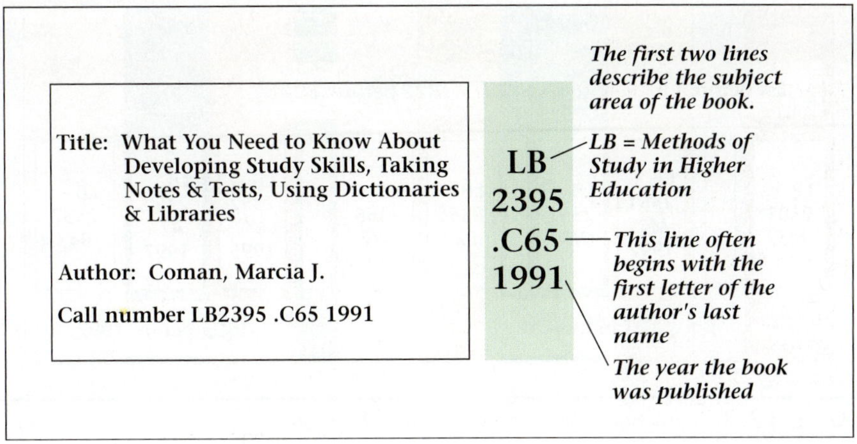

FIGURE 12.1 The library call card.

LCHS, she would quite naturally use *bipolar disorder* to search for books and articles on the subject, and no doubt she'd find some material. But if she checked the *LCSH* under *bipolar disorder,* Gracie would discover that the term preferred by librarians is *manic-depressive illness.* Searching with that term will open up many more doors for her.

The *LCHS* will not only help you find books. Many of the companies that develop databases of articles use Library of Congress terms, too. Equally important, however, for searching these periodical databases is Boolean operators.

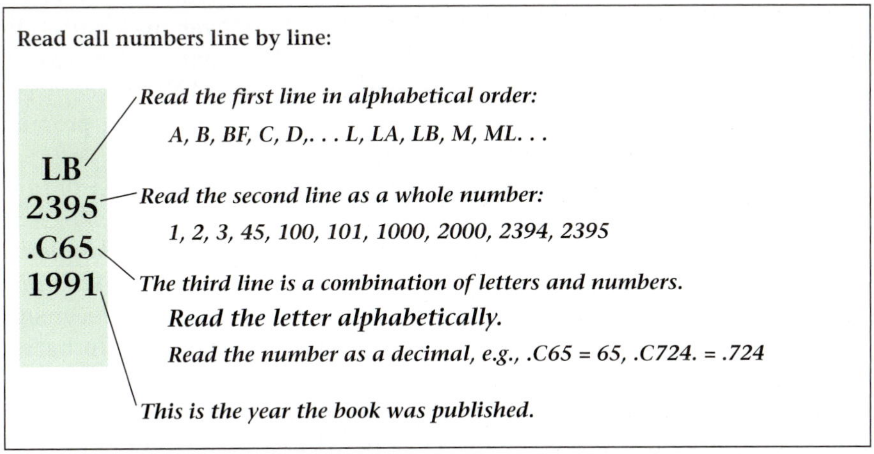

FIGURE 12.2 How to read call numbers.

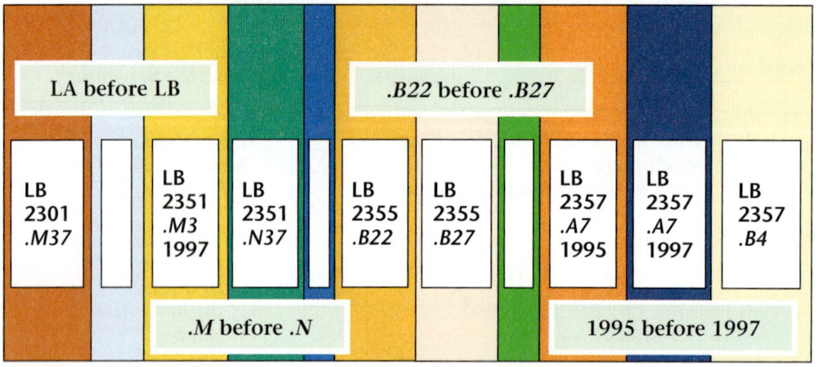

FIGURE 12.3 How books are arranged on the library shelf.

Google Your Boole

George Boole is the eighteenth-century mathematician who came up with the system for using the words AND, OR, and NOT to help researchers design logical queries. Boole's professional legacy is something every modern college researcher should know. Consider Paul's situation. His grandmother has Alzheimer's disease, and his initial research question was, *What are the best therapies for treating Alzheimer's?* When Paul consulted PsycINFO, a popular database of citations from journals relating to psychology, his instinct was simply to enter the word *Alzheimer's* in the online search form. The result was 13,392 citations, and only a portion of these were relevant. But when Paul put the word AND between two key terms from his research question—*Alzheimer's AND therapy*—he managed to reduce his results to 1,955 more relevant citations (see Figure 12.4). As he was looking over his results, Paul became interested specifically in music therapies. His next search was even more focused when he typed in the words *Alzheimer's AND therapy AND music.* That produced 74 citations, and nearly all of these seemed promising (see Figure 12.5).

The Boolean operator AND helped Paul search the PsycINFO database much more efficiently because it asked the computer to look for documents that had all three words in the title or abstract. What would happen if Paul left the AND operators out and simply searched using the three terms *Alzheimer's music therapy?* The result would have been 184,532 documents because the search software would assume that keywords with no operators in between them imply the Boolean operator OR. In other words, *Alzheimer's music therapy* is interpreted as *Alzheimer's OR music OR therapy* (see Figure 12.6). That means it would return citations for documents that had only one of the three words in the title or abstract. For a database of psychology publications, that's a lot of documents.

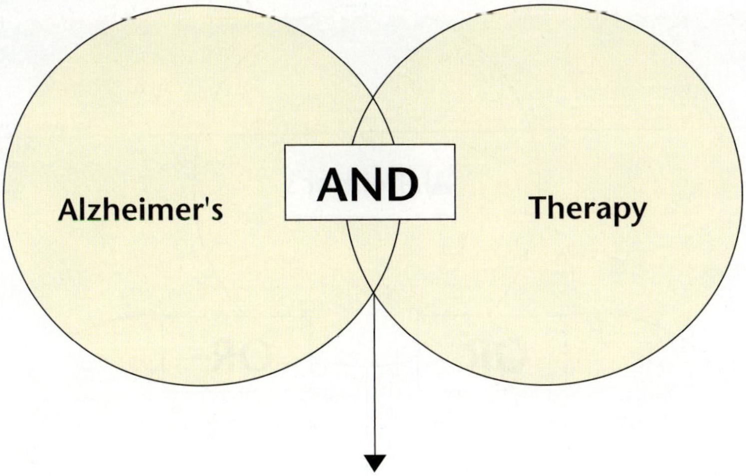

FIGURE 12.4 This query searches all documents that contain *both* words in the abstract or title. PsycINFO returned a list of 1,955 citations for *Alzheimer's AND therapy.*

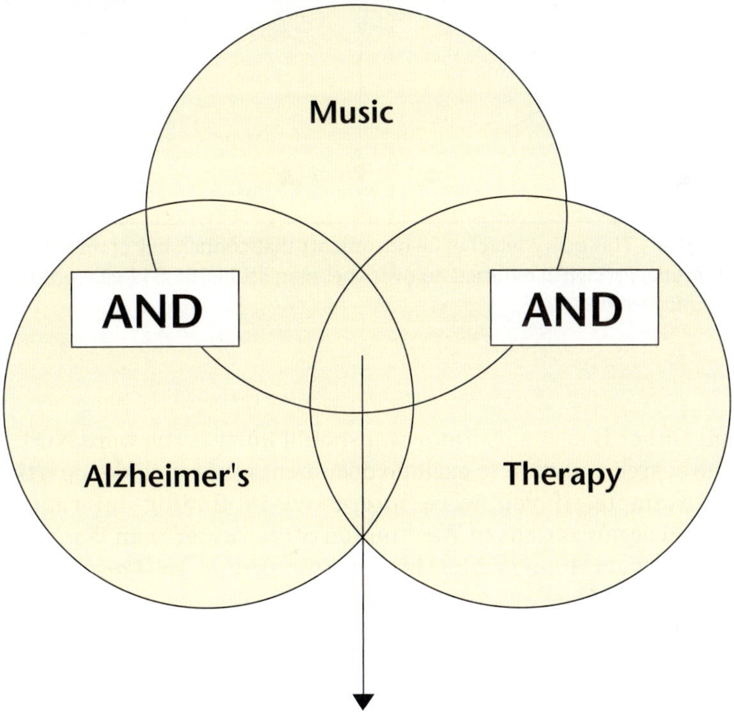

FIGURE 12.5 This focused query finds documents that include all the keywords. It generated a list of 74 citations, many of which were relevant and useful, for *Alzheimer's AND therapy AND music.*

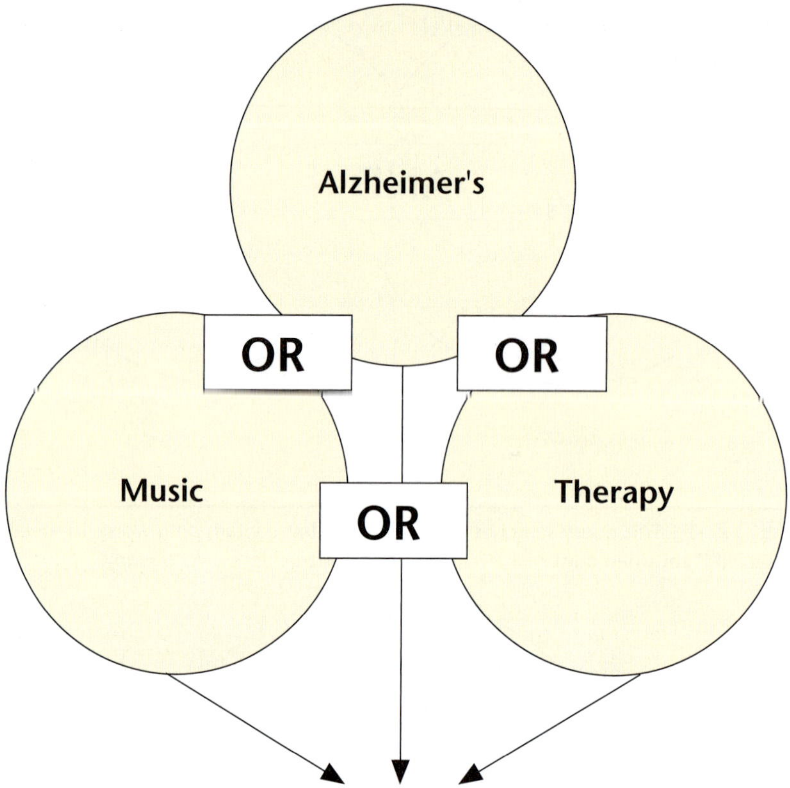

FIGURE 12.6 This query searches all documents that contain *any of* these three words in the abstract or title. PsycINFO returned an overwhelming list of 184,532 citations for *Alzheimer's music therapy*.

The only other Boolean operator you should know is the word NOT. This simply tells the search software to exclude documents that include a particular keyword. For example, if you were interested in finding information about environmental organizations in Washington State rather than Washington, D.C., you might construct a query like this: *environmental AND organizations AND Washington NOT D.C.*

The real art of designing queries using the Boolean system is combining the operators to refine your search. For example, let's take the last search on environmental groups in Washington State. Suppose the previous query didn't produce enough results. Let's broaden it a bit: *(environmental OR conservation) AND organizations AND Washington NOT D.C.* This search would find documents that use either *environmental* or *conservation* in the title or abstract, probably returning a longer list. The parentheses simply group the keywords *environmental OR conservation* together as an expression that the search software evaluates first. You can use multiple parentheses in a query to control the order in which expressions are evaluated, beginning with the innermost parenthetical expressions. Librarians call the use of parenthesis to group keywords in this manner *nesting.*

Increasingly, search pages for databases make it easy to exploit Boolean language in a search. For example, in the accompanying photo you can see how the advanced search page for Academic Search Premier, an EBSCOhost database, allows you to enter search terms, and then use drop-down menus to add the Boolean connectors AND, OR, or NOT. The search page adds even more refinement by allowing you to relate a particular term to a type or source or search. For example, you might want to search for Alzheimer's articles by a particular author whose work is relevant to your project. Using the advanced search page, you could simultaneously use *Alzheimer's* as a subject search, with *Smith* as an author search.

Knowing your Boolean operators will help you search library databases because most of the search software relies on the system. Some Web search engines do, too. But more often, search engines such as Google use a somewhat different language that accomplishes the same thing. The accompanying table shows both Boolean and typical Web search engine search terms.

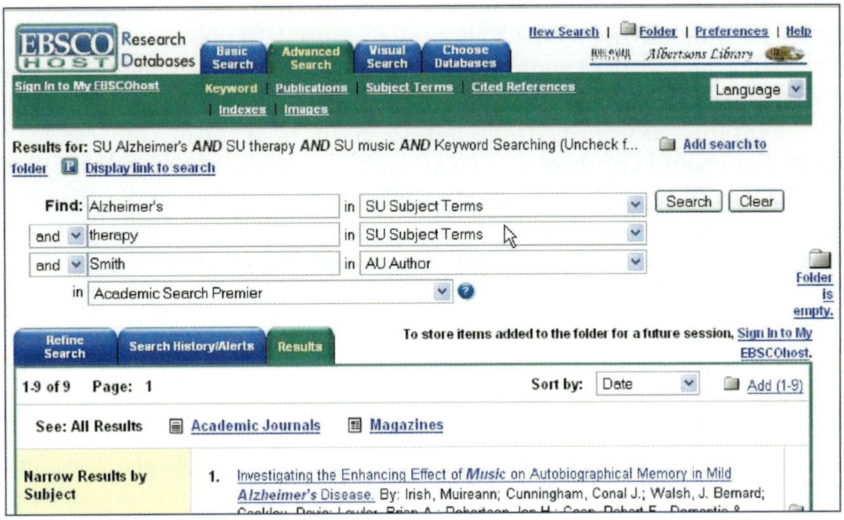

Advanced search pages such as the EBSCOhost database allow you to exploit Boolean terms using drop-down menus. Further refinements allow the researcher to link terms to different kinds of searches or sources.

SEARCH TERMS: BOOLEAN AND THEIR EQUIVALENTS IN GOOGLE

Boolean	Example	Google	Example
OR	*Romeo OR Juliet*	Add connector between keywords	*Hansel OR Gretel*
AND	*Romeo AND Juliet*	Plus sign in front of keyword, or omit connector	*Hansel + Gretel; Hansel Gretel*
NOT	*Romeo NOT Juliet*	Minus sign in front of keyword	*Hansel – Gretel*
( )	*(Romeo and Juliet)*	No equivalent	
No equivalent		Quotation marks around exact phrase	*"Hansel and Gretel"*

Today, search engines such as Google have an advanced search option that allows you to simply fill in a form if you want to search for certain keywords or phrases. I've found that, by far, the most useful syntax to use when searching the Web is quotation marks—an exact phrase search—and carefully ordered keywords, if possible more than three. For example, let's return to Paul's topic of Alzheimer's therapy. If he searched the Web using Google and the keywords *Alzheimer's therapy,* a syntax that implies an AND between the two words, Google would return about 9.9 million documents. But because the phrase *Alzheimer's therapy* or *therapies for Alzheimers* would likely appear in many relevant documents, Paul would be better off to try a phrase search. The result? Searching for *Alzheimer's therapy* produced 10,000 sites.

That's better, but Paul could further focus his research by querying Google with multiple terms, listed in order of importance because search engines usually evaluate keywords from left to right in level of importance. For example, Paul could try this: + *Alzheimer's* + *research "music therapy,"* and this time focus the search on journal articles using Google Scholar. The results of this search were about 900 sites and a rich list of scholarly sources on his topic. There is much more to know about composing queries, but you now know enough to make a significant difference in the effectiveness of your searches.

DEVELOPING WORKING KNOWLEDGE

Every day we make decisions about how much we need to know about something. Twenty-five years ago, I decided to know enough to tune up my own car. Fifteen years ago I decided I was't interested in keeping up with the changes in electronic ignitions and fuel injection, so now I leave car repair to Davey at State Street Auto. A scholar is someone who, like Davey, has committed their professional lives to keeping up with the knowledge in his or her field. College professors

Writing with Computers

RESEARCHING ONLINE

Today's researchers can conduct scholarly research over the Internet, but their strategy must be more sophisticated than just using Internet search engines. Internet search engines search only items in public places on the Internet. Most college and research libraries have sophisticated Web sites with large subscription-based databases. Internet search engines can't access this information. Generally, you can search the library's holdings in a catalog database. In addition, many libraries subscribe to third-party article indexes. These indexes catalog articles published in magazines, journals, and other periodicals. They can help scholars identify individual articles. The researcher can then use the library's catalog to find the physical location of the journal that contains the article. Large strides in the digitizing of journals over the last few years have made it possible for researchers to find full-text and electronic versions of many articles directly in the indexes or through the library's full text databases. Just ten years ago a college student would have to spend hours in the library pulling hardbound journals or spooling microfilm to access such information. Today's college student can eliminate most of this tedious labor by becoming familiar with his or her library's database services. Currently the digitizing of journals is not universal, so students must still use traditional library bindings and microfilm, but in the near future students may be able to complete all of their research without leaving their computers.

Beyond the databases and indexes of libraries, some scholarly projects place their research on the Internet. These projects use the Internet as a means of immediately displaying their ongoing discoveries and results. One example of such a project is Making of America (http://www.hti.umich.edu/m/moagrp/), which contains scanned images from books, journals, and newspapers from the nineteenth century. This database allows researchers to see the actual pages of rare publications with historical significance. Often search engines aren't able to return results from within these projects or place them in the context of individual search queries. A good researcher should attempt to discover such projects and conduct research directly on these Web sites. If you're unaware of specific online projects in a particular academic field, ask your professor for suggestions.

possess *expert knowledge* of their discipline (see Figure 12.7). Five hundred years ago, the French writer Montaigne was a "scholar of the self," proposing that self-knowledge was the important kind of knowing of all. If you wrote a personal essay in Chapter 4, you also tapped expert knowledge.

How much we need to know about a subject is, in part, a personal choice, but a college education does at least two things: Challenge you to develop new knowledge about things that will make you a better citizen and more productive professional, and teach you *how* to better acquire the new knowledge that you might seek by choice. A research project like this is driven by both goals—you'll be challenged to go beyond superficial knowledge about a meaningful topic, and you'll learn some of the methods for doing that.

Mental illness ***(May Subd Geog)***

Here are entered popular works and works on social aspects of mental disorders. Works on the legal aspects of mental illness are entered under Insanity. Works on clinical aspects of mental disorders, including therapy, are entered under Psychiatry

UF Diseases, Mental
Madness
Mental disorders
Mental diseases
BT Diseases
Psychiatry
Psychology, Pathological
RT Mental health
NT Dual diagnosis
Genius and mental illness
Insanity
Neurobehavioral disorders

— **Alternative treatment**
— **Diagnosis**
BT Psychodiagnostics
NT Psychiatric disability evaluation
— **Epidemiology**
USE Psychiatric epidemiology
— **Prevention**
— **Surgery**
USE Psychosurgery
— **Treatment**
— **Evaluation**
NT Psychiatric rating scales

- The abbreviation means "May be Subdivided Geographically." That means you might also find the topic listed by state, country, region, and so on.
- A helpful summary of how the topic is broken down.
- Mental illness is "Used For" these other terms.
- These are "Broader Terms" for mental illness, and these are "Narrower Terms." Sometimes the narrower terms will give you new ideas for a focus.
- This is a "Related Term"
- The term "USE" is among the most helpful. It tells you the preferred language to *use* to search for materials on the topic of subtopic.

FIGURE 12.7 How to read a Library of Congress Subject Headings entry. At first glance, the *Library of Congress Subject Headings* (*LCSH*) looks like a secret code, one reason that such a valuable research tool initially puts off some student researchers. But using the terms suggested by the *LCSH* can make your research more efficient, particularly when looking for library books or searching databases. Look at the example here. If you are looking for information on bipolar disorder, you might first look in the *LCHS* under *mental disorders*, but because the preferred term is *mental illness*, the book refers you to this page. What does it tell you? A lot.

You will not end up a scholar on anorexia, college dating, the medical effects of music, or whatever topic you're researching. But you will go way beyond superficial knowledge of your subject, and when you do, it will be like opening a door and entering a crowded room of intelligent strangers, all deep in conversation about your topic. At first you simply listen in before you speak, and that begins with a *working knowledge*.

Before you actually start researching a topic, it's unlikely that you could talk about it for one minute without stopping or repeating yourself. But when you can, according to librarian William Badke, you have a "working knowledge" of your topic. Depending on the nature of your project, a working knowledge may be quite enough. For example, suppose you're writing a personal essay about being the target of relational aggression, or to put it less technically, being victimized by a group of girls who express their aggression in often subtle ways. Because of the genre (the personal essay) and your purpose in writing about the topic—say, to come to a clearer understanding why a best friend turned against you—you probably don't need to know a great deal about research done in this field. It would probably be enough to understand the basic theory of relational aggression, a few people who have interesting things to say about it, and perhaps something about how other victims handled their feelings.

You might go beyond a working knowledge of your topic and develop "focused knowledge," the kind often required if you're writing a research essay (focused knowledge is discussed later in this chapter). But if you don't know much about your topic you will always develop a working knowledge first. It's the foundation for further research.

The material that follows will help you develop a working knowledge of a topic using the university library and the Internet. In addition to helping you know enough to talk for a minute without repeating yourself, a working knowledge of a topic helps you understand the following:

1. How your topic fits into the *context* of other subjects. Where does it fall relative to larger and smaller categories of relevant knowledge? This is helpful to know because it can help you narrow your topic.
2. Some of the areas of controversy, debate, questions, or unresolved problems that ripple through the ongoing published conversations about your topic. What, generally, are the people who know something about your topic talking about?

Steps for Developing Working Knowledge

1. Frame a research question or identify your topic as narrowly as you can.
2. Find appropriate search terms in the *Library of Congress Subject Headings.*
3. Check general and specialized encyclopedias.
4. Consult the *Guide to Reference Books* for other references.
5. Do a subject search and a keyword search on the World Wide Web.

Searching Key Library References

Your first inclination when starting research is probably to boot up your computer and do a Web search on your topic. You should resist this temptation, however; laying some groundwork in the library at the start of your research will save you time later. Begin in the reference room of your university library. As a first step, before you begin researching your topic, describe it briefly in a phrase or a sentence, or write out your tentative research question in your journal. It helps enormously to know from the start, if possible, that your topic covers a smaller part of the entire landscape. There's a big difference between wanting to know about *college athletics* versus *college football recruiting practices*.

A good next step is to consult the *Library of Congress Subject Headings*. These several fat volumes are often set out on a table or shelved near the reference desk. Ask a librarian where they are. Because you're probably not familiar with the *LCSH*, you may have to skim the introduction in the front. But basically, try to look up your topic in the book's alphabetically arranged index. Each heading often has lists of subheadings. These may suggest broader terms (BT) or narrower terms (NT) (see Figure 12.7 for an example). You might also notice the abbreviations UF and USE. UF means "used for," or less suitable terms for the topic; USE indicates the standard Library of Congress wording and the one you should use in your library searches. Write down any headings that the *LCSH* suggests for your topic. There may be more than one.

Laying some groundwork in the library at the start of your research will save you time later.

We all grew up with encyclopedias, and while they are pretty useful for that eighth-grade paper on China, general encyclopedias such as *Encyclopaedia Britannica* are less useful as major sources for a college paper. Yet encyclopedias are a good thing to check when developing a working knowledge of your topic. There are, of course, computer-based encyclopedias such as *Encarta,* but these don't hold a candle to the venerable bound version of *Encyclopaedia Britannica*, also in your reference room.

Begin by looking for your topic in a Britannica's *Macropaedia,* a kind of index and abstract of subjects that may point you to longer treatments in the *Micropaedia*. Sometimes you will also find information about your topic *within* articles about other subjects.

Alternatively, see if you can find a specialized encyclopedia in your topic's subject area. These are more focused, obviously, and often have a wealth of information on a topic that's lacking in the more general encyclopedia. Ask the reference librarian whether your library has a specialized encyclopedia in your subject area. A list of some of the more common of these can be found in the accompanying table.

SOME COMMON SPECIALIZED ENCYCLOPEDIAS

Humanities
Encyclopedia of World Art
Encyclopedia of Religions
Encyclopedia of Philosophy
Encyclopedia of African-American Culture and History
Encyclopedia of Social History

Social Sciences
Encyclopedia of Marriage and Family
Encyclopedia of Psychology
The Blackwell Encyclopedia of Social Psychology
Encyclopedia of Educational Research
Encyclopedia of Sociology
Encyclopedia of Social Work
Encyclopedia of World Cultures
Encyclopedia of Democracy
Guide to American Law: Everyone's Legal Encyclopedia
Worldmark Encyclopedia of the Nations

Science
Encyclopedia of the Environment
Concise Encyclopedia of Biology
Encyclopedia of Bioethics
Encyclopedia of Science and Technology
Macmillan Encyclopedias of Chemistry and Physics
Food and Nutrition Encyclopedia

Sports
The Baseball Encyclopedia
Encyclopedia of Women and Sports
Encyclopedia of World Sport
Encyclopedia of Sports Medicine and Science

When you find interesting or relevant information in an encyclopedia, jot down the encyclopedia where you found it and record the information by summarizing it, paraphrasing it, or quoting it directly (see the "Inquiring into the Details: Methods of Recording Information" box). You may find using the double-entry journal method here particularly useful for coming up with ideas and questions you will want to explore in your essay. Summarize, paraphrase, and quote information on the left page of your journal and then fastwrite some of your thoughts in response to that information on the right page. Use questions to direct your fastwriting: *What strikes you most about this information? What do you find interesting? How does the information challenge your initial assumptions about your topic?*

As a final step in the library, consult the *Guide to Reference Books.* This is another one of those incredibly useful and woefully underused reference books that can lead you to a mother lode of sources. The *Guide* includes more than 16,000 indexes, bibliographies, special encyclopedias, almanacs, and other references in several thousand general topic areas. It's organized by field of study (Humanities, Social and Behavioral Sciences, History, Science and Technology, and so forth), but probably the best place to begin is with the index at the back. Try to locate your topic directly, or find some larger subject category that seems relevant. The General Works section in each subject category is a great place to begin if the index at the back fails you.

Inquiring into the Details

METHODS OF RECORDING INFORMATION

The default mode for many student researchers is to simply quote information from a book, article, or Web page, writing down excerpts word for word. Jotting down quotations is fine. But it's often far more useful to summarize and paraphrase a source in your own words. Here's a brief description of each method.

1. **Summary.** One of the more useful ways of taking notes because it challenges you to condense, in your own words, a longer text, capturing key concepts or claims.
2. **Paraphrase.** This also tests your understanding of what you read, prompting you to translate a passage from a source into your own words; your paraphrase will be roughly the same length as the original.
3. **Quotation.** A perennial favorite approach to note taking because it's mere transcription, ranging from a few key words to several paragraphs. Remember to always transcribe the words of the original source exactly.
4. **"Paraquote."** One of the most useful methods of note taking is to cast part of an original passage in your own words, and then integrate a key term or phrase in quotations. For example: *Ballenger claims that the "paraquote," a combination of paraphrase and quotation in a single sentence, is "one of the most useful methods of note taking."*

Write down the name and publication information about any reference source listed in the *Guide* that seem promising on your topic; find out if your library has it, and if it's an encyclopedia, almanac, or some other general reference source, do some reading on your topic. Again, consider using the double-entry journal method to get the most out of the information.

Conducting Subject Surveys on the Web

One of the useful qualities of the World Wide Web is how much it offers researchers who want to quickly develop a working knowledge of their topics. The Web is probably where you wanted to start your research rather than in your library's reference room, but if the campus library reflects reference librarians' passion for order and logic in a chaotic universe, the Web is more like the mind of my nine-year-old daughter Julia. She has lots of passions, but one look at her bedroom and it's clear that order isn't one of them. She does try from time to time, as the bins in her closet show: the contents of each bin roughly corresponds to an area of interest, but the stuff is often mixed up and I'm not surprised when she can't find what she's looking for.

Librarians and scholars have tried to bring some order to the similar chaos of the Internet, perhaps with more success. They've introduced plastic bins, too, and these are subject directories such as the Virtual Library, or the Internet Public Library. Unfortunately, these sites are often ignored by student researchers who opt instead to begin with a Google search, an effort that will produce some useable results that will be scattered among much less reliable documents. Consulting the subject directories may not generate as much information, but what you find will be better quality for academic research.

A good way to start your research on the Web is to visit one or more of the following subject directories:

- Academic Info (http://www.academicinfo.net)
- Infomine (http://infomine.ucr.edu)
- The Librarians Index to the Internet (http://lii.org)
- Best Information on the Net (http://library.sau.edu/bestinfo/Default.htm)
- The Internet Public Library (http://www.ipl.org)
- Virtual Library (http://vlib.org)
- The Google Directory (http://directory.google.com)
- Yahoo! Directory (http://dir.yahoo.com)

The way to use the directories is to work from the general to the specific, beginning with broad subject categories relevant to your topic and then mouse-clicking your way down to narrower categories until you find a good match with your topic. If one directory yields little, try another.

Print out copies of any useful documents you find, and consider composing one- or two-paragraph summaries, or *annotations,* for each of the sources you find. *What are the key ideas? What seems most important and relevant to your project?* If your instructor requires you to develop a working bibliography or annotated bibliography on your topic, this might be the beginning of it (see the "Inquiring into the Details: The Working Bibliography" box).

Finish your Web research by using so-called metasearch engines. This software deploys multiple search engines in the service of a single search. For example, when you type your keywords into Dogpile it simultaneously searches using Google, Yahoo!, LookSmart, Ask.com, MSN Search, and others. If this

INQUIRING INTO THE DETAILS

THE WORKING BIBLIOGRAPHY

A working bibliography lists sources you've collected that you think will be helpful when you draft your essay. These may include annotations, or brief summaries of what the source says that you find relevant to your research question. Consider the following examples:

Topic: Relational Aggression

Print Sources

Simmons, Rachel. *Odd Girl Out: The Hidden Culture of Aggression in Girls.* New York: Harcourt, 2002.

Simmons argues that the "secret world of girls' aggression"—the backstabbing, the silent treatment, the bartering of friendship for compliance to a group's "rules"—can be just as bad as the less subtle aggression of boys. Her basic thesis is that girls in American culture are supposed to be "nice," and therefore have no outlet for their anger except for exploiting the one thing they do covet: relationships. Because my essay focuses on the popularity phenomenon in high school—How does it affect girls when they are adults?—Simmons's chapter on parents of these girls seems particularly useful because it shows how the parents' responses are often shaped by their own experiences in school.

Web Sources

"What Is Relational Aggression?" *The Ophelia Project.* 22 Sept. 2003 <http://www.opheliaproject.org/issues/issues_RA.shtml>.

The page defines relational aggression by contrasting it with physical aggression. It argues that most research, naturally, has focused on the latter because of need to limit physical injury between children. But girls tend to avoid physical aggression and instead indulge in actions that harm others by disrupting their social relationships, like giving someone the silent treatment. The Ophelia Project is a nonprofit group created in 1997 by parents who wanted to address the problem.

sounds too good to be true, it is; metasearch engines tend to skim off the top of the results for each individual search engine, so you often get a breadth of results but not depth. Still, metasearches are worth doing because they help extend your coverage of the Web.

Use one or more of the following metasearch engines to search on your topic:

- Metacrawler (http://www.metacrawler.com)
- Dogpile (http://www.dogpile.com)
- Mamma (http://www.mamma.com)
- Search.com (http://www.search.com)

Remember to play around with the number and order of keywords to get the best results. Several of these sites also provide subject searches. You might try one of those as well.

Add promising sites or documents to your working bibliography, writing summaries or annotations for each individual source. Be sure to list the bibliographic information on each source following the appropriate documentation style (see Chapter 13 for MLA and APA guidelines).

A working knowledge may be all you need, depending on your project. With a working knowledge, you know enough to search with more efficiency and read with more understanding if you want or need to learn more. If you are writing a research paper, you will need to develop focused knowledge about your topic, discussed later in the chapter. But first, consider this: How do you determine which sources you can trust, and which will be most persuasive for your readers? The next sections should help you decide.

EVALUATING LIBRARY SOURCES

One of the huge advantages of finding what you need at the campus library is that nearly everything there was chosen by librarians whose job it is to make good information available to academic researchers. Now that many of the university library's databases are available online, including full-text articles, there really is no excuse for deciding to exclusively use Web pages you downloaded from the Internet for your essays. But even in the campus library, some sources are more authoritative than others. The "Pyramid of Library Sources" (see Figure 11.1 in Chapter 11) gives you a general idea of the hierarchy of authority for most library sources.

In general, the more specialized the audience for a publication, the more authoritatively scholars view the publication's content. Academic journals are at the bottom of this inverted pyramid because they represent the latest thinking and knowledge in a discipline, and most of the articles are reviewed by specialists in the field before they are published. At the top of the inverted pyramid are general encyclopedias and general-interest magazines such as *Newsweek* and *Time*. These have broader audiences and feature articles that are written by nonspecialists. They are rarely peer reviewed. As a rule, then, the lower you draw from this inverted pyramid, the more authoritative the sources from an academic point of view. Here are some other guidelines to consider:

- *Choose more recent sources over older ones.* This is particularly good advice, obviously, if your subject is topical; the social and natural sciences also put much more emphasis on the currency of sources than humanities disciplines.
- *Look for often-cited authors.* Once you've developed a working knowledge of your topic, you'll start noticing that certain authors seem to be mentioned or cited fairly frequently. These are likely to be the most listened-to authors, and may be considered the most authoritative on your topic.
- *If possible, use primary sources over secondary sources.* In literary research, primary sources are the original words of writers—their speeches, stories, novels, poems, memoirs, letters, interviews, and eyewitness accounts. Secondary sources would be articles that discuss those works. Primary sources in other fields might be original studies or experiments, firsthand newspaper accounts, marketing information, and so on.

EVALUATING WEB SOURCES

One of the more amusing sites on the Web is titled "Feline Reactions to Bearded Men." At first glance, the site appears to be a serious academic study of the physiological responses of cats—heartbeat, respiration, and pupil dilation—to a series of photographs of men with beards. The researchers are listed with their affiliations with respected universities. The article includes an abstract, methodology, and results section, as well as a lengthy list of works cited.

The conclusions seem genuine and include the following:

1. Cats do not like men with long beards, especially long dark beards.
2. Cats are indifferent to men with shorter beards.
3. Cats are confused and/or disturbed by men with beards that are incomplete and to a lesser degree by men whose beards have missing parts.

The study is a hoax, a fact that is pretty obvious to anyone who critically examines it. For one thing, it was "published" in the *Annals of Improbable Research,* but I can usually fool about a third of my class with the site for five to ten minutes as I discuss the conventions of academic research, some of which are accurately reproduced in the "study."

Everyone knows to be skeptical of what's on the Web. But this is even more crucial when using Web sources for college writing. Because it's dominated by commercial sites, much of the World Wide Web has limited usefulness to

the academic researcher, and although very few online authors are out to fool researchers with fake scholarship, many have a persuasive purpose. Despite its "educational" mission, for example, the purpose of the Web site ConsumerFreedom.com is to promote industry views on laws relating to food and beverages. That doesn't make the information it offers useless, but a careful researcher would be wary of the site's claims and critical of its studies. At the very least, the information on ConsumerFreedom.com should be attributed as a pro-industry view.

Imagine as you're researching on the Web that you've been dropped off at night in an unfamiliar neighborhood. You're alert. You're vigilant. And you're careful about whom you ask for directions. You can also be systematic about how you approach evaluating online sources. In general, follow these principles:

- *Favor governmental and educational sources over commercial ones.* These sites are more likely to have unbiased information. How can you tell which are institutional sites when it's not obvious? Sometimes the domain name—the abbreviation *edu*, *org*, or *gov* at the end of an Internet address—provides a strong clue, as does the absence of ads on the site.

A cat reacts to a picture of a bearded man from the study "Feline Reactions to Bearded Men."

- *Favor authored documents over those without authors.* There's a simple reason for this: You can check the credentials of authors if you know who they are. Sometimes sites provide e-mail links so you can write to authors, or you can do a search on the Internet or in the library for other materials they've published.
- *Favor documents that are also available in print over those available only online.* Material that is published in both forms generally undergoes more scrutiny. An obvious example would be newspaper articles, but also some articles from journals and magazines are available electronically and in print.
- *Favor Web sources that document their claims over those that don't.* This familiar academic convention is strong evidence that the claims an online author is making are supported and verifiable.
- *Favor Web pages that were recently updated over those that haven't changed in a year or more.* Frequently at the bottom of a Web page there is a line indicating when the information was posted to the Internet and/or when it was last updated. Look for it.

For a more systematic approach to evaluating Web sources, follow the steps in Figure 12.8. This method begins by dividing Web documents into two broad categories: those with authors and those without authors. Web sites that list authors for documents are generally more trustworthy because you can evaluate who the authors are and whether they have appropriate expertise or a particular bias. But many Web documents have no stated authors, forcing you to resort to other ways of evaluating them.

The term *peer reviewed* means that an article was evaluated by other experts in the field and was published because it passed muster. Many of the articles in academic journals are peer reviewed, but very few Web documents undergo that kind of scrutiny; if they were, they usually tell you so.

By far, the most common method of analyzing the value of what you find on the Web is simply considering the source: Is it a commercial or an academic institution? Is it a lone ranger with no affiliations or government group? Are there ads on the page (which suggests a commercial site) or none (which suggests a noncommercial organization)?

DEVELOPING FOCUSED KNOWLEDGE

If working knowledge equips you to sustain a one-minute monologue on your topic, then focused knowledge is enough for you to make a fifteen- to twenty-minute presentation to your class. You'll probably be able to answer all of your classmates' questions, too.

On acquiring focused knowledge on your topic, you won't become an expert but you should know enough to do the following:

1. Be familiar with some of the *key people* who have participated actively in the professional conversation about your topic.

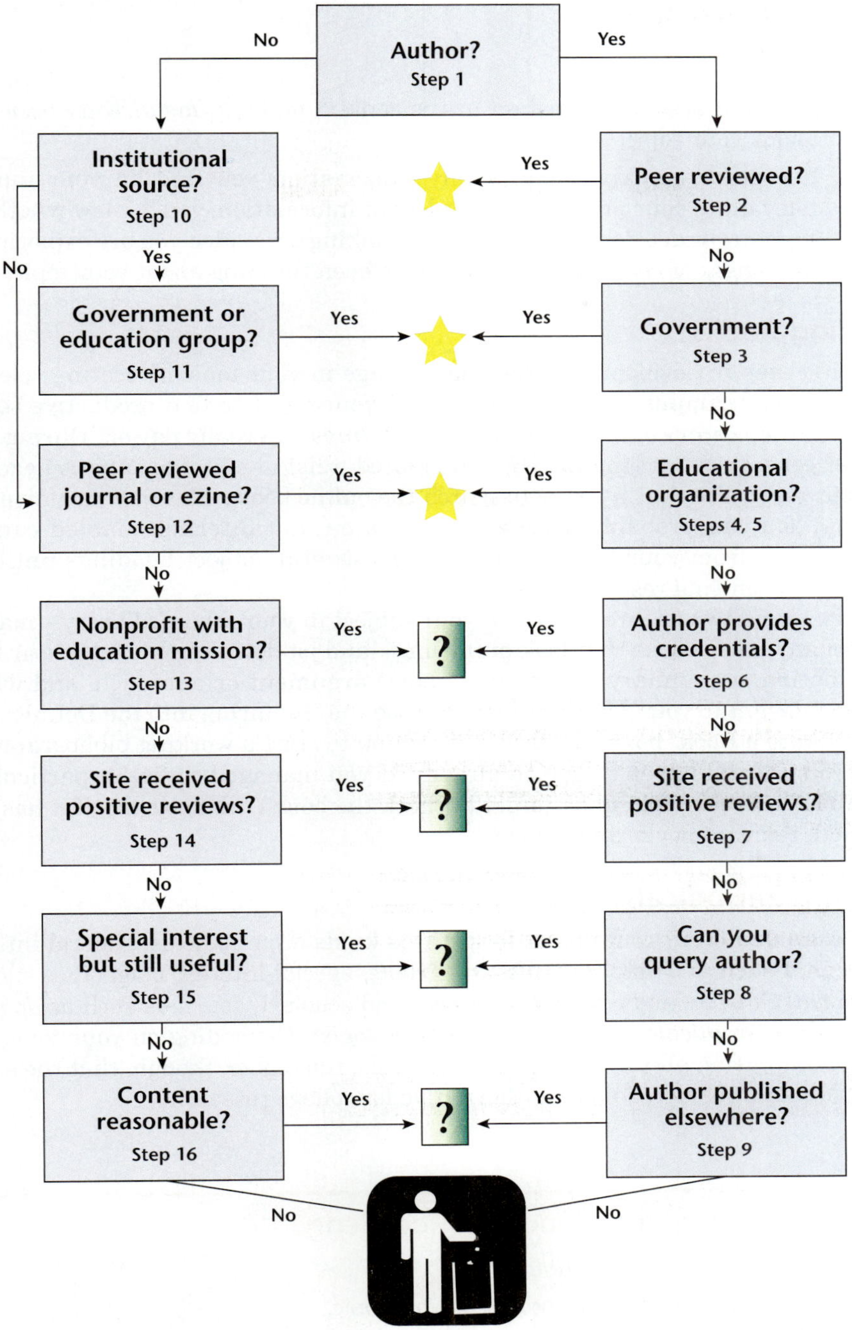

FIGURE 12.8 **Steps for evaluating Web sources.** Begin by trying to find an author of a Web document, and then follow one of the two columns. If subsequent answers to the questions that follow lead you to a star, then you've probably found a credible source. A question mark suggests one that may be useful, depending. If you end up at the trash can at the bottom, well, the implication is clear.

2. Put your research question in the context of *what has already been said* about your topic.
3. Recognize quickly whether any information you find on your topic is relevant to your project. If it is relevant information, you'll know whether it *supports or develops* a claim you are making or an idea you are exploring, or *challenges or complicates* what you've been thinking about your topic.

Finding Books

The first step in developing focused knowledge in your topic is locating relevant books in your campus library. Here's where your effort to find productive search terms in the *Library of Congress Subject Headings* will really pay off. During your earlier consultation of the *LCSH,* you created a list of suitable subject headings on your topic. Use that list now to search the online book index in your university library. You can probably access this index on any Internet-enabled campus computer or from your home computer. Try several subject headings until you generate promising results.

Next, find two or three books on your subject in your school's library—making note of any other books that look promising—and jot down complete bibliographic information, a summary of the book's basic argument or approach, and why it seems relevant to your research question (see the "Inquiring into the Details: How to Annotate a Book" box). Use this information to start a working bibliography on your topic if you haven't done so already. If you managed to find a particularly good book on your topic, don't forget to check the book's bibliography, if it has one, for more relevant books and articles.

Finding Periodicals

Your campus library contains at least three kinds of periodicals: general-interest magazines such as *Time, Harper's,* and *People;* special-interest magazines such as *PC World, Outside*, and *Sports Illustrated*; and scholarly journals such as *Journal of Mass Communication* and *American Sociologist.* Depending on your topic, you may end up using all three types of periodicals; remember, though, that the scholarly ones are considered more authoritative for college research.

Steps for Developing Focused Knowledge

1. Find relevant books on your topic.
2. Find relevant articles in periodicals on your topic.
3. Find relevant newspaper articles on your topic.
4. Find relevant sources on the Web.
5. Synthesize source information and your own ideas using techniques such as the double-entry journal and research log.

Inquiring into the Details

HOW TO ANNOTATE A BOOK

The brevity of articles and most Web pages makes them much easier to annotate than a book. You can usually summarize the argument or relevant ideas of such sources fairly easily. But how do you do that with a book that may have hundreds of pages of information and an extended argument? Read strategically.

1. To summarize a book's approach or basic argument, skim the preface and introduction. Sometimes there's a concluding chapter that neatly summarizes things, too. Even the back cover or jacket flap can be helpful for this overview.
2. To explain the relevance of the book to your research question or topic, you may focus on a particular chapter or chapters. Again, at this point you can probably skim the text quickly to discover its relevance. Later, you may do a more careful reading.
3. Evaluate *part* of the author's treatment of your topic rather than the whole book. Search the table of contents for what you suspect are the most relevant chapters, and focus your reading on those.

These days, searching for periodicals is easier than ever. Your university library likely has a Web page that includes a long list of databases that index periodicals by discipline (for example, PsycINFO) or that cover periodicals in a range of subjects (for example, Reader's Guide Abstracts or Academic Search Premier).

Find your library's Web site that lists databases for periodicals and choose a subject-specific database relevant to your topic or a general subject database. In fact, consider checking both. Again, your knowledge of Boolean logic and your familiarity with search terms suggested by the *Library of Congress Subject Headings* will give you a head start when using the search forms for each database.

As you did before with the books you found, add promising articles to your working bibliography, jotting down the bibliographic information on each article (see Chapter 13 for MLA and APA guidelines) and annotating each entry with a brief paragraph describing the article.

Finding Newspapers

Newspaper databases are also available online at your university library. The most common of these include the National Newspaper Index, Newspaper Source, and Proquest National Newspapers. Most such databases index major newspapers such as The *New York Times*, The *Wall Street Journal*, and The *Washington Post*, but you might find a database for the local or state paper as well.

Search for newspaper articles on your topic. This will be a particularly important search if you're interested in a current topic, something that has drawn the attention of daily news reporters or columnists. Some of the databases will provide you with full-text articles online, but more often you'll need to find the article on microfilm in the reference room of your university library. As before, add noteworthy newspaper articles to your working bibliography, citing bibliographic information and annotating each article.

Finding Sources on the Web

Build on the working knowledge of your topic that you developed during your preliminary search on the Web. You can maximize your coverage of the Web using various individual search engines. But why bother when a single popular search engine such as Google has such an enormous database? The extra effort is worthwhile because the overlap between individual search engines actually is quite small, particularly if your topic is uncommon.

Search the Web using at least two or three of the following popular search engines:

- Google (http://www.google.com)
- MSN Search (http://search.msn.com)
- AltaVista (http://www.altavista.com)
- Yahoo! (http://www.yahoo.com)
- Hotbot (http://www.hotbot.com)
- Search.com (http://www.search.com)
- AllTheWeb.com (http://www.alltheweb.com)
- Ask.com (http://www.ask.com)

Remember that whenever possible, you should use three or more words in a keyword search, listing the most important term first. Phrases, usually enclosed in quotation marks, can be especially helpful in generating useful results.

Writing in the Middle: Synthesizing Source Information and Your Own Ideas

It's not news that there is an epidemic of plagiarism and it's not just a problem on the college campus. Recently, several well-known historians admitted to being a bit sloppy about giving their sources proper credit. Naturally, a lot of people assume that the problem of plagiarism has to do with ethics. Students cheat. They confuse means and ends. And so on. There's some truth to this, but I contend that the real cause of the problem comes not from what students do, but what they don't do—they don't "write in the middle."

The plagiarism problem usually surfaces when writers are rushed, madly composing drafts at the last minute, and they simply haven't made the time to make the information they've collected their own. As a result, they're controlled *by* the information rather than controlling it for their own purposes. "How can I improve on what this guy says?" The thinking goes, "I guess I should just get it down in my paper." The result is sometimes unintentional plagiarism—some quotation marks were omitted or the paraphrase was too close to the original—but more often the paper suffers from another problem: the absence of an author. The writer doesn't seem to be in charge of where the essay goes and what it says.

There's a solution to this that is really quite simple. Write about what you're reading *as you collect it.*

Note cards aren't what I have in mind unless you use them to do more than simply jot down what a source says. Instead, I strongly recommend that you keep a double-entry journal or a research log that will serve two purposes: collecting information and exploring your reactions to what you've found. This is merely an extension of what I've been suggesting from the beginning of *The Curious Writer*—that you can move dialectically from creative thinking to critical thinking and back again—but this time you'll be creatively exploring information and then reflecting on how it addresses your research question.

The suggestion that you take time to write about the information you have collected in the middle of the process may come across as needing a pretty tough sell. *Save the writing for the draft,* you're thinking. But you are essentially *beginning* your draft with thoughtful note taking, which will save you time later.

Double-Entry Journal. You already are familiar with the double-entry journal. This approach uses opposing pages of your notebook to encourage dialectical thinking. On the left page take notes—paraphrases, summaries, and quotations—as you might usually do with conventional note taking, and on the opposing right page *explore* your responses, reactions, and questions about the information you've collected on the left page (for a full description of the double-entry notebook method, see "Using the Double-Entry Journal" in Chapter 2).

Research Log. Another method of note taking that also exploits dialectical thinking is the research log. Rather than using opposing pages, you'll layer your notes and responses, one after another. This is a particularly useful method for those who would prefer to work with a keyboard rather than a pencil. Here's how it works:

1. Begin by taking down the full bibliographic information on the source, something you may already have in your working bibliography.

2. Read the article, book chapter, or Web page, marking up your personal copy as you typically do, perhaps underlining key facts or ideas or information relevant to your research question.

3. Your first entry in your notebook or on the computer will be a fastwrite, an open-ended response to the reading under the heading What Strikes Me

Writing with Computers

PLAGIARISM AND THE INTERNET

Plagiarism is theft of intellectual property without acknowledging the source. Most students think of plagiarism as copying words, but plagiarism includes unacknowledged acquisition of another's words, ideas, information, or even structural presentation. Plagiarism is an academic crime with serious consequences, including expulsion. In academic circles, plagiarism can have a destructive effect on careers.

Unfortunately, the Internet makes plagiarism easier than ever before. It also increases the potential for accidental plagiarism because the efficiency of quickly finding large quantities of information causes many students to overlook proper management of their source material. The convenience of copying and pasting also causes some students to fail to distinguish outside sources from their own work. Accidental plagiarism can be avoided through diligent research practices.

The Internet also facilitates intentional plagiarism. Many Web sites collect and distribute essays. Some Web sites charge for essays while others operate under a reciprocity agreement by which a student can copy an essay from the database after uploading one of his or her own. Some services even offer to write original papers for a fee.

While the Internet might seem like a plagiarist's dream, it also makes detecting plagiarism easy. Internet services allow teachers to upload manuscripts and search for similar copies online. Most of these databases are sophisticated enough to search past minor textual changes that a coy plagiarist might make to avoid detection. These services then send a highlighted report showing where suspected similarities occur and direct the teacher to the source Web sites. Keep in mind too, that because the Internet is not regulated like traditional publications, plagiarism is rampant within Internet publications, so an essay or source material may be found on multiple Web sites, increasing the chance that a plagiarist might be caught.

If you publish on the Internet, you can reasonably assume that others may plagiarize your work. While you cannot completely protect your own intellectual property, the low cost and convenience of Internet publication appeals to many writers. A service called Copyscape.com helps writers control their work. A free version of the service allows writers to search for Web sites that have duplicated their work. A subscription version continuously monitors the Internet for duplications and notifies authors if duplicates are found on other Web sites. For those who enjoy self-publishing on the Internet, the fee of such a service might be well worth it.

Most. As the title implies, you're dealing with first thoughts here. Consider some of the following approaches to this initial response to the source:

- First play the believing game, exploring how the author's ideas, arguments, or findings seem sensible to you. Then shift to the doubting game, a more critical stance in which you look for gaps, raise questions, or express doubts about what the source says.
- What strikes you as the most important thing the author was trying to say?

- What do you remember best? What surprised you most after reading the source?
- What seemed most convincing? Least convincing?
- How does the source change your thinking on the topic? What do you understand better now than you did before you read the piece?
- How does it compare to other things you've read?
- What seems most relevant to your research question?
- What other research possibilities does it suggest?

4. Next, take notes on the source, jotting down summaries, paraphrases, quotations, and key facts you glean from it. Title this section Source Notes.

5. Finally, follow up with another episode of fastwriting. Title this The Source Reconsidered. This is a *more focused* look at the source; fastwrite about what stands out in the notes you took. Which facts, findings, claims, or arguments shape your thinking now? If the writing stalls, skip a line, take another look at your source notes, and seize on something else to write about.

One Student's Response

CLAUDE'S RESEARCH LOG

SOURCE

Source Letawsky, Nicole R., et al. "Factors Influencing the College Selection Process of Student Athletes." *College Student Journal* 37.4 (2003): 604–11. *Academic Search Premier.* EBSCOhost Databases. Albertson's Lib. 5 Apr. 2004.

WHAT STRIKES ME MOST

Really interesting article that studied about 130 student athletes at a large 1-A university. Noted that there have been a lot of research studies on why students choose a particular school but not so much on why student-athletes choose a school. Everyone assumes, of course, that student-athletes go somewhere because they're wined and dined and promised national TV exposure. In other words, it all has to do with the glamour of playing 1-A, particularly the so-called revenue sports like basketball and football. But this study had some surprising findings. They found that the number one reason that student-athletes chose a school was the degree options it offers. In other words, the reasons student-athletes choose a school aren't that much different that the reason regular students choose one. The study also found that the glamour stuff—getting awards, getting on TV, and future professional possibilities—mattered the least to the student-athletes. This study challenges some of the myths about student recruiting, and should be read by recruiters especially. If you want to get a blue-ribbon player at your school, tell them about the academic opportunities there.

SOURCE NOTES (CUT-AND-PASTE FROM ELECTRONIC VERSION)

"This study found that the most important factor for student-athletes was the degree program options offered by the University. Other important factors were the head coach, academic support services, type of community in which the campus is located, and the school's sports traditions. Two of the top three factors were specifically related to the academic rather than athletic environment. This is a key finding and should be understood as recruiting efforts should be broad based, balancing academics and athletics if they are to be effective."

"A somewhat surprising result of the study concerned relatively low ratings associated with factors considered essential to 'Big-Time College Sports.' Television exposure, perceived opportunity to play immediately, and perceived future professional sporting opportunities were among the lowest-ranked factors. Furthermore, the participants rated athletic rewards (a 5-item survey scale containing these and other reward items) consistently lower than both the campus and athletic environment. These results may be due to the fact that respondents were from each of the sports offered by the University. Many of the sports (e.g., swimming, track), although funded and supported similar to the other sports, do not receive the national attention, large crowds, and television exposure."

SOURCE RECONSIDERED

This article did more than anything I've read so far to make me question my thesis that big-time college sports recruiting is way out of control. It's pretty convincing on the point that athletes care about the academic programs when they're choosing a school. But then the second quotation has an interesting part that I just noticed. This study surveyed athletes in all sports, not just the big-time sports like football and basketball at the university where the study was conducted. It seems to me that that would really skew the findings because someone participating in a sport like tennis that doesn't get a lot of attention and doesn't necessarily lead to professional opportunities after school *would* be more interested in academics. They're not dreaming of making a name for themselves, but getting a scholarship to pay for school. Seems like a better study would focus on the big-time sports . . .

Whichever note-taking method you choose—the double-entry journal or the research log—what you are doing is taking possession of the information and making it yours by evaluating it for your own purposes. One of the hardest parts of writing with outside sources is doing exactly that—using someone else's ideas or information in the service of your own questions. And that's why taking the time to write in the middle is so important: you're doing the most important intellectual work *as* you encounter the perspectives of others. This will make writing the draft much easier, and will also, I believe, lower the risk of unintentional plagiarism, a mistake that often occurs in the mad rush to begin writing the draft the night before it's due.

INTERVIEWS

Tethered as we are these days to the electronic world of the Web and the increasingly digital university library, it's easy to forget an old-fashioned source for research: a living, breathing human being. People are often the best sources of information because you can have a real conversation rather than the imagined one simulated by the double-entry notebook. Some kinds of writing, such as the profile, fundamentally depend on interviews; with other genres, such as the personal essay or the research paper, interviews are one of several sources of information. But they can be central to bringing writing to life because when we put people on the page, abstract ideas or arguments suddenly have a face and a voice. People on the page make ideas matter.

The principal advantage of doing interviews is that you ask the questions that you are most interested in learning the answers to.

Arranging Interviews

Whom do you interview? Basically, there are two kinds of interviews: (1) the interviewee is the main subject of your piece, as in a profile, and (2) the interviewee is *a source of information* about another subject.

The interviewee as a source of information is the far more common type of interview, and it usually involves finding people who either are experts on the topic you're writing about or have been touched or influenced in some way by it. For example, Tina was writing a research essay on the day care crisis in her community. Among those affected by this issue are the parents of small children, their day care teachers, and even the kids themselves; all were good candidates for interviews about the problem. Experts were a little more difficult to think of immediately. The day care teachers might qualify—after all, they're professionals in the area—but Tina also discovered a faculty member in the College of Health and Social Sciences who specialized in policies related to child care. Interviewing both types of people—experts and those influenced by the issue—gave Tina a much richer perspective on the problem.

How do you find experts in your topic? Here are a few strategies for locating potential interviewees:

- *Check the faculty directory on your campus.* Many universities publish an annual directory of faculty and their research interests, which may be online. In addition, your university's public information office might have a similar list of faculty and areas of expertise.
- *Ask friends and your instructors.* They might know faculty who have a research interest in your topic, or might know someone in the community who is an expert on it.
- *Check the phone book.* The familiar Yellow Pages can be a gold mine. Want to find a biologist who might have something to say about the effort to bring back migrating salmon? Find the number of the regional office of U.S. Fish

and Wildlife Service in the phone book and ask for the public information officer. He or she may help you find the right expert.

- *Check your sources.* As you begin to collect books, articles, and Internet documents, note their authors and affiliations. I get calls or e-mails from time to time from writers who came across my book on lobsters, posing questions I love to try to answer because no one in Idaho gives a hoot about lobsters. Google searches of authors who are mentioned in your sources may produce e-mail addresses or Web sites with e-mail links that you might query.
- *Check the* Encyclopedia of Associations. This is another underused book and database in your university's reference room that lists organizations in the United States with interests as varied as promoting tofu and saving salmon.

Conducting the Interview

The kinds of questions you ask fundamentally depend on what type of interview you're conducting. In a profile, your questions will focus on the interview subject (see Chapter 5). To some extent, this is also true when you interview nonexperts who are *affected* by the topic you're writing about. For example, Tina is certainly interested in what the parents of preschoolers *know* about the day care crisis in her town, but she's also interested in the feelings and *experiences* of these people. Gathering this kind of information leads to some of the questions you may have used in a profile, but with more focus on the subject's experience with your topic:

- What was your first experience with ____________? What has most surprised you about it?
- How does ____________ make you feel?
- Tell me about a moment that you consider most typical of your experience with ____________.

More often, however, your motive in an interview will be to gather information. Obviously, this will prompt you to ask specific questions about your topic as you try to fill in gaps in your knowledge. But some more general, open-ended questions may be useful to ask. For example:

- What is the most difficult aspect of your work?
- What do you think is the most significant popular misconception about ____________?
- What are the significant current trends in ____________?
- If you had to summarize the most important thing you've learned about ____________, what would that be?
- What is the most important thing other people should know or understand?
- What do you consider the biggest problem?
- Who has the power to do something about it?

- What is your prediction about the future? Ten years from now, what will this problem look like?

Once you have a list of questions in mind, be prepared to ignore them. Good interviews often take turns that you can't predict, and these journeys may lead you to information and understandings you didn't expect. After all, a good interview is like a good conversation; it may meander, speed up or slow down, and reveal things about your topic and your interview subject that you don't expect. But good interviewers also attempt to control an interview when the turns it's taking aren't useful. You do this through questions, of course, but also more subtle tactics. For example, if you stop taking notes most interview subjects notice, and the astute ones quickly understand that what they're saying has less interest to you. A quick glance at your watch can have the same effect.

E-mail interviews produce a ready-made text with both your questions and the subject's answers. This is pretty wonderful. Live interviews, on the other hand, require more skill. It's usually a good idea to use a tape recorder (with your subject's permission), but never rely exclusively on it especially since machines can fail and batteries can expire unexpectedly. *Always take notes.* Your notes, if nothing else, will help you know where on the tape you should concentrate later, transcribing direct quotations or gathering information. Note taking during interviews is an acquired skill; the more you do it, the better you get, inventing all sorts of shorthand for commonly occurring words. Practice taking notes while watching the evening news.

Most of all, try to enjoy your interview. After all, you and your interview subject have something important in common—you have an interest in your topic—and this usually produces an immediate bond that transforms an interview into an enjoyable conversation.

Using the Interview in Your Writing

Putting people on the page is one of the best ways to bring writing to life. This is exactly what information from interviews can do—give otherwise abstract questions or problems a voice and a face. One of the most common ways to use interview material is to integrate it into the lead or first paragraph of your essay. By focusing on someone involved in the research question or problem you're exploring, you immediately capture reader interest. For example, here's the beginning of a *Chronicle of Higher Education* essay, "What Makes Teachers Great?"[1] Quite naturally, the writer chose to begin by profiling someone who happened to be a great teacher, using evidence from the interviews he conducted.

> When Ralph Lynn retired as a professor of history at Baylor University in 1974, dozens of his former students paid him tribute. One student, Ann Richards, who became the governor of Texas in 1991, wrote that Lynn's classes were like "magical tours into the great minds and movements of history." Another student, Hal Wingo,

1. Ken Bain, "What Makes Teachers Great?" *Chronicle of Higher Education* (April 9, 2004): B7–B9.

> the editor of *People* magazine, concluded that Lynn offered the best argument he knew for human cloning. "Nothing would give me more hope for the future," the editor explained, "than to think that Ralph Lynn, in all his wisdom and wit, will be around educating new generations from here to eternity."

This is a strong way to begin an essay because the larger idea—the qualities that make a great teacher—is grounded in a name and a face. But information from interviews can be used anywhere in an essay—not just at the beginning—to make an idea come to life.

Information from interviews can also provide strong evidence for a point you're trying to make, especially if your interview subject has expertise on the topic. But interviews can also be a *source* of ideas about what you might want to say in an essay. The essay on great teaching, for instance, offers seven qualities that great teachers embrace in their classrooms, things such as "create a natural critical learning environment" and "help students learn outside of class." All of these claims grew from interviews with sixty professors in a range of disciplines.

The principal advantage of doing interviews is that *you* ask the questions that you're most interested in learning the answers to. Rather than sifting through other sources that may address your research questions briefly or indirectly, interviews generate information that is often relevant and focused on the information needs of your essay. In other words, interviews are a source of data that can also be a *source* of theories or ideas on your topic. And this is often the best way to use interview material in your essay.

SURVEYS

The survey is a fixture in American life. We love surveys. What's the best economical laptop? Should the president be reelected? Who is the sexiest man alive? What movie should win Best Picture? Some of these are scientific surveys with carefully crafted questions, statistically significant sample sizes, and carefully chosen target audiences. In your writing class, you likely won't be conducting such formal research. More likely it will be like Mike's—fairly simple, and although not necessarily statistically reliable, your informal survey will likely be more convincing than anecdotal evidence or your personal observation, particularly if it's thoughtfully developed.

Defining a Survey's Goals and Audience

A survey is a useful source of information when you're making some kind of claim regarding "what people think" about something. Mike observed that his friends all seem to hate pennies, and he wanted to generalize from this anecdotal evidence to suggest that most people probably share that view. But do they? And which people are we really talking about? As we discussed this in his writing group, Mike pointed out that his grandfather grew up during the Great Depression, and that he has a very different perspective on money than Mike.

"So your grandfather would probably pick up a penny in the parking lot, right?" I asked. Probably, Mike said.

Quickly, Mike not only had a survey question but began to think about qualifying his claim. Maybe younger adults—Mike's generation—in particular share this attitude about the lowly penny. To confirm this, Mike's survey had both a purpose (to collect information about how people view pennies) and an audience (students on his campus). If he had the time or inclination, Mike could conduct a broader survey of older Americans, but for his purposes the quad survey would be enough.

Types of Survey Questions

You can typically ask two types of questions on a survey: *open-ended questions* and *direct questions.* Open-ended questions often produce unexpected information, while direct questions are easier to analyze. Open-ended questions are like those on the narrative evaluations students might fill out at the end of the semester, such as, "What did you learn in this course?" and "What were the instructor's strengths and weaknesses?" Direct questions are the kind used on quizzes and tests, the kind that have a limited number of answers. The simplest, of course, would be a question or statement that people might agree or disagree with: "Would you pick up a penny if you saw it lying on the street?" Yes? No? You don't know?

How do you decide which types of questions to ask? Here are some things to consider:

- *How much time do you have to analyze the results?* Open-ended questions obviously take more time, while direct questions often involve mere tabulation of responses. The size of your sample is a big factor in this.
- *How good are you at crafting questions?* Direct questions need to be more carefully crafted than open-ended ones because you're offering limited responses. Are the responses appropriate to the question? Have you considered all the alternative ways of responding?
- *Do you want statistical or qualitative information?* Qualitative information—anecdotes, stories, opinions, case studies, observations, individual perspectives—are the stuff of open-ended questions. This can be wonderful information because it is often surprising, and it offers an individual's voice rather than the voiceless results of statistical data. On the other hand, statistical information—percentages, averages, and the like—is easily understood and can be dramatic.

Crafting Survey Questions

To begin, you want to ask questions that your target audience can answer. Don't ask a question about a campus alcohol policy that most students in your survey have never heard of. Second, keep the questions simple and easy to understand. This is crucial because most respondents resist overly long survey questions and won't answer confusing ones. Third, make sure the questions will produce the information you want. This is a particular hazard of open-ended questions. For example, a broad open-ended question such as, "What do you think of the use of animals in the testing of cosmetics?" will probably produce a verbal shrug or an answer of "I don't know." A better question is more focused: "What do you think about the U.S. Food and Drug Administration's claim that animal testing by cosmetic companies is 'often necessary to provide product safety'?"

Such a question could be an open-ended or direct question, depending on the kind of responses you're seeking. Focusing the question also makes it more likely to generate information that will help you compose your essay on the adequacy of current regulations governing animal testing. Also note that the question doesn't necessarily betray the writer's position on the issue, which is essential—a good survey question isn't biased or "loaded." Imagine how a less neutral question might skew the results: "What do you think of the federal bureaucrats' position that animal testing for cosmetics is 'often necessary to provide product safety'?" An even more subtle bias might be introduced by inserting the term *federal government* rather than *Food and Drug Administration* in the original question. In my part of the world, the Rocky Mountain West, the federal government is generally not viewed favorably, no matter what the issue.

Keep your survey questions to a minimum. It shouldn't take long—no more than a few minutes at most—to complete your survey, unless you're lucky enough to have a captive audience such as a class.

Finally, consider beginning your survey with background questions that establish the identity of each respondent. Typical information you might collect includes the gender and age, or, with student-oriented surveys, the class ranking of the respondent. Depending on your topic, you might be interested in particular demographic facts, such as whether someone has children or comes from a particular part of the state. All of these questions can help you sort and analyze your results.

Inquiring into the Details

TYPES OF SURVEY QUESTIONS

These are a few of your options when deciding what type of questions to ask in a survey.

1. Limited choice

Do you believe student fees should be used to support campus religious organizations?

☐ Yes

☐ No

☐ I'm not sure

At what point in the writing process do you usually get stuck?

- ☐ Getting started
- ☐ In the middle
- ☐ Finishing
- ☐ I never get stuck
- ☐ Other______________________________.

2. Scaled response

The Student Film Board should show more foreign films.

- ☐ Strongly agree
- ☐ Agree
- ☐ Neither agree or disagree
- ☐ Disagree
- ☐ Strongly disagree

3. Ranking

Which of the following do you consider important in designing a classroom to be conducive to learning? Rank them from 1 to 5, with the most important a "1" and the least important a "5."

Comfortable seating	
Natural light from windows	
Carpeting	
Effective soundproofing	
Dimmable lighting	

4. Open-ended

Describe three things you learned in this course.

What steps do you think the university should take to increase attendance at women's soccer games?

Conducting a Survey

People who design surveys for a living always test them first. Invariably this turns up problems: a survey is too long, a question is poorly worded, the response rate to a particular question is low, and so on. You won't be able to test your draft survey nearly as thoroughly as the experts do, but before you put your faith in an untested survey, ask as many people as you can to try it out and describe their experience answering your questions. Was there any confusion? How long did it take? Is the survey generating relevant information?

Once you're confident in the design of your survey, plan how you'll distribute it. How do you reach the audience you've selected for your survey? Professional pollsters have all sorts of methods, including computerized dialing in some regions of the country and purchasing mailing lists. Your project is much more low tech. Begin by asking yourself whether your target audience tends to conveniently gather in a particular location. For example, if you're surveying sports fans, then surveying people by the main gate at the football stadium on Saturday might work. If your target audience is first-year college students and your university requires freshman English composition, then surveying one or more of those classes would be a convenient way to reach them.

In some situations, you can leave your survey forms in a location that might produce responses from your target audience. For example, a student at my university wanted to survey people about which foothill's hiking trails they liked best, and she left an envelope with the forms and a pencil at several trailheads.

A new possibility for tech-savvy students is the online survey. Software for designing online surveys is available now, but unless the survey is linked to a Web site that is visited by the target audience whose opinions you seek, the response rates can be low. Telephone surveys are always a possibility, but they are often time consuming and unless you can target your calls to a specific audience—say, people living in the dorms on your campus—it's hard to reach the people you most want to query. Postal mail is usually too slow and expensive, although intercampus mail can be an excellent option for distributing surveys. Response rates, however, may not meet your expectations.

Using Survey Results in Your Writing

The best thing about conducting an informal survey is that you're producing original and interesting information about your topic's local relevance. This can be an impressive element of your essay and will certainly make it more interesting.

Because analysis of open-ended questions can be time consuming and complicated, consider the simplest approach: as you go through the surveys, note which responses are worth quoting in your essay because they seem representative. Perhaps the responses are among the most commonly voiced in the entire sample, or they are expressed in significant numbers by a particular group of respondents. You might also quote a response because it is particularly articulate, surprising, or interesting.

In a more detailed analysis, you might try to nail down more specifically the *patterns* of responses. Begin by creating a simple coding system—perhaps numbers or colors—that represent the broadest categories of response. For example, perhaps you initially can divide the survey results into two categories: people who disagree with the university's general-education requirements and those who agree with it, Group 1 and Group 2. The next step might be to further analyze each of these groups, looking for particular patterns. Maybe you notice that freshmen tend to oppose the requirement in larger numbers than seniors and voice similar criticisms. In particular, pay attention to responses you didn't expect, responses that might enlarge your perspectives about what people think about your topic.

Direct questions that involve choosing limited responses—true/false, yes/no, multiple choice, and so on—often involve tabulation. This is where knowledge of a spreadsheet program such as Microsoft Excel is invaluable.

Your analysis of the responses to direct questions will usually be pretty simple—probably a breakdown of percentages. What percentage of the sample, for example, checked the box that signaled agreement with the statement that their "main goal for a college education was to get a good job"? In a more sophisticated analysis, you might try to break the sample down, if it's large enough, to certain categories of respondents—men and women, class ranking, respondents with high or low test scores, and so on—and then see if any response patterns correlate to these categories. For example, perhaps a much higher percentage of freshmen than seniors sampled agreed that a good job was the most important reason to go to college.

What might this difference mean? Is it important? How does it influence your thinking about your topic or how does it affect your argument? Each of these questions involves interpretation of the results, and sample size is the factor that most influences the credibility of this kind of evidence. If you surveyed only five freshmen and three seniors about their attitudes toward your school's general-education requirements, then the comparisons you make between what they say are barely better than anecdotal. It's hard to say what the appropriate sample size for your informal survey should be—after all, you aren't conducting a scientific survey and even a small sample might produce some interesting results—but, in general, the more responses you can gather the better.

Using What You Have Learned

You will have countless opportunities, in school and out, to apply your research skills. But have you learned enough about *research techniques* to find good information efficiently? Consider the following situations. What would you suggest to the writer as a good research technique?

1. Casey is revising his essay on the effectiveness and accuracy of Internet voting. His workshop group says he needs more information on whether hackers might compromise the accuracy of computers used for voting. Casey says he's relied pretty heavily on Internet sources. Where else would you suggest he search for information? What search terms might he use?
2. Alexandra needs to find some facts on divorce rates in the United States. Where might she find them fairly easily?
3. The university is proposing to build a new parking lot on a natural area near the edge of campus. Sherry wants to investigate the proposal to write a paper on whether the parking lot might be built with minimal environmental damage. What steps might she take to research the topic? Where should she look for information first? And then?

When researching we often wrestle for control. We gather information from experts, yet as writers we're expected to demonstrate some authority on the topic. Which experts make the most sense? What claims do we find persuasive? Most of all, what do *we* think? The impulse to plagiarize is a form of surrender, a willingness to let the other guy push us around.

Part Four RE-INQUIRING

Chapter 14 Revision Strategies

Chapter 15 The Writer's Workshop

Rewriting necessarily involves some time staring off into space. But the work gets done much more quickly when you're *doing* things—exploring different beginnings, fastwriting in your journal about what seems to be working and what needs work, talking to someone about your topic or ideas, doing fresh research, or pruning sentences to make your writing clear. Revision is work. But it's also an opportunity for surprise. The trick is to see what you have written in ways you haven't seen before.

14

Revision Strategies

RE-SEEING YOUR TOPIC

"I don't really revise," Amy told me the other day. "I'm usually pretty happy with my first draft."

Always? I wondered.

"Well, certainly not always," she said. "But I know I work better under pressure so I usually write my papers right before they're due. There usually isn't much time for revision, even if I wanted to do it, which I don't, really."

Amy is pretty typical. Her first-draft efforts usually aren't too bad, but I often sense tentativeness in her prose, endings that seem much stronger than beginnings, and promises that aren't really kept. Her essay promises to focus on the dangers of genetically engineered foods to teenagers who live on Cheeze-Its and Cheetos, but she never quite gets to saying much about that. The writing is competent—pretty clear and without too many awkward passages—but ultimately it's disappointing to read.

You can guess what I'm getting at here—Amy's work could be much stronger if it were rewritten—but the logic of last-minute writing is pretty powerful: "I really think I need to bump up against a deadline."

The writing process has three phases: prewriting, drafting, and rewriting. Prewriting refers to a range of activities writers might engage in before they attempt to compose a first draft, including fastwriting, listing, clustering, rehearsing lines or passages, preliminary research, conversations, or even the kind of deep thought about a topic that for some of us seems to occur best in the shower. The drafting stage is hardly mysterious. It often involves the much slower, much more focused process of putting words to paper, crafting a draft that presumably grows from some of the prewriting activities. Rewriting is a rethinking of that draft. Although this typically involves tweaking sentences, it's

What You'll Learn in This Chapter

- How genuine revision involves exactly that: revision, or *re-seeing* your topic.
- Basic revision strategies for "divorcing the draft."
- How to become a reader of your own work.
- The five categories of revision.
- Advanced revision strategies.

much more than that. Revision, as the name implies, is a *re-seeing* of the paper's topic and the writer's initial approach to it in the draft.

Revision, as the name implies, is a re-seeing *of the paper's topic and the writer's initial approach to it in the draft.*

DIVORCING THE DRAFT

Sometimes I ask my students to generalize about how they approach the writing process for most papers by asking them to divide a continuum into three parts corresponding to how much time, roughly, they devote to prewriting, drafting, and rewriting. Then I play "writing doctor" and diagnose their problems, particularly resistance to revision. Figure 14.1 below depicts a typical example for most of my first-year writing students:

FIGURE 14.1 How some writers who resist revision typically divide their time between the three elements of the writing process: prewriting, drafting, and rewriting. The most time is devoted to writing the first draft, but not much time is given to prewriting and rewriting.

The writing process shown in Figure 14.1 obviously invests lots of time in the drafting stage and very little time in prewriting or rewriting. For most of my students, this means toiling over the first draft, starting and then starting over, carefully hammering every word into place. For students who use this process, strong resistance to revision is a typical symptom. It's easy to imagine why. If you invest all that time in the first draft, trying to make it as good as you can, you'll be either too exhausted to consider a revision, delusional about the paper's quality, or, most likely, so invested in the draft's approach to the topic that revision seems impossible or a waste of time.

There also is another pattern among resistant revisers. Students who tend to spend a relatively long time on the prewriting stage also struggle with revision. My theory is that some of these writers resist revision as a final stage in the process because *they have already practiced some revision at the beginning of the process.* We often talk about revision as occurring only after you've written a draft, which of course is a quite sensible idea. But the process of revision is an effort to *re-see* a subject, to circle it with questions, to view it from fresh angles, and many of the open-ended writing methods we've discussed in *The Curious Writer* certainly involve revision. Fastwriting, clustering, listing, and similar invention techniques all invite the writer to re-see. Armed with these discoveries, some writers may be able to write fairly strong first drafts.

What is essential, however, whether you revise at the beginning of the writing process or, as most writers do, after you craft the draft, is achieving some separation from what you initially thought, what you initially said, and how you said it. To revise well, writers must divorce the draft.

WRITING WITH COMPUTERS

WHEN YOUR COMPUTER MAKES IT HARD TO DIVORCE A DRAFT

Divorcing yourself from a draft can be more difficult with a computer. The polished look of text on the screen and in printouts can give you a false sense of completion. After all, the text looks as clean and crisp as a published book or magazine. Because of this polished look, you may limit yourself to editorial changes instead of conducting actual revision. Additionally, because the computer makes it easy to copy, move, delete, insert, and preview multiple arrangements of text, it is easy to think of revision as only a process of rearranging the existing text. Because of this flexibility, writers tend to limit themselves to working only with what is already on the screen. Keep in mind that it may not be possible to repair a passage without writing new material. Being completely divorced from the draft means that you are willing to completely re-envision a sentence, paragraph, or even the whole project and compose completely new material. If a sentence or paragraph doesn't work, open a new document and try a new approach to communicate the same idea. You might be surprised how much more effective starting from scratch can be.

STRATEGIES FOR DIVORCING THE DRAFT

You can do some things to make separation from your work easier, and spending less time on the first draft and more time on the revision process is one of them. But aside from writing fast drafts, what are other strategies for re-seeing a draft that already has a hold on you?

1. **Take some time.** Absolutely the best remedy for revision resistance is setting the draft aside for a week or more. Professional writers, in fact, may set a piece aside for several years and then return to it with a fresh, more critical perspective. Students simply don't have that luxury. But if you can take a week or a month—or even a day—the wait is almost always worth it.

2. **Attack the draft physically.** A cut-and-paste revision that reduces a draft to pieces is often enormously helpful because you're no longer confronted with the familiar full draft, a version that may have cast a spell on you. By dismembering the draft, you can examine the smaller fragments more critically. How does each piece relate the whole? Might there be alternative structures? What about gaps in information? (See Revision Strategy 14.17 later in this chapter for a useful cut-and-paste exercise.)

3. **Put it away.** Years ago I wrote a magazine article about alcoholism. It was about 25 pages long and it wasn't very good. I read and reread that draft, completely

puzzled about how to rewrite it. One morning, I woke up and vowed I would read the draft just once more, then put it away in a drawer and start all over again, trusting that I would remember what was important. The result was much shorter and much better. In fact, I think it's the best essay I've ever written. Getting a troublesome draft out of sight—literally—may be the best way to find new ways to see it.

4. **Ask readers to respond.** Bringing other people's eyes and minds to your work allows you to see your drafts through perspectives other than your own. Other people have a completely different relationship with your writing than you do. They will see what you don't. They easily achieve the critical distance that you are trying to cultivate when you revise.

5. **Write different leads.** The nonfiction writer John McPhee once talked about beginnings as the hardest thing to write. He described a lead as a "flashlight that shines down into the story," illuminating where the draft is headed. Imagine, then, the value of writing a new beginning, or even several alternative beginnings; each may point the next draft in a slightly different direction, perhaps one that you didn't consider in your first draft.

6. **Conduct research.** One of the central themes of *The Curious Writer* is that research isn't a separate activity but a source of information that can enrich almost any kind of writing. Particularly in genres such as the personal essay, in which the writer's voice, perspective, and experience dominate the draft, listening to the voices and knowledge of others about a topic can deepen and shift the writer's thinking and perspectives.

7. **Read aloud.** I often ask students in workshop groups to read their drafts aloud to each other. I do this for several reasons, but the most important is the effect that *hearing* a draft has on a writer's relationship to it. In a sense, we often hear a draft in our heads as we compose it or reread it, but when we read the words aloud the draft comes alive as something separate from the writer. As the writer listens to herself—or listens to someone else read her prose—she may cringe at an awkward sentence, suddenly notice a leap in logic, or recognize the need for an example. Try reading the work aloud to yourself and the same thing may happen.

8. **Write in your journal.** One of the strategies you can use to divorce the draft is to return to your notebook and fastwrite to yourself about what you might do to improve the piece. You can do this by asking yourself questions about the draft and then—through writing—attempt to answer them. The method can help you see a new idea that may become key to the structure of your next draft. Too often we see the journal exclusively as a prewriting tool, but it can be useful throughout the writing process, particularly when you need to think to yourself about ways to solve a problem in revision.

Later in this chapter, we'll build on some of these basic strategies with specific revision methods that may work with particular kinds of writing and with drafts that have particular problems. All of these methods encourage a separation between the writer and his or her draft or rely on that critical distance to be effective.

PHOTOGRAPHY AS A METAPHOR FOR REVISION

For several years, I taught composition by asking students to bring along a camera. The idea grew out of an experience I had in a graduate seminar with my friend and mentor Donald Murray in which we were asked to apprentice to a creative activity, and then write about how the process seemed to compare to the ways we write. I chose photography. It became clear almost immediately that there were dramatic parallels between the composing processes in each; the most striking was how much taking pictures taught me about revision.

What does it really mean to revise, or put another way, to *re-see?* What might be rewarding about such an effort? For many, revision may involve little more than proofreading a first draft. But when most experienced writers imagine revision, they mean something much less superficial (not that proofreading is unimportant!). Rewriting may involve adding or cutting information, reorganizing the draft, or even rebuilding around a new angle or purpose. This kind of revision grows from the conviction that when we first look at a topic there is much we don't notice, and this is a lesson photography teaches as well.

When I first ask my students to go out and take pictures, the only instruction I provide is that they must shoot an entire roll of film. I don't suggest photographic subjects, and I don't offer tips on technique. "Just go out and take a roll of pictures," I say, "and bring back the slides next week." The results are almost always the same: every student in the class takes one photograph of every subject, a shot that usually captures it in the most familiar angle and light conditions—the school building from across the street, the roommate or friend squinting into the sun, the long shot down the beach at midday. Rarely were these particularly interesting pictures.

The same might be said of first drafts, especially those written in a rush the night before the paper is due. The writer pretty much goes with the first picture of his topic that he sees, and revision is pretty limited to "fixing" things here and there at the last minute. One common characteristic of these one-draft papers is that they often seize on the most obvious point or idea about their topics. A paper on the accuracy of "smart bombs" argues that they aren't always smart. Or a personal essay on fading friendships concludes that "true friends are hard to find." There isn't anything wrong with stating the obvious in a first draft *if* in a revision you plan to dig more deeply, working toward a fresher argument, a better insight, a less familiar way of seeing.

My students' first roll of film makes this point really well. When you take only one picture of a subject, you're not likely to see beyond what you've already seen. Our first look at almost anything is likely to reveal only what's most obvious about it. If we *really* want to see, if we really want to learn something we don't already know, we have to look and then look again. Speaking photographically, deep revision requires that we take more than one picture.

The value of taking more than one picture becomes apparent to my students when I ask them to complete a second assignment with their cameras. This time,

I say, choose only two subjects from the first roll and take twelve shots of each one. Make every shot different by varying distance, angle, and light conditions. By composing multiple "drafts" of their subjects, even novice photographers discover new ways of seeing things they've seen before. They see the pattern of three kinds of stone that come together on the corner of Thompson Hall—something they never really noticed before although they walk by the building every day. They see the way the fire escapes cling like black iron insects to the west side of the building, its bricks bloodied by the setting sun. They see the delicate structure of a tulip or their best friend's hand, roughened by a summer of carpentry. Once my students get past the first few pictures of a subject, they really begin to see it freshly. More often than not, the twelfth picture is much more interesting than the fifth or sixth. The principle is simple: *The more you look, the more you see.*

Although the Greek meaning of the word is "light writing," photography of course is *not* writing. It really isn't hard to look through a camera, take a bunch of pictures, and re-see a subject. Doing this in writing is more difficult, because we must "see" through language. Words often get in the way. Yet the motive for revision in writing isn't much different from a photographer's inclination to take more than one shot—both writer and photographer know not to trust their first look at something. They know they won't see it well enough, so both writers and photographers use a process that helps them to see their subjects in new ways. The rewards for doing this are similar, too: the pleasure of surprise and discovery, of learning something new about their subjects and about themselves.

The motive for revision in writing isn't much different from a photographer's inclination to take more than one shot—both writer and photographer know not to trust their first look at something.

FIVE CATEGORIES OF REVISION

The following are some characteristics of writers who most need to revise:

1. Writers of fast drafts
2. Writers who compose short drafts
3. Writers who indulge in creative, but not critical, thinking
4. Writers who rarely go past their initial way of seeing things
5. Writers who have a hard time imagining a reader other than themselves
6. Writers who rely on limited sources of information
7. Writers who still aren't sure what they're trying to say
8. Writers who haven't found their own way of saying what they want to say
9. Writers who haven't delivered on their promises
10. Writers who think their draft is "perfect"

These are the usual suspects for revision, but there are many more. In general, if you think there's more to think about, more to learn, more to say, and better ways to say it, then revision is the route to surprise and discovery. Most writers agree that rewriting is a good idea, but where should they start?

Problems in drafts vary enormously. But the diagnosis tends to involve concerns in five general areas: purpose, meaning, information, structure, and clarity and style. Here are some typical reader responses to drafts with each kind of problem:

1. **Problems with Purpose**
   - "I don't know why the writer is writing this paper."
   - "The beginning of the essay seems to be about one thing, and the rest of it is about several others."
   - "I think there are about three different topics in the draft. Which one do you want to write about?"
   - "So what?"
2. **Problems with Meaning**
   - "I can't tell what the writer is trying to say in the draft."
   - "There doesn't seem to be a point behind all of this."
   - "I think there's a main idea, but there isn't much information on it."
   - "I thought the thesis was pretty obvious."
3. **Problems with Information**
   - "Parts of the draft seemed really pretty vague or general."
   - "I couldn't really *see* what you were talking about."
   - "It seemed like you needed some more facts to back up your point."
   - "It needs more detail."
4. **Problems with Structure**
   - "I couldn't quite follow your thinking in the last few pages."
   - "I was confused about when this happened."
   - "I understood your point but I couldn't figure out what this part had to do with it."
   - "The draft doesn't really flow very well."
5. **Problems with Clarity and Style**
   - "This seems a little choppy."
   - "You need to explain this better. I couldn't quite follow what you were saying in this paragraph."
   - "This sentence seems really awkward to me."
   - "This doesn't have a strong voice."

PROBLEMS OF PURPOSE

When you're fulfilling a specific writing assignment for a class—for instance, you are instructed to write on the question, *What were the initial causes of U.S. intervention in Vietnam?*—then you begin, knowing your purpose. Essay exams are a familiar example of this. But more often, even if you've been assigned a topic, one of the early challenges of the writing process is to discover how you're going to answer the *So what?* question. Why exactly are you writing about this? (And you can't answer, "Because I have to.") Quite simply, readers need a reason to read, and if the writer doesn't supply them with one then they'll be understandably frustrated and bored.

It's a little like riding a tandem bike. The writer sits up front and steers while the reader occupies the seat behind, obligated to pedal but with no control over where the bike goes. As soon as the reader senses that the writer isn't steering anywhere in particular, then the reader will get off the bike. Why do all that pedaling if the bike seems to be going nowhere?

Frequently, when you begin writing about something, you don't have any idea where you're headed; that's exactly *why* you're writing about the subject in the first place. When we write such discovery drafts, revision often begins by looking for clues about your purpose. What you learn then becomes a key organizing principle for the next draft, trying to clarify this purpose to your readers. The first question, therefore, is one writers must answer for themselves: "Why am I writing this?" Of course, if it's an assignment it's hard to get past the easy answer—"Because I have to"—but if the work is going to be any good there must be a better answer than that. Whether your topic is open or assigned, you have to find your own reason to write about it, and what you discover becomes an answer to your bike partner's nagging question, yelled into the wind from the seat behind you: "If I'm going to pedal this hard, you better let me know where we're going."

In general, the motives behind writing reflect the four ways of inquiring, but writing can and often does involve more than one of these following four purposes.

1. **To explore.** One way to handle complicated questions is to approach the answers in an open-ended way; the writer writes to discover what he thinks or how he feels and reports to the reader on these discoveries.

2. **To explain.** Much of the writing we encounter in daily life is meant simply to provide us with information: This is how the coffeemaker works or this is the best way to prepare for a trip to New Zealand. Expository writing frequently explains and describes.

3. **To evaluate.** In a sense, all writing is evaluative because it involves making judgments. For instance, when you explain how to plan a New Zealand vacation, you're making judgments about where to go. But when the explicit purpose is to present a judgment about something, the writer encourages readers to see the world the way the writer does. He or she may want the reader to think or behave a certain way: It makes sense to abolish pennies because they're more

trouble than they're worth, or you should vote for the bond issue because it's the best way to save the foothills.

4. **To reflect.** Less frequently, we write to stand back from what we're writing about and consider *how* we're thinking about the subject, the methods we're using to write about it, and what we might learn from this writing situation that might apply to others.

Revision Strategy 14.1: What's Your Primary Motive?

It may help to begin revision by attempting to determine your *primary motive* for the next draft. Do you want to explore your topic, explain something to your readers, offer a persuasive judgment, or step back and reflect on what you're saying or how you're saying it? The genre of writing has a great deal to do with this (see the following table). If you're writing a personal essay, your purpose is likely to be exploratory. If you're writing a review, a proposal, a critical essay, or an argument essay, it's likely your primary motives are to evaluate. One way, then, to get some basic guidance for the next draft is to carefully craft the second half of the following sentence: *My primary motive in writing this paper is to explore/evaluate/explain/reflect about* ________.

GENRE	PRIMARY MOTIVES
Personal essay	Explore
Profile	Explore or explain
Review	Evaluate
Proposal	Evaluate
Argument	Evaluate
Critical essay	Evaluate
Ethnographic essay	Explore or evaluate
Research essay	Explore or evaluate
Reflective essay	Reflect

Of course, any one essay may involve all four motives, but for the purpose of this exercise, choose your *main* purpose in writing the essay. Composing the second half of the sentence may not be so easy because it challenges you to limit your subject. For instance, the following is far too ambitious for, say, a five-page essay: *My main motive in writing this paper is to evaluate the steps taken to deal with terrorism and judge whether they're adequate.* That's simply too big a subject for a brief persuasive paper. This is more reasonable: *My main motive in writing this paper is to evaluate passenger screening procedures in Europe and decide whether they're better than those in the United States.*

Since largely exploratory pieces often are motivated by questions, a writer of a personal essay might compose the following sentence: *My main motive in writing this essay is to explore why I felt relieved when my father died.*

After you craft your motive sentence, put it on a piece of paper or index card and post it where you can see it as you revise the draft. Periodically ask yourself,

What does this paragraph or this section of the draft have to do with my main motive? The answer will help you decide what to cut and what needs more development in the next draft. Remember, the essay should be organized around this motive from beginning to end.

Revision Strategy 14.2: What Do You Want to Know About What You Learned?

Because inquiry-based writing is usually driven by questions rather than answers, one way to discover your purpose in a sketch or draft is to generate a list of questions it raises for you. Of course, you hope that one of them might be behind your purpose in the next draft. Try the following steps with a draft that needs a stronger sense of purpose.

1. Choose a draft or sketch you'd like to revise, and reread it.
2. On the back of the manuscript, craft an answer to the following question: *What do I understand about this topic now that I didn't understand before I started writing about it?*
3. Next, if you can, build a list of questions—perhaps new ones—that this topic still raises for you. Make this list as long as you can, and don't censor yourself (see the following "One Student's Response").
4. Choose one or more of the questions as a prompt for a fastwrite. Follow your writing to see where it leads and what it might suggest about new directions for the revision.
5. If you can't think of any questions, or find you didn't learn much from writing about the topic (step 2), you may have several options. One is to abandon the draft altogether. Is it possible that this topic simply doesn't interest you anymore? If abandoning the draft isn't possible, then you need to find a new angle. Try Revision Strategy 14.3.

Revision Strategy 14.3: Finding the Focusing Question

The best topics, and the most difficult to write about, are those that raise questions for you. In a sketch or first draft, you may not know what these questions are. But if your subsequent drafts are going to be purposeful and focused, then discovering the main question behind your essay is essential. This is particularly important in essays that are research based because the drafts are longer and you're often trying to manage a lot of information. This revision strategy works best when it's a class activity.

1. Begin by simply putting your essay topic on the top of a large piece of paper such as newsprint or butcher paper. If yours is a research topic—say, Alzheimer's disease—jot that down. Post your paper on the classroom wall.

2. Spend a few minutes writing a few sentences explaining why you chose to write about this topic in the first place.

3. Make a quick list of everything you *already know* (if anything) about your topic—for instance, surprising facts or statistics, the extent of the problem, important people or institutions involved, key schools of thought, common misconceptions, familiar clichés that apply to the topic, observations you've made, important trends, and typical perspectives. Spend about five minutes on this.

4. Now spend fifteen or twenty minutes brainstorming a list of questions about your topic that you'd love to learn the answers to. Make this list as long as possible.

5. As you look around the room, you'll see a gallery of topics and questions on the walls. You can help each other. Circulate around the room and do two things: add a question that you're interested in about a particular topic, and check the question (yours or someone else's) that seems most interesting.

One Student's Response

JULIA'S DRAFT

What do I understand about this topic now that I didn't understand before I started writing about it?

After writing this essay, I understand more clearly that there's a relationship between a girl's eating disorders and how her father treats her as a child.

LIST OF QUESTIONS

- Why the father and not the mother?
- What is it about father/daughter relationships that make them so vulnerable to feminine body images?
- Is the father's influence on a girl's body image greater at certain ages or stages in her life?
- How can a father be more informed about his impact on a daughter's body image?

When you return to your newsprint or butcher paper, it should be covered with questions. How will you decide which of them might provide the best focus for the next draft? Consider the following criteria as you try to make this decision:

- **What question do *you* find most intriguing?** After all, it's your essay, and it should be driven by your own interests in the subject.
- **Which question seems most manageable?** This mostly has to do with the level of generality or specificity of the question. You want a focusing question that isn't too general or too specific. For example, a question such as *What causes international terrorism?* is a landscape question—it contains so much possible territory that you'll never get a close look at anything. But a question such as *How effective has the Saudi royal family been*

in limiting terrorist activities? is a much more focused, and therefore manageable, question.

- **What question seems most appropriate for the assignment?** For example, if you're assigned a research essay, certain questions are more likely than others to send you to the library. If you're writing a persuasive essay, gravitate toward a question that might point you toward a claim or thesis.
- **What seems most relevant to the information you've already collected?** It would be convenient if information from your research or first draft is relevant to the question that's behind the next draft. While this might make the revision go more quickly, always be open to the possibility that a question that takes you in new directions might simply be more interesting to you.
- **What question is likely to yield answers that interest your readers?** You already have a sense of this from the questions that students in your class added to your newsprint about your topic. The challenge in any piece of writing, of course, is to answer the *So what?* question. Does your focusing question promise to lead you somewhere that readers would care to go?

Revision Strategy 14.4: What's the Relationship?

One of the more common purposes for all kinds of essays is to explore a relationship between two or more things. We see this in research all the time. What's the relationship between AIDS and IV drug use in China? What's the relationship between gender and styles of collaboration in the workplace? What's the social class relationship between Huck and Tom in *The Adventures of Huckleberry Finn?*

One way, then, to clarify your purpose in revision is to try to identity the relationship that may be at the heart of your inquiry. Relationships between things can be described in several different ways.

- **Cause and effect.** What is the relationship between my father's comments about my looks and my eating disorder when I was a teenager? What is the relationship between the second Iraqi war and destabilization in Saudi Arabia? What is the relationship between the decline of the Brazilian rain forest and the extinction of the native eagles? What is the relationship between my moving to Idaho and the failure of my relationship with Kevin?
- **Compare and contrast.** How is jealousy distinguished from envy? How might writing instruction in high school be distinguished from writing instruction in college? What are the differences and similarities between my experiences at the Rolling Stones concert last month and my experiences at the Stones concert fifteen years ago?

Review your sketch or draft to determine whether what you're really trying to write about is the relationship between two (or more) things. In your journal, try to state this relationship in sentences similar to those listed here. With this knowledge, return to the draft and revise from beginning to end with this purpose in mind. What do you need to add to the next draft to both clarify and develop the relationship you're focusing on? What should you cut that is irrelevant to that focus?

PROBLEMS WITH MEANING

Fundamentally, most of us write something in an attempt to say something to someone else. The note my wife Karen left for me yesterday said it in a sentence: "Bruce—could you pick up some virgin olive oil and a loaf of bread?" I had no trouble deciphering the meaning of this note. But it isn't always that easy. Certain poems, for example, may be incredibly ambiguous texts, and readers may puzzle over them for hours, coming up with a range of plausible interpretations of meaning.

Implicit or Explicit Meaning

Two broad categories of writing are texts that embody *implicit* or *explicit* meaning. Certain literary forms such as poems or short stories are often implicit—writers may not step forward and say what they mean—while much nonfiction prose (although some of it, like the essay, is also literary) may be much more explicit.

College writing is almost always explicit in meaning, and one of the most common complaints I hear about student writing is that it's not explicit enough. Recently, the theater faculty at my university told me that their Theater 101 students have difficulty producing writing that has a clear thesis. "Some of them have never even heard the word," one professor told me. *Thesis,* of course, is only one (scientific) term to describe how meaning can be expressed in a piece of writing. Other terms include *main point, theme, controlling idea,* and *central claim* or *assertion.* I've used some of these words interchangeably in *The Curious Writer* because they basically mean pretty much the same thing: *Most well-written essays have a single dominant meaning that should be clear to the reader.*

In certain genres of academic writing, the thesis is stated very early on in a paper. This was true, for example, of the essays the theater faculty asked students to write in their 101 class. This kind of essay is often called the *thesis / support paper,* and the basic structure is probably familiar to you: Say what you're going to say, say it with supporting evidence, and say it again to conclude.

Terms to Describe Dominant Meaning

- Thesis
- Main point
- Theme
- Controlling idea
- Central claim or assertion

Other genres, including the personal and even some persuasive essays, may follow a less formal structure, working their way less directly to an important idea or point. Such essays may have a delayed thesis that appears toward the end of the piece. But make no mistake—*all* essays have some kind of controlling idea or question at their hearts. An essay that fails to make that meaning clear will frustrate the reader because the essay will seem pointless.

Looking Beyond the Obvious

Sketches and first drafts often have problems with meaning. Frequently they are written because their authors are trying to discover what they want to say. These discovery drafts then provide guidance about what that meaning might be, and the revision then will be more focused and more explicit about meaning. The challenge, of course, is learning how to read your drafts for clues about your thesis or main idea.

However, sometimes the problem isn't so much that you don't know what you're trying to say as that what you're saying seems obvious. Clichés, conventional wisdoms, or broad generalizations are typical examples of this. You're writing about the performance you saw of Tennessee Williams's *A Streetcar Named Desire* and your draft's thesis is something like, "This was a really sad play." Okay, true . . . but that's pretty obvious. Or perhaps you're writing about losing touch with your childhood buddy, and in the last paragraph of your essay you write, "True friends are hard to find." Well, that sounds familiar. Isn't there more to say that might be a little less obvious?

The revision strategies that follow address each of these problems separately. Featured first are techniques that should help you discover what you're trying to say in a sketch or draft when you're not sure. These are followed by techniques that will help you refine a thesis or theme to make it more insightful (and less obvious) or more accurate and truthful.

Methods for Discovering Your Thesis

Use the following strategies if you're not quite sure whether you know what you're trying to say in a sketch or draft. How can you discover clues about your main point or meaning in what you've already written?

Revision Strategy 14.5: Find the "Instructive Line"

It may seem odd to think of reading your own drafts for clues about what you mean. After all, your writing is a product of your own mind. But often a draft can reveal to us what we didn't know we knew—an idea that surfaces unexpectedly, a question that we keep asking, or a moment in a narrative that seems surprisingly significant. Part of the challenge is to recognize these clues to your own meanings, and understand what they suggest about the revision.

This isn't always easy, which is one reason it's often so helpful to share your writing with other readers; they may see the clues that we miss. However, this revision strategy depends on reading your own drafts more systematically for clues about what your point might be. What do you say in this draft that might suggest what you really want to say in the next one?

1. **Find the "instructive line."** Every draft is made up of many sentences. But which of these is *the most important sentence or passage?* What do I mean by *important?* Which line or passage points to a larger idea, theme, or feeling that seems to rise above much of the draft and illuminates the significance or relevance of many other lines and passages? The writer Donald Murray calls this the "instructive line," the sentence that seems to point upward toward the meaning of what you've set down. Underline the instructive line or passage in your draft. It may be subtle, only hinting at larger ideas or feelings, or quite explicitly stated. In a narrative essay, the instructive line might be a moment of stepping back to reflect—"As I look back on this now, I understand that . . ." In a review or persuasive essay, it might be an assertion of some kind—"American moviegoers are seduced by the 'twist' at the end of a film, and learn to expect it."

2. **Follow the thread of meaning.** If the instructive line is a ball of string, tightly packed with coils of meaning that aren't readily apparent, then to get any guidance for revision you need to try to unravel it. At the top of a journal page, write the line or passage you selected in your draft as most important. Use it as a prompt for five minutes of exploratory writing, perhaps beginning with the following seed sentence: *I think/feel this is true because . . . And also because . . . And also . . . And also . . . .*

3. **Compose a thesis.** Reread your fastwriting in the preceding step and, keeping your original passage in mind, craft a single sentence that best captures the most important idea or feeling you'd like to bring into the next draft. For example, *Because of the expectation, encouraged by Hollywood, that every good movie has a surprise ending, American moviegoers often find even superior foreign films a disappointment.*

4. **Post it.** Put this thesis on the wall above your computer, or use a Post-it note and place the thesis on your computer screen. Revise with the thesis in mind, from beginning to end. Add information that will *illustrate, extend, exemplify, complicate, clarify, support, show, background,* or *prove* the thesis. Cut information from the draft that does none of these things.

Revision Strategy 14.6: Looping Toward a Thesis

I've argued throughout *The Curious Writer* for a dialectical approach to writing, moving back and forth between creative and critical modes of thinking, from your observations of and your ideas about, from generating and judging, from specifics and generalities. This is how writers can make meaning. The approach can also be used as a revision strategy, this time in a technique called *loop writing.* When you loop write you move back and forth dialectically between both modes of thought—opening things up and then trying to pin them down. I imagine that this looks like an hourglass.

1. Reread the draft quickly, and then turn it upside down on your desk. You won't look at it again but trust that you'll remember what's important.

2. Begin a three-minute fastwrite on the draft in which you tell yourself the story of your thinking about the essay. When you first started writing it, what did you think you were writing about, and then what, and then . . . Try to focus on your ideas about what you were trying to say and how it evolved.

3. Sum up what you said in your fastwrite by answering the following question in a sentence: *What seems to be the most important thing I've finally come to understand about my topic?*

4. Begin another three-minute fastwrite. Focus on scenes, situations, case studies, moments, people, conversations, observations, and so on that stand out for you as you think about the draft. Think especially of specifics that come to mind that led to the understanding of your topic that you stated in the preceding step. Some of this information may be in the draft, but some may *not* yet be in the draft.

5. Finish by restating the main point you want to make in the next draft. Begin the revision by thinking about a lead or introduction that dramatizes this point. Consider a suggestive scene, case study, finding, profile, description, comparison, anecdote, conversation, situation, or observation that points the essay toward your main idea (see the "Inquiring into the Details: Types of Leads" box on page 623). For example, if your point is that your university's program to help second-language learners is inadequate, you could begin the next draft by telling the story of Maria, an immigrant from Guatemala who was a victim of poor placement in a composition course that she was virtually guaranteed to fail. Follow this lead into the draft, always keeping your main point or thesis in mind.

Revision Strategy 14.7: Reclaiming Your Topic

When you do a lot of research on your topic you may reach a point when you feel awash in information. It's easy at such moments to feel as if you're losing control of your topic, besieged by the voices of experts, a torrent of statistics and facts, and competing perspectives. Your success in writing the paper depends on making it your own again, gaining control over the information for your own purposes, in the service of your own questions or arguments. This revision strategy, a variation of Revision Strategy 14.6, should help you gain control of the material you collected for a research-based inquiry project.

1. Spend ten or fifteen minutes reviewing all of the notes you've taken and skimming key articles or passages from books. Glance at your most important sources. If you have a rough draft, reread it. Let your head swim with information.

2. Now clear your desk of everything but your journal. Remove all your notes and materials. If you have a rough draft, put it in the drawer.

3. Now fastwrite about your topic for seven full minutes. Tell the story of how your thinking about the topic has evolved. When you began, what did you

think? What were your initial assumptions or preconceptions? Then what happened, and what happened after that? Keep your pen moving.

4. Skip a few lines in your notebook, and write *Moments, Stories, People, and Scenes.* Now fastwrite for another seven minutes, this time focusing more on specific case studies, situations, people, experiences, observations, facts, and so on that stand out in your mind from the research you've done so far, or perhaps from your own experience with the topic.

5. Skip a few more lines. For another seven minutes, write a dialogue between you and someone else about your topic. Choose someone who you think is typical of the audience you're writing for. If it helps, think of someone specific—an instructor, a fellow student, a friend. Don't plan the dialogue. Just begin with the question most commonly asked about your topic, and take the conversation from there, writing both parts of the dialogue.

6. Finally, skip a few more lines and write these two words in your notebook: *So what?* Now spend a few minutes trying to summarize the most important thing you think your readers should understand about your topic, based on what you've learned so far. Distill this into a sentence or two.

As you work your way to the last step, you're reviewing what you've learned about your topic without being tyrannized by the many voices, perspectives, and facts in the research you've collected. The final step, Step 6, leads you toward a thesis statement. In the revision, keep this in mind as you reopen your notes, reread your sources, and check on facts. Remember in the rewrite to put all of this information in the service of this main idea, as examples or illustrations, necessary background, evidence or support, counterexamples, and ways of qualifying or extending your main point.

Revision Strategy 14.8: Believing and Doubting

In persuasive writing such as the argument, review, proposal, or research paper, we often feel that a thesis involves picking sides—"the play was good" or "the play was bad," "the novel was boring" or "the novel was fun to read." Instead of *either/or*, consider *both/and*. This might bring you to a more truthful, more sophisticated understanding of your subject, which rarely is either all bad or all good. One way to do this is to play Peter Elbow's doubting game and believing game.

1. Draw a line down the middle of a page in your notebook. First, on the right side, make a list of the things in response to the following questions:

The Believing Game	**The Doubting Game**
Give the author, performer, text, or performance the benefit of the doubt. Suspend criticism.	Adopt a critical stance. Look for holes, weaknesses, omissions, problems.
1. What seems true or truthful about what is said, shown, or argued?	1. What seems unbelievable or untrue?

2. How does it confirm your own experiences or observations of the same things?
3. What did you like or agree with?
4. Where is it strongest, most compelling, most persuasive?
5. How does it satisfy your criteria for being good, useful, convincing, or moving?

2. What does it fail to consider or consider inadequately?
3. Where is the evidence missing or insufficient, or where do the elements not work together effectively?
4. How does it fail to meet your criteria for good in this category of thing?
5. Where is it the least compelling or persuasive? Why?

2. From this work in your notebook, try to construct a sentence—a thesis—that is more than a simple statement of the worth or worthlessness of the thing you're evaluating, but an expression of *both* its strengths and weaknesses: *Although* __________ *succeeds (or fails) in* __________, *it mostly* __________. For example: *Although reality television presents viewers with an often interesting glimpse into how ordinary people handle their fifteen minutes of celebrity, it mostly exaggerates life by creating drama where there often is none.*

Methods for Refining Your Thesis

You may emerge from writing a draft with a pretty clear sense of what you want to say in the next one. But does this idea seem a little obvious or perhaps too general? Does it fail to adequately express what you really feel and think? Use one or more of the following revision strategies to refine a thesis, theme, or controlling idea.

Revision Strategy 14.9: Questions as Knives

Imagine that your initial feeling, thesis, or main point is like an onion. Ideas, like onions, have layers and to get closer to their hearts you need to cut through the most obvious outer layers to reveal what is less obvious, probably more specific, and almost certainly more interesting. Questions are to ideas as knives are to onions: They help you slice past your initial impressions. The most important question—the sharpest knife in the drawer—is simply *Why? Why* was the Orwell essay interesting? *Why* do you hate foreign films? *Why* should the university do more for second-language speakers? *Why* did you feel a sense of loss when the old cornfield was paved over for the mall?

Why may be the sharpest knife in the drawer, but there are other *W* questions with keen blades, too, including *What, Where, When,* and *Who?* In Figure 14.2 you can see how these questions can cut a broad thesis down to size. The result is a much more specific, more interesting controlling idea for the next draft.

1. Subject your tentative thesis to the same kind of narrowing. Write your theme, thesis, or main point as a single sentence in your notebook.
2. Slice it with questions and restate each time.

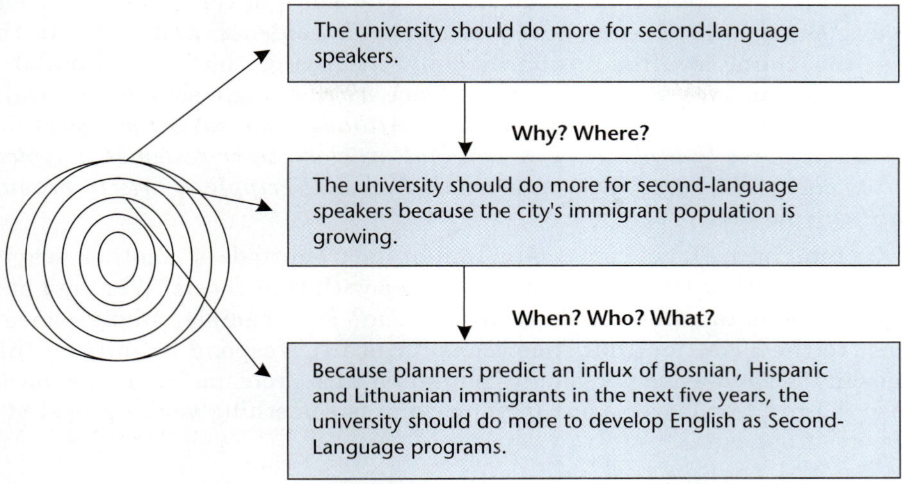

FIGURE 14.2 **Why? where? when? who? and what?** Using questions to narrow the focus of a thesis is like using a knife to cut into the heart of an onion.

3. Continue this until your point is appropriately sliced; that is, when you feel that you've gone beyond the obvious and stated what you think or feel in a more specific and interesting way.

As before, rewrite the next draft with this new thesis in mind, reorganizing the essay around it from beginning to end. Add new information that supports the idea, provides the necessary background, offers opposing views, or extends it. Cut information that no longer seems relevant to the thesis.

Revision Strategy 14.10: Qualifying Your Claim

In your research you discovered that while 90 percent of Americans think that their fellow citizens are too "fat," only 39 percent would describe themselves that way. This evidence leads you to make the following claim: *Although Americans agree that obesity is a national problem, their response is typical: it's somebody else's problem, an attitude that will cripple efforts to promote healthier lifestyles.* This seems like a logical assertion if the evidence is reliable. But if you're going to try to build an argument around it, a claim should be rigorously examined. Toulmin's approach to analyzing arguments provides a method for doing this (see the "Inquiring into the Details: Using Toulmin to Analyze Arguments" box on page 301).

1. Toulmin observes that sometimes a claim should be *qualified* to be more accurate and persuasive. The initial question is simple: *Is what you're asserting always or universally true?* Essentially, you're being challenged to examine your certainty about what you're saying. This might lead you to add

words or phrases to it that acknowledge your sense of certainty: *sometimes, always, mostly, in this case, based on available evidence,* and so on. In this case, the claim is already qualified by specifying that it is limited to Americans, but it is also based on evidence from a single source. The claim, therefore, might be qualified to say this: *Although one survey suggests that Americans agree that obesity is a national problem, their response is typical: it's somebody else's problem, an attitude that will cripple efforts to promote healthier lifestyles.*

2. Imagining how your claim might be rebutted is another way to strengthen it. How might someone take issue with your thesis? What might be the exceptions to what you're saying is true? For example, might someone object to the assertion that Americans "typically" respond by putting their heads in the sand when personally confronted with problems? You must decide then whether this clever aside in your claim is something you're prepared to support. If not, cut it.

PROBLEMS WITH INFORMATION

Writers who've spent enough time generating or collecting information about their topics can work from abundance rather than scarcity. This is an enormous advantage because the ability to throw stuff away means you can be selective about what you use, and the result is a more focused draft. But as we revise, our purpose and point might shift, and we may find ourselves in the unhappy position of working from scarcity again. Most of our research, observation, or fastwriting was relevant to the triggering subject in the initial sketch or draft, not to the generated subject we decide is the better direction for the next draft. In some cases, this might require that you research the new topic or return to the generating activities of listing, fastwriting, clustering, and so on that will help provide information for the next draft.

More often, however, writers don't have to begin from scratch in revision. Frequently, a shift in the focus or refining a thesis in a first draft just means emphasizing different information or perhaps filling in gaps in later drafts. The strategies that follow will help you solve this problem.

Revision Strategy 14.11: Explode a Moment

The success of personal essays that rely on narratives frequently depends on how well the writer renders an important scene, situation, moment, or description. When you're telling a story from experience, not all parts of the story are equally important. As always, emphasis in a narrative depends on the writer's purpose in the essay. For example, Matt's essay on the irony of the slow poisoning of Butte, Montana, his hometown, by a copper mine that once gave the city life would emphasize those parts of the story that best highlight that irony. Or a description of the agonizing death of the snow geese that unwittingly landed on the acid pond—their white beauty set against the deadly dark water—might be an important scene in Matt's next draft; it nicely portrays life and death, beauty and ugliness in much the same way the town and the mine might be contrasted. Matt should "explode that moment" because it's an important part of the story he's trying to tell about his Montana home town.

If you're trying to revise a draft that relies on narratives, this revision strategy will help you first identify moments, scenes, or descriptions that might be important in the next draft, and then develop these as more important parts of your story.

1. Choose a draft that involves a story or stories.

2. Make a list in your journal of the moments (for example, scenes, situations, and turning points) that stand out in the narrative.

3. Circle one that you think is most important to your purpose in the essay. It could be the situation that is most telling, a dramatic turning point, the moment of a key discovery that is central to what you're trying to say, or a scene that illustrates the dilemma or raises the question you're exploring in the draft.

4. Name that moment at the top of a blank journal page (for example, *the snow geese on the acid pond, when the ice broke,* or *when I saw my grandfather in his coffin).*

5. Now put yourself back into that moment and fastwrite about it for seven full minutes. Make sure that you write with as much detail as possible, *drawing on all your senses.* Write in the present tense if it helps.

6. Use this same method with other moments in the narrative that might deserve more emphasis in the next draft. Remember that real time means little in writing. An experience that took seven seconds can easily take up three pages of writing if it's detailed enough. Rewrite and incorporate the best of the new information in the next draft.

Revision Strategy 14.12: Beyond Examples

When we add information to a draft we normally think of adding examples. If you're writing a research essay on living with a sibling who suffers from Down syndrome, you might mention that your brother typically tries to avoid certain cognitive challenges. Members of your workshop group wonder, "Well, what kind of challenges?" In revision, you add an example or two from your own experience to clarify what you mean. This is, of course, a helpful strategy; examples of what you mean by an assertion are a kind of evidence that helps readers more fully understand your work. But also consider other types of information it might be helpful to add to the next draft. Use the following list to review your draft for additions you might not have thought of for revision.

- **Presenting counterarguments.** Typically, persuasive essays include information that represents an opposing view. Say you're arguing that beyond "avoidance" behaviors, there really aren't personality traits that can be attributed to most people with Down syndrome. You include a summary of a study that says otherwise. Why? Because it provides readers with a better understanding of the debate, and enhances the writer's ethos because you appear fair.

- **Providing background.** When you drop in on a conversation between two friends, you initially may be clueless about the subject. Naturally, you ask questions: "Who are you guys talking about? When did this happen? What did she say?" Answers to these questions provide a context that allows you to understand what is being said and to participate in the conversation. Background information like this is often essential in written communication, too. In a personal essay, readers may want to know when and where the event occurred or the relationship between the narrator and a character. In a critical essay, it might be necessary to provide background on the short story because readers may not have read it. In a research essay, it's often useful to provide background information about what has already been said on the topic and the research question.
- **Establishing significance.** Let's say you're writing about the problem of obesity in America, something that most of us are generally aware of these days. But the significance of the problem really strikes home when you add information from research suggesting that 30 percent of American adults are overweight, up from 23 percent just six years ago. It is even more important to establish the significance of a problem about which there is little awareness or consensus. For example, most people don't know that America's national park system is crumbling and in disrepair. Your essay on the problem needs to provide readers with information that establishes the significance of the problem. In a profile, readers need to have a reason to be interested in someone—perhaps your profile subject represents a particular group of people of interest or concern.
- **Giving it a face.** One of the best ways to make an otherwise abstract issue or problem come to life is to show what it means to an individual person. We can't fully appreciate the social impact of deforestation in Brazil without being introduced to someone such as Chico Mendes, a forest defender who was murdered for his activism. Obesity might be an abstract problem until we meet Carl, a 500-pound 22-year-old who is "suffocating in his own fat." Add case studies, anecdotes, profiles, and descriptions that put people on the page to make your essay more interesting and persuasive.
- **Defining it.** If you're writing about a subject your readers know little about, you'll likely use concepts or terms that readers will want you to define. What exactly do you mean, for example, when you say that the Internet is vulnerable to cyberterror? What exactly is cyberterror anyway? In your personal essay on your troubled relationship with your mother, what do you mean when you call her a narcissist? Frequently your workshop group will alert you to things in the draft that need defining, but also go through your own draft and ask yourself, *Will my readers know what I mean?*

Revision Strategy 14.13: Research

Too often, research is ignored as a revision strategy. We may do research for the first draft of a paper or essay, but never return to the library or search the Web to fill in gaps, answer new questions, or refine the focus of a rewrite. That's crazy, particularly because well-researched information can strengthen a draft of any kind. That has been one of the themes of *The Curious Writer* since the beginning of the book: research is not a separate activity reserved only for the research paper, but a rich source of information for any type of writing. Try some of these strategies:

1. For quick facts, visit http://www.refdesk.com. This enormously useful Web site is the fastest way to find out the exact height of the Great Wall of China or the number of young women suffering from eating disorders in America today.

2. Return to the *Library of Congress Subject Headings,* the reference mentioned in Chapter 12 that will help you pinpoint the language you should use to search library databases on your topic. Particularly if the focus of your next draft is shifting, you'll need some fresh information to fill in the gaps. The *LCSH* will help you find more of it, more quickly.

3. To maximize Web coverage, launch a search on at least three single search engines (for example, Google, MSN Search, and Yahoo!), but this time search using terms or phrases from your draft that will lead you to more specific information that will fill gaps in the draft.

4. Interview someone relevant to your topic. (See Chapter 12.)

5. To ferret out some new sources on your topic, search library databases under author rather than keyword. Focus on authors that you know have something to say on your topic.

6. Return to any of the steps in Chapter 12 that involve developing deep knowledge about your topic.

Revision Strategy 14.14: Backing Up Your Assumptions

Targeted research is particularly important when you're making an argument. In addition to providing evidence that is relevant to your thesis, frequently an argument rests on the assumptions behind that assertion. Stephen Toulmin calls these assumptions *warrants* (see the "Inquiring into the Details: Using Toulmin to Analyze Arguments" box on page 301). For example, suppose your claim is the following: *Although most Americans agree that obesity is a national problem, most don't describe themselves as fat, an attitude that will cripple efforts to promote healthier lifestyles.* Every claim rests on assumptions, or warrants. In other words, what do you have to believe is true to have faith in the accuracy of the claim?

1. Write your claim on the top of a journal page, and then list the assumptions or warrants on which it seems to rest. For example, the claim about obesity includes an assumption that most Americans equate the words *obesity* and *fat.* Also there's an assumption that public attitudes—particularly the view that there is a problem but it isn't my problem—hinder progress on public policy.

2. Which of the warrants behind your claim would be stronger if there were "backing" or evidence to support them? This will give you new direction for research. It might strengthen the argument on the obesity problem, for example, to draw on evidence from the civil rights struggle. Is there any evidence that attitudes toward personal responsibility for racism lagged behind acknowledgment of racial inequality as a national problem? Was progress finally made when this gap narrowed?

PROBLEMS WITH STRUCTURE

When it's working, the structure of a piece of writing is nearly invisible. Readers don't notice how the writer is guiding them from one piece of information to the next. When structure is a problem, the writer asks readers to walk out on a shaky bridge and trust that it will help them get to the other side, but the walkers can think of little else but the shakiness of the bridge. Some professional writers, such as John McPhee, obsess about structure, and for good reason—when you're working with a tremendous amount of information, as McPhee often does in his research-based essays, it helps to have a clear idea about how you'll use it.

Formal Academic Structures

In some academic writing, the structure is prescribed. Scientific papers often have sections—Introduction, Methodology, Results, Discussion—but within those sections writers must organize their material. Certain writing assignments may also require you to organize your information in a certain way. The most common of these is the thesis/support structure. In such essays you typically establish your thesis in the first paragraph, spend the body of the paper assembling evidence that supports the thesis, and conclude the essay with a summary that restates the thesis in light of what's been said.

Thesis/support is a persuasive form, so it lends itself to arguments, critical essays, reviews, proposals, and similar pieces. In fact, you may have already structured your draft using this approach. If so, the following revision strategy may help you tighten and clarify the draft.

Revision Strategy 14.15: Reorganizing Around Thesis and Support

Because the thesis/support structure is fairly common, it's useful to master. Most drafts, even if they weren't initially organized in that form, can be revised into a thesis/support essay. (Personal essays would be an exception.) The order of information in such in an essay generally follows this design:

- **Lead paragraph:** This paragraph introduces the topic and explicitly states the thesis, usually as the last sentence in the paragraph. For example, a thesis/support paper on the deterioration of America's national parks system might begin this way:

    Yellowstone National Park, which shares territory with Idaho, Montana, and Wyoming, is the nation's oldest park, and to some, its most revered. Established on March 1, 1872, the park features the Old Faithful geyser, which spouts reliably every 76 minutes on average. What isn't nearly as reliable these days is whether school groups will get to see it. Last year 60% of them were turned away because the park simply didn't have the staff. This essay will argue that poor funding of our national park system is a disgrace that threatens to undermine the Park Service's mission to preserve the areas "as cumulative expressions of a single national heritage" ("Famous Quotes").

The thesis (underlined) is the final sentence in the paragraph, for emphasis.

- **Body:** Each succeeding paragraph until the final one attempts to prove or develop the thesis. Often each paragraph is devoted to a single *reason* why the thesis is true, frequently stated as the topic sentence of the paragraph. Specific information then explains, clarifies, and supports the reason. For example, here's a typical paragraph from the body of the national parks essay:

    One aspect of the important national heritage at risk because of poor funding for national parks is the pride many Americans feel about these national treasures. Newsweek writer Arthur Frommer calls the national park system among the "crowning glories of our democracy." He adds, "Not to have seen them is to have missed something unique and precious in American life" (12). To see the crumbling roads in Glacier National Park, or the incursion of development in Great Smoky Mountains National Park, or the slow strangulation of the Everglades is not just an ecological issue; it's a sorry statement about a democratic nation's commitment to some of the places that define its identity.

  The underlined sentence is the topic sentence of the paragraph and is an assertion that supports and develops the thesis in the lead of the essay. The rest of the paragraph offers supporting evidence of the assertion, in this case a quotation from a *Newsweek* writer who recently visited several parks.

- **Concluding paragraph:** This paragraph reminds the reader of the central argument, not simply by restating the original thesis from the first paragraph but by reemphasizing some of the most important points. This may lead to an elaboration or restatement of the thesis. One common technique is to find a way in the end of the essay to return to the beginning. Here's the concluding paragraph from the essay on national park funding:

    We would never risk our national heritage by allowing the White House to deteriorate or the Liberty Bell to rust away. As the

National Park Service's own mission states, the parks are also "expressions" of our "single national heritage," one this paper contends is about not only preserving trees, animals, and habitats, but our national identity. The Old Faithful geyser reminds Americans of their constancy and their enduring spirit. What will it say about us if vandals finally end the regular eruptions of the geyser because Americans didn't support a park ranger to guard it? What will we call Old Faithful then? Old Faithless?

Note that the underlined sentence returns to the original thesis but doesn't simply repeat it word for word. Instead, it amplifies the original thesis, adding a definition of "national heritage" to include national identity. It returns to the opening paragraph by finding a new way to discuss Old Faithful. Revise your draft to conform to this structure, beginning with a strong opening paragraph that explicitly states your thesis and with an ending that somehow returns to the beginning without simply repeating what you've already said.

Revision Strategy 14.16: Multiple Leads

A single element that may affect a draft more than any other is how we begin it. There are many ways into the material, and of course you want to choose a beginning or lead that a reader might find interesting. You also want to choose a beginning that makes some kind of promise, providing readers with a sense of where you intend to take them. But a lead has less obvious effects on both readers and writers. How you begin often establishes the voice of the essay; signals the writer's emotional relationship to the material, the writer's ethos; and might suggest the form the essay will take.

This is, of course, why beginnings are so hard to write. But the critical importance of where and how we begin also suggests that examining alternative leads can give writers more choices and more control over their essays. To borrow John McPhee's metaphor, if a lead is a "flashlight that shines down into the story," then pointing that flashlight in four different directions might reveal four different ways of following the same subject. This can be a powerful revision strategy.

1. Choose a draft that has a weak opening, doesn't have a strong sense of purpose, or needs to be reorganized.

2. Compose four *different* openings to the *same* draft. One way to generate ideas for this is to cluster your topic, and write leads from four different branches. Also consider varying the type of lead you write (see the "Inquiring into the Details: Types of Leads" box).

3. Bring a typed copy of these four leads (or five if you want to include the original lead from the first draft) to class and share them with a small group. First simply ask your classmates to choose the beginning they like best.

4. Choose the lead *you* prefer. It may or may not be the one your classmates chose. Find a partner who was not in your small group and ask him or her the following questions after sharing the lead you chose:

- Based on this lead, what do you predict this paper is about?
- Can you guess the question, problem, or idea I'm writing about in the rest of the essay?
- Do you have a sense of what my thesis might be?
- What is the ethos of this beginning? In other words, how do I come across to you as a narrator or author of the essay?

If the predictions were fairly accurate using the lead you preferred, this might be a good alternative opening to the next draft. Follow it in a fastwrite in your notebook to see where it leads you. Go ahead and use the other leads elsewhere in the revision, if you like.

Inquiring into the Details

TYPES OF LEADS

Writer John McPhee says beginnings—or leads—are "like flashlights that shine down into the story." If you imagine that information about your topic is collected in a darkened room, then where and how you choose to begin an essay will, like a flashlight, illuminate some aspect of that room. Different beginnings point the flashlight in different directions and imply the different directions the essay might develop. Consider a few types of leads:

1. **Announcement.** Typical of a thesis/support essay, among others. Explicitly states the purpose and thesis of the essay.
2. **Anecdote.** A brief story that nicely frames the question, dilemma, problem, or idea behind the essay.
3. **Scene.** Describe a situation, place, or image that highlights the question, problem, or idea behind the essay.
4. **Profile.** Begin with a case study or description of a person who is involved in the question, problem, or idea.
5. **Background.** Provide a context through information that establishes the significance of the question, problem, or idea.
6. **Quotation or Dialogue.** Begin with a voice of someone (or several people) involved or whose words are relevant.
7. **Comparison.** Are there two or more things that, when compared or contrasted, point to the question, problem, or idea?
8. **Question.** Frame the question the essay addresses.

If your reader's predictions were off, the lead may not be the best choice for the revision. However, should you consider this new direction an appealing alternative for the next draft? Or should you choose another lead that better reflects your current intentions rather than strike off in new directions? Either way, follow a new lead to see where it goes.

Revision Strategy 14.17: The Frankenstein Draft

One way to divorce a draft that has you in its clutches is to dismember it; that is, cut it into pieces and play with the parts, looking for new arrangements of information or new gaps to fill. Writing teacher Peter Elbow's cut-and-paste revision can be a useful method, particularly for drafts that don't rely on narrative structures (although sometimes playing with alternatives, particularly if the draft is strictly chronological, can be helpful). Research essays and other pieces that attempt to corral lots of information seem to benefit the most from this strategy.

1. Choose a draft that needs help with organization. Make a one-sided copy.

2. Cut apart the copy, paragraph by paragraph. (You may cut it into smaller pieces later.) Once you have completely disassembled the draft, shuffle the paragraphs to get them wildly out of order so the original draft is just a memory.

3. Now go through the shuffled stack and find the *core paragraph*. This is the paragraph the essay really couldn't do without because it helps answer the *So what?* question. It might be the paragraph that contains your thesis or establishes your focusing question. It should be the paragraph that explains, implicitly or explicitly, what you're trying to say in the draft. Set this aside.

4. With the core paragraph directly in front of you, work your way through the remaining stack of paragraphs and make two new stacks: one of paragraphs that don't seem relevant to your core (such as unnecessary digressions or information) and those that do (they support the main idea, explain or define a key concept, illustrate or exemplify something important, provide necessary background).

5. Put your reject pile aside for the moment. You may decide to salvage some of those paragraphs later. But for now focus on your relevant pile, including the core paragraph. Now play with order. Try new leads, ends, middles. Consider trying some new methods of development as a way to organize your next draft (see the "Methods of Development" box). As you spread the paragraphs out before you and consider new arrangements, don't worry about the lack of transitions; you can add those later. Also look for gaps, places where more information might be needed. Consider some of the information in the reject pile as well. Should you splice in *parts* of paragraphs that you initially discarded?

6. As a structure begins to emerge, begin taping together the fragments of paper. Also splice in scraps in appropriate places that note what you might add in the next draft that is currently missing.

Methods of Development

- Narrative
- Problem to solution
- Cause to effect, or effect to cause
- Question to answer
- Known to unknown, or unknown to known
- Simple to complex
- General to specific, or specific to general
- Comparison and contrast
- Combinations of any of these

Now you've created a Frankenstein draft. But hopefully this ugly mess of paper and tape and scribbled notes holds much more promise than the monster. On the other hand, if you end up with pretty much the original organization, perhaps your first approach wasn't so bad after all. You may at least find places where more information is needed.

Revision Strategy 14.18: Make a PowerPoint Outline

While outlines can be a useful tool for planning a formal essay, they can also help writers revise a draft. One of the best tools for doing this is a program such as PowerPoint that challenges you to develop brief slides in sequence. The ease of moving the slides around, the imperative to be brief and to the point, and the visual display of your logic all combine to make the program an ideal medium for playing with the order of information. This is often helpful even if you don't ever make a presentation.

Your goal in creating a PowerPoint outline isn't to transfer all your text to slides and then move it around, though you could do that if you thought it helpful. Your aim is to exploit the software to help you develop a logical outline. You have several options for doing this. One is to title separate slides using some of the conventional structures of academic essays, and then making bulleted lists of the information you might include in each (see the sample slide). For example, these could be slide titles:

- Abstract, Introduction, Literature Review, Thesis/Purpose, Methods, Results, Discussion, Conclusion
- The Problem/Question, Purpose of the Essay, Claim, Reasons and Evidence (separate slide for each reason), Conclusion
- Introduction, Thesis, Example 1, Example 2, Example 3, etc., Conclusion
- Lead/Introduction, Background, Research Question, Significance of the Problem or Question, Other Voices on the Question, Thesis, Conclusion

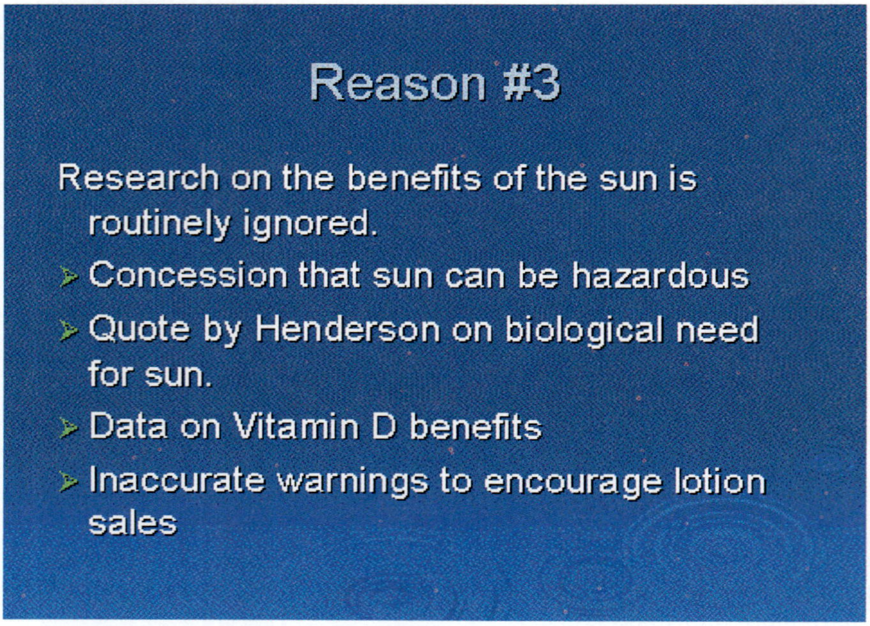

Sample PowerPoint slide outlining a plan for an essay.

Alternatively, you might use less formal methods of parsing the information in the draft onto slides. For example, can you label categories of information? In a narrative essay, it might be a particular scene, description, or reflection. In an argument it might be claims, warrants or assumptions, evidence, and counterarguments. A literary essay might be grouped on slides using key passages, main idea, textual background, information on the author, and so on.

Whichever method you use, once you are able to disassemble your draft onto PowerPoint slides using some logic, don't just play with the order. Consider moving some of the information from slide to slide, too.

PROBLEMS OF CLARITY AND STYLE

One thing should be made clear immediately: problems of clarity and style need not have anything to do with grammatical correctness. You can have a sentence that follows all the rules and still lumbers, sputters, and dies like a Volkswagen bug towing a heavy trailer up a steep hill. Take this sentence, for instance:

> Once upon a point in time, a small person named Little Red Riding Hood initiated plans for the preparation, delivery and transportation of foodstuffs to her grandmother, a senior citizen residing at a place of residence in a wooded area of indeterminate dimension.

This beastly sentence opens Russell Baker's essay "Little Red Riding Hood Revisited," a satire about the gassiness of contemporary writing. It's grammatically correct, of course, but it's also pretentious, unnecessarily wordy, and would be annoying to read if it wasn't pretty amusing. This section of the chapter focuses on revision strategies that improve the clarity of your writing and will help you consider the effects you want to create through word choice and arrangement. Your questions about grammar and mechanics can be answered in the handbook at the back of the book.

Strong writing at the sentence and paragraph levels always begins with clarity.

Maybe because we often think that work with paragraphs, sentences, and words always involve problems of correctness, it may be hard to believe at first that writers can actually manage readers' responses and feelings by using different words or rearranging the parts of a sentence or paragraph. Once you begin to play around with style, however, you will discover that it's much more than cosmetic. In fact, style in writing is a lot like music in movies. Chris Douridas, a Hollywood music supervisor who picked music for *Shrek* and *American Beauty,* said recently that he sees "music as a integral ingredient to the pie. I see it as helping to flavor the pie and not as whip cream on top." Certainly people don't pick a movie for its music, but we know that the music is central to our experience of a film. Similarly, *how* you say it in a piece of writing powerfully shapes the reader's experience of *what* you say.

But style is a secondary concern. Strong writing at the sentence and paragraph levels always begins with clarity. Do you say what you mean as directly and economically as you can? This can be a real problem, particularly with academic writing, in which it's easy to get the impression that a longer word is always better than a shorter word, and the absence of anything interesting to say can be remedied by sounding smart. Nothing could be further from the truth.

Solving Problems of Clarity

Begin by revising your draft with one or more revision strategies that will make your writing more direct and clear.

Revision Strategy 14.19: Untangling Paragraphs

One of the things I admire most in my friends David and Margaret is that they both have individual integrity—a deep understanding of who they are and who they want to be—and yet they remain just as profoundly connected to the people close to them. They manage to exude both individuality and connection. I hope my friends will forgive the comparison, but good paragraphs have the same qualities: alone they have their own identities, yet they are also strongly hitched to the paragraphs that precede and that follow them. This connection happens quite naturally when you're telling a story, but in expository writing the relationship between paragraphs is more related to content than time.

The following passage is the first three paragraphs from Paul de Palma's essay on computers, with the clever title "http://www.when_is_enough_enough?.com." Notice the integrity of each paragraph—each is a kind of mini-essay—as well as the way each one is linked to the paragraph that precedes it.

A paragraph should be unified, focusing on a single topic, idea or thing. It's like a mini-essay in that sense.

Note how the first sentence in the new paragraph links with the last sentence in the preceding one.

As before, the first sentence links with the last sentence in the previous paragraph.

The final sentence is the most important one in a paragraph. Craft it carefully.

In the misty past, before Bill Gates joined the company of the world's richest men, before the mass-marketed personal computer, before the metaphor of an information superhighway had been worn down to a cliché, I heard Roger Schank interviewed on National Public Radio. Then a computer science professor at Yale, Schank was already well known in artificial intelligence circles. Because those circles did not include me, a new programmer at Sperry Univac, I hadn't heard of him. Though I've forgotten details of the conversation, I have never forgotten Schank's insistence that most people do not need to own computers.

That view, of course, has not prevailed. Either we own a personal computer and fret about upgrades, or we are scheming to own one and fret about the technical marvel yet to come that will render our purchase obsolete. Well, there are worse ways to spend money, I suppose. For all I know, even Schank owns a personal computer. They're fiendishly clever machines, after all, and they've helped keep the wolf from my door for a long time.

It is not the personal computer itself that I object to. What reasonable person would voluntarily go back to a typewriter? The mischief is not in the computer itself, but in the ideology that surrounds it. If we hope to employ computers for tasks more interesting than word processing, we must devote some attention to how they are actually being used, and beyond that, to the remarkable grip that the idol of computing continues to exert.

Well-crafted paragraphs like these create a fluent progression, all linked together like train cars; they make readers feel confident that this train is going somewhere. This might be information that clarifies, extends, proves, explains, or even contradicts. Do the paragraphs in your draft work well on their own and together?

1. Check the length of every paragraph in your draft. Are any too long, going on and on for a full page or more? Can you create smaller paragraphs by breaking out separate ideas, topics, discussions, claims?

2. Now examine each paragraph in your draft for integrity. Is it relatively focused and unified? Should it be broken down further into two or more paragraphs because it covers too much territory?

3. In Figure 14.3, note the order of the most important information in a typical paragraph. Is each of your paragraphs arranged with that order in mind? In particular, how strong is the final sentence in each paragraph? Does it prepare readers to move into the next paragraph? In general, each paragraph adds some kind of new information to the old information in the paragraphs preceding it. This new material may clarify, explain, prove, elaborate on, contrast, summarize,

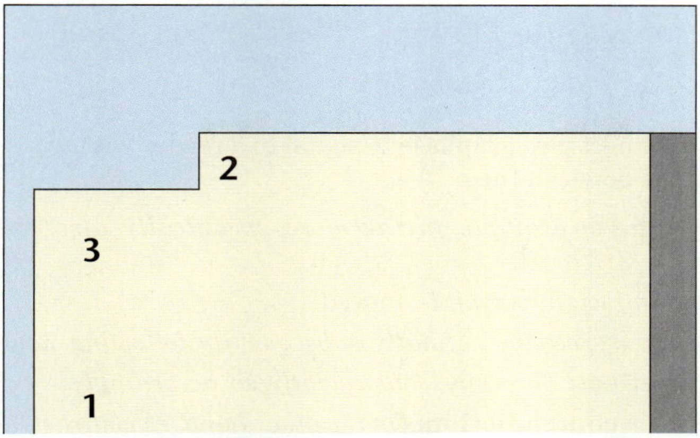

FIGURE 14.3 **Order of important sentences in a paragraph.** Often the first sentence is the second most important sentence in a paragraph. The third most important sentence follows immediately thereafter. The most important sentence usually comes at the end of the paragraph.

contradict, or alter time. Sometimes you should signal the nature of this addition using transition words and phrases (see the "Inquiring into the Details: Transition Flags" box). Are there any awkward transitions? Should you smooth them using transition flags?

Revision Strategy 14.20: Cutting Clutter

Russell Baker's overinflated version of "Little Red Riding Hood" suffered from what writer and professor William Zinsser called "clutter." This disease afflicts much writing, particularly in academic settings. Clutter, simply put, is saying in three or four words what you might say in two, or choosing a longer word when a shorter one will do just as well. It grows from the assumption that simplicity means simplemindedness. This is misguided. Simplicity is a great virtue in writing. It's respectful of the readers, for one thing, who are mostly interested in understanding what you mean without unnecessary detours or obstacles.

In case Russell Baker's tongue-and-cheek example of cluttered writing isn't convincing because it's an invention, here's a brief passage from a memo I received from a fellow faculty member some years ago. I won't make you endure more than a sentence.

> While those of us in the administration are supporting general excellence and consideration of the long-range future of the University, and while the Faculty Senate and Caucus are dealing with more immediate problems, the Executive Committee feels that an ongoing dialogue concerning the particular concerns of faculty is needed to maintain the quality of personal and educational life necessary for continued educational improvement.

Inquiring into the Details

TRANSITION FLAGS

One way to connect paragraphs is to signal to a reader with words what the relationship is between them.

- **Clarifying:** *For example, furthermore, specifically, also, to illustrate, similarly.*
- **Proving:** *In fact, for example, indeed.*
- **Time:** *First . . . second . . . finally, subsequently, following, now, recently.*
- **Cause or effect:** *Therefore, consequently, so, accordingly.*
- **Contrast or contradiction:** *On the other hand, in contrast, however, on the contrary, despite, in comparison.*
- **Summarizing:** *Finally, in the end, in conclusion, summing up, to conclude.*

That's a 63-word sentence, and while there is nothing inherently wrong with long sentences, I'm pretty sure that at least half of the words are unnecessary. For the fun of it, see if you can cut at least thirty words from the sentence without compromising the writer's intent. Look for ways to say the same things in fewer words, and look for shorter words that might replace longer ones. What kinds of choices did you make to improve the clarity of the sentence?

Now shift your attention to one of your own drafts and see if you can be as ruthless with your own clutter as you were with the memo writer's.

1. One of the most common kinds of clutter is stock phrases, things we mindlessly say because we've simply gotten in the habit of saying them. *Due to the fact that* . . . is the one that drives me most crazy. Why not the simpler word *Because?* The following table lists some of the most common stock phrases used in student writing. Read your draft from beginning to end and when you see one of these, cut it down to size.

Stock Phrase	Simpler Version
Due to the fact that . . .	Because
At the present time . . .	Now
Until such time as . . .	Until
I am of the opinion that . . .	I think
In the event of . . .	When
This is an appropriate occasion to . . .	It's time
Proceed with the implementation of . . .	Begin
Referred to as . . .	Called
Until such time as . . .	Until

Totally lacked the ability to . . .	Couldn't
A number of . . .	Many
In the event of . . .	If
There is a need for . . .	Must

2. Another thing to consider is choosing a shorter, simpler word rather than a longer, more complicated word. For example, why not say *many* rather than *numerous,* or *ease* rather than *facilitate,* or *do* rather than *implement,* or *found* rather than *identified*. Go through your draft and look for opportunities such as these to use simpler, more direct words.

3. In his book *Style: Ten Lessons in Clarity and Grace,* Joseph Williams cleverly calls the habit of using meaningless words "verbal tics." These are words, he writes, that "we use unconsciously as we clear our throats." My favorite verbal tic is the phrase *in fact*, which I park at the front of a sentence when I feel like I'm about to clarify something. Mostly I can do without it. In fact, most of us have verbal tics, and we should learn to recognize them. Williams mentions a few common ones, including *kind of, actually, basically, generally, given, various,* and *certain*—for example, *It's generally assumed that certain students have various reasons for being apolitical these days*. A better version would be, *Students have reasons for being apolitical these days*.

Go through your draft and search for words and phrases that you use out of habit, and cut them if they don't add meaning.

Revision Strategy 14.21: The Actor and the Action Next Door

I live in a relatively urban neighborhood, and so I can hear Kate play her music across the street and Gray powering up his chainsaw to cut wooden pallets next door. I have mixed feelings about this. Kate and I have different taste in music and Gray runs the saw at dusk. But I am never confused about who is doing what. That's less obvious in the following passage:

> A conflict that was greeted at first with much ambivalence by the American public, <u>the war in Iraq</u>, which caused a tentativeness that some experts call the "Vietnam syndrome," <u>sparked protests</u> among Vietnam veterans.

The subject or actor of the sentence (*the war in Iraq)* and the action (*sparked protests*) are separated by a few city blocks. In addition, the subject is buried behind a long introductory clause. As a result, it's a bit hard to remember who is doing what. Putting actor and action next door to each other makes the writing livelier, and bringing the subject up front helps clarify who is doing what.

> The <u>war in Iraq sparked</u> protests among Vietnam veterans even though the conflict was initially greeted with public ambivalence. Some experts call this tentativeness the "Vietnam syndrome."

Review your draft to determine whether the subjects in your sentences are buried or in the same neighborhood as the verbs that modify them. If not, rewrite to bring the actors up front in your sentences and to close the distance between actors and actions.

Improving Style

These revision strategies will improve the style of your writing. In the same way that a John Williams score can make movies such as *Indiana Jones and the Temple of Doom* and *Star Wars* more memorable and moving, style in writing can add to readers' experiences of a text. These are often calculated moves. Writers adopt a style because it serves a purpose, perhaps encouraging a certain feeling that makes a story more powerful, enhancing the writer's ethos to make an essay more convincing, or simply giving certain information particular emphasis. For example, here's the beginning of an article about Douglas Berry, a Marine drill sergeant.

> He is seething, he is rabid, he is wound up tight as a golf ball, with more adrenalin surging through his hypothalamus than a cornered slum rat, he is everything these Marine recruits with their heads shaved to dirty nubs have ever feared or ever hoped a drill sergeant might be.

The style of this opening is calculated to have an obvious effect—the reader is pelted with words, one after another, in a breathless sentence that almost simulates the experience of having Sgt. Douglas Berry in your face. There's no magic to this. It is all about using words that evoke action and feeling, usually verbs or words based on or derived from verbs.

Revision Strategy 14.22: Actors and Actions

My favorite verb yesterday was *shattered.* I often ask my writing students to come to class and share their favorite verb of the day; last spring, my senior seminar consistently selected *graduate* as their favorite.

As you know, verbs make things happen in writing, and how much energy prose possesses depends on verb power. Academic writing sometimes lacks strong verbs, relying instead on old passive standbys such as *the study concluded* or *it is believed.* Not only are the verbs weak, but the actors, the people or things engaged in the action, are often missing completely from the sentence. *Who* or *what* did the study? *Who* believes?

This is called *passive voice,* and while it's not grammatically incorrect, passive voice can suck the air out of a room. While reasons exist for using passive voice (sometimes, for instance, the writer wants the reader to focus on the action, not the actor), you should avoid it in your own writing. One of the easiest ways to locate passive voice in your drafts is to conduct a *to be* search. Most forms of the verb *to be* (see the box on the next page) usually signal passive voice. For example,

> It is well known that medieval eating habits were unsavory by contemporary health standards. Cups were shared, forks were never used, and the same knives used to clean under fingernails or to gut a chicken were used to cut and eat meat.

What is missing, of course, are the actors. To revise into active voice you simply need to add the actors, whenever possible:

> Medieval diners had unsavory eating habits by contemporary health standards. Friends shared cups, never used forks, and they used their knives, the same ones they used to clean under their fingernails or gut a chicken, to cut and eat their meat.

1. Conduct a *to be* search of your own draft. Whenever you find passive construction, try to put the actor into the sentence.

2. Eliminating passive voice is only one strategy for giving your writing more energy. Try to use lively verbs as well. Can you replace weak verbs with stronger ones? How about *discovered* instead of *found,* or *seized* instead of *took, shattered* instead of *broke.* Review every sentence in the draft and when appropriate revise with a stronger verb.

Revision Strategy 14.23: Smoothing the Choppiness

Good writing reads like a Mercedes drives—smoothly, suspended by the rhythms of language. One of the most important factors influencing this rhythm is sentence length, or, more precisely, pauses in the prose that vary as the reader travels from sentence to sentence and paragraph to paragraph. We rarely notice either the cause or the effect, but we certainly notice the bumps and lurches. Consider the following sentences, each labeled with the number of syllables:

> When the sun finally rose the next day I felt young again.(14) It was a strange feeling because I wasn't young anymore.(13) I was fifty years old and felt like it.(10) It was the smell of the lake at dawn that thrust me back into adolescence.(18) I remembered the hiss of the waves.(9) They erased my footprints in the sand.(9)

This really isn't awful; it could pass as a bad Hemingway imitation. But do you notice the monotony of the writing, the steady, almost unvarying beat that threatens to dull your mind if it goes on much longer? The cause of the plodding rhythm is the unvarying length of the pauses. The last two sentences in

Forms of *To Be*

- Is
- Are
- Was
- Were
- Has been
- Have been
- Will be

the passage each have 9 syllables, and the first two sentences are nearly identical in length as well (14 and 13 syllables, respectively).

Now notice how this choppiness disappears by varying the lengths of the pauses through sentence combining, insertion of other punctuation, and dropping a few unnecessary words.

> When the sun finally rose the next day I felt young again,(14) and it was a strange feeling because I wasn't young.(11) I was fifty years old.(6) It was the smell of the lake at dawn that thrust me back into adolescence and remembering the hiss of the waves as they erased my footprints in the sand.(35)

The revision is much more fluent and the reason is simple: The writer varies the pauses and the number of syllables within each of them—14, 11, 6, 35.

1. Choose a draft of your own that doesn't seem to flow or seems choppy in places.
2. Mark the pauses in the problem areas. Put slash marks next to periods, commas, semicolons, dashes, and so on—any punctuation that prompts a reader to pause briefly.
3. If the pauses seem similar in length, revise to vary them, combining sentences, adding punctuation, dropping unnecessary words, or varying long and short words.

Revision Strategy 14.24: Fresh Ways to Say Things

It goes without saying that a tried-and-true method of getting to the heart of revision problems is to just do or die. Do you know what I mean? Of course you don't, because the opening sentence is laden with clichés and figures of speech that manage to obscure meaning. One of the great challenges of writing well is to find fresh ways to say things rather than relying on hand-me-down phrases that worm their way into our speech and writing. Clichés are familiar examples: *home is where the heart is, hit the nail on the head, the grass is greener,* and all that. But even more common are less figurative expressions: *more than meets the eye, rude awakenings, you only go around once, sigh of relief,* and so on.

Removing clichés and shopworn expressions from your writing will make it sound more as if you are writing from your own voice rather than someone else's. It gives the work a freshness that helps readers believe that you have something interesting to say. In addition, clichés especially tend to close off a writer's thoughts rather than open them to new ideas and different ways of seeing. A cliché often leaves the writer with nothing more to say because someone else has already said it.

1. Reread your draft and circle clichés and hand-me-down expressions. If you're not sure whether a phrase qualifies for either category, share your circled items with a partner and discuss them. Have you heard these things before?

2. Cut clichés and overused expressions and rewrite your sentences, finding your own way to say things. In your own words, what do you really mean by "do or die" or "striking while the iron is hot" or becoming a "true believer"?

Using What You Have Learned

Take a few moments to reflect on what you learned in this chapter and how you can apply it.

1. Which revision strategy has proved most helpful to you so far? Does it address one of your most common problems in your drafts?
2. Here's a common situation: You're assigned a paper for another class and the professor doesn't require you to hand in a draft. She's just interested in your final version. What incentive do you have to work through a draft or two?
3. If revision is rhetorical, then the kinds of revision strategies you need to use depend on the particular situation: to whom you're writing and why, and in what form. The kind of writer you are—and the kinds of problems you have in your drafts—also matters. Consider the following forms: the essay exam, the review, the annotated bibliography, the letter, the formal research paper, and the reading response. Which of the five revision strategies would probably be most important for each form?

Writers rarely experience the impact their writing has on readers. When they do experience this in a writing workshop, the idea of writing for an audience ceases to be an abstraction. Writers actually witness and hear readers' responses. In some ways, though, it doesn't matter what readers say or what advice they give; it's that experience of writing for a real audience that matters most of all.

15

The Writer's Workshop

What You'll Learn in This Chapter

- The purpose of peer review.
- The most common approaches for organizing writing workshops.
- How to plan to make the most of the chance to share your draft.
- What can go wrong and how to deal with it.
- Response formats for guiding how readers evaluate your drafts.

MAKING THE MOST OF PEER REVIEW

Sharing your writing with strangers can be among the most frightening and gratifying social experiences. It can be a key to the success of the next draft or a complete waste of time. One thing sharing your writing can't be, however, is avoided, at least in most composition courses, which these days frequently rely on small and large group workshops to help students revise. This is a good thing, I think, for three reasons:

1. It's useful to experience *being* read by others.
2. Workshops can be among the most effective ways for writers to divorce the draft.
3. The talk about writing in workshops can be enormously instructive.

Being Read

Being read is not the same thing as being read to. As we share our writing, sometimes reading our own work aloud to a group, we are sharing ourselves in a very real way. This is most evident with a personal essay, but virtually any piece of writing bears our authorship—our particular ways of seeing and saying things—and included in this are our feelings about ourselves as writers.

Last semester, Matthew told me that he felt he was the worst writer in the class, and that seemed obvious when I watched him share his writing in his workshop group. Matthew was quiet and compliant, readily accepting suggestions with little comment, and he seemed to rush the conversation about his draft as if to make the ordeal end sooner. When Matthew's drafts were discussed, his group always ended in record time, and yet he always claimed that they were "helpful."

Tracy always began presenting her drafts by announcing, "This really sucks. It's the worst thing I've ever written." Of course it wasn't. But this announcement seemed intended to lower the stakes for her, to take some of the pressure off of her performance in front of others, or, quite possibly, it was a hopeful invitation for Tracy's group members to say, "You're too hard on yourself. This is really good."

To *be read* in a workshop group can mean more than a critique of your ideas or sentences; for students like Matthew and Tracy it is an evaluation of *themselves,* particularly their self-worth as writers. Of course, this isn't the purpose of peer review at all, but for those of us with sometimes nagging internal critics, it's pretty hard to avoid feeling that both your writing and your writing self are on trial. This is why it's so helpful to articulate these fears before being read. It's also helpful to imagine the many positive outcomes that might come from the experience of sharing your writing.

While taking workshop comments about your writing personally is always a risk, consider the really rare and unusual opportunity to *see* readers respond to your work. I often compare my published writing to dropping a very heavy stone down a deep well and waiting to hear the splash. And waiting. And waiting. But in a workshop, you can actually hear the murmurs, the sighs, and the laughter of your readers as you read to them; you can also see the smiles, puzzled expressions, nodding heads, and even tears. You can experience your readers' experiences of your writing in ways that most published authors never can.

In a workshop, you can actually hear the murmurs, the sighs, and the laughter of your readers as you read to them; you can also see the smiles, puzzled expressions, nodding heads, and even tears.

What is so valuable about this, I think, is that audience is no longer an abstraction. After your first workshop, it's no stretch to imagine the transaction that most writing involves—a writer's words being received by a reader who thinks and feels something in response. And when you take this back to the many solitary hours of writing, you may feel you have company; that members of your workshop group are interested in what you have to say.

This is a powerful thing. In some ways, it's the most important thing about the workshop experience.

Divorcing the Draft

Our writing relationships include our emotional connection to drafts, and this often has to do with the time we spent writing them. In Chapter 14, I described the ways we can get entangled in first drafts that blind us to other ways of seeing a topic. Sometimes we need to divorce a draft, and the best remedy for this is time away from it. But students rarely have that luxury.

Workshops provide an alternative to time and are effective for the same reason some people see therapists—group members offer an "outsider's" perspective on your work that may give it new meanings and raise new possibilities. If nothing else, readers offer a preview of whether your current meanings are clear and whether what you assume is apparent *is* apparent to someone other than yourself. It's rare when a workshop doesn't jerk writers away from at least a few of their assumptions about a draft, and the best of these experiences inspire writers to want to write again. This is the outcome we should always hope to attain.

Instructive Talk

Consider a few comments I overheard during workshops recently:

- "I don't think the focus is clear in this essay. In fact, I think there are at least two separate essays here, and it's the one on the futility of antiwar protests I'm most interested in."
- "Do you think that there's a better lead buried on the third page, in the paragraph about your sister's decision to go to the hospital? That was a powerful scene, and it seemed to be important to the overall theme."
- "I was wondering about something. What is it about the idea that we sometimes keep silent not only to protect other people but to protect ourselves that surprised you? I mean, does knowing that change anything about how you feel about yourself as a parent?"
- "I loved this line. Simply loved it."

The talk in workshops is not always about writing. The "underlife" of the classroom often surfaces in workshops, a term one educator uses to describe the idle talk about the class itself. Most writing classes ask students to step out of their usual student roles. Rather than quietly listen to lectures or study a textbook, in a writing course you are asked to make your own meanings and find your own ways of making meaning. Whenever we are asked to assume new roles, some resistance can set in, and workshops can become an occasion for talk about the class, often out of earshot of the instructor. This talk isn't always complaining. Often workshops are opportunities to share understandings or approaches to assignments and especially experiences with them. They can also be a chance for students to try out new identities—"I really liked writing this. Maybe I'm an okay writer after all."

While this kind of talk may not be directly about a draft, it can help you negotiate the new roles you're being asked to assume in your writing class. This is part of becoming better writers who are confident that they can manage the writing process in all kinds of situations. However, the main purpose of workshop groups is to help students to revise their drafts. But why seek advice from writers who are clearly less experienced than the instructor?

1. By talking with other students about writing you get practice using the language you're learning in the writing classroom, language that helps you describe important features of your own work.

2. Because writing is about making choices among a range of solutions to problems in a draft, workshop groups are likely to surface possibilities that never occurred to you (and perhaps wouldn't occur to the instructor, either).

3. Your peers are also student writers and because they come from similar circumstances—demands of other classes, part-time jobs, and perhaps minimal experience with college writing—they are in a position to offer practical and realistic revision suggestions.

4. Finally, in most writing courses, the students in the class are an important audience for your work. Getting firsthand responses makes the rhetorical situation real rather than imagined.

Will you get bad advice in a peer workshop? Of course. Your group members will vary in their experience and ability to read the problems and possibilities in a draft. But in the best writing workshops, you learn together, and as time goes by the feedback gets better and better. Paradoxically, it pays off in your own writing to be generous in your responses to the work of others.

MODELS FOR WRITING WORKSHOPS

The whole idea of peer review workshops in writing classes has been around for years. Collaboration is hardly a novelty in the professional world, but small-group work in academia is a relatively recent alternative to lecture and other teaching methods in which the student listens to a professor, takes notes on what is said, and later takes a test of some kind. You won't learn to write well through lecture, although it may be a perfectly appropriate approach for some subjects. Because collaboration in the writing classroom fits in perfectly with the class's aim of generating knowledge about the many ways to solve writing problems, peer review of drafts in small groups is now fairly common. You'll find workshops in writing classes ranging from first-year composition to advanced nonfiction writing.

What will workshops be like in your course? Your instructor will answer that question, but the workshop groups will likely reflect one or more of the following models.

Full-Class Workshops

Sometimes you may not work in small groups at all. Depending on the size of your class and your instructor's particular purposes for using peer review, you may share your work with everyone in a full-class session. This approach is popular in creative writing classes, and it's typically used in composition classes to introduce students to the process of providing responses to other students' work. It also can work nicely in small classes with ten students or less.

In a full-class workshop, you'll choose a draft to share and you (or your instructor) will provide copies for everyone either a few days before the workshop, or at the beginning of the workshop session. On drafts you receive days ahead of the session, you're often expected to read and bring written comments to class with you. If you receive the draft at the beginning of the workshop session, you might make notes while the draft's author reads the piece aloud, or take some time to write some comments either immediately after the draft is read or following the group discussion.

Reading your draft aloud to your workshop group is a common convention in all kinds of workshop groups, large or small. This might be something you resist at first. It will quickly become apparent, however, how useful it is to read your own work aloud. It's an entirely different reading to literally give voice to your words. You'll stumble over passages in your draft that seemed fine when you read them silently, and you may notice gaps you glossed over. You'll hear what your writing voice sounds like in this particular essay, and whether it works for you and your readers.

Your instructor may lead the discussion in a full-class workshop, or she may sit back and wait while students share their responses. There may be guidelines and ground rules for responses as well (for some examples of these, see "The Reader's Responsibilities" section later in the chapter). If your draft is being discussed, your instructor may ask you to simply listen. Sometimes it's best to avoid defending certain choices you made in a draft and simply take in the range of responses you receive to what you have done. In other cases, you may be asked to present the large group with questions to consider. It certainly can be scary sharing your work with twenty or twenty-five people, but imagine the range of perspectives you'll get!

Small-Group Workshops

Far more typical is the workshop group of between three and seven members, either chosen randomly by your instructor or self-selected. These groups may stay together all semester or part of the semester, or you may find yourself working with fresh faces every workshop session. Each of these alternatives has advantages and disadvantages, all of which your instructor has considered in making a choice.

Ideally, your workshop group will meet in a circle, because when everyone, including the writer presenting a draft, is facing each other you'll have more of a conversation and be able to engage each other directly (see Figure 15.1). Like so many writing group methods, this is a basic principle of teamwork borrowed from the business world.

Some of the methods of distributing drafts apply to the small group as well as to the full-class workshop discussed earlier: writers will distribute copies of their drafts either a few days before their workshops or at the beginning of the sessions. You will provide written comments to each writer either before or after the workshop.

One-on-One Peer Review

Your instructor also may ask you to work with a partner, exchanging drafts and discussing them with each other. While you lose some of the range and quantity of feedback by working with a single reader, this conversation is often richer because each of you is reading the other's work with particular care and attention. You'll probably also have more time to talk because you'll be discussing only two rather than four or five drafts.

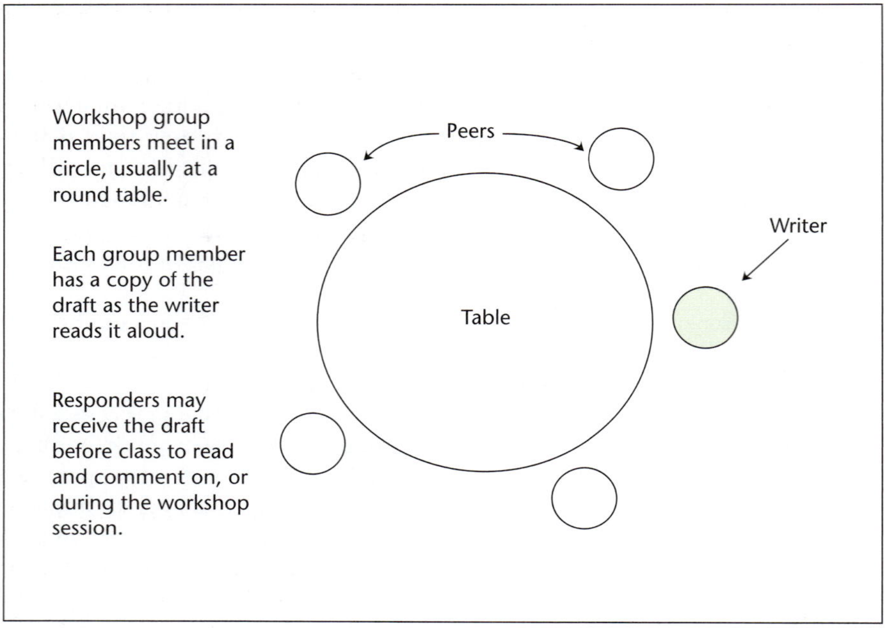

FIGURE 15.1 The small-group workshop

One variation of this kind of one-on-one peer review is the draft exchange. Your instructor will ask you to make a pile of drafts at the front of the room and ask you to take a draft from the pile, comment on it, return it, and then take another. You may return multiple times to collect, comment on, and return a draft, and the result is that each draft may have three or four readers during the class session.

THE WRITER'S RESPONSIBILITIES

No matter what model your instructor chooses, the success of the workshop depends largely on the writers themselves. Sure, it can be harder to get what you need from some groups, but in the end, you can always get *some* help with a draft if you ask the right questions and seek certain kinds of responses.

How should you prepare for a workshop to make the most of it and what are your responsibilities during the workshop? Here's a list you might find helpful:

- Make sure everyone in the group has a copy of the draft in a timely way.
- Reread and reflect on the draft before the workshop session. What kinds of responses would be most helpful from your group? What questions do you have about the draft's possible problems?

- Time the discussion so that your draft gets the allotted time and no more, particularly if there are other drafts to discuss.
- Avoid getting defensive. Listen to comments on your work in an open-minded way. Your obligation is simply to listen, not to take all the advice you're offered.
- Take notes. There are two reasons for this. First, it will help you remember other students' comments, and second, it will signal that you take those comments seriously. This increases everyone's engagement with your work.

Writing with Computers

PEER REVIEW IN CYBERSPACE

The Internet can make peer review very efficient in some situations. While it doesn't capture the nuances of face-to-face communication, it can help writers connect through difficulties such as busy schedules and great distances. With classroom management Web services such as Blackboard and WebCT, students can post their work immediately after finishing and peer reviewers can also post their responses as soon as they are finished. The advantages to peer review is that you have your peers' comments typed and saved instead of scrawled into margins or hastily written in notebooks.

Most word processors have a feature to insert comments onto a draft. This feature allows reviewers to annotate electronic files much as they would a paper copy. This feature works in conjunction with the track changes feature (see "Writing with Computers: Tracking Changes to a Draft" in Chapter 7), and inserted comments can be hidden or revealed in the same fashion. The insert comments function is found under the insert menu of most word processors, and a dedicated button can usually be made available on the toolbar. When a reviewer selects a passage and inserts a comment, the comment appears in a separate window or in a marginal balloon (depending on the word processor and the view mode you are using). Most word processors display hidden comments when you rest your cursor over them. Some word processors also include the ability to record audio comments on drafts. A reviewer can select a section of the paper and make a recording of his or her "gut" reactions. Readers who aren't up to writing comments at great length may share more substantive comments with audio recordings.

In addition to using the annotation features of word processors, writers can also connect through instant-messaging applications. Many of these applications allow users to transfer files, share their screens (allowing them to see the same thing), and have verbal discussions. These features typically need high-speed Internet connections, but they can be valuable tools when writers are separated and need to collaborate or review each other's work as if they were in the same room.

THE READER'S RESPONSIBILITIES

Tina poured her heart and soul into her personal essay draft, and she was eager to get some response to it. When it was her turn to workshop the piece, however, one of the group's members was absent, and two others failed to write her the required response. "It was so lame," she told me. "It was as if no one cared about my essay. It sure makes me feel less inclined to read their stuff carefully." If this workshop group were at Hewlett-Packard or any of the thousands of businesses that encourage teamwork, the slackers would be in trouble. But teamwork in the writing class depends more on internal motivation—a sense of responsibility to others—than any external reward or punishment. But there is some external motivation: it pays to be generous with your responses to others' work because you'll learn more about your own.

You can increase your own learning in workshop and contribute to a writer's positive experience by taking the following responsibilities seriously:

- Always read and respond to a writer's draft in a timely way. The writer may suggest the type of response that would be most helpful; if so, always keep that in mind.
- Whenever possible, focus your responses on particular parts or passages of the draft, but except in an editorial workshop, avoid a focus on grammar or mechanics.
- Offer suggestions, not directives. The word *could* is usually better than *should.* Remember that the purpose of workshop is to help identify the range of choices a writer might make to improve a draft. There is almost always more than one.
- Identify strengths in the draft. This is often a good place to begin because it sets writers at ease, but, more important, writers often build on strengths in revision.
- Consider varying the roles you play in conversation with your group (see the "Inquiring into the Details: Finding a Role" box). It's easy to fall into a rut in group work, pretty much sticking to saying the same kinds of things or developing certain patterns of response. Stay vigilant about this and try deliberating shifting the role you play in the workshop group.

WHAT CAN GO WRONG AND WHAT TO DO ABOUT IT

Lana is not a fan of workshops. In an argument essay, she complained that they "lack quality feedback" and sometimes workshop groups encourage "fault finding" that can hurt the writer and the writing. Things can go wrong in workshops, of course, and when they do students like Lana feel burned. Typically, unsuccessful

Inquiring into the Details

FINDING A ROLE

"Slacker" is a role that's easy to slide into in small-group work. It's completely passive, and it's really pretty selfish. Active roles ask more of you, but they pay off big because you learn more about your own writing. You might assume any of several active roles in a workshop group. Try them out.

Roles That Help Groups Get Things Done

Initiators: "Here's how we might proceed with this."
Information seekers: "What do we need to know to help the writer?"
Information givers: "This seems to be an important example."
Opinion seekers: "What do you think, Al?"
Opinion givers: "I think this works."
Clarifiers: "We all seem to be saying that the lead doesn't deliver, right?"
Elaborators: "I agree with Tom, and would add. . ."
Summarizers: "I think we've discussed the thesis problem enough. Should we move on to the evidence?"

Roles That Help Maintain Group Harmony

Encouragers: "I love that idea, Jen."
Expressivists: "My silence isn't because I'm not moved by the essay, but I'm still trying to figure out why. Is that why you're quiet, Leah?"
Harmonizers: "I think we disagree about this, but that's okay. Let's move on to discussing this next page."
Compromisers: "Maybe both Richard and Joseph are right, particularly if we look at it this way . . ."
Gatekeepers: "Jon, we haven't heard anything from you yet."

workshop groups suffer from two major problems: lack of commitment by group members and lack of clarity about the process of giving feedback. It's like a cold and a runny nose—when a group is afflicted with one problem it usually suffers from the other.

Lack of commitment is easy to see. The writer whose draft is to be discussed forgets to make copies for the rest of her group. Members who were supposed to provide written responses to a writer's draft before class hastily make notes on his manuscript as it's being discussed. The group is supposed to allot fifteen minutes to discuss each draft but finishes in five. Members are frequently absent and make no effort to provide responses to drafts they missed. Discussion is limited to general, not particularly thoughtful, compliments: "This is really good. I wouldn't change a thing," or "Just add a few details."

This lack of commitment is contagious and soon infects nearly every group meeting. Things rarely improve; they frequently get worse. Part of the problem may be that workshop participants may not be clear about what is expected of them, a problem that should be minimized if you reviewed the checklists about the writer's and reader's responsibilities in workshop discussed in the preceding sections. A solution that is beyond your control is that the instructor evaluates or even grades workshop participation, but a group can evaluate itself, too. Questions members should ask when evaluating their group can include: How effectively does your group work together? How would you evaluate the participation of group members? How do you feel about your own performance? How satisfied were you with the responses to your draft?

Groups that work together over a period of time should always monitor how things are going, and the group evaluations can be particularly helpful for this. If problems persist, the instructor may intervene or the group might consider intervention of its own (consider Exercise 15.1 as one option). Remember, the best workshops have a simple but powerful effect on writers who share their work: *it makes them want to write again.*

EXERCISE 15.1

Group Problem Solving

If group evaluations reveal persistent problems, devote ten minutes to exploring possible solutions.

STEP ONE: Choose a facilitator and a recorder. The facilitator times each step, directs questions to each participant, and makes sure everyone participates. The recorder takes notes on newsprint.

1. Discuss the patterns of problems identified by group members. Do writers seem dissatisfied? Do readers feel like they're performing poorly?
2. What is behind these problems? Brainstorm a list.
3. What might be done to change the way the group operates? You must come up with *at least* one concrete idea that you agree to try.

STEP TWO: After the next workshop session, set aside five minutes at the end to discuss whether the change improved the group's performance. Is there something else you should try?

One Student's Response

AMY'S PERSPECTIVE ON WORKSHOPS

WHEN THINGS GO RIGHT

In both small and large workshops things are most productive when the conversation delves deep into a couple of issues instead of skimming the surface on a broad range of topics. My best experiences have been in small workshops because the groups were willing to get more deeply involved in a piece. It probably helps that there aren't too many ideas in a small group and the ones that get thrown out for debate are well considered. I always appreciate it when the group writes notes on my paper for future reference and my absolute best workshops have been multiple sessions with the same small group. Assessing each other's progress really helps in the revision stages.

WHEN THINGS GO WRONG

Especially in a small workshop people can take things too personally and ruin the objective atmosphere, letting their own agenda take precedence over progression. In one of the worst workshops I've been a part of, we were assessing an essay by a writer who chose to write about her relationship with God. The essay had many problems, she used very vague metaphorical language, and the attempted symbolism didn't really work. It was a bit hard to read because of the overly sentimental tone of the piece. Instead of discussing these points, though, the workshop turned into an argument about outside topics and became pretty vicious. The writer was very open to most of the comments I made about some major changes that needed to happen in the piece, but very defensive (understandably) to the personal attacks. The communication simply broke down due to varying personal beliefs when they could have been a strength of the group.

In a large group a fine balance must be achieved. It is important that the conversation runs deep, but also that it covers more than one topic. Because of the multitude of opinions in a large group the entire workshop can get stuck on one topic or section of the piece. Not only is it unproductive when the debate gets stuck, but it's also really hard to sit through.

METHODS OF RESPONDING

One thing I don't need with an early draft is someone telling me that I misspelled the word *rhythm*. It is a word I'll never be able to spell, and that fact makes me eternally grateful for spell-checkers. I do like to know whether an early draft delivers on its implied promises to the reader, and especially whether there is another angle or another topic lurking there that I might not have noticed. But I don't want my wife, Karen, to read my stuff until I have a

The kinds of responses we seek to our writing in workshops depend on at least two things: where we are in the writing process and how we feel about the work in progress.

late draft to show her because I sometimes find her comments on early drafts discouraging.

The *kinds* of responses we seek to our writing in workshops depend on at least two things: where we are in the writing process and how we feel about the work in progress. This is not particularly surprising. After all, certain kinds of problems arise during different stages of the writing process, and sometimes what we really need from readers of our work is more emotional than practical. We want to be motivated, encouraged, or validated, or feel any number of things that will help us work well.

Experiential and Directive Responses

It makes sense, then, to invite certain kinds of readings of your work that you'll find timely. In general, these responses range from experiential ("this is how I experienced your draft") to more directive ("this is what you could do to make it better"). Which of these two forms would make reader comments on your work most helpful? For example, depending on who you are and how you work, it may be most helpful to get less directive responses to your work early on. Some people feel that very specific suggestions undermine their sense of ownership of rough drafts. They don't want to know what readers think they should do in the revision but how readers experienced their draft. What parts were interesting? What parts were confusing? On the other hand, other writers feel particularly lost in the early stages of the writing process; they could use all the direction they can get. You decide (or your instructor will make suggestions), choosing from the following menu of workshop response methods. These begin with the most experiential methods of response to those that invite your readers to offer quite specific suggestions about the revision.

Response Formats

The following formats for responding to workshop drafts begin with the least directive, most experiential methods and move to the more directive approaches. While many of these formats feature some particular ways of responding to drafts, remember that the writer's and reader's responsibilities described earlier apply to all of them. Participate thoughtfully and ethically (see the box "The Ethics of Responding") and you'll be amazed at what you learn about your own writing from talking with other writers about theirs.

The No-Response Workshop. Sometimes the most useful response to your work comes from simply reading it aloud to your group and asking them to just listen, nothing more. Why? You may not be ready for comments because the work is unformed and you're confident that'll you discover the direction you want to go in the next draft. Comments may confuse or distract you. It's always helpful to read your work aloud to yourself, but it's also valuable to read to an audience even if you

The Ethics of Responding

Respect the writer.

Everyone contributes.

Say "could" rather than "should."

Say "I" rather than "you," as in "I couldn't follow this" rather than "You weren't very clear."

don't invite a response. You will read with more attention and awareness. Finally, you may simply feel unprepared for a response because your confidence is low.

The method couldn't be simpler. You read your draft with little or no introduction while your group quietly listens. They will not comment unless they want you to repeat something because it was inaudible. Remember to read slowly and clearly.

The Initial-Response Workshop. Robert Brooke, Ruth Mirtz, and Rick Evans[1] suggest a method that is useful for "maintaining your motivation to write while indirectly learning what to improve in your text." It might also be appropriate for an early draft.

They suggest that you invite three kinds of responses to your work: a "relating" response, a "listening" response, and a "positive" response. These three types of response to a draft could be made in writing, in workshop discussion, or both.

- **Relating response.** As the name implies, group members share what personal associations the writer's topic inspires. Perhaps they've had a similar or a contradictory experience. Maybe they've read something or seen something that is relevant to what the writer is trying to do in the draft.
- **Listening response.** This is much like the "say back" method some therapists use with patients. Can you summarize what is it that you hear the writing saying in the draft? Is this something that is helpful to know?
- **Positive response.** What parts of the draft really work well and why? Might these be things the writer might build on in the next draft?

The Narrative-of-Thought Workshop. A writer who hears the story of readers' thinking *as they experienced the draft* can get great insight about how the piece shapes readers' expectations and how well it delivers on its promises. This method borrows a term from Peter Elbow— "movie of the mind"—to describe the creation of such a narrative response to a piece of writing.

The easiest way to create stories of your readers' experiences is to prepare your draft ahead of time to accommodate them. Before you make copies for your workshop group, create 2- to 3-inch white spaces in the manuscript immediately after the lead or beginning paragraph, and then again in the middle of the essay. Also leave at least that much white space after the end of the piece.

1. Robert Brooke, Ruth Mirtz, and Rick Evans, *Small Groups in Writing Workshops* (Urbana, IL: NCTE, 1994).

You will read your draft episodically, beginning by just reading the lead or introductory paragraph, then allowing three or four minutes for your group's members to respond in writing in the space you provided for some of the following questions. The writer should time this and ask everyone to stop writing when it's time to read the next section of the draft. Repeat the process, stopping at the second patch of white space after you've read roughly half of the essay. Give your group the same amount of time to respond in writing and then finish the essay to prompt the final episode of writing.

- **After hearing the lead:** What are your feelings about the topic or the writer so far? Can you predict what the essay might be about? What questions does the lead raise for you that you expect might be answered later? What has struck you?
- **After hearing half:** Tell the story of what you've been thinking or feeling about what you've heard so far. Has the draft fulfilled your expectations from the lead? What do you expect will happen next?
- **After hearing it all:** Summarize your understanding of what the draft is about, including what it *seems* to be saying (or not quite saying). How well did it deliver on its promises in the beginning? What part of your experience of the draft was most memorable? What part seemed least clear?

Discuss with your group each of the responses—after the lead, after the middle, and at the end of the draft. This conversation, and the written comments you receive when you collect their copies of your draft, should give you strong clues about how well you've established a clear purpose in your essay and sustained it from beginning to end. The responses also might give you ideas about directions to take the next draft that you hadn't considered.

The Instructive-Lines Workshop. Most essays balance on a thesis, theme, question, or idea. Like the point of a spinning top, these claims, ideas, or questions are the things around which everything else revolves. Essay drafts, however, may easily topple over because they lack such balance—there is no clear point, or there are too many, or some of the information is irrelevant. In discovery drafts especially, a writer may be seeking the piece's center of gravity—or *centers* of gravity—and a useful response from a workshop group is to help the writer look for the clues about where that center might be.

This format for a workshop invites the members to try to identify the draft's *most important lines and passages,* by clearly marking them with underlining or highlighter. What makes a line or passage important? *These are places where writers explicitly or implicitly seem to suggest what they're trying to say in a draft* and they may include the following:

- A line or passage where the writer seems to state his or her thesis.
- A part of a narrative essay when the writer adopts a critical stance and seems to be trying to pose a question or speculate about the meaning of an experience or some information.

- A part of the draft in which the writer seems to make an important claim.
- A scene or comparison or observation that hints at the question the writer is exploring (or could explore).
- A comment in a digression that the writer didn't seem to think was important, but you think might be.

These underlinings become the subject of discussion in the workshop session. Questions to consider include the following: Why did this particular line seem important? What does it imply about what you think is the meaning of the essay? Do the different underlined passages speak to each other—can they be combined or revised into a controlling idea or question for the next draft—or do they imply separate essays or treatments? Would the writer underline something else? How might the different interpretations of the draft be reconciled?

The Purpose Workshop. Sometimes writers know their purpose in a draft: "I'm trying to argue that the Enron collapse represented the failure of current methods of compensating CEOs," or "I'm proposing that having vegetarian fast-food restaurants would reduce American obesity," or "This essay explores the question of why I was so relieved when my father died." What these writers may need most from their workshop groups is feedback on how well the draft accomplishes particular purposes.

Before the workshop session, the writer crafts a statement of purpose similar to those in the preceding paragraph—a sentence that clearly states what the writer is trying to do in the draft. This statement of purpose should include a verb that implies what action you're trying to take—for example, *explore, argue, persuade, propose, review, explain,* or *analyze.* As you probably guessed, these verbs are usually associated with a particular form of inquiry or genre.

The writer should include this sentence *at the end* of the draft. It's important that you to make group members aware of your purpose only after they've read the entire piece and not before. Discussion and written responses should then focus on some of the following questions:

- Were you surprised by the stated purpose, or did the essay prepare you for it?
- If the stated purpose did surprise you, what did you think the writer was trying to do in the draft instead?
- Does the lead explicitly state or hint at the stated purpose?
- What parts or paragraphs of the draft seemed clearly relevant to the stated purpose, and which seemed to point in another direction?
- Did the draft seem to succeed in accomplishing the writer's purpose?

If more directive responses would be helpful to you, consider also asking some questions such as whether there might not be a stronger beginning or lead buried elsewhere in the draft, or soliciting suggestions about which parts or paragraphs should be cut or what additional information might be needed. Which parts of the draft seemed to work best in the context of the writer's stated purpose, and which didn't work so well?

The Graphing Reader Interest Workshop. What commands readers' attention in a draft and what doesn't? This is useful to know, obviously, because our overall aim is to engage readers from beginning to end—which is difficult to do, particularly in longer drafts, and reader attention often varies from paragraph to paragraph in shorter drafts. But if your draft drones on for three or four paragraphs or a couple of pages, then the piece isn't working well and you need to do something about it in revision.

One way to know this is to ask your workshop group to graph their response to your essay, paragraph by paragraph, and then discuss what is going on in those sections that drag.

For this workshop, consecutively number all the paragraphs in your draft. You or your instructor will provide each member of your group with a "Reader Interest Chart" (see Figure 15.2), on which the corresponding paragraph numbers are listed. On the vertical axis is a scale that represents reader interest, with 5 being high interest and 1 being low interest in that particular paragraph. As you slowly read your draft aloud to your group's members, they mark the graph after each paragraph to roughly indicate their interest in what the paragraph says and how it says it.

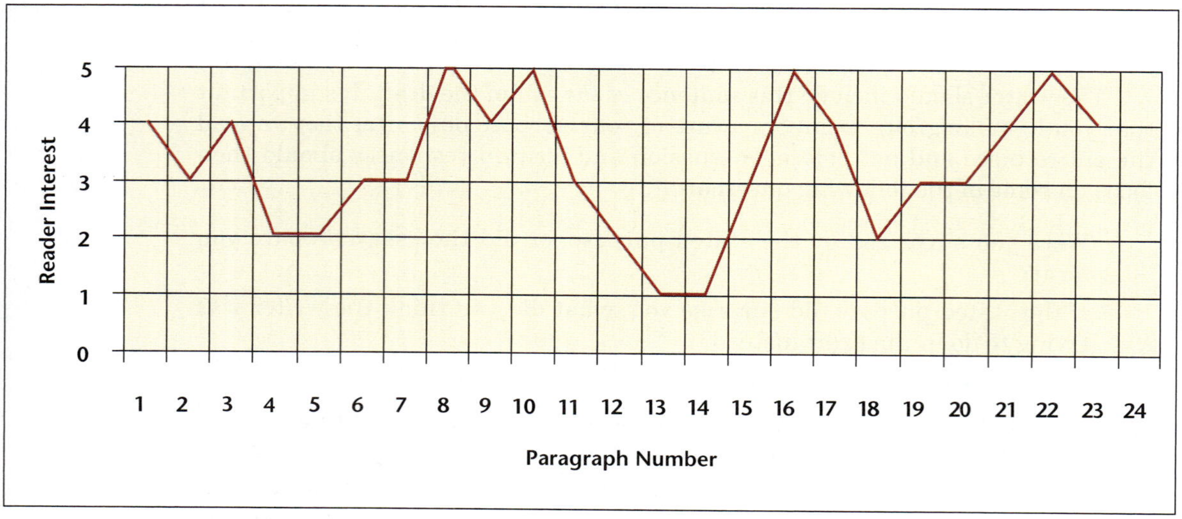

FIGURE 15.2 Reader interest chart.

When you're finished, you'll have a visual representation of how the essay worked, paragraph by paragraph, but the important work is ahead. Next, you need to discuss with your group *why* a paragraph or section of the draft failed to hold some readers' attention. What is going on in those parts of the draft?

- Are they confusing?
- Do they needlessly digress?
- Is the prose awkward?
- Is there too much or too little explanation?
- Are they too loaded with facts and not enough analysis?
- Does the writer seem to lose his voice?

One way to find out what's going on with the weaker parts of your essay is to look at the stronger ones. What do you notice about those paragraphs that were rated 4 or 5 by your group members? What are the particular strengths of these sections? Can you do more of that in other, less lively sections of the draft?

The Sum-of-the-Parts Workshop. Like a watch, a well-written essay moves fluently forward because all of its parts work together. In workshops you can never talk about all those parts; there is too little time, and often it's hard to tease apart all the gears and the springs that make an essay go. But you can try to be as thorough as you can during a workshop, essentially running through a checklist of some of the most important elements, including purpose, theme, structure, information, and style. In this workshop, you attempt to cover as much territory as possible, so the responses you get will have breadth but not depth. You also invite some directive responses from your readers—suggestions for the revision and specific areas of confusion—as well as their interpretation of your purpose and theme.

One of the best ways to solicit this information is to use a worksheet like the one that follows. Typically, this worksheet would be filled out by your group's members outside class and before you workshop the draft. It would then be attached to the copies of your draft and returned to you after the group discusses the work. If your peers respond thoughtfully to the worksheet, it can generate a wealth of information for you about your draft.

The Thesis Workshop. An alternative to the sum-of-all-parts format is to focus on a single element of the draft that you are particularly concerned about, and no part is more important than the thesis. An essay without an implicit theme or an explicit thesis is an essay without meaning. No one is particularly interested in reading a pointless story or research essay, nor are most readers interested in points that seem unrelated to the information in the draft or that are painfully obvious. For example, the idea that the death of your Aunt Trudy was sad for you is a much less compelling theme to build an essay around than the idea that her death—and the deaths of family members generally—upset the family system in ways that helped you to take on new roles, new identities.

Workshop Worksheet

Purpose: In your own words, what is the writer's motive in the draft? Use one of the following verbs to describe this in a sentence: *explore, explain, argue, analyze, review, report, propose, persuade, reflect.*

Theme: State in your own words what you think the thesis, main point, or central question is in this draft. What question does this idea or question raise for you?

Information: Name at least two specific places in the draft where you wanted more information to fully appreciate what the writer was trying to say. What kind of information do you suggest (anecdote, story, fact, detail, background, example, interview, dialogue, opposing perspective, description, case study, etc.)?

Design: Identify *at least* one paragraph or passage that seemed out of place. Any suggestions about where it belongs?

Style: Place brackets [ ] around several sentences or passages in the draft that seemed awkward or confusing to read.

A thesis workshop will help you make sure there is a controlling idea or question behind the draft, and help you think more deeply about what you're trying to say. Your workshop members can help with this because they bring a range of perspectives and experiences to a conversation about your theme that might make it richer and more informative for you.

In this workshop, group members receive the drafts ahead of time. Before the workshop session they should underline the thesis, main idea, theme, or question that seems to be behind the draft. This will be the *main thing* the writer seems to be saying or exploring. This isn't particularly difficult in essays with explicit thesis statements, such as arguments or proposals, but in personal essays and other more literary pieces, the theme may not be so explicit. In that type of essay, they should underline the passage that seems central to the meaning of the essay. This may be a reflective passage or it might be a scene or moment.

Second, at the top of a piece of paper, they should write down in a sentence or two—at most—the thesis or theme as they understand it. This may involve simply copying it down from the draft. However, if thesis or theme is not that clear or explicit, each reader should write it down in his or her own words, trying to capture the main point of the draft.

Then members should fastwrite for five minutes about their own thoughts and experiences about the writer's thesis or theme, constantly hunting for questions it raises for them. Say the draft's thesis is that the university athletic programs have become too powerful and have undermined the university's more important academic mission. In the fastwrite, explore what you've noticed about the football team's impact on the school. Where does the football program get funds? Does it compete with academic programs? Then fastwrite about what you've heard—for instance, that athletics have strong alumni support. Keep the fastwrite focused on the thesis; if it helps, stop and reread it for another prompt.

The workshop session that follows will be a conversation largely focused on what people thought was the point of the draft, and their own thoughts and feelings about it. The writer should facilitate the conversation without comment and make sure the following two things are discussed in this order:

1. What seems to be the thesis, theme, or question behind the essay? Is it clear? Are there alternative ideas about what it might be?

2. What does each group member think or feel about what the writer seems to be saying? How do the reader's experiences and observations relate to the writer's main point or question? And especially, what questions should the writer consider in the next draft?

Although it may be hard to keep quiet if your draft is being discussed, the conversation will probably surprise you. You may discover that several of your group members either failed to understand what you were trying to say in the draft or give you a completely new idea about what you were up to. At its best, the thesis workshop inspires you to think more deeply about your theme or main idea as you consider the range of experiences and questions that other people have about it. Take lots of notes.

The Editing Workshop. In a late draft, the larger issues—for example, having a clear purpose, focus, and point, as well as appropriate information to support it—may be resolved to your satisfaction, or you may feel that you already have some pretty good ideas about how to deal with them. If so, what you may need most from your workshop group is editorial advice: responses to your work at the sentence and paragraph levels.

In the editing workshop, you invite your group members to focus on style and clarity (and perhaps grammar and mechanics). The questions that direct the reading of the draft might include some or all of the following:

- Did you stumble over any awkward passages that seemed to interrupt the fluency of the writing?
- Were there any sentences or passages that you had to read a few times to understand?
- Could any long paragraphs be broken down into smaller ones? Did any paragraphs seem to be about more than one thing?
- Are the first and last lines of the essay well crafted? Are the last lines of paragraphs strong enough?
- Were there any abrupt transitions between paragraphs?
- Was the voice or tone of the draft consistent?
- (Optional) Did you notice any patterns of grammatical problems, including run-on sentences, unclear pronoun references, lack of subject–verb agreement?

Group members who see any of these problems should bracket [ ] the sentence or passage and refer to it when discussing the editorial issue with the group. The workshop discussion has the following ground rules:

- Be respectful of the writer's feelings. Some of us feel that style is a very personal issue, and that grammar problems are related somehow to our self-worth.
- Don't have arguments about editorial judgments. Group members don't have to agree. In fact, you probably won't agree about a lot of things. Offer your comments on style as suggestions and then move on, although don't hesitate to offer a differing opinion.
- Make sure to identify places in the draft where the writing is working just fine. Editorial workshops need not focus exclusively on problems. Sentences, paragraphs, or passages that work well stylistically can often help the writer see how to revise the less effective parts.
- If readers have some comments about larger issues in the draft, things such as purpose or theme, ask the writer first if he or she welcomes that kind of feedback. Otherwise, keep the workshop focused on editorial matters.

An editing workshop may sound a little harrowing. It really isn't, particularly if the group knows the ground rules. My students often tell me that these conversations about style are some of the best workshops they have had. Everybody learns something, not just the writer, a principle that applies to many workshop formats and another reason that peer review is such a useful practice in the writing classroom.

Reflecting on the Workshop

The real work follows the workshop. Then you have the task of mulling over the things you've heard about your draft and deciding how you're going to rewrite it. This calls for a way of inquiring—reflection—that you've already practiced. As soon as possible after your workshop session, reread your notes and your readers' comments, then go to your journal and fastwrite for five minutes. Choose one of the following prompts to get—and keep—you going.

- What did I hear that seemed most useful? What did I hear that I'm not sure about?
- What responses to my draft do I remember most? Why?
- What did I think I needed to do to revise the draft before the workshop? Did my peer review experience change my mind? Did it reinforce my initial plans?
- What do I plan to do to revise this draft to make it stronger?

Using What You Have Learned

The writing workshop is just one of many forms of collaboration that you'll likely experience both during and after college. Even unsuccessful workshops are instructive because they help you understand how groups work and what roles you can play to make them function better. Consider your experience so far.

1. What is the best workshop group experience you've had in this class? What made it so good? What was the worst experience? What made it so bad?
2. As you reflect on your own performance in groups, what have you learned about yourself as a collaborator? How would you describe yourself as a group member? How would you *like* to describe yourself?
3. If you're currently involved in a group project in another class, how would you compare your writing workshop with that other group project? Can what you've learned in one provide useful guidance for the other?

APPENDIX A

THE WRITING PORTFOLIO*

WHAT IS A PORTFOLIO?

You've probably heard about stock portfolios and artist portfolios, but the term *writing portfolio* may be something new. *Portfolio* in these three examples means a collection of stocks, photographs or paintings, or writings that represent something about the compiler: for example, if you have a stock portfolio in which 75 percent of your money is invested in high-risk growth funds and the other 25 percent is in safe bond funds, then you might be showing that you're a risk taker. If you are an artist and you select a range of photographs taken over a long period of time, you might be showing how you've developed and changed as a photographer.

Writing portfolios can reflect similar things about their authors. As a collection of the work you've done for a writing class, a portfolio can demonstrate how you've developed as a writer, it can show specific writing principles you've learned, or it can illustrate the range of genres you have worked with (to name a few). Often it will be a large percentage of your course grade, so the work you submit will have been revised several times and you might be asked to reflect on your assembled work, exploring what you want the portfolio to illustrate. In fact, the whole idea of using a portfolio to evaluate your work emphasizes the principles of inquiry and reflection at the heart of this book.

Instructors use portfolios in different ways: some require certain essays and assignments to be included, some allow *you* to choose what to include, others ask that you choose according to particular guidelines (for example, pieces that demonstrate your ability to conduct research, to put a lesson plan together if it's a teaching portfolio, or to revise). It's important that you understand what kind of portfolio your instructor is requiring and why. We'll talk about why later—let's look first at the different kinds of portfolios you might be asked to assemble.

*Appendixes A, B, C, and D were written by Dr. Michelle Payne, Department Chair at Boise State University.

TYPES OF PORTFOLIOS

It's important here to distinguish between *unevaluated* and *evaluated* portfolios. An unevaluated portfolio would be one in which you are collecting all your work for the course, like a journal or working folder, but your instructor will not be evaluating the material. You keep class notes, doodles, drafts of essays, exercises, and anything else that relates to the course. From that folder, you then might be asked to *choose specific assignments,* continue working on them, and turn them in for your final portfolio. A final portfolio is one type of evaluated portfolio. Your instructor either gives you the evaluation criteria for it or helps the class develop those criteria with him or her. You turn in selected pieces from the course, either freely chosen by you or required by your instructor. The work is "final" in that you have stopped revising, done your best to make it as effective an essay as possible, and are ready to have it graded. Unevaluated portfolios, then, are places in which you experiment with, collect, and play around with your ideas and your writing, not worrying about evaluation as much as you would when you assemble an evaluated portfolio. All the activities in this book, for example, would be part of a writing journal or working folder that your instructor might not evaluate. Then, as you develop essays from those exercises, you revise them into final products that your instructor can grade.

Unevaluated Portfolios

The unevaluated portfolios you are most likely to encounter in your college writing are as follows:

- *A journal or working folder.* In this type of unevaluated portfolio, keep all your work for your writing course—everything that you do in and out of class, all your assignments and drafts. It's a place where you can track your progress as a writer because you have everything there. Some instructors ask you to turn this type of portfolio in for a holistic grade (that is, the entire body of work is evaluated, not individual pieces), based on criteria that is different from the criteria used for evaluating a portfolio of final drafts (for example, in evaluating a writing journal, your instructor might consider whether you've completed all the assignments, taken risks in your writing, and experimented).
- *A learning portfolio.* For this type of unevaluated portfolio, you collect materials from your course and possibly other places that reflect something about your learning process. Let's say your writing instructor wants you to keep a record of your learning in another course, such as sociology. You might include class notes that changed the way you understood a concept, restaurant napkins scribbled with conversations you've overheard, a paper you are assigned to write, and some reflections on how the theories you've

been learning affect how you perceive your world. You can include both print and nonprint materials, such as photos or music. Learning portfolios often allow for free choice, so you have to carefully select what you will include and why. This type of portfolio may be helpful as you apply the concepts you learn in this course—about inquiry, essay writing, and reflection—to another course.

Evaluated Portfolios

Evaluated portfolios include the following:

- *A midterm portfolio.* As the name suggests, this portfolio is assembled at midterm. Your instructor might ask you to include particular assignments—such as your two best reading responses and a revised essay—and write a cover letter that explains, for example, what you've learned about writing that is reflected in these pieces. You might also be asked to evaluate the portfolio yourself and discuss your goals for the rest of the course. A midterm portfolio might be evaluated, but it might also be used as a practice run for the final portfolio at the end of the course and not be evaluated.
- *A final portfolio—limited choice.* Your instructor may require you to include specific assignments and essays in the portfolio you turn in at the end of the course. Let's say your university's writing program, for example, requires all students to write a research essay in their first-year writing course and to demonstrate that they can use documentation effectively, support their claims with evidence, and do more than simply string information together. Your instructor, then, would ask you to include one or more research essays in the final portfolio so he or she can assess whether you have learned what is required. That might be the only required essay and you would have some choice about what else to include. Or you might be required to include a profile, an argument, and an ethnographic essay, as well. In addition, instructors might ask you to include a reflective essay with your final portfolio (explained in more detail next). In general, a final portfolio emphasizes the final products of the course, the revised and polished work that shows what you've learned for the entire term.
- *A final portfolio—open choice.* While all your work will be revised and polished, your instructor may ask you to choose your best writing for the course and not require particular essays. She might ask that you only choose from the essays you've written or that you choose from the informal writing you've done, as well (such as the writing exercises in this book). She may require a certain number of pages (say, twenty to twenty-five pages) or a certain number of assignments (three out of the five essays required in the course) or leave the length and number of assignments

open. Here are a couple of examples: If you feel your research essay is better than your ethnographic essay, then you might include it and not work any further on your ethnographic essay. You might also include your personal essay, an argument, and your response to particular writing exercises. You would include these pieces because you believe they are your best work, but you want to be sure you can talk specifically about *why* they are the best and *what* they show your instructor about what you've learned. For instance, do you want to show your growth, your success in using writing as inquiry, or what you've learned about crafting paragraphs?

WHY REQUIRE A PORTFOLIO?

Before we talk more about how to choose the materials to include in your portfolio, we should talk about why you will be expected to assemble one. If you are keeping an unevaluated portfolio, your instructor wants to emphasize your learning process at least as much as your final product. We rarely take the time to reflect on how we learn, but doing so can help you learn better in your other courses. Are you a visual learner? Do you learn best when you have a relationship with your teacher or when the teacher is more removed? If you learn more outside school, why? Learning portfolios enable you to develop even better learning strategies and understand why you might struggle with certain learning situations. The same is true for a writing journal or working folder. As you collect everything you do in a writing course, you can pause periodically and reflect on which writing strategies seem to sabotage your efforts, which seem to work well, how you might work through writer's block, or what principles about writing you've been learning. Many of the exercises in this book prompt you to reflect on your writing process, your reading strategies, and your learning and thinking, so if you've been doing them, you have already seen the benefits of reflecting on your process.

In both kinds of unevaluated portfolios, the *process* of whatever you're doing is being emphasized and valued. You don't have to worry about writing beautifully styled sentences the first time around or having a complicated reading all figured out the first time through. An unevaluated portfolio allows for—in fact encourages—the messiness of writing and thinking instead of focusing only on polished work. These kinds of portfolios emphasize risk, experimentation, and reflection on the process of writing and learning, all of which are central to the ideas in this book. These types of portfolios, then, reflect and reinforce what you've been learning about writing so far.

Evaluated portfolios are important for very similar reasons. In order to get your drafts to the point that they are ready to be evaluated, you are encouraged all term to experiment, rewrite, and critique them. In fact, most of the term you are working in your writing journal, exploring ideas, commenting on peers' drafts in workshop, revising your own drafts, and taking them apart again, all in an effort to learn more about writing and make your essays more effective. Portfolios allow you to do all that over a long period of time and in a relatively "evaluation-free" zone, so you are graded based on your final product at the end, not in the middle, of the process.

Your final product, though, is the result and reflection of all that work you did throughout the semester. In addition, the reflection exercises in this book have had you thinking about your learning all term. You will be more conscious of the writing and reading strategies that work best for you, and so will be better prepared to write the reflective essay that your instructor may require in the portfolio.

Of course, the final product is what is evaluated in a final portfolio, so while this kind of portfolio reinforces the process of inquiry and reflection, it also emphasizes the way a sentence is crafted, the way an essay is organized, and the way a writer explores an idea. A portfolio, then, allows an instructor to evaluate *both* the process of writing and the quality of the final product.

ORGANIZING PORTFOLIOS

Because a writing portfolio emphasizes the *process* of writing and learning as much as the final product, you'll want to keep your course materials organized—that is, the materials that reflect your process. Whether or not your instructor assigns a journal or working folder, it's a good idea to keep one yourself. You can do this on the computer or in a notebook. You can organize your writing journal or working folder in several ways, including these options:

1. **Organize by chronological order.** Keep everything that you do in the course in the order you complete it.
2. **Organize by assignments.** Within each category, include all the writing you've done (fastwriting, drafts, exercises), peer and teacher responses, notes, research materials, and so on. As an example, your portfolio might be broken out into the following categories:
   - Profile
   - Ethnographic essay
   - Review
   - Argument
   - Reflective exercises
   - Reading responses
   - Essay exam

3. **Organize by subjects.** Here you place your writing into categories defined by the subject or theme of the writing. For example:
   - Racism (profile, research essay)
   - Italy trip (personal essay, review, argument)

   With this approach, you have a better sense of how you've explored a topic through different genres, comparing what you've learned about the subject as well as about the form.

4. **Organize by stage of process.** Here you place your writing into categories based on what place in the writing process it falls, starting with your fastwriting and journal writing and ending with your final drafts and reflective writing. For example:
   - Fastwriting/journal writing
   - Exercises
   - Sketches
   - Early drafts
   - Peer responses
   - Instructor responses
   - Revisions
   - Final drafts
   - Reflective writing

You can also create your own categories to organize your class work. However you choose to organize your writing, be sure to keep everything you write for the course; don't throw anything away. If you are using a computer, *save all of your writing files and keep a separate backup copy.*

If you are expected to include a reflective letter or essay as a preface to your portfolio, it's a good idea to create a separate section in your journal or folder for all the reflective writing you've done in the class. You can do all the reflective exercises in that separate section, or you can include them for each separate assignment. However you do it, keeping your reflective writing in one place will make it easier to compose your reflective letter or essay.

WRITING A REFLECTIVE LETTER OR ESSAY

You may have to preface your final portfolio with a letter or essay that introduces the pieces you've included and reflect on what you've learned about writing, reading, and inquiry. For some instructors, this letter or essay becomes crucial in evaluating the whole portfolio because it gives coherence and purpose to the material and articulates what you've learned. In my own classes, the reflective essay can make the difference of half a letter grade in the overall evaluation of the portfolio. As always, clarify with your instructor what is expected in the reflective letter or essay and how it will be weighed in the portfolio grade. While some instructors require a five- to seven-page essay or letter that begins the portfolio, others may require a prefatory letter for *each piece* you include in the portfolio. Some want only a reflection on the writing process for each essay, others may want only a narrative of how your thinking changed about each subject you wrote about. Regardless, you'll want to spend some time going through your writing journal or folder and reflecting on what you notice. Here are some questions that might help:

- **Patterns.** As you flip through the pages of your writing journal or folder, what patterns do you notice? What seems to happen frequently or stand out to you? For example, you might notice that you always begin your essays the same way, or you ended up writing about the same subject the whole semester without realizing it, or you got better at organizing your essays and using significant detail.
- **Reflective writing.** As you look only at the reflective writing you've done throughout the course (the reflective exercises in this book), what do you notice? What five things have you learned about writing, reading, and inquiry based on that early reflective writing?
- **Change over time.** How did you describe your writing process (and/or reading process) at the beginning of the course? How would you describe it now? If it has changed, why and how?
- **Writing principles.** List five to seven principles about writing that you have learned in this course, the five to seven most important things you've learned about writing, reading, and inquiry. Or, list five to seven strategies for writing and reading that you will take with you into other writing situations.
- **Revision.** For each of the essays you are including in your portfolio, what would you do differently if you had more time?
- **Writing processes.** For each of the essays in your portfolio, describe the writing and thinking process that led to the final product. Emphasize the most important changes you made and why you made them.
- **Most and least effective writing.** Which essay in the portfolio is your strongest? Your weakest? Why?
- **Effect of peer response.** How have your peers and other readers of your work affected the revisions you've made?
- **Showing what you've learned.** What does your portfolio demonstrate about you as a writer, a student, a reader, a researcher? How? Be as specific as possible.

Typical Problems in Reflective Essays/Letters

- Use of overly general and vague comments.
- Not enough specific details.
- Giving the teacher only what you think he or she wants whether it's true or not.
- Critiquing the course (usually this is reserved for end-of-term evaluations that are confidential and anonymous); it's not wise to risk criticizing the person who is evaluating you.
- Comments that suggest you don't take the assignment seriously.

- **What's missing.** What is *not* reflected in your portfolio that you believe is important for your instructor to know?
- **Expectations.** How does your portfolio meet the expectations for effective writing defined in your class?
- **Applying the textbook.** How have you applied the principles about each essay form that are outlined in this textbook?
- **Personal challenge.** In what ways did you challenge yourself in this course?

Your instructor might ask you to address only three or four of these questions in the letter or essay itself, but it's a good idea to do some fastwriting on all of them. Doing so will help your essay or letter be more specific, thoughtful, and persuasive.

As with any essay, you'll want to take this one through several revisions and get feedback from readers before you include it in the portfolio. Your instructor might even ask you to workshop a draft of this with your group. If you've done some fastwriting on the preceding questions, you are in good shape to compose a first draft of your reflective letter or essay. Keep in mind who your audience is—your teacher, teachers unknown to you, and/or your peers—and address what that audience expects. Be as specific as possible, citing examples from your work, drawing on the terms and principles you've discussed in class and read about in this book.

If you've been doing reflective writing all term, you will have plenty of material to draw from to make your reflective essay or letter concrete, substantive, and as honest as it can be (given the circumstances). You'll probably surprise yourself with all that you've learned.

FINAL PREPARATIONS

Before you turn your portfolio in, take time to proofread it carefully, possibly asking one of your peers for help. Check again to be sure you've met all the criteria for the portfolio, including what is required, assembling it appropriately, and formatting it as required. This is work that you are proud of, so the way you present it should reflect that pride. It should meet high standards for presentation and quality.

CREDITS

Text Credits

Page 139. Anonymous. "Soup" from THE NEW YORKER. Copyright © 1989 The New Yorker. All rights reserved. Originally published in The New Yorker. Reprinted by permission.

Page 142. Lauren Slater. "Dr. Daedalus" by Lauren Slater. Copyright © 2001 by Harper's Magazine. All rights reserved. Reproduced from the July issue by special permission.

Page 190. Ann Hodgman. "No Wonder They Call Me a Bitch" by Ann Hodgman from SPY MAGAZINE. Copyright © 1989 by Sussex Publishers, Inc. Reprinted by permission of the author.

Page 319. Leslie Marmon Silko. "Lullaby" from STORYTELLER by Leslie Marmon Silko. Copyright © 1981 by Leslie Marmon Silko reprinted with the permission of The Wylie Agency Inc.

Page 375. Rachel Simmons. Excerpt from "Intimate Enemies" in ODD GIRL OUT: THE HIDDEN CULTURE OF AGGRESSION IN GIRLS, Copyright © 2002 by Rachel Simmons, reprinted by permission of Harcourt, Inc.

Page 79. Frank Bruni. From "It Died For Us" by Frank Bruni from THE NEW YORK TIMES, June 25, 2006. Copyright © 2006 The New York Times Co. Reprinted by permission.

Page 278. Ellen Goodman. "Getting Real in the Classroom" by Ellen Goodman from THE BOSTON GLOBE, July 7, 2006. Copyright © 2006, The Washington Post Writers Group. Reprinted with permission.

Page 380. Patricia Leigh Brown. "For the Muslim Prom Queen, there are No Kings Allowed" by Patricia Leigh Brown from THE NEW YORK TIMES, June 9, 2003, p. A1. Copyright © 2003 The New York Times Co. Reprinted by permission.

Page 328. Joyce Carol Oates. "Where Are You Going, Where Have You Been?" by Joyce Carol Oates. Copyright © 1970 Ontario Review. Reprinted by permission of John Hawkins & Associates, Inc.

Page 434. "Courting Confusion" by The Editors of CHRISTIAN CENTURY. Copyright 2001 Christian Century. Reprinted with permission from the August 15-22, 2001 issue of the Christian Century. Subscriptiosn: $49/yr. from P.O. Box 378, Mt. Morris, IL 61054. 1-800-208-4097.

Page 99. "Long Overdue" by Naomi Shihab Nye. Reprinted by permission of the author, Naomi Shihab Nye, 2006.

Page 341. "Who Is Ellie? Oates' Where Are You Going, Where Have You Been?" by Alice Hall Petry from STUDIES IN SHORT FICTION 25.2 (Spring 1988): 155–157. Reprinted by permission of the author.

Page 146: "Learning About Work from Joe Cool" by Gib Akin from JOURNAL OF MANAGEMENT INQUIRY, March 2000, pp. 59–61. Copyright © 2000. Reprinted by permission of Sage Publications, Inc.

Page 95. Reprinted from Ann Marie Oomen, PULLING DOWN THE BARN, 2004, pp. 17–21, wit the permission of Wayne State University Press.

Page 103. "One More Lesson" is reprinted with permission from the publisher of SILENT DANCING: A PARTIAL REMEMBRANCE OF A PUERTO RICAN CHILDHOOD by Judith Ortiz Cofer (Arte Publico Press—University of Houston, 1990).

Page 137. "Thumb-sucking girl" by Sonja Livingston from CREATIVE NONFICTION 27, 2005. Reprinted by permission of the author.

Page 283. "Still Trying to Kick the Kink" by Erin Aubry Kaplan as appeared in LOS ANGELES TIMES, July 12, 2006. Reprinted by permission of Erin Aubry Kaplan, Op-ed columnist, Los Angeles Times.

Page 186. "Review of Peter Guralnick's 'Lost Highways'" by Lester Bangs from PSYCHOTIC REACTIONS AND CARBURETOR DUNG edited by Greil Marcus, Copyright © 1987 by The Estate of Lester Bangs. Used by permission of Alfred A. Knopf, a division of Random House, Inc.

Page 225. "How Bingeing Became the New College Sport" by Barrett Seaman from TIME, August 21, 2005. Copyright © 2005 Time Inc. Reprinted by permission.

Page 436. "The Worth of a Date" by Bailey, Beth L. from FRONT PORCH TO BACK SEAT: Courtship in Twentieth-Century America, pp. 57–76. Copyright © 1988 The Johns Hopkins University Press. Reprinted with permission of The Johns Hopkins University Press.

Page 183. "Jack's still splashing about in the shallows" by Mark Kermode from THE OBSERVER, July 9, 2006. Copyright Guardian News and Media Limited 2006. Reprinted by permission.

Page 231. James Howard Kunstler and Nikos A. Salingaros. "The End of Tall Buildings" by James Howard Kunstler and Nikos A. Salingaros as appeared in Planetizen.com, September 17, 2001. Reprinted by permission of the authors.

Page 281. George Will. "Teach Johnny to Write" by George Will from THE WASHINGTON POST, July 9, 1995. Copyright © 1995, The Washington Post Writers Group. Reprinted with permission.

Page 384. Rebekah Nathan. Reprinted from Rebekah Nathan: MY FRESHMAN YEAR: WHAT A PROFESSOR LEARNED BY BECOMING A STUDENT. Copyright © 2005 by Rebekah Nathan. Used by permission of the publisher, Cornell University Press.

Page 441. Tracey Lambert. "Pluralistic Ignorance and Hooking Up" by Tracey Lambert et al from JOURNAL OF SEX RESEARCH 40.2 (May 2003): 129–133. Reprinted by permission of The Journal of Sex Research.

Photo Credits

Page 2. Reg Charity/Corbis

Page 19. AP WideWorld Photos

Page 32. Royalty Free/Corbis

Page 37. Jackson Pollock One (Number 31, 1950) (c) The Museum of Modern Art/Licensed by SCALA/Art Resource, NY

Page 37. © 2006 The Pollock-Krasner Foundation/Artist Rights Society (ARS), New York

Page 37. Major League Baseball trademarks and copyrights are used with permission of MLB.com. All Rights Reserved.

Page 53. Photofest NYC

Page 55. Kraft Foods

Page 56. The Advertising Archives

Page 58. "All I got was a letter from my girl. He got a tube of non-alcoholic Wildroot Cream Oil!" Item BH0636. Ad*Acess. 1999. Rare book, Manuscript and Special Collections Library, Duke University. http://scriptorium.lib.duke.edu/adaccess

Page 59. Francis G. Mayer/CORBIS

Page 60. Pepper No. 30 Photograph by Edward Weston. Collection Center for Creative Photography. © 1981 Arizona Board of Regents.

Page 60. Swim Ink 2, LLC/CORBIS

Page 61. Swim Ink 2, LLC/CORBIS

Page 61. Photograph by Milton Rogovin, copyright 1952–2002

Page 66. Courtesy of Paramount Pictures

Page 68. Library of Congress Prints and Photographs Division

Page 77. Yann Arthus-Bertrand /CORBIS

Page 80. Ji Lee

Page 106. Getty Images

Page 132. James Amos/Corbis

Page 151. Library of Congress Prints and Photographs

Page 176. Photos 12.com - Collection Cinema

Page 194 Courtesy of Oakland Museum of California

Page 194. Library of Congress Prints and Photographs Division

Page 194. Library of Congress Prints and Photographs Division

Page 194. Library of Congress Prints and Photographs Division

Page 194. Library of Congress Prints and Photographs Division

Page 194. Library of Congress Prints and Photographs Division

Page 215. Sunset Boulevard/Corbis

Page 218. Joseph Sohm; ChromoSohm Inc./CORBIS

Page 228. Courtesy of the Lower Manhattan Development Corporation

Page 242. Courtesy of Drug Free Arizona

www.drugfreeaz.org

Page 266. Getty Images

Page 286. Photo B.D.V./CORBIS

Page 300. Guess. Advertisement from Guess.com website. Reprinted by permission fo GUESS Inc.

Page 347. *Christina's World* 1948 Tempera on Panel © Andrew Wyeth / The Museum of Modern Art/Licensed by SCALA/Art Resource, NY

Page 370. Peter Lilja / Taxi / Getty

Page 388. Royalty-Free / Corbis

Page 455. Aaron Douglas, *Aspiration,*1936. Oil on Canvas 60" × 60" (152.4 × 152.4 cm). Fine Arts Museums of San Francisco, Museum Purchase, the estate of Thurlow E. Tibbs Jr., the Museum Society Auxiliary, American Art Trust Fund, Unrestricted Art Trust Fund, partial gift of Dr. Ernest A. Bates, Sharon Bell, Jo-Ann Beverly, Barbara Carleton, Dr. and Mrs. Arthur H. Coleman, Dr. and Mrs. Maxwell C. Gillette, Mr. and Mrs. Richard Goodyear, Zuretti L. Goosby,

Marion E. Greene, Mrs. Vivian S. W. Hambrick, Laurie Gibbs Harris, Arlene Hollis, Louis A. and Letha Jeanpierre, Daniel and Jackie Johnson, Jr., Stephen L. Johnson, Mr. and Mrs. Arthur Lathan, Lewis & Ribbs Mortuary Garden Chapel, Mr. and Mrs. Gary Love, Glenn R. Nance, Mr. and Mrs. Harry S. Parker Ill, Mr. and Mrs. Carr T. Preston, Fannie Preston, Pamela R. Ransom, Dr. and Mrs. Benjamin F. Reed, San Francisco Black Chamber of Commerce, San Francisco Chapter of Llinks, Inc. San Francisco Chapter of the N.A.A.C.P., Sigma Pi Phi Fraternity, Dr. Ella Mae Simmons, Mr. Calvin R. Swinson, Joseph B. Williams, Mr. and Mrs. Alfred S. Wilsey, and the people of the Bay Area, 1997.84

Page 490. 1996–98 AccuSoft Inc., All right /Robert Harding World Imagery/Corbis

Page 499. BSCO Publishing

Page 511. Robert Bull Design

Page 530. Owen Franken /CORBIS

Page 596. Michael Prince /CORBIS

Page 636. Steven Rubin /The Image Works

INDEX

B

C

D

E

J

K

L

M

S

T

Y